Human Security, Transnational Crime and Human Trafficking

In recent years, drug use, illegal migration and human trafficking have all become more common in Asia, North America and Europe: the problems of organized crime and human trafficking are no longer confined to operating at the traditional regional level. This book fills a gap in the current literature by examining transnational crime, human trafficking, and its implications for human security from both Western and Asian perspectives. The book:

- provides an outline of the overall picture of organized crime and human trafficking in the contemporary world, examining the current trends and recent developments;
- contrasts the experience and perception of these problems in Asia with those in the West, by analyzing the distinctive Japanese perspective on globalization, human security, and transnational crime;
- examines the policy responses of key states and international institutions in Germany, Canada, the United States, the European Union, Japan, and Korea.

This book argues that any effort to combat these crimes requires a response that addresses the welfare of human beings alongside the standard criminal law response. It represents a timely analysis of the increasingly serious problems of transnational crime, human trafficking, and security.

Shiro Okubo served as Professor of Law and the Director of the Institute of International Studies and Area Studies and the Institute of Humanities, Human and Social Science at Ritsumeikan University, Japan. Since his retirement, he serves as a specially appointed professor at the Research Institute of Ritsumeikan University. He is the author of *The Individual and Associations as Human Rights Actors in Post-War Japan* (Nihon Hyoron-sha Publishing Co., 2003), and co-editor of *Challenges to Criminal Justice: Crime and Human Rights in the Borderless Society* (Nihon Hyoron-sha Publishing Co., 2001).

Louise Shelley is Professor in the School of Public Policy at George Mason University, United States; she is the founder and Director of the Terrorism, Transnational Crime and Corruption Center (TraCCC). She recently published *Human Trafficking: A Global Perspective* (Cambridge University Press, 2010).

Routledge Transnational Crime and Corruption Series
Published in association with the Terrorism, Transnational Crime and Corruption
Center, School of Public Policy, George Mason University, USA

1 **Russian Business Power**
The role of Russian business in foreign and security relations
Edited by Andreas Wenger, Jeronim Perovic and Robert W. Orttung

2 **Organized Crime and Corruption in Georgia**
Edited by Louise Shelley, Erik Scott and Anthony Latta

3 **Russia's Battle with Crime, Corruption and Terrorism**
Edited by Robert W. Orttung and Anthony Latta

4 **Human Trafficking and Human Security**
Edited by Anna Jonsson

5 **Irregular Migration from the Former Soviet Union to the United States**
Saltanat Liebert

6 **Human Security, Transnational Crime and Human Trafficking**
Asian and Western perspectives
Edited by Shiro Okubo and Louise Shelley

Human Security, Transnational Crime and Human Trafficking
Asian and Western perspectives

Edited by Shiro Okubo and Louise Shelley

LONDON AND NEW YORK

First published 2011
by Routledge
2 Park Square, Milton Park, Abingdon, Oxon, OX14 4RN

Simultaneously published in the USA and Canada
by Routledge
711 Third Avenue, New York, NY 10017

Routledge is an imprint of the Taylor & Francis Group, an informa business

© 2011 Shiro Okubo and Louise Shelley for selection and editorial matter;
individual contributors their contribution

The right of Shiro Okubo and Louise Shelley to be identified as editors
of this work has been asserted by them in accordance with the Copyright,
Designs and Patent Act 1988.

Typeset in Times New Roman by Pindar NZ, Auckland, New Zealand

First issued in paperback 2013

All rights reserved. No part of this book may be reprinted or reproduced or
utilised in any form or by any electronic, mechanical, or other means, now
known or hereafter invented, including photocopying and recording, or in
any information storage or retrieval system, without permission in writing
from the publishers.

British Library Cataloguing in Publication Data
A catalogue record for this book is available from the British Library

Library of Congress Cataloging in Publication Data
Human security, transnational crime, and human trafficking : Asian and
Western perspectives / edited by Shiro Okubo and Louise Shelley.
       p. cm. — (Routledge transnational crime and corruption series)
    Includes bibliographical references and index.
    1. Transnational crime. 2. Transnational crime—Asia. 3. Human trafficking
4. Human trafficking—Asia. 5. Human smuggling. 6. Human smuggling—
Asia. I. Okubo, Shiro, 1943- II. Shelley, Louise I.
    HV6252.H86 2011
    364.1'35—dc22   2010031380

ISBN: 978-0-415-72619-1 (pbk)
ISBN: 978-0-415-43701-1 (hbk)
ISBN: 978-0-203-83195-3 (ebk)

Dedicated to Mariko Okubo

Contents

List of illustrations		ix
List of contributors		xi
Introduction		1
SHIRO OKUBO AND LOUISE SHELLEY		

PART I
Transnational crime and human security   7

1	Globalization, human security, and the right to live in peace	9
	SHIRO OKUBO	
2	Human security objectives and the fight against transnational organized crime and terrorism	36
	YVON DANDURAND AND VIVIENNE CHIN	

PART II
Transnational organized crime and the legal response   57

3	Transnational organized crime: the German response	59
	HANS-JOERG ALBRECHT	
4	International organized crime operating in Western Europe: the judicial and police approach against organized crime in the European Union	81
	JOAQUÍN GONZÁLEZ IBÁÑEZ	

5 Crime in Japan and its relation to international organized crime 96
KAN UEDA

6 Drug trafficking in Korea 114
SUNG-KWON CHO

PART III
Human smuggling and trafficking 133

7 International trafficking: an important component of transnational crime 135
LOUISE SHELLEY

8 Foreign women's life and work in the entertainment sector of Korea from the human trafficking perspective 152
DONG-HOON SEOL AND GEON-SOO HAN

9 Trafficking in persons in the Americas: an overview 180
JOHN T. PICARELLI

PART IV
Responding to human smuggling and trafficking 195

10 The EU combat against illegal immigration, smuggling, and trafficking in human beings: its impact on Spanish law 197
EMILIANO GARCÍA COSO

11 Japanese experience and response in combating trafficking 216
ATSUSHI KONDO

12 The trafficking of Thai women to Japan and countermeasures of the Thai government 233
YURIKO SAITO

Index 253

Illustrations

Figures

3.1	Wire-taps per 100,000 of the population	71
3.2	Wire-taps (per 100,000) and convictions per wiretap	71
9.1	Generic human trafficking network	188
9.2	Corporate trafficking syndicate example	191

Tables

6.1	Confiscations of main narcotic drugs	116
6.2	Yearly price for illegal sales of methamphetamine (pilophone)	117
6.3	Illegal importation of new narcotic drugs	117
6.4	Crackdown on narcotic drug criminals	119
6.5	Arrests of offenders for different drug crimes	120
6.6	Arrests of foreigners for drug offenses	121
6.7	Source countries for Chinese-produced methamphetamine	124
6.8	The share of drug arrests of criminals and members of criminal organizations by the Police and Prosecutors' Office and Customs	127
8.1	Awareness of Korea prior to migration	155
8.2	Source of information on work in Korea	156
8.3	Type of visa	159
8.4	Place of work	162
8.5	Job descriptions (multiple responses)	163
8.6	Services that migrant women offer (multiple responses)	164
8.7	Distribution of customers by nationality	167
8.8	Freedom to go out during free time	173
8.9	Desired job in Korea	174
8.10	Composition of monthly income	174
9.1	Forms and routes of trafficking in South America	183
9.2	Forms and routes of trafficking in Latin America and the Caribbean	185
11.1	The number of new entrants on "entertainer" visas (2004–6)	223
11.2	The number of special residence permission and regular residence granted to trafficking victims (2005–6)	224

x   *Illustrations*

11.3	The number of victims protected at Women's Consulting Office	225
11.4	Number of identified trafficking cases and victims	226
12.1	Trafficking victims at House for Women Saalaa (1992–2001)	236
12.2	Estimated annual income accruing to agents in migrant fees in major markets for illegal Thai workers, 1993–1995	242
12.3	Nationality and number of women and children visitors to Social Development and Welfare Bureau-run facilities (January 1999–July 2004)	244
12.4	Number of Thai women returning from abroad using Social Development and Welfare Bureau-run Facilities, according to country repatriated (2000–4)	245

Contributors

Hans-Joerg Albrecht is director of the Max Planck Institute for Foreign and International Criminal Law in Freiburg, Germany. He teaches criminal law, criminal justice, and criminology at the University of Freiburg. Albrecht's research interests cover various legal, criminological, and policy topics ranging from sentencing theory, juvenile crime, drug policies, environmental crime, and organized crime, evaluation research and systems of criminal sanctions, police powers, criminal procedure, and telecommunication surveillance. He is particularly interested in international comparative and cross-cultural research. He has published various books on topics including sentencing, day-fine systems, recidivism, child abuse and neglect, drug policies.

Vivienne Chin is an international justice consultant and a principal of Dandurand, Chin and Associates. She is an Associate of the International Centre for Criminal Law Reform and Criminal Justice Policy (Vancouver), a part of the United Nations Crime Prevention and Criminal Justice Programme Network of Institutes. She specializes in international cooperation and the implementation of international criminal justice and human rights standards and treaties. Her previous experience includes three years as Secretary General of the Commonwealth Magistrates' and Judges' Association (London, U.K.), and seven years as a Senior Commonwealth Fraud Officer/Chief Mutual Assistance Officer, for the Legal and Constitutional Affairs Division, Commonwealth Secretariat, an intergovernmental organization based in London (U.K.).

Sung-Kwon Cho is an advisory member of the Center for International Crime Information, Korean National Intelligence Service as well as a professor in the Department of Narcotics Studies at the Graduate School of Public Administration, Hansung University. His fields of research include terrorism, drug trafficking, transnational organized crime, political corruption, cyber warfare, and intelligence studies. He has published *The History of Korean Organized Crime: Organized Crime and Political Power* (in Korean) (Seoul, Korea: Hansung University Press, 2006) and *Globalization and Human Security*, with Woo Sang (Paju, Korea: Jijmoon, 2005), and has a forthcoming book, *The History of Transnational Criminal Organizations*.

xii *Contributors*

Yvon Dandurand is a criminologist who has taught criminology and sociology of law in various Canadian universities, including the University of Ottawa, Carleton University, and Queens University. He currently is the Dean of Research and Industry Liaison at the University College of the Fraser Valley (Abbotsford, B.C.) and a member of the institution's senior management team. Dandurand is also a Senior Associate and a former Director of Policy Development and Human Rights of the International Centre for Criminal Law Reform and Criminal Justice Policy. He has served on numerous United Nations experts committees, including committees on firearms regulation, victims of crime, violence against women, juvenile justice, restorative justice, terrorism, and organized crime.

Emiliano García Coso is a professor at the University Pontificia Comillas, School of Law, Madrid, Spain. He was a visiting Scholar at Washington College of Law in 2008–2009. He is one of the Spanish members of the Odysseus Network of experts on European Immigration and Asylum Studies sponsored by the European Commission. He has written on consumer protection, Spain as a European frontier, European regulation of migration, and human smuggling and trafficking.

Geon-Soo Han is a professor in the Department of Cultural Anthropology, Kangwon National University in Korea. He earned his Ph.D. from the University of California at Berkeley. His published work includes "Foreign Migrant Workers and Social Discrimination in Korea," "African Migrant Views on Korean People and Culture," "Multicultural Korea: Celebrating or Challenge of Multiethnic Shift in Contemporary Korea?" and numerous articles in Korean on the issue of migrant workers, marriage-based immigration, and human trafficking victims in Korea.

Joaquín González Ibáñez is a lecturer and researcher of International Law and European Union Law at University Alfonso X el Sabio of Madrid, and was a Fulbright-Schuman Visiting Scholar at the Washington College of Law in 2008–9. He is the author of several papers on Human Rights and International Law, as well as of the book *Educación y Pensamiento republicano cívico (Civic and Republican Thought and Education)*. He is also the editor of the book *Derechos Humanos, relaciones internacionales y globalización (Human Rights, International Relations and Globalization)* published by Ediciones Jurídicas in 2006.

Atsushi Kondo is a professor of Constitutional Law at Meijo University, Nagoya, Japan. His research interests are immigration and integration policies in Japan and developed countries. He edited *Citizenship in a Global World* (New York: Palgrave Macmillan, 2001); *New Concept of Citizenship* (Stockholm: CEIFO at Stockholm University, 2003); *Migration and Globalization* (Tokyo: Akashi Shoten, 2008). His journal articles (written in English) are "The Development of Immigration Policy in Japan," *Asian and Pacific Migration Journal*, 2002; "Summary of the Legal Position of Migrants in Japan," *Meijo Hogaku*, 2008.

Contributors   xiii

Shiro Okubo served as a professor of Constitutional Law at Ritsumeikan University Law School, Kyoto, Japan and presently serves as a specially appointed professor at the Research Institute of Ritsumeikan University. He covers a wide range of Japanese constitutional law issues such as human rights, judicial review, and national security as well as human security in the context of globalization. He was director of the Institute of International Relations and Area Studies and the Institute of Humanities, Human and Social Sciences of Ritsumeikan University. He was a visiting professor at the School of International Service and the Washington College of Law, American University. He is the author of *Individual and Group as a Core of Human Rights* (Nihonhyoronsha, 2003); "Japan's Constitutional Pacifism and United Nations Peacekeeping" in *Japan's Quest*, W. S. Hunsberger, ed. (M.E. Sharpe, 1997) and chief editor of *Human Security and Transnational Organized Crime* (4 volumes, Nihonhyoronsha, 2007).

John T. Picarelli is a social science analyst for the International Center of the National Institute of Justice (NIJ). Dr. Picarelli's expertise lies in the intersection of international affairs and homeland security, with a particular emphasis on issues related to organized crime, human trafficking, terrorism, arms proliferation, and gangs. At NIJ, he is responsible for promoting international research and locating international programs and policies that benefit U.S. criminal justice agencies. Dr. Picarelli has published extensively on the topics of organized crime, terrorism, cybercrime, and human trafficking, with over two dozen journal articles and book chapters. He is an adjunct faculty member at American University and George Washington Universities.

Yuriko Saito is an associate professor of International Studies, Meijigakuin University, Yokohama, Japan. She is an expert on the trafficking of Thai women to Japan and the social reintegration of human trafficking survivors. She is the co-author of *To Japan and Back: Thai Women Recount their Experiences in Japan* (International Organization for Migration, 1999), the author of *Who are the Victims of Trafficking in Persons? The Problem of Victim Recognition and Japanese Government Measures against Trafficking in Persons* (University Asia Pacific Research Center, 2006) and "Trafficking in Japan: Past, Present and Future," *New Internationalist Japan*, 2007.

Dong-Hoon Seol is a professor in the Department of Sociology, Chonbuk National University in Korea. His main research interests are economic globalization, sociology of labor markets, international migration, and human trafficking. He has published many articles, books and government-sponsored reports including *Foreign Workers in Korean Society, 1987–1998* (Seoul National University Press, 1999), *Global Capitalism and International Labor Migration* (Seoul National University Press, 2000), "South Korea: Importing Undocumented Workers" (in *Controlling Immigration: A Global Perspective*, 2004), "International Sex Trafficking in Women in Korea: Its Causes, Consequences, and Countermeasures,"

xiv *Contributors*

Asian Journal of Women's Studies, 2004, and "International Marriages in South Korea: The Significance of Nationality and Ethnicity," 2006.

Louise Shelley is a professor in the School of Public Policy, George Mason University and the founder and Director of the Terrorism, Transnational Crime and Corruption Center (TraCCC). She is the recipient of the Guggenheim, NEH, IREX, Kennan Institute, and Fulbright Fellowships and received a MacArthur Grant to establish the Russian Organized Crime Study Centers. She is on the advisory group on illicit trade of the World Economic Forum. She is the author of *Policing Soviet Society* (Routledge, 1996), *Lawyers in Soviet Worklife* and *Crime and Modernization* and has just published *Human Trafficking: A Global Perspective* (Cambridge University Press, 2010). She has written extensively on all aspects of transnational crime and the links with corruption and terrorism.

Kan Ueda is a professor of criminal law and criminology at the School of Law, Ritsumeikan University, Kyoto, Japan. He is a leading expert on basic theory of criminology and problems of criminality with a particular focus on the former Soviet Union. He is the author of *Study of the History of the Soviet Criminology Theory* (Seibundo, 1984), *Lectures in Criminal Law* (Yuhikaku, 1987), *Criminality and Criminology in Contemporary Japan* (Progress: Moscow, 1989), *Lectures in Criminology* (Seibundo, 2004), *The Unfinished Criminal Law: What was Soviet criminal law?* (Seibundo, 2008) as well as numerous articles and book chapters on all aspects of criminal law and criminology. He is also an editor of *Contemporary View of Transnational Organized Crime* (Nihonhyoronsha, 2007).

Introduction

Shiro Okubo and Louise Shelley

This book is an outgrowth of research done over a five-year project at Ritsumeikan University on human security carried out with a grant for Scientific Research from the Ministry of Education, Culture, Sports, Science and Technology. It represents a real international collaboration. It develops from previous work published in 2001 by two of the contributors to this volume, Kan Ueda and Shiro Okubo, entitled *Criminal Justice under Challenges: Crimes and Human Rights in the Borderless Society* (Tokyo: Nippon Hyoron Sha) and from previous work of Louise Shelley and her collaborators at the Terrorism, Transnational Crime and Corruption Center (TraCCC). Over the course of five years, with support from this project, many international scholars came to Ritsumeikan from Asia, North America, and Europe to present their research and exchange ideas and analysis on transnational crime and human security. The following institutions played a key role in its international development: the Washington College of Law and TraCCC of the American University, Graduate School of International Studies, University of Denver, the University of British Columbia Law School, the International Centre for Criminal Law Reform and Criminal Justice Policy, Canada, and organizations of the United Nations. The results of this project were published in a four volume set in Japan called *Human Security and Transnational Organized Crime* (Nihonhyoronsha, 2007).

We want to thank Ms. Keiko Yamada, Ms. Kaoru Yamamoto, Ms. Mina Yamamoto, and Mr. Tomokazu Takagi who provided strong support for this project from the Office of Humanities and Social Sciences Research, Ritsumeikan University, Kyoto, Japan. We want to thank Ms. Joyce Horn in Washington, D.C. for her strong editorial support in bringing this book to fruition.

The research published here focuses on particular aspects of this project. It examines the nature of transnational crime and of human trafficking in a comparative perspective. An international human rights and human security perspective shape the analyses presented in this collection. The causes of these problems, the different forms they assume in different societies, and the diverse social and legal policy reactions developed to address them are emphasized. All of the studies document the rise of the problems that they are studying in their countries and their regions. Drug use, illegal migration, and human trafficking have all grown more common in Asia, North America, and Europe in recent decades. Yet in not one of these

2 S. Okubo and L. Shelley

societies have measures taken to address these problems had a significant impact in stemming their growth.

However, examples are provided of efforts made to alleviate the suffering of the victims. For example, in Korea more treatment is provided to drug addicts than in the past and in Japan shelters have been opened to help female victims of human trafficking. But as the authors of these studies point out, those who are assisted represent a small minority of the victims. All too often, the criminalization of drug use, human trafficking, and illegal migration, according to the authors, leads to great suffering by the victims. The human security perspective of the book suggests that there needs to be more than a criminal law response to these crimes. A response that addresses human beings and their welfare is crucial in any effort to combat transnational crime, human trafficking, and smuggling.

All of the studies point out the limits of national governments in addressing these transnational problems. But bilateral, regional, and multilateral efforts to combat these problems have also failed to be successful because criminals exploit the loopholes in the legal systems. For example, in many countries, including Japan, punishments are applied only to criminals who commit relatively serious crimes abroad. Moreover, it is hard to punish a foreign criminal who leaves the country after having committed a crime. This allows many transnational criminals to commit human trafficking crimes with impunity. Moreover, some "Internet crimes" (such as trafficking in prohibited goods, gambling, and the display of child pornography) are punished differently in different countries, reflecting cultural and political differences. Therefore, criminals take advantage of the gap in the criminal justice systems between countries. Therefore, the diverse chapters in the collection make it clear that there needs to much more international cooperation in developing and implementing laws and policies to address transnational crime. Examples are given in the Japanese-Thai context and in the European context of measures to counter illegal migration and human trafficking, but these are still too limited in the face of such significant growth of the problems and such significant violations of human rights.

The chapters discuss the development in recent years of regional and international legal frameworks to address transnational crime, human trafficking, and smuggling. The background for these more focused measures came in the years following World War II with the adoption of the Universal Declaration of Human Rights in 1948 and subsequently the International Covenant on Economic, Social and Cultural Rights and the International Covenant on Civil and Political Rights Convention on the Elimination of All Forms of Discrimination Against Women. These international agreements laid the groundwork for later and more specific measures to address transnational crime and human trafficking such as the Single Convention on Narcotic Drugs of the UN, the United Nations Convention Against Illicit Traffic in Narcotic Drugs and Psychotropic Substances and a decade ago the United Nations Convention on Transnational Crime and its accompanying protocols. The Protocol to Prevent, Suppress and Punish Trafficking in Persons, especially Women and Children and The Protocol against the Smuggling of Migrants by Land, Sea and Air are discussed extensively in both the legal framework chapters and the more specific chapters on the manifestation of these phenomena.

The European contributors point out that the European Union treaty establishes the framework for cooperation on diverse forms of transnational crime. More specific legislation has also been adopted by such multilateral European bodies as the European Union and the Council of Europe to address transnational crime. This involved specific targeted bodies as well as legal instruments. Yet this multinational framework to address transnational crime on a regional basis is not replicated in North America or Asia as the chapters from these regions illustrate.

The previously cited legislation, as many of the authors point out, focuses on the coercive role of the state in addressing transnational crime and pays scant attention to those victimized by the criminals. Almost all the contributors point to the need for greater attention to the needs of victims. The chapters analyze what can be done at the national and international level to achieve a more victim-centered approach in the law and in social and legal assistance to the victims. Only by considering these elements can we be addressing transnational crime and human trafficking from a human security perspective.

Organization of the book

The book is organized thematically rather than regionally. In an effort to show the universality of the problems we are confronting and the limitations of the legal response globally, we have divided the book into four parts. Each part of the book brings together authors from different regions of the world—Asia, Europe and North America. This sets the book apart from many that discuss transnational crime, emphasizing the unique regional dimensions of the problem.

The first part lays out the intellectual framework of the book, focusing on the human security dimension of transnational crime. Shiro Okubo explains why human security is such an important concept in Japan in the post World War II period and how it frames Japanese foreign policy. This focus on the human being and his/her welfare, rather than on military solutions to problems, he believes is particularly suited to addressing transnational crime and corruption because there are so many victims and the harm is not caused by states but by individuals and groups. He argues for a legal framework that is not based on repression but on humanistic concerns. Yvon Dandurand and Vivienne Chin believe that transnational crime needs to be analyzed not just as a threat to national and international security. They argue for a victim-centered approach to these problems that does not rely exclusively on a law enforcement response. Using Canadian examples, they illustrate how coercive and intrusive approaches are often prioritized to combating transnational crime and terrorism rather than ones that focus on the needs of the individual who suffers as a result of the commission of this crime.

The next two parts of the book focus on the legal response to transnational crime and human smuggling and trafficking. These chapters examine the domestic and international effects of these crimes in the post-Cold War period. Chapters address how the collapse of the Soviet Union, the domestic changes in China, the collapse of the economic bubble in Japan, and the increasing economic discrepancies between the developing and developed world have contributed to the growth

4   *S. Okubo and L. Shelley*

of these phenomena. The rise of regional conflicts and the decline of traditional communities are discussed as contributing to these problems. Specific illustrations of these phenomena are provided, such as the greater number of women trafficked from former socialist states and conflict regions in Southeast Asia, the expansion of drug production in China with the lessening of state controls, and many trying to move illegally to Europe to escape endemic poverty and absence of opportunity in their home countries.

The second part on transnational organized crime and the legal response begins with a broad discussion of the topic by Hans-Joerg Albrecht as well as a more specific focus on the German response to the phenomenon. He points out how the illicit movement of people and goods is part of a larger problem of an illicit economy and the presence of demand for goods and services makes these phenomena hard to control. Like all the authors, he points out the suffering of the victims. He also discusses that while laws and law enforcement are becoming more international, the judicial response remains national. Therefore, this dichotomy makes it hard to respond to these transnational crimes.

Joaquín González Ibáñez discusses the mechanisms adopted in Europe to respond to cross-border crime. These include, for example, Europol established to promote police cooperation and Eurojust to promote cooperation on the judicial level. A European Anti-Fraud Office (OLAF) was founded to fight fraud in the EU and it has initiated large cases with success. Yet cooperation against transnational crime has not been sufficient to stem its growth or prevent widespread victimization. Like other contributors, he points to the need for an approach centered on the rights of the individual.

Kan Ueda discusses the dramatic change in crime and its status within Japan in recent decades. In the 1980s, Japan was cited as a country with little crime that had been able to successfully control its criminality. This is no longer the case. The shocking crime of the Aum Shinrikyo sect as well as the rise of juvenile delinquency, the drug trade, and human trafficking show that Japan is no longer immune to the crime problems known in other parts of the world. As Sung-Kwon Cho discusses regarding drug trafficking in Korea, Korea's drug problems are appreciably worse than those which exist in Japan. Both authors suggest that the internationalization of Japanese organized crime groups, *yakuza*, has had an important impact on the rise of the drug trade and drug abuse in Japan. Professor Ueda suggests that these transnational crimes contradict Japan's conception of itself as a safe country and require the development of both an international and citizen-based approach to these problems. Cho points out that South Korea remains more of a transit country for drugs than a major consumer, although the problems of drug abuse are growing. He sees the Korean perspective as relying excessively on the criminal law and not providing sufficient treatment for the victim.

The third part, on human smuggling and trafficking, focuses on the regional and international developments of the problem and the contribution of organized crime to its growth. Louise Shelley discusses the reasons for the rise of human trafficking, placing growth of the phenomenon in its economic, political, and social contexts. She points out that rural to urban migration, the rise of regional conflicts, and the

Introduction 5

rise of the HIV/AIDS epidemic have all been conducive to the rise of trafficking. Because inadequate attention is being paid by the international community to economic and social needs, people, especially women and children, remain vulnerable to traffickers. She sees human trafficking remaining as a key component of transnational crime in the future.

Geon-Soo Han and Dong-Hoon Seol provide a very rich ethnographic study of the diverse groups of foreign women who work in the entertainment sector in Korea. All report high degrees of abuse including long working hours, humiliation, and violence perpetrated by customers and those who control them. Professors Han and Seol examine the segmentation of the market with women from different countries serving diverse components of the sex industry. Women from the former Soviet Union work in nightclubs frequented by Koreans whereas Filipinas serve Americans near military bases. As South Korea has cracked down on trafficking, the practice has been driven underground.

John Picarelli argues that the trade in human beings is closely related to the historical evolution of every country in the Americas, given that trade in humans has existed in the Americas almost since the arrival of the Europeans. He reviews the different kinds of crime groups that now control trafficking and contrasts those with past ones. Despite the changes in the traffickers, the routes of contemporary trafficking follow the same patterns as the routes used by slavers in the seventeenth and eighteenth centuries. Debt bondage schemes continue to ensnare migrants as they did in the 1900s.

The fourth part of the book focuses on the response to human smuggling and trafficking. It examines the validity and limits of the traditional Western (including Japanese) criminal justice systems, and the need for improved domestic and international laws. These articles also examine the problems of protection of human rights for victims who have been harmed by transnational crime groups. Attention is paid to the problems of foreign nationals in different countries and the difficulties in protecting their rights.

Emiliano García Coso discusses the priority given to transnational crime by the EU and the effort to adopt a legal framework that will address transnational crime and immigration crime in particular. In the aftermath of 9/11, the EU detected flaws in residence permits and there was concern that a clear relationship existed between illegal immigration, terrorism, a lack of security, and delinquency. This resulted in the drafting of European legislation to combat direct and indirect criminal activities related to illegal migration. There has been a focus on combating traffickers but also on returning illegal immigrants and strengthening Europe's external border controls.

Atsushi Kondo's chapter on Japan, like that of Picarelli's, points to the long history of trafficking within Japan and of the domestic legislation to deal with the phenomenon. He examines the impact of the UN 2000 Protocol and the U.S. 2004 Trafficking in Persons Report (TIP) that heavily criticized Japan for its failure to respond to trafficking. He examines the changes that have occurred since the passage of the UN protocol and the challenges that still need to be overcome. He points to the need for much more victim assistance with the rise of foreign trafficking victims in Japan.

6   S. Okubo and L. Shelley

Yuriko Saito has been involved with the movement to help foreign trafficking victims in Japan, particularly those from Thailand. She discusses the incredible hardship of the trafficked women and the suffering that has resulted in a few trafficking victims even killing their female traffickers. In light of this analysis, it makes Seol and Han's conclusion that women in Korea face even worse conditions particularly disturbing. In discussing actual cases of some of the women victims, she points out how poverty in Southeast Asia has been a driving force in bringing women to Japan. Professor Saito analyzes the development of measures to help Thai victims by their government and the role of Japanese women in providing assistance and shelters for foreign victims.

The diverse contributions to this collection lead to the conclusion that much remains to be done to address transnational crime and human trafficking. Traditional criminal law has been based on the structure of the nation-state founded on the concept of citizenship. However, globalization and the accompanying internationalization of crime have already broken down much of that structure. Many who are victims are not citizens of the state in which they are victimized. Nonetheless, Japan and many other countries are stuck at a certain level of response to such issues by relying on outdated international law enforcement organizations and "judicial cooperation." International treaties have been successful in preventing hijackings, but they have not been entirely successful in the area of regulating drugs or combating trade in humans. In light of this situation, the countries of North America, Europe, and Asia must aim at combating such problems by considering practical international crime policies at a variety of levels that respect individual rights. These should be combined with global cooperation to save and aid victims by offering them social and economic assistance and the conditions necessary to rebuild their lives.

Part I

Transnational crime and human security

1 Globalization, human security, and the right to live in peace

Shiro Okubo

Introduction

At the turn of the new century, unexpected events occurred one after another. We have to realize that we are in the midst of a historical transformation, a global structural change named "globalization." People, goods, capital, information, and technology move and spread across borders with a scale and speed that have never been experienced. Globalization causes many, sometimes serious, changes in politics, economics, society, and culture in individual countries, communities, and regions as well as on the international level.

Along with globalization, people face new types of risks, insecurity, and large-scale threats: civil war and internal armed conflicts; famine, poverty, unemployment, and disease; natural disasters and global environmental change. Expanding transnational organized crime and human trafficking are also part of the negative consequences.

Among various opinions and debates on the features of contemporary globalization, we think the following three perspectives allow us to analyze the chaotic situations surrounding globalization clearly. First, the multifaceted and multidimensional aspects of globalization should be considered in a structural context as a whole. Second, a historical approach would give a useful perspective of developments of globalization. Third, and most important, globalization should be analyzed from the perspective of people whose lives, human rights, and safety are often most vulnerable.

This chapter consists of six sections. Sections 1 and 2 cover present situations: three events at the turn of the century; globalization of the free market; and globalization of democracy. Section 3 follows a "human security" approach to people's life and safety and traces the emergence and evolution of the "human security" concept in the United Nations and in Japan's foreign policy. Section 4 argues "freedom from fear and want" as the historical origin of both "human security" and "the right to live in peace" in the Japanese constitution. Section 5 analyzes the emerging process of "the right to live in peace" in post-war Japan and the judiciary.

10 S. Okubo

Three events at the turn of the century

A series of important occurrences that took place at the end of the twentieth and the beginning of the twenty-first century surprised us by their scale, rapid pace of development, and the magnitude of their consequences.

The first occurrence was the fall of the Berlin Wall on November 9, 1989, followed by the collapse of socialist states in Eastern Europe and the Soviet Union. It gave us a sudden end to the Cold War confrontation with nuclear arms. It appeared at the time that humankind could finally be liberated from fear of the total destruction of the world by a nuclear war. In a longer time perspective, it also appeared to be a decisive turning point in modern history, putting an end to the ideological and regime conflicts between capitalism and socialism that swept over the world in the nineteenth and twentieth centuries.[1]

What actually transpired in the "post-Cold War" era, however, was a chaotic and unstable world; a mono-polar military dominance by the United States was constantly undermined by destabilization in various regions of the world. We have witnessed civil wars and internal conflicts brought about by regional, ethnic, or religious causes—widespread poverty, hunger, refugees, diseases—as well as transnational organized crimes and human trafficking. In addition, we face global environmental changes, contributing to far more serious and larger scale natural disasters than in the past.

The second occurrence of importance was the terrorist attack of September 11, 2001, on the United States and the subsequent events. Having been alarmed by the unprecedented assault on its mainland, the United States declared "war on terror" throughout the world. After attacking Afghanistan in retaliation, the United States, together with a "coalition of willing" countries, invaded and occupied Iraq. Brushing aside worldwide objections and protest against the invasion, the United States waged war. The subsequent occupation led to untold suffering by Iraqi citizens, quickly turning into a bottomless pit of confrontations between occupation forces, a resistance movement, and an armed insurgency.

By this invasion, the United States lost the legitimacy and credibility that it had accumulated during and after World War II and by its dedication to establishing freedom and democracy in the world.[2] The wartime mobilization by the Bush administration went beyond the enforcement of an anti-terrorist strategy to include the abrogation of international agreements such as the ban on nuclear tests, the global warming Kyoto Protocol, and approval for the International Criminal Court. The oppressive pressure against "axis of evil" countries induced them to further nuclear proliferation. The military hegemony and unilateral behavior of the United States did not contribute to peace and stability in the world, but rather caused serious cracks even in U.S. public opinion.

The third occurrence was the economic and financial crisis in fall 2008. The width and the depth of its repercussion cannot yet be determined. Each country adopted its own ad hoc measures. A G-8 summit financial meeting was not sufficient, so a G-20 summit was called. The crisis obviously means a failure of the neoliberal economy spearheaded by global financial firms since the end of the 1970s, but, more

Globalization, human security, and the right to live in peace 11

profoundly, it reflects a failure of the U.S.-led international financial system since World War II, the Bretton Woods regime. The crisis calls for far more than ad hoc policy interventions. What must be considered is a kind of total strategy to rectify current worldwide poverty and disparity and to deal with global environmental change caused by modern industrialization.

These three occurrences involved and will involve changes across the realms of politics, economies, societies, and cultures, even extending to biological and ecological issues, and may take generations or even centuries to address. They may suggest that we are in the midst of global structural change at the beginning of the new century. What do we need in order to understand the meaning and the characteristics of such a total change? Two tentative viewpoints should be considered.

The first viewpoint is related to our understanding of the multifaceted and multidimensional structure of globalization. There are various opinions but no single definition or theory can explain it. We should consider globalization as a historically dynamic process with inconsistent motion and frictions. In this chapter, we will discuss two aspects of globalization—the free market and democracy—and very briefly analyze their characteristics, historical background, and driving factors.

The second is related to what happens in people's consciousness in a period of such total change. The unprecedented speed, scale, and multifaceted nature of the changes often leave us struggling to digest each change, unconscious of our place in history.[3] As a result, people have an "identity crisis." not knowing what, why, and where we are heading. To understand the various aspects of contemporary globalization as a whole, we need some basic, original idea or at least a frame of thinking to acknowledge our existence as human beings I think one possible option is the concept of "human security."

Two globalizations and the "security" concept

In understanding globalization as a multidimensional and structural formation, there are two underlying driving forces: globalization of the free market and globalization of democracy.

Globalization of the free market

Contemporary globalization has been led by the spread of the free market across borders. Globalization of the free market was accelerated during the late 1970s and 1980s by the policies of "neoliberalism," Thatcherism in the United Kingdom, and Reaganomics in the United States, which propelled not only privatizations and deregulations within their economies but also global liberalization of trade, investments, and information services. As a result, financial markets and investors came to dominate the world economy. Then, the collapse of the socialist regime decisively designated this free market economy as a global economic system.

Main actors in the global economy are global multinational corporations that have aggressively conducted speculation, mergers and acquisitions, restructurings and reorganizations on a global scale. Susan Strange argued that globalization of

12   *S. Okubo*

the free market caused a structural power shift in security, credit, knowledge and information, and production. She characterized transnational non-state actors as those with "authority beyond the state."[4]

In developed countries, globalization of the free market started a never-ending pursuit of both more free markets and improved efficiency. By dismantling "welfare states" created after World War II, neoliberalism eventually succeeded in redistributing wealth and power to favor the upper class and increased social inequality and disparity, disturbing the "law and order" of the state.[5]

Developing countries were forced into the world's market economy through consolidation of accumulated debts and the structural adjustment loans of the International Monetary Fund (IMF) and the World Bank. Disparity and poverty were spread throughout the world, as evidenced by repeated famines in Africa and accelerated deterioration of the environment in the 1980s. Some states were driven into bankruptcy. On the other hand, countries such as South Korea, Singapore, and Taiwan joined the world free market in the 1980s and then China and India emerged as new powers in the 1990s. The uneven economic development and the instability in the world economy impact not only economies but also politics, society, culture, and religion.

The most striking impact of globalization is the transformation of the power structure among nation-state and non-state authorities—in other words, the decline of sovereign nation-states. The balance of power between nation-states with political and military capacity versus multinational corporations and international markets with rapidly expanding social and economic power is tilting toward the latter. Not only multinational corporations but also various non-state organizations, including transnational organized crime, are now powerful actors in international relations. In fact, transnational criminal organizations have grown most rapidly in the process of globalization.[6] Those non-state authorities have their own *raison d'être* and various functions that have brought about the "decline" of sovereign nation-states.

Still, the "decline" of nation-states does not necessarily mean the "retreat" of nation-states from international relations, because globalization grows through the concurrent process of rearrangement of national infrastructures and legal systems, including denationalization of governmental institutions. For example, multinational corporations as the main actors of economic globalization are concentrating their vital functions within particular nation-states, asking for and adjusting to governmental policies and regulations. Accordingly, it could be said that while nation-states are maintaining political and military powers, they have to reconfigure their waning traditional powers of sovereignty, and they also must add new roles in the globalization process.[7]

Globalization of democracy

Another globalization force is that of democracy. The globalization of democracy started during the late 1970s and the 1980s when people resisted the oppressive governance of authoritarian regimes. In Asia, despotic rule of the Philippines ended in 1986, and the single-party governance by the Kuomintang in Taiwan collapsed

Globalization, human security, and the right to live in peace 13

between 1986 and 1989. The Korean military regime finally collapsed in 1987 and moved to democratization in the 1990s, while many Central and South American countries swept away military governments in the 1980s. In South Africa, after a series of popular uprisings and protests, governance by and for whites was finally replaced by majority rule. Then, starting in fall 1989, socialist regimes in Eastern Europe and the Soviet Union collapsed one after another.

Although the concept of "democracy" is controversial and multidimensional, we define it as a form of governance in which the supreme power is vested in the people and exercised substantially by them. Although globalized democracy during the 1980s through the 1990s was mostly pitted against military or authoritative regimes, democracy has been one of the main driving forces of modern history.[8]

Second, the globalization of democracy was realized not only in the form of "governance by the people" but also in the form of constitutional democracy, in which freedom and rights of the people and human dignity are essential components.[9] The quality of democracy came to be evaluated by the quality and extent of protection of human rights in governance. In the 1990s, an "overlapping consensus"[10] that not democracy in general but constitutional democracy should be a vital principle of governance was formulated in the contemporary world.

Third, the human rights principle was gradually globalized, overcoming various challenges on its way.[11] Although the international political pressure for human rights started to be reflected in laws and regulations with the foundation of the United Nations in 1945 and the promulgation of the Universal Declaration of Human Rights in 1948, development was slow. In the midst of the Cold War, the International Covenant on Economic, Social and Cultural Rights and the International Covenant on Civil and Political Rights were finally adopted in 1966 and came into effect ten years later in 1976. The Convention on the Elimination of All Forms of Discrimination Against Women was opened for signature and ratification in the late 1970s. The preamble of the Convention regarded eliminating gender and sexual discrimination as part of "peace, security, equality and development" and the third generation of human rights, such as the "right to development," was introduced. During the 1980s, the international human rights law was further advanced and institutionalized. Many regions enacted human rights in their own legal system, such as the European Convention on Human Rights and the African Charter on Human and People's Rights.

As the universality of human rights expanded in the 1990s, there were various approaches to human rights with social and cultural differences, leading to a controversy over such universality.[12] One typical case was the "Asian value on human rights" debate, which was a hot issue during the Vienna World Conference on Human Rights in 1993.[13] Embedded in universality and legitimacy of human rights, the globalization of democracy has proceeded as constitutional democracy.

The fourth element of globalization of democracy is the rise of "civil society," or non-governmental organizations (NGOs) as parties acting in the politics of international relations. Various NGO movements have spread across the world, diminishing "the North-South Divide" or "structural violence"[14] since the 1960s and 1970s. These NGOs started as anti-nuclear movements and were joined by

14   *S. Okubo*

environmental movements in the 1980s, all of which form part of the global civic movement. During the 1990s, activities and alliances of NGOs took aggressive actions against the G-7, the IMF, and the World Bank as well as multinational corporations.[15] Now it is common for international politics to be conducted not only by sovereign nation-states, but also by different kinds of NGOs, most of which advocate democracy and human rights.

Transformation of the global power structure

In the modern era, it is believed that sovereign nation-states offer security for the people. The traditional concept of "security" was defined as the relationship between state and individuals, and assumed that the nation-state eliminated external threats by its military capability and the people as a nation enjoyed their peace and freedom under constitutional order within its boundaries. Such national security was the basis of international relations.

However, "succeeding generations" experienced "the scourge of war, which twice in our lifetime has brought untold sorrow to mankind," as stated in the United Nations Charter. The same situation continues. The Cold War led major states to belong to one of two ideological camps—capitalism or communism—which required a more escalated super-national security system. On both sides, a worldwide military security system was constructed, leveraging on the fear of nuclear war. During the Cold War the notion of national security was comprehensively established on the pretext of "power politics," "real politik," and even the "realism" of international relations, which deeply influenced and controlled our way of thinking about "security."

It was only in the late stage of the Cold War era that the concept of national security began to be questioned. A report by the Club of Rome, *The Limits to Growth*, published in 1972,[16] warned of the limits in the growth of the world economy and called for "sustainable development." The 1970s were the turning point for people to be conscious of security issues, focusing on the economy, energy, food, and environment, rather than on military means by which the traditional security regime predominantly governed. Among academics, an emerging study of peace, elaborated under the Cold War environment, uncovered "structural violence" between the North and the South, scrutinized the real beneficiaries of the then prevailing security system, and asked what and for whom the very concept of security existed.

In the 1980s a prevalent idea was that of "common security," which called for control of nuclear power and disarmament. The Report of the Palme Commission of 1982[17] criticized seriously the theory of nuclear deterrence based on "the balance of nuclear terror," and called for restrictions or bans on nuclear, chemical, and biological weapons as well as regular armaments. The report also argued that "common security" over both the North and the South could be achieved by economic development of the third world.

The situation in the aftermath of the Cold War elucidated the limit of traditional concepts of international relations and national security based on sovereign nation-states. In 1992, "An Agenda for Peace," prepared by then-Secretary-General

Globalization, human security, and the right to live in peace 15

of the United Nations Boutros Boutros-Ghali, suggested a transition from "containment" to "prevention" and proposed that the United Nations should play a larger role in "conflict prevention," "peace keeping," "peace making," and "peace building." However, this raised questions as to who would be responsible for each region's security and policing. There was no clear accord as to what enforcing role the United Nations should take beyond its traditional peacekeeping activities.

Regional conflicts, frequently triggered by racial or ethnic or socio-economic disputes, often result in social and political disorder. In these situations, establishing policing and public order are only part of the challenge to reconstruct the daily lives and safety of people and their community. The traditional concept of national security, which has prioritized the rebuilding of military capacity and police order, has to be reconsidered and changed.

Emma Rothschild argues that the idea of security proposed in the 1990s has a "dizzy complexity" that can be characterized by four attributes. First, security is extended downward from security of nations to security of groups and individuals. Second, it is extended upward from nations to the biosphere. Third, it is extended horizontally to different entities, such as individuals, nations, and systems, and in contexts from military to political, economic to social, environmental to human security. And the fourth extension is that of political responsibility in all dimensions to ensure security. She concludes that this extension is aimed finally at security of humans or individuals.[18] Her re-examination of the concept of "security" is one of the best considerations of Western liberal political thought. The critical issues here are the risks to which individuals are exposed and the conditions under which they can maintain their daily lives in safety.

Emergence and evolution of human security

Emergence of human security

After the end of the Cold War, the United Nations Development Program (UNDP) introduced a new concept of human security, replacing the then-prevailing idea of national security. Until the 1980s, the UNDP had been engaged in international projects to aid economic development. It then started publishing annual reports on "Sustainable Human Development" as part of its aim to create an environment enabling people to enjoy long, healthy, and creative lives.[19]

Concerned at the fact that UN peacekeeping activities in 1992 came to include more military actions under the "Agenda for Peace" proposed by Boutros Boutros-Ghali, the 1993 UNDP report proposed "human security as a new concept of security."[20] The 1994 report extended this new concept of "human security" as a part of the UNDP proposal for the 1995 World Summit for Social Development marking the fiftieth anniversary of the United Nations.

The 1994 report presented several significant ideas in theory and in policy-making. First, recalling "freedom from fear and want" as the starting idea for the foundation of the United Nations, it clearly defined the fundamental change of security theory from national security to human security. The report repeatedly proposed that we

16   S. Okubo

should move away from a nation-state concept of security to one that was human oriented and from a military concept to a socio-economic one.

Second, a human security concept requires reconsideration of the traditional view of international relations—shifting from focusing on the relations of sovereign nation-states to a new multidimensional approach to the political economy of international relations as being a global one. With ongoing globalization, each nation-state finds itself in the midst of the ongoing structural power change in the world, but it still must maintain its inherent role of providing physical security, ensuring human rights, and responding to the adverse effects of globalization of the free market.

Third, seven categories of human security (economic, food, health, environmental, personal, community, and political) are proposed as universal and comprehensive guarantees to all people regardless of state, region, and community. But the priority of the basic needs will differ among and within the seven categories. The UNDP 1994 report stated that although "people in rich nations seek security from the threat of crime and drug wars in their streets" rather than hunger and disease, "people in poor nations demand liberation from the continuing threat of hunger, disease," although the threat of crime could be still at present in their daily lives.[21]

The fourth is related to the concept of the individual. The critical point of the human security concept is how to respect and ensure individual self-determination under existing conditions. In the policy-making context we should ask "for whom, by whom, and how should human security be realized?"

"Open Letters on Human Security" submitted by 36 scholars to the Commission on Human Security raised this fundamental issue.[22] The letters warned that discussions on human security often avoid critical evaluation of specific structural and institutional issues and stressed four points for consideration:

- everyday insecurity—all are determining factors in the everyday conditions of people's security;
- the most vulnerable—preference should be given to eliminating the roots of insecurity of the most vulnerable people, individuals, and groups;
- pluralism—a process of pluralistic interactions, dialogue, and consultation among all parties concerned has to be adopted in identifying situations of human insecurity;
- multilateralism—implies the involvement of the people themselves in the processes to reduce and eliminate the sources of their insecurity; also the full mobilization of civil society, especially local, national, and international NGOs, in full cooperation with the UN.

The letters pointed out the risk that UN organizations will often execute their policies in "protectionist" form and stress quantitative measures. In ensuring human security, the most important objective is to find out what the individuals or populations need and respond to such needs.

The fifth is related to the manner in which various actors become involved. Non-state institutions, groups, and individuals can simultaneously threaten and provide for

Globalization, human security, and the right to live in peace 17

human security. To realize human security effectively, it is important to consider the complex and ambivalent relations among parties who provide human security.

Finally, there have been many criticisms of and reservations about the concept of human security since the UNDP proposal.[23] Insofar as the human security concept emerged in the midst of globalization, a great deal of criticism would be inevitable, but the most important is the idea that "human" security should be considered and tested in situations where the people, searching for peace and freedom from fear and want, actually need the minimum necessities for their human dignity and capability to live by themselves.

Evolution of human security in the United Nations

As it happened, the proposal of human security had to cope with the worst timing and the worst situations. Since the middle of the 1990s, a series of serious conflicts have occurred, including genocide, war crimes, and ethnic cleansing in Kosovo and Rwanda. Additionally, the United States committed itself to "the War on Terror" following the September 11, 2001 attack, and started the invasion of Iraq. Then-Secretary-General of the United Nations Kofi Annan announced: "The war in Iraq severely tested the principle of collective security and the resilience of the Organization. Rarely in its fifty-eight-year history have such dire forecasts been made about the United Nations."[24]

The United Nations had opportunities to review worldwide issues to "maintain international peace and security" at the 2000 Millennium and the 2005 "World Summit" for the Sixtieth Anniversary of its birth. As the UN discussed reform in the twenty-first century, the concept of human security came to center stage in the discussion and resolutions in the Assembly.

The 2000 Millennium Report of the UN Secretary-General[25] and the 2000 United Nations Millennium Declaration[26] effectively placed the human security proposal by UNDP in the historical and contemporary situation of the United Nations. The Millennium Report asked "Who are we, the peoples? And what are our common concerns?" and then confirmed that although globalization had become a positive force for people, it left billions of them behind in squalor, bringing disparity, inequality, and insecurity to the world and giving rise to crime, narcotics, terrorism, pollution, disease, weapons, refugees, and migrants. It also tried to re-examine two problem areas: "Freedom from Want" and "Freedom from Fear."[27]

At The United Nations Millennium Summit held in September 2000, leaders of 189 nations adopted the United Nations Millennium Declaration. This declaration set forth eight goals: (1) values and principles; (2) peace, security, and disarmament; (3) development and poverty eradication; (4) protecting our common environment; (5) human rights, democracy, and good governance; (6) protecting the vulnerable; (7) meeting the special needs of Africa; and (8) strengthening the United Nations. As part of the third item, "development and poverty eradication," they set The Millennium Development Goals, which are to be achieved by 2015.

In response to the UN Summit, the Commission on Human Security was organized[28] and submitted its final report to the UN Secretary-General in 2003.[29] The

18   *S. Okubo*

report further strengthened the concept of human security presented by UNDP with policy proposals and recommendations. The human security theory set forth in the report clearly identified and discussed issues and means of resolution. It did not hesitate to warn against and criticize the unilateral action of the United States in pursuit of its national security at that time[30] and called for caution on possible military intervention in developing countries.[31]

In the same period, the international community had to face the controversial and difficult question of how to respond to extremely inhumane situations such as genocide and ethnic cleansing, which happened in civil wars and conflicts. The report "The Responsibility to Protect" by the International Commission on International and State Sovereignty examined these issues in detail and concluded that military intervention for humanitarian purposes is an exceptional and extraordinary measure, but it may be warranted in particular situations and conditions.[32] The report stated "it is no longer viable for any state to assert unrestricted national sovereignty while acting in its own interests, especially where others are affected by its actions"[33] and tried to redefine sovereignty as the responsibility to protect.

The relation between human security and humanitarian intervention is close but ambivalent. The former is designed to target the global structure of poverty and economic disparity and to offer the basic need to empower people to live through non-coercive, non-military means. The aim of humanitarian intervention is to save the lives of the people, but the means of doing so is coercive and requires use of force. Humanitarian intervention in the name of freedom from fear is often selective and risks military commitment from the North to the South in real international politics.

The 2004 Report of the Secretary-General's High-level Panel on Threats, Challenges, and Change[34] argued for "a new security consensus" and that the target for maintaining international peace and security has changed from states waging aggressive war to "poverty, infectious disease and environmental degradation; war and violence within States; the spread and possible use of nuclear, radiological, chemical and biological weapons; terrorism; and transnational organized crime."[35] The report examined rules and guidelines for the legitimacy of using force[36] and recommended post-conflict peace-building.[37]

A report of the Secretary-General, "In Larger Freedom,"[38] prepared for the "World Summit," showed acceptance of the aforementioned suggestions from the high-level panel. With respect to "the responsibility to protect," Kofi Annan, being well aware of the sensitivities involved in this issue, said, "I believe that we must embrace the responsibility to protect, and, when necessary, we must act on it."[39] Rather than setting standards for humanitarian intervention, the more imminent issue was the proposal to create an intergovernmental peace-building commission.[40]

On September 16, 2005, the sixtieth UN General Assembly adopted the 2005 "World Summit Outcome."[41] The "Outcome" reaffirmed participating countries' faith in the United Nations and their commitment to the purposes and principles of the UN Charter and international laws, demonstrating determination to build sustainable and equitable peace in the world. The General Assembly confirmed establishment of a Peace-building Commission,[42] and the creation of a Human

Rights Council.[43] The "Outcome" also provided that although "Each individual State has the responsibility to protect its populations from genocide, war crimes, ethnic cleansing and crimes against humanity," the international community, through the United Nations, is "prepared to take collective action, in a timely and decisive manner, through the Security Council, in accordance with the Charter, including Chapter VII, on a case-by-case basis."[44]

The "World Summit Outcome" for the first time defined human security, noting:

> (W)e stress the right of people to live in freedom and dignity, free from poverty and despair. We recognize that all individuals, in particular vulnerable people, are entitled to freedom from fear and freedom from want, with an equal opportunity to enjoy all their rights and fully develop their human potential. To this end, we commit ourselves to discussing and defining the notion of human security in the General Assembly.[45]

It did not adopt the "concept," but rather the "notion" of human security, which means that defining the concept of human security has been left for future discussion in the UN.[46] It should be noted here that, as pointed out in the report "A More Secure World," the concept of human security is the basic idea that demonstrates "the indivisibility of security, economic development and human freedom."[47]

Human security in foreign policy: Japan

The Japanese and Canadian governments formed government-level policies in line with the concept of human security proposed by UNDP. Although the Japanese government focused on "freedom from want," the Canadian government focused on "freedom from fear."[48]

After the 1997 Asian economic crisis, the Japanese government introduced the concept of human security in making official foreign policy. Foreign Minister Keizo Obuchi, who later became Prime Minister, took the first initiative. In a series of addresses and speeches starting in Singapore on May 4. 1998, he repeatedly stated that Japan would form its foreign policy based on human security.[49]

In December 1998, in "An Intellectual Exchange to Make the Future of Asia," Obuchi stated, "We need to deal with the Asian Crisis with sensitivity for people in socially weak positions, viewing them in light of Human Security." He also stated, "We must seek new strategies of economic development, putting importance on Human Security." Referring to poverty, refugees, human rights, HIV, terrorism, and anti-personnel landmines, Obuchi appealed to Japan to make stronger efforts to combat these sources of insecurity to ensure human security. He also stated that human security is a comprehensive idea to protect people from any and all threats against cohabitation in peace, satisfactory level of standards of living, and human dignity.[50]

Keizo Takemi, then parliamentary undersecretary of foreign affairs, explained the political contexts of the aforementioned Japanese policy on human security.[5] He stated that, in principle, Japan aimed to attain and maintain national security

20 *S. Okubo*

by non-military means. Behind such non-militant thoughts lie "the Japanese constitution, which forfeits the use of armed forces as a means to solve international disputes," and "learning from history what military methods brought to the world and to Japan."

In 1999, the Japanese government founded a Human Security Foundation in the United Nations,[52] and at the UN Millennium General Assembly in 2000 proposed establishment of a Commission on Human Security.[53] In a 2003 policy guideline on official development assistance (ODA) the Japanese government addressed human security and set forth a policy goal not only to aid regions and nations on development but to aid individuals in protecting themselves from direct threats, set up grant assistance for grassroots human security projects, and revise Japan's Official Development Assistance Charter, which had been approved more than ten years earlier.[54] Changes included consideration of the perspective of human security in its policies on ODA. Japan launched its Medium-Term Policy on ODA in February 2005, explaining six concrete approaches to adopt the perspective of "Human Security" in the process of policy and project formulation, implementation, and evaluation. (Japanese human security diplomacy, however, was heavily disrupted by the September 11 attack.[55])

The 1999 *Diplomatic Blue Book* stated that

> Human security comprehensively covers all the menaces that threaten human survival, daily life and dignity—for example, environmental degradation, violations of human rights, transnational organized crime, illicit drugs, refugees, poverty, anti-personnel landmines, and infectious diseases such as AIDS—and strengthens efforts to confront these threats.

It further stated that "as these are all cross-border issues, coordinated action by the international community will be important, as will linkages and cooperation among governments, international organizations, NGOs and other parts of civil society."[56] Since then, the human security concept has been one of the major themes of Japanese diplomacy.

However, as Japan declined to engage in the "war on terror" led by the United States, human security diplomacy eventually was positioned in a complementary role in the overall security policy of Japan. The 2003 *Diplomatic Blue Book* emphasized the traditional role of national security policies against international crises and threats, and finally the 2006 *Diplomatic Blue Book* explained the concept of human security as efforts to provide "protection by the state and international society."[57] Such an explanation of human security is nothing more than the very concept of national security.

The merit of Japanese human security diplomacy lies in the concept embracing various types of threats and strengthening efforts to combat risks in line with the UNDP concept of human security. In the first years of the new century, its usefulness was limited to diplomatic activities, ODA activities, and support of the Human Security Fund of the United Nations. The Japanese government has now faced the need to redefine the concept of human security in its diplomatic policy-making.

Globalization, human security, and the right to live in peace 21

Difference from the Canadian concept

The government of Canada introduced the concept of human security in its foreign policy before other countries did, and organized a human security network together with other countries such as Norway. The Canadian initiative started when Lloyd Axworthy became foreign minister in 1996.[58] The Canadian government recognized the significance of the concept of human security, ranging from the state-oriented view of security to the human-oriented view. Because this concept is too comprehensive to treat as a policy guideline, the government focuses on "the continuing insecurity resulting from violent conflict."[59] It took two initiatives to create the campaign to ban landmines (the Ban Treaty and the Ottawa Conference) and the effort to create the International Criminal Court.

A recent bulletin of the Department of Foreign Affairs and International Trade of Canada emphasizes counter-terrorism and protection of human rights, particularly the prosecution of anti-humanitarian crimes. It states that the international community should contribute to the protection of citizens in time of threats such as genocide and ethnic cleansing, even with military force if necessary.[60] However, the policy of Canada focuses on "freedom from fear" from a West European perspective of rights and freedom and is inclined to seek direct effects from its human security policy, rather than to change the structure of human security. Canadian initiatives on human intervention tend to invite antipathy from Asian and other developing nations. The opposition to a recent report of the Canada-led International Commission on Intervention and State Sovereignty (ICISS) from the group of 77 countries is one such case.[61]

In contrast to the Canadian concept, the Japanese human security policy has a specific focus on freedom from want and empowerment of people through economic and human development. The most conspicuous merit of this approach is to advance human security policy through non-military means.[62] Japanese government officials and diplomats continue to use human security as the key concept in their speeches. Further, Japan continues to contribute to the Human Security Fund, the largest fund among UN programs. Japan also organized the "Friends of Human Security" network in October 2006 as a follow-up to the 2005 "World Summit Outcome."[63] Japan is also an active contributor to peace-building commissions and other similar activities of the UN.

The human security concept stands out as one of the most unique aspects of post-war Japan's diplomacy. Although national security policies centered on the Japan–U.S. military alliance constitute the backbone of Japanese diplomacy, the human security concept can act at least as a counterbalancing force in Japanese diplomacy.

Freedom from fear and freedom from want

"Freedom from fear and want" as the purpose of World War II

The Charter of the United Nations adopted on June 26, 1945 states that the purpose of establishing the United Nations is "to save succeeding generations from

22   S. Okubo

the scourge of war," "to reaffirm faith in fundamental human rights, in the dignity and worth of the human person," and "to promote social progress and better standards of life in larger freedom" (the preamble). Thus, the basic tasks of the UN are "to maintain international peace and security" and "to achieve international co-operation . . . in promoting and encouraging respect for human rights and for fundamental freedoms" (Article 1).

The phrase "free from fear and want" as the historical origin of human security has its direct root in the Atlantic Charter of 1941. Article Six provides that

> after the final destruction of the Nazi tyranny, they hope to see established a peace which will afford to all nations the means of dwelling in safety within their own boundaries, and which will afford assurance that all the men in all the lands may live out their lives in freedom from fear and want.[64]

The Declaration by the United Nations on January 1, 1942, clearly recognized the principles of the Atlantic Charter, stating that it seeks "to defend life, liberty, independence and religious freedom, and to preserve human rights and justice in their own lands as well as in other lands."[65]

In the Dumbarton Oaks Conference where the foundation of the United Nations was established, promoting "respect for human rights and fundamental freedom" was deemed one of the tasks of a new international organization, but it was not explicitly listed among the "purposes" of the proposed "general international organization" as a form of uniting nations.

In light of the international criticism against the omission, it was decided in the United Nations Conference held in 1945 in San Francisco to incorporate the following provision in Article 1 of the UN Charter defining the purposes of the organization:

> To achieve international co-operation in solving international problems of an economic, social, cultural, or humanitarian character, and in promoting and encouraging respect for human rights and for fundamental freedoms for all without distinction as to race, sex, language, or religion.

Edward Stettinius, U.S. Secretary of State, reported to the government on the developments at the San Francisco Conference for foundation of the United Nations as follows.

> The battle of peace has to be fought on two fronts. The first is the security front where victory spells freedom from fear. The second is the economic and social front where victory means freedom from want. Only victory on both fronts can assure the world of an enduring peace. No provisions that can be written into the Charter will enable the Security Council to make the world secure from war if men and women have no security in their homes.[66]

Globalization, human security, and the right to live in peace 23

The UN Charter and the Constitution of Japan

The preamble of the Constitution of Japan adopted the same composition as the UN Charter, declaring the country had "resolved that never again shall we be visited with the horror of war through the action of government, do proclaim that sovereign power resides with the people and do firmly establish the constitution." It further states: "we recognize that all peoples of the world have the right to live in peace, free from fear and want." The Constitution of Japan was a historical product of World War II and accepted being "free from fear and want" as the purpose of the war.[67]

The difference between the UN Charter and the Constitution of Japan lies in how to preserve peace and security. In the UN Charter, prevention of war and maintenance of international peace and security rest on coercive military measures. The Security Council has the primary responsibility of maintaining international peace and security and

> may take such action by air, sea, or land forces as may be necessary to maintain or restore international peace and security. Such action may include demonstrations, blockade, and other operations by air, sea, or land forces of Members of the United Nations [Article 42]

The Security Council also admits the inherent right of individual or collective self-defense of member states (Article 51).[68]

In contrast, the Japanese constitution provides the total and absolute renunciation of military action; not only to "renounce war as a sovereign right of the nation," but also to renounce "the threat or use of force as means of settling international disputes," and further to prohibit maintenance of "land, sea, and air forces, as well as other war potential." This historical background was clear. Japan ignited the war and was defeated completely. Drawing lessons from this experience, the Japanese Constitution was an unprecedented constitutional doctrine for peace.

The UN Charter included provisions for promoting respect for human rights, Articles 55 and 56, in which member states pledge to promote international economic and social cooperation and universal respect for human rights. The Charter also included Article 68, which sets forth the creation of commissions to promote human rights. Discussions in the commission led to the Universal Declaration of Human Rights in 1948. The inseparable relation between respect for international human rights and world peace was crystallized in the preamble of the Declaration as "recognition of the inherent dignity and of the equal and inalienable rights of all members of the human family is the foundation of freedom, justice and peace in the world" and "advent of a world in which human beings shall enjoy freedom of speech and belief and freedom from fear and want has been proclaimed as the highest aspiration of the common people."

The Constitution of Japan provides a series of fundamental human rights from civil liberties to social rights in chapter three as the Bill of Rights, but also mentions "the right to live in peace" in the preamble. That, combined with the total denial of war and military measures in Article 9, urged us to take a Copernican conversion

24 *S. Okubo*

in the conception of security from a state-oriented view to a people-oriented view. "The right to live in peace" of "all peoples of the world" can create a real sense of self-determination. In addition, prescribing that "the right to live in peace" is being "free from fear and want" concisely suggests the real causes of war and how we can stop warfare and reclaim our lives. Thus, the peace doctrine of the Japanese constitution may be considered a high point in the history of political and constitutional thought on war and peace.

The right to live in peace

Post-war Japan and the peace doctrine

The legislative process of the peace doctrine in Japan's constitution is already well known.[69] It has two aspects. One derives from both the world pacifism that emerged from the terrible experiences of two world wars and the historical movement to make war illegal, such as the Kellogg-Briand pact of 1928 and the UN Charter. The other aspect is reflected in the political situations in 1945–6. At that time, the most critical issue was how to treat the emperor. The U.S. government sought to make use of the emperor with his pre-war conservative group for building a pro-American government in post-war Japan.[70]

But maintaining any form of imperial rule, even when the renewed one became merely a symbol of state with no political power, demanded a clear guarantee to avoid the suspicion of a resurgence of Japanese militarism in the post-war world. To accomplish this occupation policy, General Douglas MacArthur, Supreme Commander of the Allied Powers, decided to draft a clear provision that provided a total ban on the maintenance of any form of military force in post-war Japan.[71]

After the promulgation, Japan undertook a delicate balancing act between the peace doctrine of the constitution and the military alliance with the United States, which fundamentally contradicted each other, but reconciled them in post-war politics. In other words, the constitutional peace doctrine constantly faced the possibility of being disposed of or substantively changed, but has survived throughout the whole post-war period up to today. The real factor in maintaining the peace doctrine was not the occupation policy, the post-war government, or governmental parties, but its own vitality and the continuous support of people inside and outside Japan. Japan has consistently avoided involvement in armed conflicts overseas and concentrated its human and material resources on its own socio-economic development under the constitutional peace doctrine. This post-war process in line with the constitutional doctrine is the basis for Japanese foreign policy on human security.

Emergence of the right to live in peace

The constitutional significance of the concept of "the right to live in peace" in the preamble was not recognized in the early post-war period. However, as Article 9 became a heated issue in post-war politics, the constitutional debates over the peace doctrine discovered the link between Article 9 and the preamble. "The right

Globalization, human security, and the right to live in peace 25

to live in peace" gradually obtained a position as a constitutionally protected right among legal academics as well as in social movements. In the 1960s, the phrase began to be reviewed in court. Thus, for nearly a half-century Japan had discussed "freedom from fear and want" as the substance of "the right to live in peace" before the emergence of the concept of human security in the international community in the 1990s.[72]

The beginning of the Cold War brought major changes in the U.S. occupation policy. Its priority turned to building Japan as a base against communist expansion in Asia. Following the peace treaty of 1952, combined with the Japan–U.S. Mutual Security Treaty, Japan was able to re-enter international society. Immediately, the conservative government attempted to revise Article 9 completely, but finally failed in the mid-1950s.[73] As the Cold War tension prodded memories of horrible wartime experiences, a public movement was organized against the involvement in the "hot war" in Asia and rearmament of Japan under the Japan–U.S. alliance.[74]

After the 1960 political crisis concerning the revision of the Japan–U.S. Security Treaty, the majority of the party in government, the Liberal Democratic Party (LDP), abandoned their attempt to return to the old regime and moved decisively to so-called "post-war governance." The policy strategy to put special emphasis on socio-economic developments conformed with U.S. global strategy.[75] To deal with U.S. demands for Japan to build a large military, the LDP government fully exploited the constitutional peace doctrine and the strong tendency to support the peace constitution. On one hand, the conservative government always had to pay attention to the people's sense of pacifism, and on the other, the United States had to respect the political stability of Japan under the LDP government.

In fact, the government strengthened the Japanese Self-Defense Forces (SDF) and the Japan–U.S. military alliance step by step, manipulating the constitutional interpretation of Article 9.[76] Initially, the government's interpretation was that the SDF is not in the normal sense "military" or of "war potential"; that is, capable of waging "modern wars." It then proceeded to the official opinion of the cabinet that aggressive military force is prohibited but "necessary minimum force for defense" is permitted under the Constitution.[77] The government position was continuously met by strong opposition based on the words clearly used in Article 9, which meant the government had to consider the constitutionally "minimum" limitations of the Self-Defense Forces.[78] Such limitations are a prohibition against joining in collective security, the so-called non-nuclear policy, the budgetary parameter of spending no more than 1 percent of GNP for defense, and a prohibition on exporting military hardware.[79]

The contradiction between the constitution and governmental security policy has produced many constitutional law suits. The Supreme Court has been bureaucratically conservative, but it could not disregard the clear provision of Article 9. In the Sunagawa case[80] in the late 1950s, although the Tokyo district court declared the Japan–U.S. Security treaty unconstitutional, the Supreme Court declined to rule on the constitutionality of the treaty because of the "political question" that the judiciary would not be able to decide.[81] Since then the Supreme Court has maintained such a judicial doctrine to avoid the constitutional issue, but when any

26   *S. Okubo*

constitutional suits were filed, the trial attracted the attention of the entire nation and public concern could not be avoided.[82]

Initially, "the right to live in peace" was interpreted as an idealistic right deriving from natural law and beyond positive law. However, along with heated debates in a series of so-called peace litigations, "the right to live in peace" became not simply an ideal. It required that total renunciation of war and military capability be constitutionally protected by legal academics, public opinion, and the courts.

The most controversial case in the 1970s was that of the Naganuma Nike Missile Base. The residents in Naganuma challenged the constitutionality of an administrative decision for the construction of an anti-aircraft missile base for the Self-Defense Forces. The Sapporo district court confirmed "the right to live in peace" in the preamble as the plaintiffs' suit and determined that the size and the capabilities of the Self-Defense Forces were unconstitutional. The court declared that the right to live in peace is "crystallized and stipulated in the form of specific fundamental rights under each clause of Chapter Three of the Constitution," and that

> to understand each provision of Forest Law in context of the constitutional order, . . . it is just to interpret that the said provision aims to protect "the right to live in peace" of the local people. Accordingly, if the right of the area residents to peaceful existence is infringed upon by the defendant's official act . . . this base, with anti-aircraft facilities, radar and so forth, would be the first target of an attack from another country at the time of an emergency. Consequently, the danger exists that the plaintiffs' right to live in peace is being infringed upon.[83]

Although the higher court reversed the district court decision on technical grounds, avoiding the constitutional issue,[84] the right to live in peace has been one of the critical constitutional issues in subsequent law suits in the era of global nuclear confrontation. The actual possibility of nuclear war and the extinction of human life gave rise to the idea that we cannot make the decision that war is just or unjust and so the right to maintain peace becomes the "most fundamental human right" in the nuclear age.[85] Through discussions of the significance and legal character of "the right to live in peace" it became clear that issues of peace and war or national security do not belong exclusively to the government, but rather that the people's self-determination should be guaranteed in their daily lives.

The international role of Japan and the right to live in peace

Since the late 1970s, the main topic in the constitutional struggle over Article 9 has moved from the meaning of "the right for self-defense" to "the right of collective self-defense" under the Japan–U.S. Alliance as a part of the global military strategy of the United States.[86]

Entering the post-Cold War era, Japan is looking for an international role in a new controversy over the constitutional peace doctrine. One issue is whether Japan should be a "normal" country, equipped with a military force. This would lead to changing the constitutional interpretation of Article 9 and to total constitutional reform.[87]

Globalization, human security, and the right to live in peace   27

There are two different types of international roles: "collective self-defense" within the U.S. global strategy,[88] and "collective security" with the UN.

Since the Guidelines for the U.S.–Japan Defense Cooperation of 1978 and 1997, Japan has engaged in U.S.-led military operations under the greatly expanded notion of self-defense.[89] In 1990, Japan was asked to cooperate with the U.S.-led multinational forces in the Middle East. After heated controversy in the Diet, the Japanese government dispatched mine sweepers of the Maritime Self-Defense Force to the Persian Gulf in 1991.[90] In 1992, the UN Peacekeeping Act was enacted and "the UN Peace Cooperation Corps," including 600 SDF personnel, were sent to Cambodia with the coalition forces.[91] The majority of public opinion approved active cooperation with the UN, but opposed the use of force, or any military activities, even for the UN forces.

Since the late 1990s, the major political parties have moved to prepare for constitutional reform and public opinion appeared to be shifting to accept the revision of the constitution. The call for constitutional reform in general peaked in 2004 through 2005 and the major parties, conservative media, and business organizations prepared the drafts for the revision.[92] The majority of the people, however, consistently opposed revision of Article 9[93] and popular civic movements led by liberal intellectuals, such as the Article 9 Society, strongly defended the peace provisions of the constitution.

After the September 11, 2001 attacks, Japan accepted U.S. pressure to cooperate with the worldwide military strategy and enacted the Anti-Terrorism Special Measures Law of 2003, which authorized government contribution to the international community in the "prevention and eradication" of international terrorism. Further, the Iraq Special Measures Law of 2003 was enacted, authorizing the deployment of the SDF to Iraq for strictly humanitarian and reconstruction assistance in non-combat areas. Many law suits were filed challenging the deployment and the enactment as being unconstitutional.

The Nagoya High Court declared the operations of the SDF in Iraq illegal and unconstitutional.[94] Although the court dismissed the plaintiffs' claims both for damages and for an injunction against the deployment of the Air Self-Defence Force (ASDF), the court held that ASDF operations in Iraq violated the limits imposed by the Iraq Special Measures Law and the prohibition on the use of force in Article 9(1) of the Constitution. The court said that the ASDF activities in Iraq did not involve any use of force, but that transporting coalition forces was an essential element of combat and although the Special Measures Law of 2003 is constitutional, the activities of the ASDF contravene both the Special Measures Law and Article 9, section 1 of the Constitution, which forbid "the threat or use of force as a means of settling international disputes."

The Court then defined "the right to live in peace" as follows: (1) As no basic human right exists without peace, "the right to live in peace" is the right every person should have and is the foundation upon which all human rights rest. It is not limited to constitutional ideals and principles but is a constitutionally legal right. (2) The Constitution clearly states that all Japanese citizens have "the right to live in peace" and Article 9 instructs the government to abandon war and not

28 *S. Okubo*

to use force. Moreover, Article 13 instructs the government to respect and uphold individual human rights. (3) "The right to live in peace" is founded on rights of freedom, social rights, and the right to vote, and therefore is a tangible subject and right that can be protected in court if action is taken by the government in violation of Article 9. In such a case, action can be taken to stop the violation and to request damages.

The decision to declare the operations of the SDF unconstitutional has been epoch-making since the Naganuma case in the Sapporo district court more than 30 years ago. That decision demonstrated that Article 9 of the Constitution is still enforced not only by effectively restricting military activities of the SDF with U.S. forces but also by revealing the political context—that the Japanese government is under legitimate and widespread national pressure based upon the people's quest for the right to live in peace.[95]

Conclusion

We are surely in the midst of dramatically changing circumstances. A series of events at the beginning of the new century demonstrates dramatically that the traditional concepts, theories, and policies on economics, politics, and international relations have not been capable of responding to the present situations. What looks clear is, first, that we are asking what we are and how we should preserve ourselves. Second, using violence to preserve our existence is the worst way to respond. For example, the contemporary terrorism is surely an ultimate form of violence, but the use of force to eradicate such violence is another form of violence. Violence cannot change the situation at all; rather, it makes it worse.

We should be aware that the answer for these situations was found and clearly set out more than a half-century ago just after World War II—"freedom from fear and want." "Human security" is another name for "freedom from fear and want," which was conceived about 50 years after its origin. The issue now is how to establish human security. What we should stress is that human security does not require any form of violence, war or use of force.

Notes

1 1989 is one of the four '89s in modern history. Yoichi Higuchi proposed a historical schema of four '89s in modern constitutional history: the Bill of Rights of England in 1689; the Declaration of the Rights of Man and Citizen in the French Revolution in 1789; the Meiji Constitution of Japan in 1889, the first Western type constitution in Asia, although it was neither liberal nor democratic, but rather was most authoritarian. Then we had the fall of the Berlin Wall in 1989. See Y. Higuchi, "Les quatre 'Quantre-vingt-neuf' ou la signification profonde de la Révolution Française pour le développement du constitutionnalisme d'origine occidentale dans le monde," p. 989.

2 J. Habermas, "Interpreting the fall of a Monument." This essay originally appeared in German in the *Frankfurter Allgemeine Zeitung*, April 17, 2003.

3 Yoshikazu Sakamo wrote that although looking at each event is easy, understanding the true nature of worldly structural changes is difficult, because changes are happening on a large scale and are multiple in character and in the areas where they occur. No

Globalization, human security, and the right to live in peace   29

nation-state, government, or political party has clearly defined responsibilities, while corporations and work places do not know what to do in global markets. People are not sure even about what school education and home bring to them. Y. Sakamoto, *Soutaika no Jidai* (*the Era of Relativity*), preface.

4 S. Strange, *The Retreat of the State*, identified the control of communications, organized crime, insurance businesses, the Big Six accountant firms and multinational businesses, cartels, and international organizations such as IMF and World Bank as being an "authority beyond the state."

5 D. Harvey, *A Brief History of Neoliberalism*.

6 See L. Shelley, "Transnational Organized Crime: An Imminent Threat to the Nation State"; Strange, *Retreat of the State*, 110–21; J. Mittelman, *The Globalization Syndrome*, pp. 203–22.

7 S. Sassen, *Losing Control: Sovereignty in an Age of Globalization*.

8 For the classic consideration on the relations between market capitalism and democracy, see C. B. Macpherson, *The Life and Times of Liberal Democracy*.

9 The concept of "constitutionalism" can be defined in different contexts. It originally included a restraint of popular will or sovereignty and, above all, could be a fear of the consequences of democratic power and rule. We use "constitutional democracy," which makes democracy more substantial and more concerned with human rights. I refer here to constitutional democracy as distinct from liberal democracy.

10 E. Kelly, ed., *Justice as Fairness: A Restatement by John Rawls*, Part 1, §11, 32–8; John Rawls, *The Law of the Peoples*, §6–3, pp. 172–4.

11 See, e.g., J. Donnelly, *International Human Rights*, pp. 3–18.

12 J. Bauer and D. Bell, eds., *East Asian Challenge for Human Rights*; A. Langlois, *The Politics of Justice and Human Rights*.

13 The World Conference on Human Rights, 1993, reaffirming "the universal nature of these rights and freedoms is beyond question," declared, "All human rights are universal, indivisible and interdependent and interrelated. The international community must treat human rights globally in a fair and equal manner, on the same footing, and with the same emphasis. While the significance of national and regional particularities and various historical, cultural and religious backgrounds must be borne in mind, it is the duty of States, regardless of their political, economic and cultural systems, to promote and protect all human rights and fundamental freedoms."

14 J. Galtung, "Violence, Peace, and Peace Research"; Johan Galtung, "Human Needs, Humanitarian Intervention, Human Security, and the War in Iraq," presented at a 2004 conference on Human Security, <http://www.aa.tufs.ac.jp/humsecr/report/040110top.html> (accessed September 30, 2006).

15 See, e.g., Mittelman, *The Globalization Syndrome*.

16 D. H. Meadows, D. L. Meadows, J. Randers, W. W. Behrens, *The Limits to Growth: A Report for the Club of Rome's Project on the Predicament of Mankind*.

17 Report of the Independent Commission on Disarmament and Security Issues, *Common Security: A Programme for Disarmament*.

18 E. Rothschild, "What Is Security?" She referred to the phrase of Vaclav Havel, "the sovereignty of the community, the region, the nation, the state makes sense only if it is derived from one genuine sovereignty—that is, from the sovereignty of the individual."

19 Mahbub ul Haq was well-known for taking the initiative by publishing an annual human development report. See Mahbub ul Haq, *Reflections on Human Development*.

20 The 1993 report stated, "During 1992, the UN had to intervene in several internal conflicts, from Bosnia to Somalia . . . (b)ut military force is only a short-term response. The long-term solution is faster economic development, greater social justice and more people's participation. The new concepts of human security demand people-centred development, not soldiers," overview, p. 3.

21 Human Development Report 1994, p. 24.

30   *S. Okubo*

22 "Open Letter on Human Security to the Chairs of the United Nations Independent Commission on Human Security," September 15, 2001, <http://www.mushakoji.com/gyoseki/openleter.php> (accessed September 30, 2008).
23 For recent work on the human security concept, see R. Joly and D. B. Ray, "Human Security Framework and National Human Development Reports: A Review of Experiences and Current Debates," NHDR Occasional Paper 5, May 2006. See also S. Tdadbakhsh, "Human Security in International Organization: Blessing or Scourge?", p. 8.
24 Report of the Secretary-General on the Work of the Organization, General Assembly, A/58/1, introduction, p. 1.
25 K. Annan, "We the Peoples—The Role of the United Nations in the 21st Century," A/50/2000, UN.
26 United Nations Millennium Declaration A/55/2, September 8, 2000.
27 Annan, "We the Peoples," p. 14.
28 Japan addressed the UN Summit Assembly, stating that Japan "positioned human security as one of the key perspectives of Japanese diplomacy" and called for the establishment of an international commission on human security to further deepen the concept, <http://www.mofa.go.jp/policy/other/bluebook/2001/chap1-g.html> (accessed November 10, 2009).
29 Final Report of the Commission on Human Security, "Human Security Now," May 1, 2003, <http://www.humansecurity-chs.org/finalreport/index.htm> (accessed November 10, 2009).
30 Ibid., p. 12.
31 Ibid., p. 28.
32 Canada organized the International Commission on Intervention and State Sovereignty (ICISS) in September 2000 and the commission submitted a report to the UN Secretary-General. The report formalized that for humanitarian intervention there must be serious and irreparable harm occurring to human beings, or imminently likely to occur, of the following kind: (a) large scale loss of life, actual or apprehended, with genocidal intent or not, which is the product either of deliberate state action, or state neglect or inability to act, or a failed state situation; or (b) large scale "ethnic cleansing," actual or apprehended, whether carried out by killing, forced expulsion, acts of terror or rape, <http://www.iciss.ca/report-en.asp> (accessed November 10, 2009).
33 Ibid., p. 12.
34 "A More Secure World: Our Shared Responsibility? Report of the Secretary-General's High Level Panel on Threats, Challenges and Change," 2004, UN Document A/59/565.
35 Ibid., p. 1.
36 "A More Secure World" adopted the concept of "responsibility to protect" and humanitarian intervention, paras. 199–209.
37 "In Larger Freedom: Towards Development, Security, and Human Rights for All," Report of the General Secretary, UN Doc.A/59/2005, March 21, 2005.
38 "In Larger Freedom," para. 8.
39 "In Larger Freedom," para. 135.
40 "In Larger Freedom," paras. 114–19.
41 General Assembly, "World Summit Outcome," UN Doc.A/Res/60/1, 24, October 24, 2005.
42 2005 "World Summit Outcome," para. 97. The report strongly recommended establishment of a single intergovernmental organ dedicated to peace-building, para. 225. The report of "In Larger Freedom" proposed creation of an intergovernmental Peace-building Commission and a Peace-building Support Office within the UN Secretariat, para. 114.
43 "World Summit Outcome," para. 157. The report recommended reform of the Commission of Human Rights, para. 284, and "In Larger Freedom" proposed a Human Rights Council, para. 183.
44 "World Summit Outcome," paras. 138–9.

Globalization, human security, and the right to live in peace 31

45 "World Summit Outcome," para. 143.
46 After the 2005 UN Summit, the General Assembly had the first thematic debate on human security in March 2008, available at <http://www.un.org/ga/president/62/statement/crhumansecurity220508.shtml> (accessed November 8, 2009).
47 "A More Secure World," Synopsis, p. 1.
48 See S. Edson, *Human, Security: An Extended and Annotated International Bibliography*; S. Alkire, "A Conceptual Framework for Human Security". p. 20; R. Jolley and D. B. Ray, "The Human Security Framework and National Human Development Reports."
49 Ministry of Foreign Affairs of Japan, International Symposium on Development, "Development: With a Special Focus on Human Security," <http://www.mofa.fo.jp/policy/human-secu/sympo9906.htm> (accessed September 30, 2009).
50 Ministry of Foreign Affairs of Japan, *Diplomatic Blue Book*, 1999, p. 244.
51 K. Takemi, "On Human Security," lecture at Keio University, May 19, 1999.
52 The Trust Fund for Human Security was established in March 1999 with an initial contribution of about ¥500 million. By FY 2009, total contributions amounted to some ¥39 billion (approximately $US346.58 million), making the trust fund one of the largest of its kind established in the UN. The fund implemented 195 projects totaling $US312 million in 118 countries and one area. Moreover, in FY 2006–2008, Japan appropriated ¥31 billion for the Grant Assistance for Grassroots Human Security Projects, which incorporates the concept of human security. See, Ministry of Foreign Affairs, The Trust Fund for Human Security, <http://www.mofa.go.jp/policy/human_secu/t_fund21.pdf> (accessed November 9, 2009).
53 "Human Security Now."
54 Japan's Official Development Assistance (ODA) Charter was revised in 2003 after more than ten years in operation. The revision included consideration of the perspective of human security in its policies on ODA. Japan launched its Medium-Term Policy on ODA in February 2005, which explains six concrete approaches to adopt the perspective of "human security" in the process of policy and project formulation, <http://www.mofa.go.jp/policy/oda/mid-term/policy> (accessed November 9, 2009).
55 The 2002 *Diplomatic Blue Book* stated that "The terrorists' attack on the United States on September 11th urged international society to be aware of risks that multiple issues such as conflicts and poverty create conditions for terrorism to grow." It also argues that "an important focus of Japanese foreign policy, in an aim to realize human security, is to create a society where each individual can realize his/her potential and make it sustainable . . . in order to deal with increasingly multiple and complex threats." Japan had correctly pointed out the background of the terrorists' attack and indicated that problems cannot be solved simply with military actions, <www.mofa.go.jp/policy/other/bluebook/2002> (accessed February 3, 2010).
56 The 1999 *Diplomatic Blue Book*, Section 3, An Overview, <http://www.mofa.go.jp/POLICY/other/bluebook/1999/II-3-a.html> (accessed November 9, 2009).
57 The 2006 *Diplomatic Blue Book*, p. 183, <http://www.mofa.go.jp/POLICY/other/bluebook/2006/12.pdf> (accessed November 9, 2009).
58 See L. Axworthy, "Canada and Human Security: The Need for Leadership."
59 L. Axworthy, *Human Security: Safety for People in a Changing World*.
60 "Freedom from Fear," Department of Foreign Affairs and International Trade, Canada, 2000.
61 P. Evans, "Human Security and East Asia: in the Beginning," p. 263.
62 The Japanese government has succeeded in defining a human security concept in line with the 1994 UNDP report. Ambassador Yukio Takasu, Permanent Representative for the UN, defined this concept as a common understanding that "all individuals, particularly vulnerable people, are entitled to freedom from fear and want, with an equal opportunity to enjoy all their rights and fully develop their human potential" at the General Assembly Thematic Debate on Human Security, New York, May 22, 2008, <www.mofa.go.jp/announce/speech/un2008/un0805–6.html> (accessed February 3, 2010).

32 S. Okubo

63 The first meeting of Friends of Human Security (FHS) was held on October 19, 2006, as an informal forum for Member States as well as relevant international organizations to discuss the concept of human security. The second meeting was held on April 30, 2007 and the third on November 7, 2007, <http://www.mofa.go.jp/mofaj/gaiko/hs/friends.html> (accessed November 10, 2009).

64 Dating back to January 6, 1941, its origin can be found in the presidential message of Franklin Roosevelt declaring support of "the Four Freedoms" —freedom of speech and expression, freedom of every person to worship God, freedom from want, and freedom from fear.

65 On February 11, 1945, with the end of World War II approaching, the Yalta Declaration Conference confirmed that "(b)y this declaration we reaffirm our faith in the principles of the Atlantic Charter, our pledge in the Declaration by the United Nations and our determination to build in cooperation with other peace-loving nations world order, under law, dedicated to peace, security, freedom and general well-being of all mankind."

66 U.S. Secretary of State Edward R. Stettinius, Jr. reporting to his government on the results of the San Francisco meeting that established the United Nations, 1945. Cited in United Nations Development Programme, 1994, *Human Development Report 1994*, UNDP, p. 24.

67 For the legislative process of the Constitution of Japan, see S. Koseki, *The Birth of Japan's Postwar Constitution*.

68 Article 51 of the UN Charter provides that the right of individual or collective self-defense is confirmed "until the Security Council has taken measures necessary to maintain international peace and security."

69 Shiro Okubo, "Japan's Constitutional Pacifism and the United Nations Peacekeeping" in *Japan's Quest: The Search for International Role, Recognition, and Respect*, p. 102.

70 The U.S. Occupation policy was "to bring about the eventual establishment of a peaceful and responsible government which will respect the rights of other states and will support the objectives of the United States," United States Initial Post-Surrender Policy I(b), 29 August 1945.

71 The first draft was drastic: "War as a sovereign right of the nation is abolished. Japan renounces it as an instrumentality for settling its disputes and even for preserving its own security . . . no Japanese army, navy, or air force will ever be authorized and no rights of belligerency will ever be conferred upon any Japanese force," the second of three principles by MacArthur for drafting the constitution of Japan, March 3, 1946. The first paragraph of the draft of Article 9, however, was "[the Japanese people] forever renounce war as a sovereign right of the nation and the threat or use of force as means of settling international disputes" and the second paragraph included "land, sea, and air forces, as well as other war potential, will never be maintained. The right of belligerency of the state will not be recognized."

72 For the relation between "the right to live in peace" and the domestic policy of "The Three Non-Nuclear Principles" (not to produce, not to possess, and not to permit the introduction of nuclear weapons into Japan), see K. Urata, *Reflections of Global Constitutionalism*, pp. 214–19.

73 A two-thirds majority in both houses of the Diet is the constitutional requirement to initiate an amendment for a national ratification (Article 96). The conservative government tried to change the electoral law in the mid-1950s, but failed.

74 The United States pressed Japan to establish a "national police reserve" in 1950 during the Korean War, a "national safety force" in 1952, and then the Self-Defense Forces in 1954, which is now in force.

75 The opinion that rearmament may disturb economic growth was strong even in the conservative camp and the business community.

76 Most governmental interpretations were apologetic and later changed, but had highly political functions in reconciling the gap between the provisions of the constitution and reality.

Globalization, human security, and the right to live in peace   33

77 Since 1954 the Legislation Bureau has taken the initiative of the governmental interpretation of Article 9; see James Auer, "Article Nine: Renunciation of War," p. 74.

78 The LDP government has recognized a series of constitutional limitations—prohibition to dispatch the SDF overseas for military action in the 1950s and prohibition to join in collective security agreements to defend other nations in the 1980s—but the government announced that the non-nuclear principles were as a self-imposed limitation rather than a constitutional prohibition.

79 See C. Martin, "Binding the Dogs of War: Japan and the Constitution of Jus ad Bellum."

80 The people who opposed extension of the U.S. military air base were arrested and prosecuted for violating the special criminal law for the Japan–U.S. Security Agreement.

81 The Supreme Court said that although there is nothing in Article 9 that would deny the right of self-defense inherent in our nation as a sovereign power, the Security Treaty features an extremely high degree of political consideration, having bearing upon the very existence of our country, unless it is clearly unconstitutional and invalid, *Sakata v. Japan*, 13 keishu 3225, case No.1959(A)No.710(Sup.Ct.)GB12/16/59. See John M. Maki, *Court and Constitution in Japan: Selected Supreme Court Decisions, 1948–60.*

82 The Eniwa case, *Nozaki v. Japan*, 9 lower keishu 359, March 29, 1967, was well known in the 1960s.

83 *Ito, et al. v. Minister of Agriculture, Forestry, and Fisheries*, District Court, 1973; see H. Itoh and L. W. Beer, *The Constitutional Case Law of Japan: Selected Supreme Court Decisions, 1961–70*, pp. 83–122.

84 *Minister of Agriculture, Forestry, and Fisheries v. Ito, et al.*, Sapporo High Court, 1976; *Uno, et al. v. Minister of Agriculture, Forestry, and Fisheries*, Supreme Court, 1982. As to the right to live in peace, the high court said that although the Preamble has a legal character, it is not concrete and peace is no more than an ideal or a goal.

85 See "The inherent right to life in peace," Declaration on the Preparation of Societies for Life in Peace, UN Doc., Resolution of the General Assembly, 33/73, December 15, 1978; "the inalienable right of every nation and every human being to live in peace," Declaration on International Disarmament, Resolution of the General Assembly, 34/88, December 11, 1979.

86 Auer, "Article Nine."

87 For the Gulf War controversy over whether Japan should be "a normal country," see Okubo, "Japan's Constitutional Pacifism," pp. 106–8.

88 Japan's Cabinet Legislation Bureau repeated its interpretation that the exercise of the right of collective self-defense exceeds the limit on self-defense authorized under Article 9 of the Constitution and is not permissible.

89 See R. Fisher, "The Erosion of Japanese Pacifism: The Constitutionality of 1997 U.S.-Japan Defense Guidelines."

90 This was the first overseas deployment of Japanese military force since World War II.

91 Okubo, "Japan's Constitutional Pacifism."

92 In May 2007, the government parties in the House of Councillors passed the National Referendum Law for revision of the constitution, but it was defeated in the Upper House in July 2007. The government parties then lost control of the Diet to the Democratic Party of Japan—then the leading opposition party; now the government party—which opposed the National Referendum Law. For the constitutional situation of Article 9 generally, see C. Pence, "Reform in the Rising Sun: Koizumi's Bid to Revise Japan's Pacifist Constitution"; P. Boyd and R. Samuels, "Nine Lives?: Politics of Constitutional Reform in Japan."

93 In 2004, the *Yomiuri Shinbun* newspaper opinion poll showed 65 percent of the respondents in favor of a constitutional amendment in general, 23 percent against, but the support decreased to 42.5 percent in 2008 and opposition 43.1 percent. The approval of article 9 was 44 percent, with 47 percent against in 2004, and in 2008 31 approved, 60 percent opposed. The *Asahi Shinbun* opinion poll of 2008 revealed 66 percent opposed to revision of Article 9, and 17 percent approved, *Asahi Shinbun*, May 3, 2008.

34 S. Okubo

94 Nagoya High Court, April 17, 2008, Hanreijiho no. 2956, p. 74, <http://www.hahei sashidome.jp/english/index.htm> (accessed November 10, 2009).
95 The Nagoya case is one of the 12 lawsuits, joined by more than 6,000 plaintiffs, against the dispatch of the SDF to Iraq.

References

Alkire, S. (2001) "A Conceptual Framework for Human Security," Centre de Recherche et d'Intervention sur le Suicide et l'Euthanasie, working paper 2.

Auer, J. (1993) "Article Nine: Renunciation of War," in *Japanese Constitution*, P. R. Luney, Jr. and K. Takahashi, eds., Tokyo: Tokyo University Press.

Axworthy, L. (1997) "Canada and Human Security: The Need for Leadership," *International Journal* 52, no. 2: 183–96.

Axworthy, L. (1999) *Human Security: Safety for People in a Changing World*, Department of Foreign Affairs and International Trade, Canada.

Bauer, J. and Bell, D., eds. (1999), *East Asian Challenge for Human Rights*, Cambridge: Cambridge University Press.

Donnelly, J. (1998) *International Human Rights*, 2nd edn, Boulder, CO: Westview Press.

Edson, S. (2001) *Human, Security: An Extended and Annotated International Bibliography*, Centre for History and Economics: King's College, Cambridge.

Evans, P. (2004) "Human Security and East Asia: in the Beginning," *Journal of East Asian Studies* 4, no. 2: 263–84.

Final Report of the Commission on Human Security, "Human Security Now." May 1, 2003, <http://www.humansecurity-chs.org/finalreport/index.htm> (accessed November 10, 2009).

Fisher, R. (1999) "The Erosion of Japanese Pacifism: The Constitutionality of 1997 U.S.-Japan Defense Guidelines," *Cornell International Law Journal* 32: 393–430.

Galtung, J. (1969) "Violence, Peace, and Peace Research," *Journal of Peace Research* 6, no. 3: 167–91

Galtung, J. (2004) "Human Needs, Humanitarian Intervention, Human Security, and the War in Iraq," presented at a 2004 conference on Human Security, <http://www.aa.tufs.ac.jp/humsecr/report/040110top.html> (accessed September 30, 2006).

Habermas, J. (2003) "Interpreting the fall of a Monument," *German Law Journal*, 4, no. 7 (July): 701–8.

Harvey, D. (2005) *A Brief History of Neoliberalism*, Oxford: Oxford University Press.

Higuchi, Y. (1989) "Les quatre 'Quantre-vingt-neuf' ou la signification profonde de la Révolution Française pour le développement du constitutionnalisme d'origine occidentale dans le monde," *L'image de la Revolution française*, M. Vovell, Paris/Oxford: Pergamon Press.

Itoh H. and Beer, L. W. (1996) *The Constitutional Case Law of Japan: Selected Supreme Court Decisions, 1961–70*, Seattle: University of Washington Press.

Jolley, R. and Ray, D. B. (2006) "The Human Security Framework and National Human Development Reports: A Review of Experiences and Current Debates," National Day of Healing and Reconciliation, Occasional Paper 5, May.

Kelly, E. ed. (2001), *Justice as Fairness: A Restatement by John Rawls*, Cambridge, MA: Harvard University Press.

Koseki, S. (1997) *The Birth of Japan's Postwar Constitution*, edited and translated by R. A. Moore, Boulder, CO: Westview Press.

Globalization, human security, and the right to live in peace   35

Langlois, A. (2001) *The Politics of Justice and Human Rights*, Cambridge: Cambridge University Press.

Macpherson, C. B. (1977) *The Life and Times of Liberal Democracy*, Oxford: Oxford University Press.

Maki, John M. (1964) *Court and Constitution in Japan: Selected Supreme Court Decisions, 1948–60*, Seattle: University of Washington Press.

Martin, C. (2008–9) "Binding the Dogs of War: Japan and the Constitution of Jus ad Bellum," *University of Pennsylvania Journal of International Law* 30: 267–357.

Meadows, D. H., Meadows, D. L., Randers, J. and Behrens, W. W. (1972) *The Limits to Growth: A Report for the Club of Rome's Project on the Predicament of Mankind*, New York: Universe Books.

Ministry of Foreign Affairs of Japan (2009) The Trust Fund for Human Security, <http://www.mofa.go.jp/policy/human_secu/t_fund21.pdf> (accessed November 9, 2009).

Ministry of Foreign Affairs of Japan, International Symposium on Development, "Development: With a Special Focus on Human Security," <http://www.mofa.fo.jp/policy/human-secu/sympo9906.htm> (accessed September 30, 2009).

Ministry of Foreign Affairs of Japan. (1999), *Diplomatic Blue Book*.

Mittelman, J. (2000) *The Globalization Syndrome*, Princeton, NJ: Princeton University Press.

Okubo, Shiro (1966) "Japan's Constitutional Pacifism and the United Nations Peacekeeping" in *Japan's Quest: The Search for International Role, Recognition, and Respect*, Warren. S. Hunsberger, ed., Armonk, NY: M. E. Sharpe, Inc.

"Open Letter on Human Security to the Chairs of the United Nations Independent Commission on Human Security". September 15, 2001, <http://www.mushakoji.com/gyoseki/openleter.php> (accessed September 30, 2008).

Pence, C. (2006–7). "Reform in the Rising Sun: Koizumi's Bid to Revise Japan's Pacifist Constitution", *North Carolina Journal of International Law and Commercial Regulation* 32.

Rawls, J. (1999) *The Law of the Peoples*, Cambridge, MA: Harvard University Press.

Report of the Independent Commission on Disarmament and Security Issues. (1982), *Common Security: A Programme for Disarmament*, London: Pan Books.

Rothschild, E. (1995) "What Is Security?," *Daedalus* 124, no. 3: 53–98.

Sakamoto, Y. (1997) *Soutaika no Jidai* (*the Era of Relativity*), Tokyo: Iwanami Publishing Co.

Samuels, R and Boyd, J. P. (2005). "Nine Lives?: Politics of Constitutional Reform in Japan," *Policy Studies* 19.

Sassen, S. (1996) *Losing Control: Sovereignty in an Age of Globalization*, New York: Columbia University Press.

Shelley, L. (1995) "Transnational Organized Crime: An Imminent Threat to the Nation State," *Journal of International Affairs* 48, no. 2 (Winter): 463–89.

Strange, S. (1996) *The Retreat of the State*, Cambridge: Cambridge University Press.

Tdadbakhsh, S. (2007) "Human Security in International Organization: Blessing or Scourge?" *Human Security Journal* 4, Summer.

ul Haq, Mahbub (1995) *Reflections on Human Development*, Oxford: Oxford University Press.

United Nations Development Programme. (1994), *Human Development Report 1994*, UNDP.

Urata, K. (2005) *Reflections on Global Constitutionalism*, Institute of Comparative Law, Waseda University.

2 Human security objectives and the fight against transnational organized crime and terrorism

Yvon Dandurand and Vivienne Chin

Because organized crime tends to be associated with the exploitation of various illicit markets (drugs, firearms), it is easy to forget that organized crime is not necessarily victimless. In fact, it rarely is. There are very few organized criminal activities that do not sooner or later involve a serious form of victimization. Organized crime victimizes a great number of people, even if many of the victims do not necessarily understand exactly how they have been victimized and by whom. We can think of victims of elaborate frauds, human trafficking, trafficking in firearms, drug dealing, or extortion. Criminal organizations never hesitate to use fear and intimidation. That is precisely how they usually perpetuate themselves and avoid detection and prosecution. The sad reality is that, given the opportunity, criminal groups will always prey on economically, culturally, or otherwise isolated or excluded groups.

The 2004 Annual Report on Organized Crime in Canada underlines the fact that intimidation, assaults, or homicides are an integral part of organized crime: "The violence is a serious threat to public safety, resulting in injuries and a sense of insecurity in communities." It adds that "large and small communities across the country continue to be negatively affected by the often subtle yet complex effects or organized crime."[1]

The same report, based on criminal intelligence, attempts to demonstrate how violence and the threat of violence from organized criminal groups is a significant threat to public safety. These groups use violence to protect and promote their criminal interests. The violence is often also intended to intimidate and coerce individuals and communities, creating what the report calls a "general sense of insecurity in communities."[2]

Why then is organized crime increasingly defined as a national security problem and not as a fundamental human security issue? Why are human rights and human security concerns receiving so little attention in our anti-crime and anti-terrorism efforts? Have we lost sight of what organized crime does to people and to communities?

Beare argues that the concept of organized crime "has become stretched and mythologized to the point of total distortion, rendering it useless for anything but political mileage and the bargaining for resources by law enforcement."[3] There certainly is a lot of truth in that statement. We will argue that a human security approach to the problem of organized crime compels us to focus more clearly on

Human security objectives   37

its impact on victims. This, in turn, leads us to acknowledge the many ways in which law enforcement and criminal justice agencies fail to prevent victimization, to protect victims, and to respond to their needs. Adopting a human security perspective with respect to organized crime and terrorism redirects our attention toward the plight of victims and the need to protect and assist them. The rights of organized crime victims are too often ignored in the name of some abstract security objective. Researchers and policy-makers should therefore re-examine our criminal justice system's current response to organized crime and its current neglect of basic human security objectives.

Many countries, including Canada, have made a concerted and sustained effort to fight transnational organized crime and terrorism. They have invested a considerable amount of resources in this effort and in doing so have created great public expectations. Laws have been adopted that have created new offenses and developed new methods of tracking and seizing the proceeds of crime. Treaties and conventions have been adopted that have formalized the countries' commitment to cooperate with each other and work more closely together to fight transnational organized crime and terrorism. Complex and expensive systems have been put into place to support that collaboration. In the process, some long-standing legal protections for basic rights are sometimes being abandoned in the name of pursuing greater public safety and security.

In Canada, in September 2000, Federal, Provincial, and Territorial Ministers Responsible for Justice declared the fight against transnational organized crime a "national priority." Subsequently, a host of new measures have been adopted over the last several years, including major amendments to the Criminal Code. Canada has ratified all the relevant international conventions. In 2005, a new law against human trafficking was adopted. In spite of all these measures, it is still not clear that any significant progress is being achieved in terms of reducing or stopping organized crime. In fact, most people seem to be prepared to agree that we are indeed losing the so-called "war against transnational crime."

Every year, new reports from national and international law enforcement agencies, crime commissions, and Parliamentary committees announce that the problem is getting worse. For example, in August 2003, Commissioner of the Royal Canadian Mounted Police (RCMP) Giuliano Zaccardelli, commenting on a report released by the Criminal Intelligence Service of Canada, stated that organized crime was still on the rise in Canada and that new cross-border alliances were being forged among criminal organizations.[4] Similar types of alarmist statements are regularly made by law enforcement officials and politicians. Such statements may serve to fuel public fear and mobilize public support for law enforcement demands for more resources. They, unfortunately, are based on weak intelligence and guesswork. The truth is that organized crime activities are mostly clandestine and very rarely come fully to the attention of the authorities. No one is really able to systematically assess how much organized crime there is and how many people are victimized by it in one way or another.

Because of the panic created by criminal justice officials and the media, a fear is growing that the battle against transnational organized crime cannot be won. Most

38 Y. Dandurand and V. Chin

people, at least in Canada, are prepared to assume that the "war" is in fact being lost every day, little by little. In Canada, major law enforcement agencies[5] have begun to reflect that general attitude by formulating their own objectives no longer in terms of "stopping" organized crime, but in terms of simply "disrupting" it. The change in rhetoric may reflect nothing more than a clever attempt to manage public expectations. Nevertheless, the public feelings of insecurity that are thus being fed are now part of a growing "human security deficit."

We would all be well advised to reflect on the "human security" objectives that we must pursue with respect to transnational crime. If we are really committed to human security as a fundamental social objective, we need to understand how it should direct our approach to the control of organized crime. We may also need to reflect on whether our current response to organized crime is the best one to achieve these objectives. Perhaps we ought to reconsider the strategies we have espoused and the goals we are pursing. All of this may lead us to admit that our current approaches largely fail to advance any basic human security objectives. We may also be led to engage in a more systematic query about how some radically different responses to transnational organized crime could perhaps yield more significant results in terms of achieving our fundamental human security objectives. We might ask, for instance, whether our laws and our law enforcement practices and priorities would be the same if they were genuinely aligned with our human security objectives.

A focus on the vulnerability of certain groups

Organized crime and terrorism now tend to be approached by the international community primarily as direct threats to national and international security, which they most certainly are, and not so clearly as matters of human security and human rights. National security objectives have had a tendency to take precedence over human security concerns. In the process, some significant human security and human rights concerns have been neglected.

As is generally the case with moral panics, claims that public safety or national security are at risk produce a disaster mentality; fear and anxiety over crime and terrorism can be used by governments to restrict people's rights, in particular the rights of minority groups and foreigners.[6] After September 11, 2001, members of many minority groups felt under siege in their own country.[7] Furthermore, as various social groups are able to successfully associate the problems of terrorism and organized crime with a perceived lack of control of immigration and refugees, Canadian intolerance of immigrants is growing, as was confirmed by a September 2003 survey conducted for Citizenship and Immigration Canada.[8]

Similarly, in the fight against organized crime, we seem to be prone to suspect immigrants and more likely to define them as part of the problem rather than as potential victims. Even if the relation between ethnicity and organized crime is a problematic one, the concept of organized crime has always had a strong ethic connotation.[9] And, as Van Duyne noted, in the "organized crime against us" representation of the problem, the "they-us" dimension is very often amplified by the assumption that the "they" is of foreign origin.[10]

Human security objectives 39

In North America, since the 1950s, a dominant explanation and social representation of organized crime has been in terms of an "alien conspiracy."[11] Just as the theory was losing credibility, it re-emerged even more strongly around the fear of terrorism in the late 1990s. In a recent more subtle incarnation of the conspiracy theory, the conspiracy element is often abandoned in favour of the idea that criminals, terrorists, and other villains are essentially foreign, especially when xenophobic feelings and fears are being exacerbated. The police and the media can thus rely on the "ethnic assumption" to provide a simple framework to explain and justify various interventions.

We all know how easily, particularly in a democratic society, the rights, safety, and security of various vulnerable groups can be compromised by the activities of terrorist agents and organized criminals. Some communities can basically be held hostage by criminal or radical groups, living under a climate of fear, as victims of violence and intimidation. We also know how easily and quickly the rights and liberty of the same vulnerable groups can be sacrificed by a society in the pursuit of some illusion of safety. Why have we not therefore focused on developing effective strategies to offer protection to these vulnerable groups? Are we really expecting members of these groups to stand up alone, without any assistance, against organized crime or terrorist organizations?

Vulnerable groups frequently complain that they do not receive effective protection from law enforcement agencies. During national consultations that were recently organized by the Canadian federal government, several groups have expressed their concerns that they do not always receive equal protection from the authorities. As Sheptycki noted, "the notion of transnational organized crime is often read against a background of crude stereotyping"[12] and so is terrorism. Because many members of ethnic minorities fear prejudice, racial profiling, and racism, they often do not know whom they should fear the most: the criminals or the authorities. Should they decide to denounce their oppressor or collaborate with law enforcement, they do not know what protection they can really expect to obtain from the authorities.

Canada is apparently a frequent destination for international terrorists and their supporters. The Canadian Security Intelligence Service Public Report for 1999 pointed out that Canadians mirror the population of the globe; therefore, when violence grips some region torn by conflict, it often resonates in Canada.[13] A 1999 Report of the Special Senate Committee on Security and Intelligence noted that groups with terrorist affiliations conduct fundraising activities in Canada. Such groups and other criminal organizations are often able to exploit the particular vulnerability of diasporas, recent immigrants, and minority religious groups to further their own ends.

The widespread intimidation of potential witnesses and informers within a community as a whole can take place when it is infiltrated and eventually controlled by radical elements or criminal gangs. One must understand that that kind of intimidation is particularly hard to detect and especially difficult to combat. For example, Bolan described how the intimidation of the Indo-Canadian community was a factor in defeating the efforts of investigators and prosecutors in the Air India case: "For fifteen years, intimidation had been a successful tactic to silence potential witnesses."[14]

40   Y. Dandurand and V. Chin

In that particular case, radical elements were hiding within and controlling large segments of the Indian Diaspora in Canada. According to Bolan, it was not until a journalist was shot that the police understood the danger faced by anyone in a position to expose the militants or who dared speak against them. "They were threatened and attacked for writing or speaking their mind on issues of extremism, but police did not treat the crimes against them seriously." She adds that:

> A certain level of cynicism was building in the Sikh community. Many people wondered if the Canadian authorities were being completely inept in dealing with criminals and terrorist thugs just because they were from a minority, non-English speaking community? . . . Some also thought that race and culture played a factor. They asked themselves whether white Canadians would tolerate the same lawlessness in their community if threats, beatings, and shootings were going unpunished.[15]

Despite being designated a terrorist group by India and several Western nations, the Babbar Khalsa managed to get charitable status from Revenue Canada in the early 1990s. This occurred while many people in the community had reasons to believe that some of the directors of the organization were perhaps involved in terrorist activities. "It was a common tactic of the separatists to invite politicians to the temple under one guise and advertise it in Punjabi as something else. They would then claim that the politicians were supportive of the separatist cause."[16] The community felt that it could not count on the authorities for protection. The *Report of the Honourable Bob Rae on Outstanding Questions with Respect to the Bombing of Air India Flight 182* refers to "evidence of a culture of fear within communities that has stopped people telling the truth about what happened."[17] In that case, various forms of low-level intimidation and ostracism were reinforced by violent retaliation and even murder.

During the last several years, Canadians have become much more aware of how the vulnerability of certain minority groups can increase the vulnerability of the country as a whole. As organized crime groups and terrorist organizations have become increasingly internationalized, they have learned to rely on their ability to obtain support, through deception, coercion, and other means, from various vulnerable groups.

In the fight against terrorism and organized crime, recent immigrants and other minority groups with potential ties with insurgent or criminal groups in other countries are often on the "front line." Exclusion or discrimination on the basis of ethnic origins or religious affiliation is often compounded by political, as well as economic and social exclusion. Marginalization, alienation, and the resulting sense of victimization can encourage extremism and facilitate the exploitation of communities by radical elements.[18] These marginalized groups are often victimized, terrorized, and pressed and coerced into supporting criminal elements for which they have no sympathy. Yet, they are too easily and too often labeled as part of the problem and left to fend for themselves against these powerful and dangerous enemies.

Intimidation

As Dedel pointed out, community residents should ideally be committed to reporting crime and giving evidence in court; and in return, police should be committed to providing support, information, and protection to the community and to potential witnesses.[19] Things are seldom that simple when it comes to organized crime and communities that are being intimidated.

Intimidation can be "community-wide," acts by gangs and criminal organizations intended to foster a general atmosphere of fear and non-cooperation within a community.

> Examples of mass intimidation given by police and prosecutors suggest that fear is only one factor contributing to the reluctance of witnesses to step forward; strong community ties and a deep-seated distrust of law enforcement may also be strong deterrents to cooperation.[20]

Community-wide intimidation involves acts that are intended to create a general sense of fear and an attitude of non-cooperation with police and prosecutors within a particular community.[21]

The Council of Europe defines criminal intimidation as:

> Any direct, indirect or potential threat to a witness, which may lead to interference with his/her duty to give testimony free from influence of any kind whatsoever. This includes intimidation resulting from the mere existence of a criminal organization having a strong reputation for violence and reprisal, or from the mere fact that the witness belongs to a closed social group and is a position of weakness therein."[22]

People who live in communities that have direct knowledge of the activities of criminal organizations are often effectively deterred from cooperating with authorities.

Prosecutors often complain that the mere fact that a crime is gang-related can be sufficient to prevent an entire neighborhood from cooperating. Some authors have noted that this kind of community-wide intimidation is particularly frustrating for prosecutors and police investigators "because, while no actionable threat is ever made in a given case—thereby precluding conventional responses—witnesses and victims are still discouraged form testifying."[23] Witness are often aware that by communicating with the police about a crime, they have transgressed community norms. In some cases, community hostility can force those who have collaborated with the authorities to leave their home.[24]

Many members of minority and ethnic groups avoid cooperating with the criminal justice system for cultural reasons, including a sense of group loyalty that makes them reluctant to testify against members of their own culture. Illegal immigrants who are often found within these communities are typically reluctant to have contact with law enforcement because they are vulnerable to the threat of deportation.[25]

Intimidation can be of varying severity. Some experts distinguish between "low-level" intimidation and the very serious and often life-threatening experience of other witnesses and their families, often in relation to organized criminal or terrorist groups. The number of witnesses who fall in the latter category is relatively small in comparison to witnesses who face low-level intimidation (yet, most of the attention of legislators and law enforcement and justice officials has focused on that particular group). Both forms are encountered in the manner in which terrorist and criminal groups typically maintain whole groups or communities in fear of reprisals and retaliation. At one extreme, there are individuals and their families who are at high risk of serious, even life-threatening, intimidation, typically linked to serious organized crime or terrorist groups. Such intimidation is relatively rare and tends to be used sparingly by criminal groups. More typically, communities are dealing with non-life-threatening intimidation: members of the community fear violence without a specific threat.[26]

Citizens who confront organized crime are intimidated and live in fear. They cannot count on the state's protection. Shelley has characterized this situation as a new form of authoritarianism.[27] In Toronto, this seems to have been the predicament of the Jamaican Diaspora intimidated by Jamaican gangs operating in both Canada and Jamaica. The intimidation and exploitation of immigrants and members of minority groups by transnational terrorists and other criminal organizations is a pressing issue that is woefully neglected everywhere in the world. Policymakers and law enforcement officials typically fail to grasp that, in countries such as Canada, the United Kingdom, or the United States, several minority ethnic communities find themselves on the front lines of powerful and dangerous struggles and are the immediate victims of terrorists and other criminal organizations.

The cumulative evidence of research on witness intimidation is that, like crime generally, intimidation is neither evenly nor randomly distributed socially or geographically. Some individuals in certain communities are more likely to suffer intimidation than others. Geographical proximity to the offender, within a close-knit community generally increases the risk of intimidation, given that opportunities for intimidation are higher.[28] Having examined the limited empirical data on witness intimidation, Fyfe remarked that intimidation can have an enormous impact at the level of communities.[29]

Endangered individuals who belong to these vulnerable groups are more difficult to protect (for example, by relocation) because of their close ties and sometimes their dependence on the community. Furthermore, the risk for the relatives of these endangered individuals is higher when the organized criminal groups show no reservations in the use of violence against individuals who defy their control or power over the community, individuals who report them to the authorities and their relatives.[30]

Current programs for protection of collaborators of justice deal with symptoms rather than the causes of intimidation. As was argued by Fyfe and Sheptycki, these programs are concerned with "risk minimization" not the reasons behind the intimidation.[31] One should look at the broader context of intimidation and the reasons certain groups become especially vulnerable and try to address these factors.

Collateral damage

Nikos Passas observed that the discourse of a "war on crime" or a "war against terrorism" "paves the ground for the acceptance of 'collateral damage.'"[32] The hardship imposed on these vulnerable groups by criminal/terrorist activities as well as by the official response is too easily dismissed as part of that necessary "collateral damage."

We have not paid sufficient attention to the unintended impact of the various measures taken in many countries to combat organized crime and terrorism. We have failed to look carefully at how several of these measures may have greatly enhanced the vulnerability of some diasporas, immigrants and other minority groups.

There is a long list of new measures adopted to fight organized crime and terrorism (for example, border control, control of financial transactions, preventive detention, limitation of movement, surveillance techniques, profiling, and control of informal value transfers) that have radically altered the situation of various diasporas, immigrants, and minority groups, and in some cases threaten their human rights. The precise impact of these measures on these vulnerable groups is an empirical question that has yet to receive some serious attention. Many of the measures that were adopted in order to combat terrorism and organized crime may themselves have had unintended detrimental effects on the situation of groups that are particularly vulnerable to the tactics of organized criminal groups and terrorists. In fact, not only were there *unintended* detrimental effects, it is not even clear that any of these measures were indeed achieving their *intended* effect.[33] In fact, we suspect that some of these policies and measures may have had no effect at all, yielded diminishing returns, or became counterproductive. Should we not seriously consider conducting some sort of "audit" of their impact on vulnerable groups?

In Canada, Parliament has adopted a new immigration and citizenship law, as well as major amendments to its Criminal Code to combat organized crime[34] and a comprehensive Anti-Terrorism Act.[35] These legislative measures clearly did not all receive the unconditional support of the groups that are most directly and immediately exposed to the ongoing activities of foreign terrorists and other criminal organizations. While these proposed laws were being debated prior to their adoption, several vulnerable groups cautiously expressed their concerns. They asked for greater protection under the law. They also complained that these laws increased their own vulnerability. Nevertheless, until some of the new legal dispositions are successfully challenged in Canadian courts, their impact on vulnerable groups will receive little attention.

For example, many of the dispositions of the law against terrorism were defended by the then Minister of Justice and Attorney General of Canada, the Hon. Anne McLelland, on the basis that they were necessary to detect terrorists and their supporters before they commit their terrorist crimes. The logic of "collateral damage" was slowly being introduced into the Canadian debate.

Canadian courts have begun at last to play their role in that respect. For example, in September 2006, the Hon. Mr. Justice Rutherford of the Ontario Superior Court of Justice (*R. v. Khawaja*) struck down the new article 83.01(1)9B)(i)(A) of the

44 Y. Dandurand and V. Chin

Criminal Code because it made proof under the definition of "terrorist activity" dependent on showing that the specified activity was undertaken "in whole or in part for a political, religious or ideological objective or cause." Such a definition was found to be an infringement on fundamental freedoms guaranteed in Canadian constitutional law."[36]

Justice Rutherford argued that:

> It seems to me that the inevitable impact to flow from the inclusion of the "political, religious or ideological purpose" requirement in the definition of "terrorist activity' will be to focus investigative and prosecutorial scrutiny on the political, religious and ideological beliefs, opinions and expressions of persons and groups both in Canada and abroad. . . . There will also be an indirect or re-bound effect of the sort Professor Stribopoulos described, as individuals' and authorities' attitudes and conduct reflect the shadow of suspicion and anger falling over all who appear to belong or to have any connection with religious, political or ideological grouping identified with specific terrorist acts.[37]

Kotler had already argued that "the criminalization of motive runs the risk of politicizing the investigative and trial processes, while chilling the expression of 'identifiable groups.'"[38]

One case shook the whole Canadian criminal justice system and eventually forced the resignation of the Commissioner of the RCMP.[39] Maher Arar was an innocent victim of inaccurate RCMP intelligence reports and deliberate smears by Canadian officials. A Canadian citizen, Mr. Arar was deported from the United States to Syria—where he was tortured as a terrorist suspect. Eventually, a Commission of Inquiry, over which Mr. Justice Dennis O'Connor presided, was established to look into the incident and the police wrongdoings. It was established that an inexperienced officer gave false information to American authorities—wrongfully tagging Mr. Arar as an "Islamic extremist."[40]

The report of the commission of inquiry makes several important points about vulnerable Canadians who are unfairly being profiled and targeted:

> Although this may change in the future, anti-terrorism investigations at present focus largely on members of the Muslim and Arab communities. There is therefore an increased risk of racial, religious or ethnic profiling, in the sense that the race, religion or ethnicity of individuals may expose them to investigation. . . . Profiling based on race, religion or ethnicity is the antithesis of good policing.[41]

The Commission's report is very clear about the dangers involved with some of the current counter-terrorism methods: "Because terrorism investigations today are focused on specific communities there is an understandable concern that individuals and groups as a whole may feel unfairly targeted."[42]

The need to better understand the vulnerability of various groups

The situation calls for a careful study of the complex nature of the relationship and interface between vulnerable groups and terrorist/criminal groups. Too many unexamined assumptions are being made about how members of vulnerable minority groups and diasporas are recruited and how their support is obtained or coerced by terrorists groups and criminal organizations. We suspect that many of these assumptions amount to nothing more than mere speculation on our part, an expression of our own lack of understanding of the groups, their concerns, their roots, and their struggles. Many of these assumptions are clearly tainted by our own unexamined collective willingness to blame outsiders for the violence we find in our midst.

It is often the case that ethnic communities living in ethnic enclaves are less inclined to integrate with their host society and thus become more susceptible to insurgent indoctrination and more vulnerable to intimidation by terrorists and other criminal organizations. Anything that contributes to isolate or ghettoize these groups increases the likelihood that they will be intimidated, victimized, recruited, or exploited by criminal or terrorist organizations. Our collective distrust of some of these vulnerable groups often inspires their own distrust and feeds their fears. We do not truly understand where the complex allegiances of these vulnerable groups really lie and how our own actions may be pushing them in a dangerous direction. Some of our current responses may further alienate these very same groups whose help we need in order to succeed in our efforts to combat organized crime and terror.

Should we not be trying to identify the strengths and positive elements of these groups and understand how these strengths can offer a basis for victimization prevention? The concept of resiliency has been applied successfully to other areas of crime prevention; there is no reason why it could not be applied to support vulnerable groups. For example, Finn and Healey recommend that, under these circumstances, the "implicit intimidation" must also be addressed by various measures for building community trust in the criminal justice system through community policing, community prosecution, and outreach to community groups interested in reclaiming ownership of their neighbourhoods from gang members.[43]

However, at this point, we do not really understand how these vulnerable groups organize themselves to address issues that concern them directly, including their feelings of alienation and their fear of victimization. We far too readily assume that these local groups are organized in such a way that they automatically fall under the control of some distant elements in their country of origin. In fact, the situation of these groups is evidently much more complex. Their psychology largely escapes us. Our lack of understanding of how these vulnerable groups respond to and deal with those who threaten, victimize, and exploit them reflects to a certain extent our own collective indifference to their struggle. Because we dissociate ourselves from these groups and cannot identify ourselves with their struggle, we perceive their exploitation and victimization as "their" problem, not ours. In this we make a very important mistake.

Understanding the nature of the vulnerability and the strengths of these groups is a prerequisite to offering them effective protection and, in the process, protecting ourselves. Nonetheless, numerous methodological hurdles stand in the way of developing such an understanding, including the facts that:

- official data on these groups are very unreliable;
- the more vulnerable the groups feel, the more reluctant their members are to volunteer any information;
- journalistic accounts are too often distorted;
- official information tends to adopt the form of "intelligence" that law enforcement agencies are reluctant to share;
- when cases of intimidation and retaliation are dealt with openly, there often is a long time lag between the time at which the information is obtained and the time at which the information is made public (for example, when a case comes to court);
- a lot of the information we have is incomplete, politically distorted, and outdated;
- much of what is to be studied and understood occurs abroad (including, for example, incidents of intimidation and violence directed at relatives of members of these vulnerable groups) and sometimes in several other countries at the same time.

Using the example of the Salford Witness Support Service based on strong inter-agency cooperation, Fyfe argues that it is possible for law enforcement agencies and their partners to produce a clear message to both witnesses and potential intimidators that action is being taken to ensure that witnesses can speak up knowing that help and support are available if they fear or are subject to intimidation.[44]

Protecting victims and vulnerable groups

We must ask whether we can identify concrete actions that could be taken at the national or international level to offer more effective protection to the diasporas, refugees, immigrants, and other minority groups that are particularly vulnerable to violence, threats, intimidation, extortion, and various forms of exploitation at the hands of terrorists and other transnational criminal organizations.

One wonders whether more creative approaches to work with the victims and innocent witnesses of organized crime and obtain their support and cooperation would yield more convincing results. The case has often been made that more creative approaches are necessary in relation to the need to offer greater protection to victims of trafficking and to illegal migrants, and the need to give greater emphasis to harm reduction approaches and demand reduction strategies to deal with the illicit drug trade.

Physical, economic and psychological intimidation of witnesses and their relatives can and does take place in a variety of contexts. The successful prosecution of organized crime activities, corruption, and acts of terrorism usually entails effective measures being taken for the protection of witnesses, victims, and collaborators of justice. These include legislative and practical measures to ensure that witnesses may testify freely and without intimidation, including the criminalization of acts of intimidation or reprisals, the use of alternative methods of providing evidence, physical protection, relocation programs, permitting limitations on the disclosure of information concerning their identity or whereabouts, and, in exceptional circumstances, protecting the anonymity of a person providing evidence.

At present, most countries have very limited means of protecting vulnerable victims, witnesses, and informants. Although international cooperation treaties sometimes refer to the need for countries to cooperate in protecting victims of crime, in practice these efforts have remained quite limited.

Being mindful of the impact of anti-crime and anti-terrorism measures

Many of the measures that have been adopted in recent years to combat terrorism and organized crime can have an unintended detrimental effect on the situation of groups that are particularly vulnerable to the tactics cf criminal groups. In most instances, it is very difficult to ascertain whether any of these measures are achieving their intended effect. However, it is already possible to identify some potential points of impact. They are as follows.

Preventive arrest and detention

What is the net impact on vulnerable groups of having introduced the possibility of proceeding with preventive arrests and short-term preventive detention (for example, Bill C-36 in Canada and similar new summary procedures in other jurisdictions)?

Compelling testimony

What is the net impact on vulnerable groups of adopting measures to compel individuals to be examined in court during investigations of terrorist activities, particularly when little protection is offered to them after they have produced evidence?

Border control

What is the net impact on vulnerable groups of introducing more effective border control measures such as those that are called for by UN Security Council Resolution 1373 (2001), (2)(g), involving the control of identity papers and travel documents? Can these measures add to the already existing feelings of vulnerability and insecurity of members of vulnerable groups? These new regimes are, at best, very intimidating. They feed the vulnerable groups' fears of being prevented from traveling, or prevented from visiting their home country, or after a visit, from re-entering their country of adoption. The Commission of Inquiry into the Actions

48   Y. Dandurand and V. Chin

of Canadian Officials in Relation to Maher Arar, for example, points at several issues with current practices and policies relating to the use of "border lookouts."[45]

In some cases, the new control regimes have crushed some of the immigrants' hopes of being reunited with family members, in particular when the latter no longer qualify for visitors' visas or for immigration. As the new provisions lead to the introduction of visa restrictions and requirements for more sophisticated travel/citizenship documents, some members of these vulnerable groups now have to obtain documents from their country of origin and, in some cases, they may place themselves at risk by doing so.

Furthermore, these control measures may inadvertently exert pressure on members of these groups—those with an irregular citizenship status or insufficient travel or citizenship documentation—to resort to the services of criminal organizations that will smuggle them in and out of a country. In the process, some of them may have indebted themselves to criminal organizations to a point where they can repay their debt only by participating in criminal activities.

Restricting access to a country to members of certain groups

What is the net impact on vulnerable groups of controlling or restricting entry of members of their group into the country in order to prevent the movement of terrorists? Surely, such measures are not without immediate consequences for the members of these vulnerable groups. They also affect how they are perceived and treated in their adopted community. Can this not contribute to their increasing isolation and alienation?

Restricting refugee protection

What is the net impact on vulnerable groups of the new measures to prevent people from abusing their refugee status? These measures will obviously have some impact on the refugees themselves, but also on public attitudes concerning refugees.

Restricting cross-border movement of cash and other values

What is the net impact on vulnerable groups of measures to prevent the cross-border transportation of cash (cash couriers) and bearer negotiable instruments? Such measures also affect the ability of these groups to conduct normal business transactions, to send money to relatives, or even to make legitimate investments.

Measures to monitor financial transactions

What is the impact on vulnerable groups of measures to monitor and report suspicious financial transactions? Can such measures relating to "suspicious transactions" lead to measures to react to "suspicious individuals"? Racial and ethnic profiling can easily come to play a role in the application, if not in the intent, of these regulatory regimes. In recent months, there has been a public uproar when it was announced

Human security objectives 49

that certain major banks were quietly closing and refusing to open American dollar accounts for Canadians holding dual citizenship with six countries considered to be "enemies of the United States."[46] What's more, this was not the bank's policy but rather an attempt to comply with American legislation in an effort to protect their business in that country. In other areas, some Canadian aircraft-building companies have fired some long-standing employees who belong to so-called suspicious national groups. They were doing so to comply with the laws of our American neighbors. The blatant forms of discrimination, once more, only increase the vulnerability of members of these groups.

Controlling alternative remittance systems

What will be the impact on vulnerable groups of implementing recommendations #7 and #8 of the FATF Special Recommendations on Terrorist Financing concerning alternative remittance and wire transfers? Will it adversely affect how legitimate transnational transactions are conducted between members of these vulnerable groups?

Some of the measures implemented to prevent the financing of terrorism have complicated the normal transactions between these groups (and their charitable organizations) and various financial institutions. Since these financial institutions are under new obligations to detect and report any potential evidence of financing of terrorism, a new climate may have been created in which various vulnerable groups will hesitate to trust the financial institutions and resort instead to informal financial systems that are more easily targeted by terrorists.

According to the Canadian Islamic Congress:

> Recent events, for example, have had a prolonged negative impact on the lives of ordinary Muslims and Arabs in Canada, especially among the younger generation. Since 9/11 and the widespread investigations launched into numerous Arab-Islamic organizations, Canadian (and all North American) Muslims have been afraid to donate to legitimate charities, because they have no idea which charity will be targeted next. This reduction of charitable funding is causing incredible hardship to victims of war and occupation overseas, especially women, children, the elderly and the sick, whose local care giving organizations rely solely on donations received from Muslims all over the world.[47]

Some members of vulnerable groups fear that they may one day be accused of some form of complicity with terrorists because they made bona fide donations to charitable organizations. Some of them face a moral dilemma, as they wish to contribute to a worthy cause in their country of origin, but are told by authorities (not always reliably or accurately) that their gifts go to support terrorists.

Some charitable or religious organizations can be penetrated, subverted, co-opted or literally hijacked by unscrupulous groups, including terrorists. The fear that an organization they are contributing to might be outlawed, with the resulting suspicions cast upon all those who helped it in the past, deters members of these organizations from coming forward to the authorities and seeking help when one of these organizations is being assaulted by some criminal elements.

Foreign remittances often play a crucial role in the life of immigrants who have kept strong ties with their family abroad. The immigrants often try to relate to others in countries that function largely on a cash basis. Threatening that system is tantamount to making these groups even more vulnerable. What is the impact on vulnerable groups of measures concerning "suspicious individuals"? Article 18(3)(b)(i) of the International Convention for the Suppression of the Financing of Terrorism provides that states shall cooperate with each other in "conducting inquiries" concerning "the identity, whereabouts and activities of persons in respect of whom a reasonable suspicion exists that they are involved in such offences."

The sad part of it all is, as Naylor puts it, that after 15 years of progressive escalation of its use, no one can determine with a remote degree of confidence whether or not the proceeds-of-crime approach to crime control is having any effect. "The entire exercise," he adds, "rests on a series of inaccurate or at least unprovable assumptions and involves the commission of a series of sins against decency and common sense."[48]

Expanding the definition of complicity

What will be the impact of the criminalization of various acts of complicity? In our haste to criminalize certain behavior more efficiently (for example, conduct relating to participation in organized criminal groups or acts of terrorism), we may have failed to appreciate the complex nature of the interactions between members of these vulnerable groups and between them and terrorist/criminal organizations. Should we accept the reduction, for the sake of prosecutorial efficiency, of some of these complex interactions and relationships to the simplistic legal notion of "complicity"? We have also criminalized various other forms of assistance (including "harboring" of criminals and terrorists), not realizing that such behavior necessarily has a different meaning when the person being assisted is a member of one's family or extended family. The consequences of such policy choices and their impact on the nature of the interactions that now take place in and around various vulnerable groups are not at all well understood.

Designating charitable organizations as terrorist groups

What is the real impact on vulnerable groups of measures to "designate" certain charitable organizations as "supporters" of terrorists, or to remove or deny charitable status (exemptions under tax laws) to certain organizations? Such measures are perceived as imminent threats to the survival of organizations that are vital to these groups. Measures that are ostensibly designed to preclude (mostly through regulation and closer scrutiny) the abuse of some entities (for example, non-profit organizations) by terrorists and criminals can also make it more difficult for these vulnerable groups to organize themselves for various legitimate purposes.

Increasing extraditions

What is the potential impact of various enhanced extradition measures on vulnerable groups? What do these measures mean to the members of vulnerable groups? How are they perceived? Are these measures not increasing the vulnerability of these groups, their leaders, or their members?

Increased mutual assistance

What is the impact on vulnerable groups of various measures to facilitate mutual assistance between countries? This may constitute yet another dimension of the vulnerability of these groups (or some of their members). An added (and possibly extreme) vulnerability may result from the fact that some states or their agents may be using the new international cooperation regime as a means of political oppression or as a way to gain a political or material advantage. As the chairman of the Counter-Terrorism Committee of the Security Council implied in a presentation he made in 2002, there is a risk that some governments will "use counter-terrorism as a pretext for political oppression."[49] One cannot necessarily assume that foreign law enforcement agencies with which one's country is cooperating are always beyond reproach and are never prepared to abuse the international cooperation regime in order to serve their own political or criminal ends. One cannot always assume either that these foreign officials are not corrupt. In many instances, members of minority groups who are familiar with the way some of these agencies operate "back home" are not expecting to be treated fairly by them. These new cooperation regimes can therefore become another source of fear and apprehension among these vulnerable groups.

Should we reconsider enforcement priorities?

We have become convinced that we should look at how we define our priorities for law enforcement and prevention in relation to transnational organized crime and, to a certain extent, terrorism. In fact, if we can collectively reaffirm our fundamental human security objectives in that regard, we will be compelled to look at these priorities very differently.

A study by Porteous reviewed the impact and costs of key organized crime activities in Canada.[50] The estimate of the costs that was arrived at by that researcher has been challenged. However, the analysis allowed us to start thinking in terms of the impact of organized crime on people and, from that point of view, can help us ask a few interesting questions from a human security perspective.

That analysis confirmed that the highest social and economic costs of organized crime could be attributed to the illicit drug trade. These activities were also the ones associated with the highest level of violence. In Canada, it is also the organized crime activity that receives the most attention from law enforcement agencies.

By contrast, organized crime activities related to the environment, particularly the improper storage or disposal of hazardous waste, have the second highest social

52 Y. Dandurand and V. Chin

and economic impact but receives far less law enforcement attention. The same is true of human trafficking, economic crime, and corruption, all with very costly impacts but rarely treated, it would seem, as a law enforcement priority.

The investigation of these and other types of activities requires specialized enforcement personnel and is usually prolonged and costly. It requires proactive methods and considerable investments in specialized law enforcement teams. As soon as these activities occur across borders, which they increasingly do, investigation and prosecution costs increase dramatically. In effect, because the cost of international investigations can quickly become prohibitive, most law enforcement agencies have established a financial value threshold below which they will not normally proceed with an international investigation (for example, if a cross-border fraud involves less than a certain amount of money).

Obviously, law enforcement agencies must make some choices, set priorities, and act accordingly. It is not clear, however, that relying on such crude measures to set investigation priorities is always the strategically most efficient way to fight organized crime. It amounts sometimes to creating circumstances under which criminal groups can act with relative impunity. More importantly, these priorities do not tend to be tightly aligned with the priorities that a human security agenda would dictate.

It would seem to us that our justice system ought to place the protection of those who are victimized and terrorized by criminal organizations at the heart of crime control strategies. The social costs of failing to do so would be too enormous. In a multicultural society such as Canada we cannot afford to let fear and ill-conceived crime control policies irremediably damage our ever fragile social cohesion.

We offer these comments to encourage consideration of some of the implications of adopting a human security bias in determining our collective policy and law enforcement agenda in relation to transnational organized crime.

Notes

1 *2004 Annual report on Organized Crime in Canada*, p. 3.
2 Ibid., p. 35.
3 M. E. Beare, "Introduction," in M. E. Beare (ed.), *Critical Reflections on Transnational Organized Crime, Money Laundering and Corruption*, pp. xi–xxix.
4 A. Auld, "Organized Crime on Rise, Report Says," *Globe and Mail*, August 23, 2003.
5 For example, in Canada, the Royal Canadian Mounted Police, the Criminal Intelligence Service of Canada, or the Organized Crime Agency of British Columbia.
6 M. Welch, "Ironies of Social Control and the Criminalization of Immigrants," p. 322.
7 D. Kilgour, S. Millars, and J. O'Neil, "Strength under Siege: Canadian Civil Society post-September 11th," in K.-A. Kassam, G. Melnyk, and L. Perras (eds.), *Canada and September 11th: Impact and Responses*, p. 157.
8 J. Aubry. "Canadian Intolerance of Immigrants Grows," *Vancouver Sun*, December 20, 2003.
9 F. Bovenkerk, D. Siegel and D. Zaitch, "Organized Crime and Ethnic Reputation Manipulation," p. 16.
10 P. Van Duyne, "Organized Crime, Corruption and Power," p. 202.
11 L. Bernstein, *The Greatest Menace: Organized Crime in Cold War America*.

Human security objectives 53

12 J. Sheptycki, "Against Transnational Organized Crime," in Beare, *Critical Reflections on Transnational Organized Crime*, p.144.
13 Canadian Security Intelligence Service, *1999 Public Report.*
14 K. Bolan, *Loss of Faith: How the Air-India Bombers Got Away with Murder*, p. 239.
15 Ibid., pp. 101–3.
16 Ibid., p. 101.
17 B. Rae, *Lessons to be Learned.*
18 United Nations (2006a), *Uniting Against Terrorism*; United Nations (2006b); *Alliance of Civilizations.*
19 K. Dedel, *Witness Protection*, p. 19.
20 K. M. Healey, *Victim and Witness Intimidation: New Developments and Emerging Responses*, pp. 1–2.
21 Dedel, *Witness Protection*, p. 4.
22 Council of Europe, "Witness Protection," *Combating Organised Crime: Best Practices Survey of the Council of Europe*, p. 16.
23 P. Finn. and K. M. Healey, *Preventing Gang- and Drug-Related Witness Intimidation*, p. 2.
24 N. Fyfe, *Protecting Intimidated Witnesses*, p. 84.
25 Finn and Healey, *Preventing Gang- and Drug-Related Witness Intimidation*, p. 4.
26 W. Maynard, *Witness Intimidation: Strategies for Prevention.*
27 L. Shelley, "Transnational Organized Crime: The New Authoritarianism," in H. R. Friman and P. Andreas (eds.), *The Illicit Global Economy and State Power*, pp. 25–51.
28 R. Elliot, "Vulnerable and Intimidated Witness: A Review of the Literature," in *Speaking Up for Justice*, pp. 99–207.
29 Fyfe, *Protecting Intimidated Witnesses*, p. 45.
30 Council of Europe, *Combating Organised Crime*, p. 27.
31 N. Fyfe and J. Sheptycki, "International trends in the facilitation of witness co-operation in Organized Crime Cases."
32 N. Passas, "Cross-border Crime and the Interface between Legal and Illegal Actors."
33 On the impact of anti-money laundering and anti-terrorism financing measures, see R. T. Naylor, *Wages of Crime: Black Markets, Illegal Finance, and the Underworld Economy.*
34 Bill C-24, 18 December 2001.
35 Bill C-36, 18 December 2001.
36 See also I. Macleod, "Anti-terrorism Law Struck Down," *Vancouver Sun*, October 25, 2006.
37 *R. v. Khawaja*, Ontario Superior Court of Justice, 2005/12/16, p. 22.
38 I. Kotler, "Terrorism, Security and Rights: The Dilemma of Democracies," in E. Mendes and D. M. McAllister (eds.), *Between Crime and War: Terrorism, Democracy and the Constitution*, pp. 13–19.
39 "How Zaccardelli failed RCMP, Arar and Canada," *Globe and Mail*, Editorial, September 29, 2006.
40 J. Tibbetts, and N. Cockburn, "Mounties Blamed in Arar Case," *National Post*, September 19, 2006; J. Sallot, "How Canada failed Citizen Maher Arar" *Globe and Mail*, September 19, 2006.
41 Commission of Inquiry into the Actions of Canadian Officials in Relation to Maher Arar, *Report on the Events Relating to Maher Arar*, p. 356.
42 Ibid., p. 357.
43 Finn and Healey, *Preventing Gang- and Drug-Related Witness Intimidation*, p. 3.
44 Fyfe, *Protecting Intimidated Witnesses*, p. 48.
45 Commission of Inquiry in Relation to Maher, p. 359.
46 Iraq, Iran, North Korea, Sudan, Cuba, and Burma. See A. Hanes, "RBC Takes Heat over Closing U.S. Accounts."
47 Canadian Islamic Congress, *Canada's Relations with Countries of the Muslim World*, p. 3.

54   *Y. Dandurand and V. Chin*

48   R. T. Naylor, *Wages of Crime: Black Markets, Illegal Finance, and the Underworld Economy.*
49   J. Greenstock, "Work of the Counter-Terrorism Committee of the Security Council," p. 37.
50   S. D. Porteous, *Organized Crime Impact Study.*

References

Aubry, J. (2003) "Canadian Intolerance of Immigrants Grows," *Vancouver Sun*, December 20.
Auld, A. (2003) "Organized Crime on Rise, report says," *Globe and Mail*, August 23.
Beare, M. E. (2003) "Introduction," in M. E. Beare (ed.), *Critical Reflections on Transnational Organized Crime, Money Laundering and Corruption*, Toronto: University of Toronto Press, pp. xi–xxix.
Bernstein, L. (2002) *The Greatest Menace: Organized Crime in Cold War America*, Boston, MA: University of Massachusetts Press.
Bolan, K. (2005) *Loss of Faith: How the Air-India Bombers Got Away with Murder*, Toronto: McClelland and Steward Ltd.
Bovenkerk, F., Siegel D. and Zaitch D. (2003), "Organized Crime and Ethnic Reputation Manipulation," *Crime, Law and Social Change*, 39, no. 1 (January): 23–38, New York: Springer.
Canadian Intelligence Service Canada. (2004) *2004 Annual report on Organized Crime in Canada*, Ottawa: Canadian Intelligence Service Canada.
Canadian Islamic Congress. (2003) *Canada's Relations with Countries of the Muslim World*, A Position Paper presented to the House of Commons Standing Committee on Foreign Affairs and International Trade by the Canadian Islamic Congress, May 6.
Canadian Security Intelligence Service. (1999) *1999 Public Report.* Ottawa: CSIS, Communication Branch.
Commission of Inquiry into the Actions of Canadian Officials in Relation to Maher Arar. (2006) *Report on the Events Relating to Maher Arar*, Ottawa: Public Works and Government Services Canada.
Council of Europe. (2004) "Witness Protection," *Combating Organised Crime: Best Practices Survey of the Council of Europe*, Strasbourg: Council of Europe Publishing.
Dedel, K. (2006) *Witness Protection*, Problem-Oriented Guides for Police Series, No. 42, Washington, D.C.: United States Department of Justice, Office of Community Oriented Policing Services, July.
Elliot, R. (1998) "Vulnerable and Intimidated Witness: A Review of the Literature," in *Speaking Up for Justice: Report of the Interdepartmental Working Group on the Treatment of Vulnerable and Intimidated Witnesses in the Criminal Justice System*, London: Home Office, pp. 99–207.
Finn, P. and Healey, K. M. (1996) *Preventing Gang- and Drug-Related Witness Intimidation.* Washington, D.C.: U.S. Department of Justice, Office of Justice Programs, National Institute of Justice.
Fyfe, N. (2001) *Protecting Intimidated Witnesses*, Hampshire: Ashgate Publishing Limited.
Fyfe, N. and Sheptycki, J. (2006) "International Trends in the Facilitation of Witness Co-Operation in Organized Crime Cases," *European Journal of Criminology* 3, no. 3: 319–55.
Greenstock, J. (2002) "Work of the Counter-Terrorism Committee of the Security Council," *Combating International Terrorism: The Contribution of the United Nations*, New York: United Nations.

Human security objectives   55

Hanes, A. (2007) "RBC Takes Heat over Closing U.S. Accounts," *Vancouver Sun*, January 27.

Healey, K. M. (1995) *Victim and Witness Intimidation: New Developments and Emerging Responses*, Washington, D.C.: U.S. Department of Justice. National Institute of Justice, October.

"How Zaccardelli failed RCMP, Arar and Canada," *Globe and Mail*, Editorial, September 29, 2006.

Kilgour, D., Millars, S. and O'Neil, J. (2002) "Strength under Siege: Canadian Civil Society post-September 11th," in K.-A. Kassam, G. Melnyk, and L. Perras (eds.), *Canada and September 11th: Impact and Responses*, Calgary: Detselig Enterprises Ltd, pp. 151–61.

Kotler, I. (2002) "Terrorism, Security and Rights: The Dilemma of Democracies," in E. Mendes and D. M. McAllister (eds.), *Between Crime and War: Terrorism, Democracy and the Constitution*, Toronto: Thompson Carswell, pp. 13–19.

Macleod, I. (2006) "Anti-terrorism Law Struck Down," *Vancouver Sun*, October 25.

Maynard, W. (1994) *Witness Intimidation: Strategies for Prevention*, Crime Detection and Prevention Series: Paper No. 55, London: Home Office, Police Research Group.

Naylor, R. T. (2002) *Wages of Crime: Black Markets, Illegal Finance, and the Underworld Economy*, Montreal & Kingston: McGill-Queen's University Press.

Passas, N. (2003) "Cross-border Crime and the Interface between Legal and Illegal Actors," *Security Journal* 16, no. 1: 19–37.

Porteous, S. D. (1998) *Organized Crime Impact Study*, Ottawa: Public Works and Government Services of Canada.

Rae, B. (2005) *Lessons to be Learned: The Report of the Honourable Bob Rae, Independent Advisor to the Minister of Public Safety and Emergency Preparedness, on outstanding questions with respect to the bombing of Air India Flight 182*, Ottawa: Air India Review Secretariat.

Sallot, J. (2006) "How Canada failed Citizen Maher Arar" *Globe and Mail*, September 19.

Shelley, L. (1999) "Transnational Organized Crime: The New Authoritarianism," in H. R. Friman and P. Andreas (eds.), *The Illicit Global Economy and State Power*, Lanham, MD: Rowman & Littlefield Pub., pp. 25–51.

Tibbetts, J. and Cockburn, N. (2006) "Mounties Blamed in Arar Case," *National Post*, September 19.

United Nations (2006a), *Uniting Against Terrorism: Recommendation for a Global Counter-Terrorism Strategy, Report of the Secretary General*, United Nations General Assembly, 27 April (A/60/825).

United Nations (2006b); *Alliance of Civilizations: Final report of the High-Level Group*, New York, United Nations, November 13.

Van Duyne, P. C. (1997) "Organized Crime, Corruption and Power," *Crime, Law and Social Change* 26, no. 3: 201–38.

Welch, M. (2003) "Ironies of Social Control and the Criminalization of Immigrants," *Crime, Law and Social Change* 39, no. 4: 319–37.

Part II

Transnational organized crime and the legal response

3 Transnational organized crime

The German response

Hans-Joerg Albrecht

Introduction

The emergence and course of transnational crime is closely associated with basic changes in modern societies. The changes affect labor markets, the economy, and mechanisms of social integration. Transnational crime is also linked to migration, immigration, and processes that have led to multicultural or multiethnic societies in both Europe and North America. Changes concern not only the emergence of transnational enterprises and a globalized economy but also the emergence of transnational ethnic communities that bridge borders and cultures. Transnational crimes have always been part of the crime phenomenon, but the quantity, quality, and structure of transnational crime today are determined by the market economy, organizations and networks, rational choice, and migration.

However, there is a type of transnational crime that is not characterized by borders (crossing of borders) because it falls into an area where borders and nations as well as the nation-state have become meaningless. That is cyberspace. With cyberspace a completely new environment has emerged where crime is bred in forms we now call cyber crime but that could easily be conceptualized as a very prominent form of transnational crime. Cyber crime creates a globalized threat that fuels insecurity, which in turn fuels demands (and offers) to establish security and safety through expanding social control, in particular electronically operated systems of control.[1] In a survey of businesses and commerce in Europe (N=3403) almost half of the enterprises said that cyber crime will be the most pronounced risk in the future in the field of economic crime. Thirteen percent of enterprises reported victimization through cyber crime, a fourth of them reported ten or more cyber attacks.[2]

When considering the significant characteristics of transnational crime the first concerns its cross-border nature. Transnational crime is characterized either by a cross-border criminal who perceives opportunities to commit crimes beyond national borders or by the cross-border transfer of illegal commodities.

Transnational crime refers to networks of criminals or organized crime groups.[12] From a methodological perspective, with transnational crime we address a topic not accessible through conventional instruments of criminological research such as surveys, interviews, or participant observation that are routinely used to study conventional subjects such as youth and crime.[13] That is why the United

60   H.-J. Albrecht

Nations is currently looking into possibilities of incorporating variables into the World Crime Survey that should produce information on transnational organized crime.[14]

However, the phenomenon of transnational organized crime itself is part of a trend toward the integration and convergence of social, cultural, and economic systems. The process of integration is based on general trends such as the mobility and globalization of the economy. Smuggling and trafficking in goods, services, and humans represent the "underside" of (global) legitimate trade; those activities are driven by laws defining the scope and content of trafficking and smuggling or the goods and services that are provided, as well as by demand, which emerges from conventional society and, for example, established sex markets.[16] Transnational organized crime also raises ideological questions in terms of responsibility and explanation,[17] and it is linked to human right issues.[18]

The concept of transnational organized crime

The phenomenon of transnational crime can be easily explained and conceptualized by a system of coordinates derived from four concepts—the market economy, organized crime, immigration and migration, and minorities (social and ethnic segmentation in modern societies)—that enable us to understand fully what transnational crime means, which forms it takes, what kind of control and investigation problems it poses, and how societies can or should respond.

Criminal markets

Transnational crime is related to the market economy. All transnational crime is part of an economy regulated by demand and supply. Modern societies in Europe and in North America have produced an enormous demand for undocumented labor, which continues to attract illegal immigration. Illegal immigration thus has become a major market where transnational crime groups are operative.

It is estimated that 60–90 percent of illegal immigrants today have been supported by organized groups in traveling to Europe and crossing European borders.[19] Estimates put the number of immigrants illegally smuggled and trafficked at some four million per year.[20] Brokerage of illegal immigrants into labor markets concentrates on the construction business, house servants, sweatshops, and agriculture as well as various types of shadow economies. Conventional organized crime, in particular the Chinese triads, is involved in trafficking immigrants.[21] In Germany, estimates put the number of illegal immigrants in the construction business at approximately 500,000. According to recent estimates, globally some 4.5 million persons are in another country illegally. International adoption practices provide a market for children.[23] The emergence of shadow economies leads to the accumulation of capital, which in turn demands reallocation of illicit capital into legal markets.[24]

There have been many "answers" to shadow economies and black markets during recent decades. However, the most important certainly seem to be disruption of local retail markets through zero-tolerance and proactive policing, and disruption of the global economy through the use of proceeds of illicit goods and services.

Anti-money-laundering and confiscation measures rank high in the policy agendas of European countries. Demands to prevent organized crime from profiting from various types of crimes, especially drug trafficking, have led to legislation facilitating seizure, freezing, and forfeiture of crime proceeds. The Council of Europe's Convention on Money Laundering and guidelines issued by the European Commission oblige member states to enact legislation forbidding money laundering and to establish systems of control to enhance the potential of identifying, freezing, and confiscating crime money. Also, the 1988 UN Convention against trafficking in illicit drugs emphasizes the need to crack down on illegal profits. Article K of the European Union Treaty makes international crime, including drug trafficking and money laundering, an important issue in police and justice cooperation. The 2000 UN Convention of Control of Transnational Organized Crime also gives special attention to money-laundering and forfeiture policies. Anti-money-laundering measures and confiscation techniques today seem to represent the most powerful weapons available in the fight against drug trafficking and other types of organized crime.[25] It is argued that the traditional response to crimes such as imprisonment and fines alone are ineffective, the better alternative being to follow the money trail.[26] In only one decade, most European countries have amended both basic criminal codes and procedural laws with the intent to facilitate seizure and forfeiture of ill-gotten gains.[27]

Both confiscation and anti-money-laundering policies have contributed to a significant change in criminal law and criminal procedure. Criminal law policies in this field have developed into international policies. Policies designed to combat organized crime are backed up by commitments to uniform legislation and joint efforts in law enforcement as expressed in international treaties and supra-national directives.[28]

The absence of victim reports leaves two options available for criminal justice agencies. The first is a proactive approach to meaningful information that can result in successful prosecutions. This option has been used extensively in combating drug markets and drug-related crime. The second option would consist of criminal justice agencies creating "artificial victims"[29] such as used in the field of environmental law. This could be applied to the field of money laundering. Persons or institutions, if somehow persuaded that they are victimized by money laundering, may be persuaded to act. Their cooperation may be hindered because confidentiality and the respect for customers' privacy have always been central values in the financial system. The second way of mobilizing the corporate world seems preferable to law enforcement systems, but it is also questionable as it privatizes the police function.

Organized crime

The concept of organized crime is based on two theoretical approaches. The first views organized crime as linked with the traditional subcultures dependent on

62   H.-J. Albrecht

shadow economies. The demand for drugs, prostitution, or gambling emerges outside shadow economies and keeps those economies alive. The arrangements vary and include various types of corruptive relationships.[30]

The second theoretical approach refers to crime as a rational and well-organized enterprise.[31] Organized crime thus has the structure of and becomes indistinguishable from other types of conventional economic behavior.

Immigration

Immigration in Europe since the early 1960s has been associated with crime and other social problems. The relevance of the relationship between safety and immigration results from the process of globalization in the economy, shrinking of the labor market, rapid expansion of shadow economies, and mass unemployment, the consequences of which become visible in feelings of "unsafety," segregation, and the emergence of inner-city ghettos,[34] and in the loss of social solidarity and massive signs of bias, hate and violence.

Immigrant groups show signs of failing to integrate and display signs of conflict. Particularly problematic is their high rate of unemployment (at least twice that among the native populations[35]) and low levels of training and education, which force immigrants (in particular immigrants from non-EU countries) to live at the margins of society.

During the 1950s and 1960s, most immigration to Western Europe was labor immigration as well as immigration based on post-colonial relationships. Immigration today is predominantly triggered by military conflicts, civil wars, and rapid processes of economic and cultural transformation in third world countries.[37] Constructing immigration as a social, economic, political, and crime problem has gained momentum with the socio-political and economic changes in Eastern Europe and the opening of formerly tightly controlled borders between western and central European countries.

At the beginning of the twenty-first century, the number of immigrants in the European Union was estimated at approximately ten million or 3 percent of the EU population. The destination of migrants is primarily determined by family and friendship networks.

The relationship between immigration and crime can be summarized as follows:[39]

- Some immigrant groups exhibit much higher rates of criminal activity than the native population.
- Some immigrant groups display the same degree of crime involvement or even less than is observed in the majority group.[40]
- First-generation immigrants of the 1950s and 1960s have been much less involved in crime than are second or third-generation immigrants and immigrants arriving in the 1980s and 1990s.
- What most immigrant groups have in common is a socially and economically disadvantaged position, which puts them at risk of becoming involved in the shadow economy, drug markets, and property crime.

Transnational organized crime   63

In general, differences between socially similarly situated groups can result in crime patterns that differ in terms of both the structure and magnitude of crime involvement.[41] Cultural differences between immigrant groups concern the capacity for community building and for the preservation of the cultural and ethnic homogeneity of the immigrant group

Multiethnic societies

Immigration is closely related to minorities and ethnic segmentation of modern societies (and horizontal social order). This, too, contributes to the distinct features of transnational crime. With changes in immigration patterns and in the economic and social structures of modern societies, we find that immigrants move into a precarious position that creates marginality and exclusion and contributes to ethnic segmentation and partiality as well as loyalty. These changes reinforce shadow economies and create new types of law enforcement problems:[42]

- Social and economic changes in the last 20 years have worked to the disadvantage of immigrants. The success stories of immigration in nineteenth and twentieth-century Europe and North America concern immigrant groups who managed to work their way up and to integrate (economically and culturally) into mainstream society. For example, at the end of the nineteenth and the beginning of the twentieth centuries several waves of Polish labor immigrants settled in western Germany (particularly in coal mining areas); they melted rather rapidly into mainstream society and became invisible as a distinct group within half a century.
- In Europe, most immigrants are from other European countries (including Turkey) or from areas neighboring Europe (such as the Maghrebian countries); this creates new networks of migration and a pluralism of "transnational communities."[43]
- The disappearance of low-skilled work and the transformation of industrial societies into service and information societies dependent on highly skilled labor[44] has changed labor markets and the basic framework of traditional mechanisms of social integration. Shadow economies and black markets, particularly in metropolitan areas, now offer precarious employment opportunities for newly arriving immigrants.[45]
- Political changes in Europe have affected the legal status of immigrants through changing the statutory framework on immigration and enforcement policies. In the 1960s and 1970s most immigrants entered European countries legally (as labor immigrants or on the basis of family reunification); today, new arrivals are frequently illegal—asylum seekers, refugees, and merely tolerated immigrants—who are subject to strict administrative controls and threatened by serious risks of criminalization.
- With the transformation of labor markets into enterprises requiring highly skilled staff, immigrants also adopted an image of being unemployed and dependent on social security. Crime policies concern not only crime and

64   H.-J. Albrecht

victimization but precursors of crime—family problems, unemployment, and lack of education and professional training.[46]

- Immigrants tend to concentrate in inner-city ghettos. Migration and immigration in Europe are headed toward metropolitan areas, which are increasingly plagued by all sorts of social problems, including the emergence of inner-city ghettos, youth gangs, drug use, and shadow economies.
- There are important changes in the structure of immigrants. Labor migrants of the 1950s and 1960s were predominantly from rural areas while immigrants from the 1980s and 1990s are from metropolitan areas where resources for migration are more readily available than in disadvantaged areas of developing countries.
- Migration and immigration in the second half of the twentieth century led to the rapidly developing phenomenon of ethnic and migration networks and the establishment of transnational communities, providing ample opportunities to move and representing an alternative to the EU master plan of free movement of goods and people.

The potential risk posed by transnational organized crime is determined by the presence of an organization or a network that represents transnational communities.

The future enemies of the nation-states and security have common characteristics: they use modern communication technology, they have a basis that guarantees trust and cooperation (such as ethnic membership, religion), they form independent but communicating small groups and develop a capacity to swarm (on the basis of a common program and developing a capacity of acting independently).[48]

New challenges for police, policing, and law enforcement

The emergence of zero-tolerance style policing and related strategies focus on the disruption of local expressions of transnational crime—local shadow economies, black markets, and related problems. Research on zero-tolerance policing has revealed that strategies to organize the relationship between police and ethnic minorities has led to the question of how such conduct can be reduced without giving up the advantages of strict policing.[53] The goal of policing is not only the reduction of crime but also to respect the value of human life and dignity and guarantee the basis of a civil and civilized society.

Most important in the attempt to make police an organization that adopts a balanced approach to crime control and a fair and impartial approach to ethnic minorities has been the representation of minorities in police forces. However, European police forces have only recently adopted policies of active recruitment of ethnic minorities.

The second challenge follows from the attempt to balance efficiency in crime control with the need to protect privacy and human rights. Demands for more sophisticated electronic control of communication and for compensation for growing mobility, globalized threats, and weakening border controls reflect the decline in informal controls of crime. There is a growing tension resulting from conflicting perspectives between the right of privacy and law enforcement objectives.

The third challenge concerns cooperation between police forces and an increasing demand for intelligence about the police and international variations in police organization, police laws, criminal procedural laws, and policing models adopted by various countries.

The German legislative response to transnational and organized crime

In 1993, the law on Control of Drug Trafficking and Other Forms of Organized Crime (*Gesetz zur Bekämpfung der Betäubungsmittelkriminalität und anderer Formen organisierter Kriminalität*) came into force. This law affected both basic criminal law and criminal procedural law. In basic criminal law new sanctions have been introduced and aggravating circumstances for certain types of crimes have been recognized, giving particular attention to property and to violent and drug offenses committed by gangs and criminal networks/criminal organizations. The penalty of confiscation added a new tool in the system of criminal sanctions. A whole range of new procedures has been introduced. These changes concern, first, the introduction of new investigative techniques and the extension of old ones—including undercover agents, computerized information screening, telephone tapping and other electronic surveillance measures, long-term observation, and the crown witness. Furthermore, emergency powers of police and public prosecution have been extended.

What was left out in the 1993 law amendment is (acoustic) electronic surveillance of private homes and private premises. Electronic surveillance of private premises, however, was introduced in a procedural law amendment in 1998 after the major political parties managed to broker an agreement on the conditions under which this type of investigative measure should be authorized.[56] This procedural law is now under review by the Federal Constitutional Court as several complaints have been filed challenging this investigative power because of disproportional interference with the right of privacy. The Crime Control Law 1994 (*Verbrechensbekämpfungsgesetz*) authorized the exchange of information between secret services and police.[57]

The 1993 amendment introduced a financial penalty that authorized confiscation of the assets of offenders (*Vermögensstrafe*, §43a of the German Criminal Code) This amendment was declared unconstitutional by the Federal Constitutional Court in 2002. A penalty of "extended forfeiture" of crime proceeds (*erweiterter Verfall*, §73d G. C. C.) was also introduced. "Extended forfeiture" requires a causal link between a criminal offense and the assets to be forfeited, but the burden of proof is reduced as a proof beyond a reasonable doubt is not required with respect to the criminal offense from which the property or assets originated (although it is not yet clear upon which facts the assumption of a link may be based and how convincing such facts must be to justify the assumption of such links). Throughout the parliamentary debates on the financial penalty and extended forfeiture, constitutional concerns have been raised. It has been argued that the penalty of confiscation as well as extended forfeiture violates the constitutional right of property, and that

66   H.-J. Albrecht

neither of these sanctions complies with the rule of law as the principle of individual guilt is violated.

In addition, the offense of money laundering was created in 1993, accompanied by the law on money-laundering control (*Geldwäschegesetz*). This statute represents a new type of criminal law aimed at risk control. The law on money-laundering control created special duties for banks, other financial institutions, and commerce to identify clients and keep documents on money transfers, and to report "suspicious" cases of money transfers to police and public prosecutors.[59]

The European Union has issued three directives (in 1991, 2001, and 2005) that oblige EU member countries to introduce legislation on money laundering and extend its reach to lawyers and notaries.[60] With this type of legislation two significant changes in criminal law arise. First, the private sector's duties to participate in crime investigation and crime control have been extended drastically. Traditionally, citizens were not obliged to report crimes nor were they in other ways compulsorily involved with the criminal justice process. Second, a field of commercial and economic action that until now has been regarded as basically legitimate and legal has fallen under suspicion and is subject to criminal investigation and monitoring. Here, the question arises whether a society can afford social control systems placing such generalized suspicion on certain individuals and organizations without having a concrete suspicion that they are potential law breakers or supporters of organized crime. Although some argue that modern societies must be capable of coping with such restraints, others express serious doubts on the legitimacy of these control approaches (let alone the problem of implementation and its outcomes, which actually are rather meager and obviously costly[61]).

In 1993, the first year of the application of money laundering controls and the money laundering offense statute, some 555 million DM have been reported to be involved in "suspicious" transfers. Of these 555 million DM, 25 million have been seized but not finally confiscated. It is expected that the proportion of crime money confiscated will be well below 1 percent of the originally reported amount. In 1996, 3,289 suspicious cases involving approximately 10,000 transactions were reported. However, 85 percent of the criminal investigations launched as a consequence of the reports ultimately were dismissed.[62] A major obstacle in implementing money-laundering laws obviously concerns the problem of establishing individual responsibility and providing sufficient evidence of the criminal offense from which profits were derived and subsequently laundered.[63]

In fact, pursuit of the "money trail" has been shown to be far less efficient in cutting off money supplies of organized crime than expected when this legal reform was introduced in the early 1990s.[64]

It comes as no surprise that the Social Democratic Party came up with the proposal for administrative measures on financial penalties and forfeiture to avoid constitutional problems. This points toward a trend of turning criminal law into administrative police law, which is not bound by the principle of individual liability but is triggered by threats to safety and order with administrative measures responding to mere risks (and not to harm done by individual offenders) and is legitimized solely by its preventive outcomes. Similar problems have become visible with

Transnational organized crime   67

respect to criminal prosecution of economic and environmental crimes committed in or through organizations. Corporate liability and corporate sanctions have been and are still being discussed in German criminal politics but have not received much support so far.

The German response to law enforcement problems seems to lower the standards for establishing individual liability, particularly in cases of negligent behavior, as demonstrated by some criminal product liability cases in the 1990s. Money-laundering offense statutes provide another facet of criminal politics that have been addressed in the fields of environmental and economic offense statutes. The new types of criminal law are likely to be associated with a greater potential for conflicts and serious problems in implementation as a consequence of (1) value conflicts not resolved during the process of creation but dislocated to the implementation process, (2) conflicts of goals among different state agencies equally involved in the process of norm implementation, (3) problems arising out of the complex organizational and economic environment to which criminal law is applied, and (4) negative side-effects in terms of black markets and related problems.[65]

New criminal investigative techniques, including a search procedure based on electronic information reduction techniques or data mining (§§98a–c of the Criminal Procedural Code), were justified mainly by law enforcement problems in the field of organized crime.[66] Modern societies produce enormous amounts of information on individuals in various public or private sectors. Credit card companies, telephone companies, social service administration, housing agencies, and many more collect data from their clients. The new provisions empower police and public prosecutors to search these information systems with using certain matching techniques in order to filter out smaller groups of individuals who, in principle, fit profiles established for certain groups of offenders (for example, drug traffickers). Critics argue that the principle of proportionality might be violated by such techniques because the privacy of a large number of innocent citizens is infringed upon and large numbers of innocent citizens fall under the scope of police investigations and public prosecutors.

New surveillance technologies have been admitted through the 1993 law amendment (§§100c, d CPC), which allows for electronic and video-based surveillance of suspects without their knowledge. Another important new investigative technique is "undercover policing" (§§110a–e CPC). This produces many legal problems that can be summarized under the topic of deception. An undercover agent, according to German criminal procedural law, is a police officer who has adopted a "legend" and thus changed his or her identity. This allows an undercover agent to penetrate gangs and organized criminal networks to procure evidence that otherwise (and with traditional methods) would not be obtainable.

The basic reason for introducing such methods of investigation lies in the conception of organized crime, which is seen to create heavy obstacles for traditional methods of criminal investigation. The legal problems that arise are the circumvention or neutralization of basic rights of suspects—among them the right to remain silent and the right not to be obliged to support investigative authorities in producing evidence against him or herself. The right to remain silent also applies to

68   H.-J. Albrecht

certain categories of relatives who are not obliged to give testimony. The legislators, therefore, have restricted the use of undercover agents to cases of serious crimes and have tried to limit such investigative techniques to cases where traditional investigative techniques presumably would not be successful.

In addition, some powers have been moved from the judiciary to the investigative authorities. Pre- or post-facto control of the use of undercover policing through the judiciary is limited to exceptional cases (§110b CPC). There is also clear evidence that this type of pre-trial investigation is merely an executive task. The investigative strategies allowed through undercover policing set further limits on the implementation of the principle of legality. Undercover policing is based on discretion and it is up to the investigative authorities to choose the crimes that should be the subject of undercover policing.

Wire-tapping was authorized in Germany by a law amendment of 1968. It was justified by the needs of intelligence services and subsequently by the needs of effective law enforcement in the field of illicit drugs. Surveillance of telecommunications must comply with requirements set out in §§100a of the German Criminal Procedural Code. According to these requirements an order of telecommunication surveillance must be issued by a judge. However, in situations of emergency a public prosecutor may order surveillance. Telecommunication surveillance may be ordered in case of suspicion of a criminal offense listed in a catalogue attached to §100a of the Criminal Procedural Code. An order is to be issued only if telecommunication surveillance is assessed to be the "last resort" in investigating a catalogued crime or in locating the suspect.

A "last resort" situation may be assumed only if other investigative methods would be unsuccessful. The order may be made only against the suspect or against third persons who either receive messages for or transmit messages from the suspect or whose telephone lines are used by the suspect. The order must be given in writing. It must indicate the name and address of the person against whom it is directed as well as the telephone number or other identification of the person's telecommunication connection. The type, extent, and period—not to exceed three months—of the measures shall be specified in the order. Information obtained by a wire-tap may be used as evidence in other criminal proceedings only as such information relates to a criminal offense listed in the catalogue of §100a. Conversations between the suspect and individuals entitled to a professional duty to remain silent (lawyers, priests, physicians) may not be intercepted nor may their content be used as evidence. Those affected by a wire-tap must be informed after completion of the criminal investigation.

Another problem related to the use of deceptive and covert investigative techniques concerns the use of information that was found by chance. Wire-taps may, for example, generate information on other crimes not related to the offense that is investigated or on suspects until then not known to police. Using covert surveillance technologies, information may be produced that is not relevant to the case investigated but could be useful to launch criminal investigations because of other offenses detected during the course of observation and surveillance. To restrict the use of so-called "random hits" (*Zufallsfunde*) German legislation has provided a

Transnational organized crime 69

compromise. If new investigative techniques produce such information, it may be used only to establish the suspicion of criminal offenses for which the surveillance techniques legally could have been applied.

Eavesdropping on private premises, according to §100c of the Criminal Procedural Law, may be authorized in cases of serious crimes listed in the catalogue annexed to §100c and under the conditions required for wire-tapping. However, other than for wire-taps judicial authorization requires a decision by the criminal chamber of the district court. Authorization of eavesdropping is limited to a period of four weeks (which can be extended to further periods of four weeks on the basis of separate judicial decisions). As with wire-taps, professional secrecy and conversations between relatives is protected.

The Federal Constitutional Court, in a March 3, 2004 decision (1 BvR 2378/98; 1 BvR 1084/99), ruled that although authorization of eavesdropping on private premises in principle complies with constitutional requirements, the current statutory framework of wire-taps and eavesdropping in Germany does not comply fully with proper protection of the fundamental right to privacy.

What was not regulated in the amendments is the role and deployment of so-called "whistle-blowers" or private informants during pre-trial investigations or provocation of criminal offenses by law enforcement officers. Such informants have been heavily used since the 1970s, essentially for the reasons that triggered legislation on undercover policing. There are two techniques applied with private informants. First, they usually are used to provoke crimes—for example, the "buy and bust" technique in drug markets in which a private informant approaches another person and asks him or her to sell illegal drugs; when drugs and money are exchanged police who have observed the transaction arrest the trafficker.

Second, private informants are used to obtain confessions or other information leading to evidence. The statutes regulating undercover policing may not be applied to private informants. However, the Supreme Court has ruled several times that private informants and provocation of criminal offenses can be used under certain conditions: offenses investigated by private informants must be crimes of a very serious nature and individuals approached by private informants must be under suspicion for the types of crimes for which they are being approached. If such conditions are not met, the trial court may mitigate punishment. The Supreme Court is still being criticized for its decisions that authorize these investigative activities, which are said to create conflicts with both procedural and other rights. The European Court of Human Rights—contrary to the decisions of the German Supreme Court—has ruled that provoking crimes under certain conditions precludes the criminal proceedings from being carried through.[67]

Finally, another newly introduced technique of criminal investigation concerns "police observation." With police observation, information on suspects or persons assumed to have contacts with a suspect can be collected routinely during police controls to facilitate location of a suspect. This measure may be run for a period of 12 months.

The lesson drawn from experiences under the terror regime of German fascism shows that there should be a strict separation of police and secret services. Today, this

70   H.-J. Albrecht

line has become blurred. In the Crime Control Act (*Verbrechensbekämpfungsgesetz* 1994) a certain exchange of information has been accepted; but voices call for further extension of information exchange. Secret services are empowered to use a wide range of covert and intrusive measures with the stipulation that no repressive action may follow this type of intelligence collection. On the other hand, police have fewer powers to collect information but are empowered to use repressive means.

Anti-terrorism legislation following 9/11 has expanded the scope of information exchange among secret services, police, and civil society. International legislation previously designed to control transnational crime, money laundering, and illegal immigration represent the core of anti-terrorist legislation after 9/11.[68] This type of legislation goes into the creation of "precursor" criminal law—for example, with offense statutes that criminalize participation or support of criminal or terrorist groups and money laundering and offense statutes designed through the Vienna Convention of 1988 and in the UN Convention of 2000 to control transnational organized crime.

We find expressions of such developments in the attempt to obtain information collected in the rapidly growing area of private telecommunication and in the creation of obligations of the private sector to support strategies of prevention and repression. These developments include deployment and extension of investigative methods initiated since the 1980s in controlling organized crime or transaction crime and in the use of conventional investigative methods such as private informants or crown witnesses.[69] The trends extend to building preventive and repressive strategies and are visible in laws on associations or political parties and on religion and religious groups.

Police laws (addressing police powers in maintaining peace and order in society as opposed to procedural laws addressing police powers in investigating crime) have changed significantly with the introduction of new investigative techniques, although they are restricted to preventive purposes and to maintaining order. These developments point to the growing relevance of prevention in both types of police work and to the essentially preventive nature of the new investigative techniques discussed above.

Research on the efficiency of new methods of criminal investigation and on the strategy of following the money trail demonstrates that anti-transnational crime legislation has limited effect.[70] Telecommunication control, widely used though rarely studied from an empirical point of view, shows wide variation among various countries followed by more or less comparable results regarding the impact such investigative techniques have on transnational organized crime.

An inverse relationship between variables can be demonstrated when comparing the use of wire-taps and the efficiency of wire-tapping. The more wire-taps launched, the lower the average number of convictions resulting from cases where they were used.

There is no available evidence that using telecommunication control helps to significantly increase the efficiency of law enforcement in the field of organized crime. From the viewpoint of proportionality such evidence is needed for evaluation research regarding the cost and benefits of investigative techniques that intrude on privacy.[71]

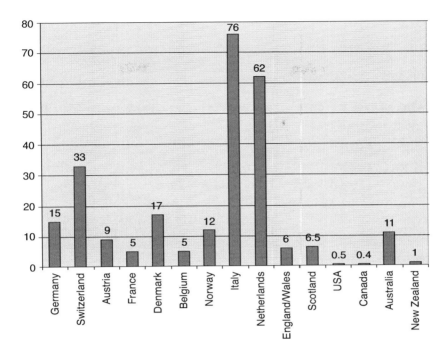

Figure 3.1 Wire-taps per 100,000 of the population.
Source: Albrecht, H.-J. *et al.*, *Kontrolle der Telekommunikation*, Freiburg, 2003.

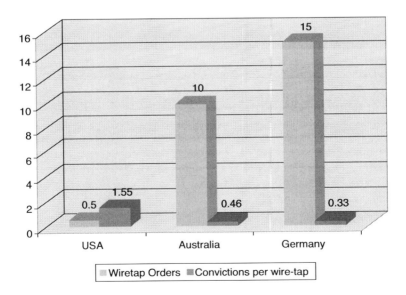

Figure 3.2 Wire-taps (per 100,000) and convictions per wire-tap.
Source: Albrecht, H.-J. *et al.*, *Kontrolle der Telekommunikation*, Freiburg, 2003.

72   H.-J. Albrecht

International cooperation and international policing

On the international level, the political will to focus on transnational organized crime and work on instruments to combat these types of crimes were first expressed in the 1988 Vienna Convention. The Vienna Convention focused on three areas perceived to be of paramount importance for the control of transnational drug trafficking: harmonization of substantial criminal law in the field of drug trafficking, harmonization of money laundering legislation, and streamlining of international judicial cooperation. Attempts to harmonize investigative techniques were of marginal importance. The 1988 Vienna Convention addressed controlled deliveries as a means to investigate major cases of transnational drug trafficking. It was followed by the 2000 UN Convention Against Transnational and Organized Crime, which included an additional protocol dealing with trafficking in humans.[72]

The 2000 Transnational Crime Convention defines transnational and organized crime beyond drug trafficking and attempts to establish a framework within which all types of transnational crimes can be dealt with effectively. According to Article 2 of the Convention an

"Organized criminal group" shall mean a structured group of three or more persons, existing for a period of time and acting in concert with the aim of committing one or more serious crimes or offences established in accordance with this Convention, in order to obtain, directly or indirectly, a financial or other material benefit.

The definition remains vague to cover the various phenomena internationally regarded as transnational crime. The convention also covers various offenses that represent core transnational crimes such as money laundering, corruption, and trafficking in humans as well as all serious offenses committed by organized crime groups. Members of the convention are urged to introduce criminal legislation that makes such membership in a criminal enterprise a criminal offense.

The Convention also suggests introducing various types of control of communication and undercover operations as well as the crown witness and witness protection programs and corporate liability. The Convention covers not only judicial cooperation in combating transnational crime but international police cooperation, which now stands independently. That reinforces a trend very visible in Europe where cross-border cooperation is dominated by police, which has provoked criticism of "policization" of criminal procedure and marginalization of the judiciary in international law enforcement.[73] In fact, the system of liaison officers, which has been strengthened considerably over the last two decades, has created a dynamic in the field of international police cooperation that does not have a parallel in judicial cooperation. What further pushed international police cooperation are the elitist forms it takes. First, police cooperation is entrusted to a small group of police officers that is, second, far from everyday police work.[74]

Summarizing the trends in the Transnational Crime Convention we may conclude that a process has taken off that aims at harmonizing special investigative techniques

Transnational organized crime 73

and special sanctioning strategies while expanding their application beyond drug trafficking to serious types of crimes at large. These developments indicate a strong commitment to crime prevention based on criminal law. Policies against organized and transnational crime tend to promise more security in face of risks resulting from globalization and the weakening of national systems of crime control. Risk orientation results in specific legislation and specific investigative practices that are unfolding today under guidelines set by international and regional bodies (United Nations, Financial Action Task Force, and so forth). Such security legislation has to face concomitant costs that encompass economic costs and social costs as well as costs in terms of restrictions of basic rights. Beside such costs affecting individuals, the emphasis on security and risk prevention impacts on the general make-up of societies that are today—as the German sociologist Beck[75] has put it—at risk of being transformed into surveillance states that undermine freedom and democracy while attempting to maximize security. The focus evidently is on efficiency in crime control and law enforcement—policing and law enforcement go international while the judiciary and judicial procedures remain national.

Notes

1 R. Fox, "Someone to Watch Over Us: Back to the Panopticon?", p. 253.
2 Pricewaterhouse/Coopers, *Europäische Umfrage zur Wirtschaftskriminalität 2001*, p. 24.
3 C. Fijnaut and L. Paoli, eds. *Organised Crime in Europe: Concepts, Patterns and Control Policies in the European Union and Beyond*, 2004.
4 J. Sheptycki, "Patrolling the New European (In)Security Field: Organisational Dilemmas and Operational Solutions for Policing the Internal Borders of Europe."
5 D. Nogala, "Policing Across a Dimorphous Border: Challenge and Innovation at the French-German Border."
6 A. Szasz, "Corporations, Organized Crime, and the Disposal of Hazardous Waste: An Examination of the Making of a Criminogenic Regulatory Structure"; G. Hayman and D. Brack, "International Environmental Crime. The Nature and Control of Environmental Black Markets," 2002; H.-J. Albrecht, "The Extent of Organized Environmental Crime," 2004.
7 Fijnaut and Paoli, *Organised Crime in Europe*.
8 V. Nicolic-Ristanovic, "Illegal Markets, Human Trade and Transnational Organised Crime"; A. Herz, *Strafverfolgung von Menschenhandel*; F. Laczko and E. Gozdziak, eds., "Data and Research on Human Trafficking: A Global Survey."
9 Financial Action Task Force (FATF), *The Forty Recommendations*.
10 C. Fijnaut and L. Huberts, eds., *Corruption, Integrity and Law Enforcement*.
11 S. Leman-Langlois and J.-P. Brodeur, "Terrorism Old and New: Counterterrorism in Canada."
12 J. Arquilla and D. Ronfeldt, eds., *Networks and Netwars: The Future of Terror, Crime, and Militancy*.
13 See J. Shapland, "Crime: A Social Indicator or Social Normality?"; H. J. De Nike, U. Ewald, C. J. Nowlin, eds., *Victimization Perception after the Breakdown of State Socialism: First Findings of a Multi-City Pilot Study 1993*.
14 Centre for International Crime Prevention, Office for Drug Control and Crime Prevention, "Global Studies on Organized Crime," United Nations Interregional Crime and Justice Research Institute, February 1999.
15 Bundeskriminalamt, Lagebild Organisierte Kriminalität 1992–2002, Wiesbaden, 1993–2003; see also NCIS, UK Threat Assessment of Serious and Organised Crime 2002, London, 2003; Bundesamt für Polizei: Bericht Innere Sicherheit 2002, Bern, 2003.

74   *H.-J. Albrecht*

16   P. Andreas, "Smuggling Wars: Law Enforcement and Law Evasion in a Changing World," pp. 86–7; L. Kelly and L. Regan, "Stopping Traffic: Exploring the Extent of, and Responses to, Trafficking in Women for Sexual Exploitation in the UK," p. 1.

17   M. Le Breton and U. Fiechter, "Frauenhandel im Kontext von Exklusions- und Differenzierungsprozessen."

18   "Trafficking in Women and Girls: An International Human Rights Violation" Fact Sheet released by the Senior Coordinator for International Women's Issues, U.S. Department of State, March 10, 1998.

19   A. A. Aronowitz, "Smuggling and Trafficking Human Beings: The Phenomenon, the Markets that Drive it and the Organizations that Promote it," p. 169.

20   Ibid., p. 164.

21   Yiu Kong Chu, *The Triads as Business*, p. 115.

22   "Out of the Shadows," *Time*, July 30, 2001, pp. 26–9.

23   H.-J. Albrecht, "Kinderhandel—Eine Untersuchung zum (gewerblichen) Handel mit Kindern"; see also P. Eisenblätter, "History and Causes of Intercountry Adoptions in a 'Receiving' Country," Contribution to the Expert Meeting, "Protecting Children's Rights in Intercountry Adoptions and Preventing Trafficking and Sale of Children"; H.-J. Albrecht, "Grenzgänger: Internationale Adoption und Kinderhandel."

24   T. Sinuraja, "Internationalization of Organized Economic Crime: The Russian Federation Case," p. 46.

25   L. Tullis, *Handbook of Research on the Illicit Drug Trade: Socioeconomic and Political Consequences*, p. 133.

26   E. U. Savona, "The Organized Crime/Drug Connection: National and International Perspectives," p. 131; M. Pieth, "Gewinnabschöpfung bei Betäubungsmitteldelikten," *Strafverteidiger*, p. 558.

27   J. Meyer, *et al.*, eds., "Gewinnabschöpfung bei Betäubungsmitteldelikten Eine rechtsvergleichende und kriminologische."

28   M. Levi, "Incriminating Disclosures: An Evaluation of Money Laundering Regulation in England and Wales"; M. Pieth, "Gewinnabschöpfung bei Betäubungsmitteldelikten," p. 559.

29   M. Levi, "Incriminating Disclosures," p. 202.

30   P. Williams, "The Geopolitics of Transnational Organized Crime," Paper presented at the Conference on Global Security, University of Pittsburgh, November 2–3, 1995, p. 5.

31   H.-J. Albrecht, "Organisierte Kriminalität—Theoretische Erklärungen und empirische Befunde."

32   H.-J. Albrecht, "Immigration, Crime and Unsafety."

33   H.-H. Kühne, *Kriminalitätsbekämpfung durch innereuropäische Grenzkontrollen? Auswirkungen der Schengener Abkommen auf die innere Sicherheit*; "Moderne Sicherheitsstrategien gegen das Verbrechen."

34   P. Wiles, "Ghettoization in Europe?"

35   P. Muus, "International Migration: Trends and Consequences," p. 45.

36   Ibid.

37   E. Reyneri, "Migrants' Insertion in the Informal Economy, Deviant Behaviour and the Impact on Receiving Societies," The Comparative Reports. Tables of Contents and Abstracts, Milano, 1999.

38   L. Hearing and R. van der Erf, "Why Do People Migrate?"

39   M. Tonry, "A Comparative Perspective on Minority Groups, Crime, and Criminal Justice."

40   Ibid.

41   See the various reports in M. Tonry, ed., *Ethnicity, Crime and Immigration: Comparative and Cross National Perspectives*.

42   H.-J. Albrecht, "Ethnic Minorities, Crime and Criminal Justice in Germany."

43   A. Portes, "La Mondialisation Par Le Bas," p. 23.

44   W. J. Wilson, *When Work Disappears*.

Transnational organized crime   75

45 Reyneri, *et al.*, "Migrants' Insertion in the Informal Economy."
46 M. Althoff, Die Herstellung von rassistischen Bildern in den Medien. Der "ideale" Asylbewerber.
47 Arquilla and Ronfeldt, *Networks and Netwars*.
48 H. Hess, "Terrorismus und Weltstaat," p. 146.
49 A. De Benoist, "Die Wurzeln des Hasses: Ein Essay zu den Ursachen des globalen Terrorismus," p. 19.
50 Ibid, p. 39.
51 J. A. Eterno, "Zero Tolerance Policing in Democracies: The Dilemma of Controlling Crime without Increasing Police Abuse of Power."
52 G. L. Kelling, "Crime Control, the Police, and Culture Wars: Broken Windows and Cultural Pluralism."
53 Eterno, "Zero Tolerance Policing," p. 191.
54 H. L. Packer, "The Courts, the Police, and the Rest of Us."
55 D. Duprez and M. Pinet, *Policiers et mediateurs. Sur le Recrutement et les Appartenances*, pp. 116–19.
56 J. Vahle, "Ein Koloß auf tönernen Füßen. Anmerkungen zur (Neu-) Regelung des sogenannten Großen Lauschangriffs."
57 M. Köhler, "Unbegrenzte Ermittlung und justizfreie Bundesgeheimpolizei: Der neue Strafprozeß?"; for a complete overview, see H.-J. Albrecht, *Counter-Terrorism Legislation in Germany*.
58 Bundesverfassungsgericht (Federal Constitutional Court), 2 BvR 794/95, 20. 3. 2002.
59 K. Oswald, *Die Implementation gesetzlicher Maßnahmen zur Bekämpfung der Geldwäsche in der Bundesrepublik Deutschland*.
60 Council Directive of June 10, 1991 on preventing use of the financial system for the purpose of money laundering; Directive 2001/97/EC of the European Parliament and of the Council of 4 December 2001 amending Council Directive 91/308/EEC on prevention of use of the financial system for the purpose of money laundering.
61 K. Oswald, *Die Implementation gesetzlicher Maßnahmen*; M. Yeandle, M. Mainelli, A. Berendt, B. Healy, *Anti-Money Laundering Requirements: Costs, Benefits and Perceptions*.
62 D. Scherp, "Lagebild Geldwäschebekämpfung. Eine Zwischenbilanz zur Gesetzesänderung vom Mai 1998," p. 460.
63 H. Fromm, "Finanzermittlungen—Ein Herzstück der OK-Bekämpfung?"
64 H.-J. Albrecht, "Money Laundering and the Confiscation of the Proceeds of Crime: A Comparative View on Different Models of the Control of Money Laundering and Confiscation."
65 H. Hoch, Die Rechtswirklichkeit des Umweltstrafrechts aus der Sicht von Umweltverwaltung und Strafverfolgung, Max-Planck-Institut, Freiburg; W. Lutterer, H. Hoch, Rechtliche Steuerung im Umweltbereich, Max-Planck-Institut, Freiburg.
66 W. Gropp, "Besondere Ermittlungsmaßnahmen zur Bekämpfung der Organisierten Kriminalität."
67 EGMR (European Court of Human Rights) *Strafverteidiger*, p. 127.
68 V. Militello, J. Arnold, L. Paoli, *Organisierte Kriminalität als transnationales Phänomen*, Freiburg: Edition iuscrim; H.-J. Albrecht, C. Fijnaut, eds., *The Containment of Transnational Organized Crime: Comments on the UN Convention of December 2000*, Freiburg: Edition iuscrim; H.-J. Albrecht, "Fortress Europe?—Controlling Illegal Immigration"; B. Huber, "Die Änderungen des Ausländer- und Asylrechts durch das Terrorismusbekämpfungsgesetz."
69 Maurer, A., "§129b und Kronzeugenregelung. Alte Instrumente in neuem Gewand"; S. Stern, "Heute Beschuldigter—morgen 'Kron'-Zeuge"; in 2006, due to continuing lobbying for again introducing a general crown witness regulation, the minister of justice presented a draft crown witness law, see <http://www.bmj.bund.de> (accessed June 12, 2006).

76   *H.-J. Albrecht*

70 H.-J. Albrecht, C. Dorsch, C. Krüpe, Rechtswirklichkeit und Effizienz der Überwachung der Telekommunikation nach den §§ 100a, 100b StPO und anderer verdeckter Ermittlungsmaßnahmen, edition iuscrim, Freiburg i. Br.; C. Dorsch, Die Effizienz der Überwachung der Telekommunikation nach den §§ 100a, 100b StPO. Berlin; C. Krüpe-Gescher, Die Überwachung der Telekommunikation nach den §§ 100a, 100b StPO in der Rechtspraxis, Berlin; H. Meyer-Wieck, Rechtswirklichkeit und Effizienz der akustischen Wohnraumüberwachung ("großer Lauschangriff") nach § 100c Abs. 1 Nr. 3 StPO. Research in Brief, Freiburg; H. Meyer-Wieck, Der Große Lauschangriff. Eine empirische Untersuchung zu Anwendung und Folgen des §100c Abs. 1 Nr. 3 StPO. Berlin.
71 For a review of research see H.-J. Albrecht, *et al.*, *Kontrolle der Telekommunikation.*
72 M. Joutsen, "Elaboration of a United Nations Convention Against Transnational Organized Crime."
73 See also H. Aden, "Convergence of Policing Policies and Transnational Policing in Europe."
74 Ibid., p. 103.
75 U. Beck, *Das Schweigen der Wörter. Über Terror und Krieg.*

References

Aden, H. (2001) "Convergence of Policing Policies and Transnational Policing in Europe," *European Journal of Crime, Criminal Law and Criminal Justice* 9, no. 2: 99–112.
Albrecht, H.-J. (1994) "Kinderhandel—Eine Untersuchung zum (gewerblichen) Handel mit Kindern," Bonn: Bundesministerium der Justiz.
Albrecht, H.-J. (1997) "Ethnic Minorities, Crime and Criminal Justice in Germany" in *Crime and Justice: A Review of Research*, Vol. 21, M. Tonry, ed., Chicago: University of Chicago Press, pp. 31–99.
Albrecht, H.-J. (1998) "Money Laundering and the Confiscation of the Proceeds of Crime: A Comparative View on Different Models of the Control of Money Laundering and Confiscation," in *The Europeanisation of Law, United Kingdom Comparative Law Series*, vol. 18, T. Watkin, ed., Oxford: Alden Press, pp. 166–207.
Albrecht, H.-J. (1998) "Organisierte Kriminalität—Theoretische Erklärungen und empirische Befunde," Deutsche Sektion der Internationalen Juristen-Kommission, *Organisierte Kriminalität und Verfassungsstaat*, Heidelberg: Müller, pp. 1–40.
Albrecht, H.-J. (2002) "Fortress Europe?—Controlling Illegal Immigration," *European Journal of Crime, Criminal Law and Criminal Justice* 10, no. 2: 1–22.
Albrecht, H.-J. (2002) "Immigration, Crime and Unsafety," in *The Governance of Safety in Europe*, A. Crawford, ed., Cullompton/UK, Portland/USA: Willan Publishing, pp. 159–85.
Albrecht, H.-J. (2002) "The Extent of Organized Environmental Crime: A European Perspective" in *Environmental Crime in Europe: Rules of Sanctions*, F. Comte and L. Krämer, eds., Amsterdam: Europa Law Publishing, pp. 71–101.
Albrecht, H.-J. (2005) "Grenzgänger: Internationale Adoption und Kinderhandel" in *Internationaler Kinderschutz. Politische Rhetorik oder effektives Recht?* T. Marauhn, ed., Tübingen, pp. 97–126.
Albrecht, H.-J. (2006) *Counter-Terrorism Legislation in Germany*, Freiburg.
Albrecht, H.-J. and Fijnaut, C., eds. (2002) *The Containment of Transnational Organized Crime: Comments on the UN Convention of December 2000*, Freiburg: Edition iuscrim.
Albrecht, H.-J. *et al.*, (2003) *Kontrolle der Telekommunikation*, Freiburg.
Albrecht, H.-J., Dorsch, C. and Krüpe, C. (2003), Rechtswirklichkeit und Effizienz der

Transnational organized crime   77

Überwachung der Telekommunikation nach den §§ 100a, 100b StPO und anderer verdeckter Ermittlungsmaßnahmen, edition iuscrim, Freiburg i. Br.

Althoff, M. (1997) Die Herstellung von rassistischen Bildern in den Medien. Der "ideale" Asylbewerber. In: Frehsee, D., Löschper, G., Smaus, G., eds., Konstruktion der Wqirklichkeit durch Kriminalität und Strafe, Baden-Baden: Nomos, pp. 392–403.

Andreas, P. (1999) "Smuggling Wars: Law Enforcement and Law Evasion in a Changing World" in T. Farer, ed., *Transnational Crime in the Americas*, New York and London: Routledge, pp. 85–98

Aronowitz, A. A. (2001) "Smuggling and Trafficking Human Beings: The Phenomenon, the Markets that Drive it and the Organizations that Promote it," *European Journal on Criminal Policy and Research* 9: 163–95.

Arquilla, J. and Ronfeldt, D., eds. (2001), *Networks and Netwars: The Future of Terror, Crime, and Militancy*, Santa Monica, CA: Rand.

Beck, U. (2002) *Das Schweigen der Wörter. Über Terror und Krieg*, Frankfurt: Edition Suhrkamp.

Centre for International Crime Prevention, Office for Drug Control and Crime Prevention. (1999), "Global Studies on Organized Crime," United Nations Interregional Crime and Justice Research Institute, February.

De Benoist, A. (2002) "Die Wurzeln des Hasses: Ein Essay zu den Ursachen des globalen Terrorismus," Berlin: Edition JF.

De Nike, H. J., Ewald, U., Nowlin, C. J. eds. (1995), *Victimization Perception after the Breakdown of State Socialism: First Findings of a Multi-City Pilot Study 1993*. Berlin: Gilinsky Publications.

Dorsch, C. (2005) Die Effizienz der Überwachung der Telekommunikation nach den §§ 100a, 100b StPO. Berlin.

Duprez, D. and Pinet, M. (2001) *Policiers et mediateurs. Sur le Recrutement et les Appartenances*, Ifresi, Lille.

EGMR (European Court of Human Rights). (1999) *Strafverteidiger*.

Eisenblätter, P. (1992) "History and Causes of Intercountry Adoptions in a 'Receiving' Country," Contribution to the Expert Meeting, "Protecting Children's Rights in Intercountry Adoptions and Preventing Trafficking and Sale of Children," Manila, Philippines, April 6–12.

Eterno, J. A. (2001) "Zero Tolerance Policing in Democracies: The Dilemma of Controlling Crime without Increasing Police Abuse of Power," *Police Practice & Research. An International Journal* 2: 189–217.

Fijnaut, C. and Huberts, L., eds. (2002) *Corruption, Integrity and Law Enforcement*, The Hague, London, New York: Springer.

Fijnaut, C. and Paoli, L., eds. (2004) *Organised Crime in Europe: Concepts, Patterns and Control Policies in the European Union and Beyond*, Dordrecht: Springer.

Financial Action Task Force (FATF). (2003) *The Forty Recommendations*, Paris: FATF Secretariat.

Fox, R. (2001) "Someone to Watch Over Us: Back to the Panopticon?" *Criminology and Criminal Justice* 1, no. 3: 251–76.

Fromm, H. (1998) "Finanzermittlungen—Ein Herzstück der OK-Bekämpfung?" *Kriminalistik* 52: 463–9.

Gropp, W. (1993) "Besondere Ermittlungsmaßnahmen zur Bekämpfung der Organisierten Kriminalität," *Zeitschrift für die Gesamte Strafrechtswissenschaft* 105: 405–29.

Hayman, G. and Brack, D. (2002) "International Environmental Crime. The Nature and Control of Environmental Black Markets," Workshop Report, Royal Institute of International Affairs.

78   H.-J. Albrecht

Hearing, L. and van der Erf, R. (2001) "Why Do People Migrate?" Statistics in Focus, Populations and Social Conditions, *EuroStat Theme* 3, no. 1.

Herz, A. (2005) *Strafverfolgung von Menschenhandel*, Berlin.

Hess, H. (2002) "Terrorismus und Weltstaat," *Kriminologisches Journal* 34: 143–9.

Hoch, H. (1994) Die Rechtswirklichkeit des Umweltstrafrechts aus der Sicht von Umweltverwaltung und Strafverfolgung, Max-Planck-Institut, Freiburg.

Huber, B. (2002) "Die Änderungen des Ausländer- und Asylrechts durch das Terrorismusbekämpfungsgesetz," *Neue Zeitschrift für Verwaltungsrecht* 7: 787–94.

Joutsen, M. (1999) "Elaboration of a United Nations Convention Against Transnational Organized Crime," *ISPAC Newsletter* 7, no. 28.

Kelling, G. L. (1998) "Crime Control, the Police, and Culture Wars: Broken Windows and Cultural Pluralism," Perspectives on Crime and Justice, 1997–1998 Public Lecture Series. NIJ, Washington, pp. 1–29.

Kelly, L. and Regan, L. (2000) "Stopping Traffic: Exploring the Extent of, and Responses to, Trafficking in Women for Sexual Exploitation in the UK," Police Research Series, Paper 125, London.

Köhler, M. (1994) "Unbegrenzte Ermittlung und justizfreie Bundesgeheimpolizei: Der neue Strafprozeß?" *Strafverteidiger*, pp. 386–89.

Krüpe-Gescher, C. (2005) Die Überwachung der Telekommunikation nach den §§ 100a, 100b StPO in der Rechtspraxis, Berlin.

Kühne, H.-H. (1991) *Kriminalitätsbekämpfung durch innereuropäische Grenzkontrollen? Auswirkungen der Schengener Abkommen auf die innere Sicherheit*, Berlin: Duncker & Humblot.

Kühne, H.-H. (1999) "Moderne Sicherheitsstrategien gegen das Verbrechen," Bundeskriminalamt, Wiesbaden.

Laczko, F. and Gozdziak, E. eds. (2005) "Data and Research on Human Trafficking: A Global Survey," *International Migration* 43, Special Issue.

Le Breton, M. and Fiechter, U. (2001) "Frauenhandel im Kontext von Exklusions- und Differenzierungsprozessen" in *beiträge zur feministischen theorie und praxis* 24: 114–26.

Leman-Langlois, S. and Brodeur, J.-P. (2005) "Terrorism Old and New: Counterterrorism in Canada," *Police Practice & Research: An International Journal* 6, no. 2: 121–40.

Levi, M. (1995) "Incriminating Disclosures: An Evaluation of Money Laundering Regulation in England and Wales," *European Journal of Crime, Criminal Law and Criminal Justice* 3, no. 2: 202–17

Lutterer, W. and Hoch, H. (1997) Rechtliche Steuerung im Umweltbereich, Max-Planck-Institut, Freiburg.

Maurer, A. (2002)"§129b und Kronzeugenregelung. Alte Instrumente in neuem Gewand," *Bürgerrechte & Polizei* 70: 20–7.

Meyer, J., *et al.*, eds. (1989) "Gewinnabschöpfung bei Betäubungsmitteldelikten Eine rechtsvergleichende und kriminologische," *Untersuchung*, Wiesbaden.

Meyer-Wieck, H. (2004) Rechtswirklichkeit und Effizienz der akustischen Wohnraumüberwachung ("großer Lauschangriff") nach § 100c Abs. 1 Nr. 3 StPO. Research in Brief, Freiburg.

Meyer-Wieck, H. (2005) Der Große Lauschangriff. Eine empirische Untersuchung zu Anwendung und Folgen des §100c Abs. 1 Nr. 3 StPO. Berlin.

Militello, V., Arnold, J., and Paoli, L. (2001) *Organisierte Kriminalität als transnationales Phänomen*, Freiburg: Edition iuscrim.

Muus, P. (2001) "International Migration: Trends and Consequences," *European Journal on Criminal Policy and Research* 9: 31–49.

Transnational organized crime   79

Nicolic-Ristanovic, V. (2004) "Illegal Markets, Human Trade and Transnational Organised Crime" in *Threats and Phantoms of Organised Crime, Corruption and Terrorism*, P. C. van Duyne, *et al.* eds., Nijmegen: Wolf Legal Publishers, pp. 117–37.

Nogala, D. (2001) "Policing Across a Dimorphous Border: Challenge and Innovation at the French-German Border," *European Journal of Crime, Criminal Law and Criminal Justice* 9, no. 2: 13–43.

Oswald, K. (1997) *Die Implementation gesetzlicher Maßnahmen zur Bekämpfung der Geldwäsche in der Bundesrepublik Deutschland*, Freiburg.

Packer, H. L. (1966) "The Courts, the Police, and the Rest of Us," *Journal of Criminal Law, Criminology and Police Science* 57: 238–40.

Pieth, M. (1990) "Gewinnabschöpfung bei Betäubungsmitteldelikten," *Strafverteidiger*, p. 558.

Portes, A. (1999) "La Mondialisation Par Le Bas" in *Delits d'Immigration, Actes de la Recherche en Sciences Sociales*, 129, P. Bourdieu, ed., pp. 15–25.

Pricewaterhouse/Coopers. (2001) *Europäische Umfrage zur Wirtschaftskriminalität 2001*, Frankfurt: Moderne Wirtschaft.

Reyneri, E. (1999) "Migrants' Insertion in the Informal Economy, Deviant Behaviour and the Impact on Receiving Societies," The Comparative Reports. Tables of Contents and Abstracts, Milano.

Savona, E. U. (1992) "The Organized Crime/Drug Connection: National and International Perspectives" in H. H. Travor and M. S. Gaylord, eds., *Drugs, Law and the State*, New Brunswick, London: Transaction Books, pp. 119–33.

Scherp, D. (1998) "Lagebild Geldwäschebekämpfung. Eine Zwischenbilanz zur Gesetzesänderung vom Mai 1998," *Kriminalistik* 52: 458–62.

Senior Coordinator for International Women's Issues, U.S. Department of State. (1998) "Trafficking in Women and Girls: An International Human Rights Violation," Fact Sheet, March 10.

Shapland, J. (1994) "Crime: A Social Indicator or Social Normality?" in *Normes et Deviances en Europe: Un Debat Est-Ouest*, P. Robert and F. Sack, eds., Paris: L'Harmaltan, pp. 101–26

Sheptycki, J. (2001) "Patrolling the New European (In)Security Field: Organisational Dilemmas and Operational Solutions for Policing the Internal Borders of Europe," *European Journal of Crime, Criminal Law and Criminal Justice* 9, no. 2: 144–60.

Sinuraja, T. (1995) "Internationalization of Organized Economic Crime: The Russian Federation Case," *European Journal of Crime Policy and Research*, 3, no. 4: 34–53.

Stern, S. (2002) "Heute Beschuldigter—morgen'Kron'-Zeuge," *Strafverteidiger* 6: 185–90.

Szasz, A. (1986) "Corporations, Organized Crime, and the Disposal of Hazardous Waste: An Examination of the Making of a Criminogenic Regulatory Structure," *Criminology* 24, no. 1: 1–27

Tonry, M. (1998) "A Comparative Perspective on Minority Groups, Crime, and Criminal Justice," *European Journal of Crime, Criminal Law and Criminal Justice* 6, no. 1: 60–73.

Tonry, M. ed. (1997) *Ethnicity, Crime and Immigration: Comparative and Cross National Perspectives*, Chicago, London: University of Chicago Press.

Tullis, L. (1991) *Handbook of Research on the Illicit Drug Trade: Socioeconomic and Political Consequences*, New York: United Nations Research Institute for Social Development.

Vahle, J. (1998) "Ein Koloß auf tönernen Füßen. Anmerkungen zur (Neu-) Regelung des sogenannten Großen Lauschangriffs," *Kriminalistik* 52: 378–81.

Wiles, P. (1993) "Ghettoization in Europe?" *European Journal on Criminal Policy and Research* 1, no. 1: 52–69.

80   *H.-J. Albrecht*

Williams, P. (1995) "The Geopolitics of Transnational Organized Crime," Paper presented at the Conference on Global Security, University of Pittsburgh, November 2–3.

Wilson, W. J. (1997) *When Work Disappears*, New York: Knopf.

Yeandle, M., Mainelli, M., Berendt, A. and Healy, B. (2005) *Anti-Money Laundering Requirements: Costs, Benefits and Perceptions*, London: Corporation of London City Research Series No. 6, June.

Yiu Kong Chu. (2000) *The Triads as Business*, London, New York: Routledge.

4 International organized crime operating in Western Europe

The judicial and police approach against organized crime in the European Union

Joaquín González Ibáñez

Introduction: the European integration process

The existence of an open European space without borders had long been a goal of European integrationists. After the European Steel and Coal Treaty in 1950 where the pillars for peace and stability were recognized, the 1957 Treaty establishing the European Community set the goal of creating a European market within "an area without internal frontiers in which the free movement of goods, persons, services, and capital is ensured in accordance with the provisions of this treaty."[1]

The idea of European integration and the struggle to reach political stability, economic development, and welfare within the European Union (EU) could not be achieved without a solid judicial framework and effective law enforcement measures to support the single market; this legal framework would be able to provide economic advantages and security for EU citizens. As a result, justice and home affairs are also at the heart of efforts to forge a real concept of European citizenship.

Developing of an area of freedom, security, and justice as outlined in the Treaty of Amsterdam (1997) after the European Council conclusions of Tampere 1999 has been a long and complex process. The competences are finally in the current European Union Treaty, also called the Treaty of Nice 2002.[2]

On January 1, 2007 the European Union became the common ground for 27 member states and approximately 450 million people who are not only economic actors—consumers—in a vast single market but also citizens of the European Union. The European Union's so-called "Third Pillar" contains the legislation of what initially was labeled as "Justice and Home Affairs" (JHA) in the UE Treaty of Amsterdam and in EU Treaty of Nice. This legislation, defined in Title VI as "Provisions on Police and Judicial Cooperation in Criminal Matters" was designed to regulate issues regarding crime and security within EU borders. These acts deal with complex issues of security, rights, and freedom and, in many ways, they lie at the heart of the concept of European citizenship. They touch on some of the most difficult and sensitive issues currently facing all 27 EU member states; including political asylum, illegal immigration, organized crime, drug smuggling, and terrorism. Justice and home affairs rules also govern the way the European Union's national courts work together when people are involved in legal proceedings in more than one EU country.[3]

82   J. G. Ibáñez

During Finland's presidency of the EU in 1999, at the Special Meeting of the European Council held in Tampere in October, the Union-wide fight against crime was one of the main subjects of the resolutions for the "creation of an area of freedom, security and justice." Since the mid-1970s member states have cooperated against organized crime in the European Community and the EU has been acting in a coordinated manner to tackle organized crime, terrorism, and drug abuse in the EU.[4] The development of a common legal structure against organized crime has been based on cooperation among police and judicial authorities of the member states, harmonization of internal norms, fluid exchange of valuable criminal information, and a political will to face organized crime operating in the European Community.[5]

Two institutions remain as the pillars of the European Union fight against crime: (1) The European Police Office (Europol) as the central police office for exchange of information among the member states and for analyzing crime, and (2) an operative European Judicial system (Eurojust), which collects, analyzes, and forwards information and findings, thus providing support to the national law enforcement authorities in their fight against serious forms of international crime.

Main crimes perpetrated by organized groups in Europe

The existence of a unique territory involving people traveling from country to country provides room for international organized crime. A by-product of economic integration in the European Union is the creation of new opportunities for criminal enterprises to commit crimes across national borders.

The Rule of Law of the European Union and its member states against organized crime has always been based on four main elements: international cooperation, adoption of efficient legal instruments and institutions, prevention, and harmonization of legislation.

The areas and activities in which organized crime groups engage are varied and far-reaching. These areas include: drug trafficking; money laundering; fraud against the EU budget; arms dealing; international car theft; loan sharking; trafficking in art, antiquities, and rare fossils; environmental crime such as black market trading in nuclear materials and the illegal disposal of hazardous waste; trafficking in endangered animals and plant species; trafficking in prostitution; pornography (including child Internet pornography); smuggling of illegal immigrants and trading in human organs; computer crime (including communication among groups for planned illegal activities through highly complex encrypted messages); and coercive labor.[6]

In the EU territory one of the key areas for all organized crime is drugs. The immense profits from drug dealing can be estimated only from the seizures made, mainly by customs officials. But there is widespread agreement that the drug trade represents a huge, and the most important, market for organized crime. In 2004 the UN Office on Drugs and Crime published a special report on *Drugs and Crime Trends in Europe*,[7] which described the relevance of drug trafficking within the EU's borders and the main destinations of different drugs emanating from Asia and Latin America. The report also showed the increasing importance of synthetic drugs produced in European member states.

International organized crime operating in Western Europe   83

Money laundering, the process by which "dirty" money is converted into "clean" untraceable funds, is another key area of organized criminal activity and it is essential to conceal the massive profits made from drug trafficking.

The theft of vehicles has been another lucrative area for organized crime in Europe. Criminals also traffic in plant machinery, agricultural equipment, and automobiles. The growth in trafficking of illegal immigrants is another lucrative market that organized crime has tapped.

BBC columnist John Simpson assesses crime as one of the four evils that threaten global stability. According to him, those who celebrated the fall of the Berlin Wall and the revolutions in Czechoslovakia and Romania never thought that one of the great evils of the century was being born. Because of globalization and transport and communication improvement, a new brand of organized transnational crime is observable from Johannesburg to Prague, and from Lagos to Macau.[8] Nevertheless, from a European point of view, unemployment remains the main fear of most Europeans. A survey conducted by the German communication group GFK revealed that unemployment is the most important fear of Europeans and the most important problem to solve; that is followed by issues of inflation, healthcare, and housing. Crime was farther down the list and only the British placed crime as the main threat to their society.[9]

During the last 20 years, various forces have contributed to the observed increase in crime in Europe: the elimination of formal borders in 1986, and more specifically in 1992 with the complete entry into the Common Market; the fall of the Berlin Wall in 1989; the collapse of communist regimes; and the proximity of the EU countries to countries in conflict and to countries in transition Europe. The EU, frequently called a "Club for Rich Countries," is a natural destination for some criminal groups from neighboring countries on the southern and eastern borders of the EU. With the entry of ten new member states (eight out of ten were former communist regimes) in January 2004 and further enlargement of the EU in January 2007 with Bulgaria and Rumania, the former distinction between crime of the East and the West has lost its importance. Now everyone is "in" with the exception of Russia and the Soviet successor states outside the Baltics. There is seemingly no limit to what is a target of organized criminals in "Old Europe." Cultural and historical objects have become increasingly sought after by collectors, creating a huge black market for stolen antiques, paintings, sculpture, and so forth.[10]

Difficulties in structuring a common response against organized crime in European treaties

Drafting EU rules on police and judicial cooperation in criminal matters has never been easy. Issues such as asylum policy, crime fighting measures, or approaches to border control and terrorism lie at the heart of the concept of national sovereignty and touch sensitive historical and contemporary issues of EU member states. The countries within the EU traditionally have been reluctant to give up any right to control criminal policy in their countries. Member states now, however, accept that shared problems need common solutions.

84   J. G. Ibáñez

For many years, all European policies on justice and home affairs were agreed on by government meetings in ad hoc groups outside the European Union's law-making structures. In 1985 the European Commission issued a White Paper on the internal market proposing that harmonization of laws should help lay the foundation for the creation of a single market by the end of 1992. The scenario was transformed in 1986 when the member states decided to cooperate on the entry, movement, and residence of third country nationals into and within the European Union. Then, in 1992, common rules for citizens of non-EU countries crossing the EU's external frontiers and for immigration policy were incorporated into the Treaty on European Union or Maastricht Treaty. (The terminology European Economic Community was definitively abandoned in favor of characterizing the relationship as a more political process with the name European Union.)

The Maastricht Treaty formally recognized that justice and home affairs were a common concern and created a special law-making structure to handle legislation linked to these concerns. This is often called "the Third Pillar" of the EU, as opposed to the majority of traditional EU responsibilities in the "First Pillar" and the common foreign and security policy in the "Second Pillar." Acts passed under the new rules were, in effect, intergovernmental agreements that were legally binding on the European Union. Bringing police and judicial cooperation in criminal matters within the ambit of the European Union was an important first step. But law making in this arena remained slow because in the second and third pillars every act had to be passed unanimously. This differed from the normal functioning of the EU, which in its First Pillar functions as a supranational international organization rather than an intergovernmental international organization as in the Second and Third Pillars, which allow states the possibility to veto the adoption of binding norms.

The leap toward a common response in the EU Treaty of Nice

The next important step in the evolution of the European Union's Justice and Home Affairs Acts came on May 1, 1999, when the Treaty of Amsterdam—which updated the Maastricht Treaty—entered into force. The Amsterdam Treaty moved several key policy areas, including asylum, immigration policy, and cooperation among civil courts, into the EU's normal law-making structures. At a special summit meeting in the Finnish city of Tampere in October 1999, EU governments pledged to adopt a series of new initiatives on asylum, fighting crime, and cooperation between courts and police forces.

The current EU Treaty provides for a stronger role for Europol in the fight against crime and drugs. The aim of the incorporation of Schengen into the Treaty is to establish an area where internal frontier controls would be abolished and police and judicial cooperation would be improved. To reinforce the external borders of the Union, the European Commission can now act to provide policy measures on visas and immigration as these areas have now been moved to the first pillar (the functioning of the European Community as a supranational organization).

The Nice Treaty goes even further than the Maastricht and Amsterdam treaties to combat the drug problems by extending the Union's responsibility in this

International organized crime operating in Western Europe   85

area. For the first time, the fight against drugs is cited as a specific objective of the Union.

With the Treaty of Amsterdam going into force in 2000, the fight against crime and drugs in the EU became an important activity. Subsequently, the Nice Treaty in 2002 established combating drugs as a specified policy of the EU, and common policies on visas and immigration were improved. To achieve these goals, greater police cooperation should be implemented to protect citizens, with enhanced standards for all.

At the Tampere Summit some important issues were identified as priorities in the field of judicial cooperation in criminal matters. The Commission drew up an action plan that addressed:

- streamlining mutual assistance;
- facilitating extradition;
- adopting mutual recognition of rulings in criminal cases;
- setting up a central coordinating team of judicial experts—Eurojust;
- developing the European judicial network (a decentralized network of judicial contact points);
- approximation—taking different and diverse legislation on common principles;
- improving compensation for victims of criminal offenses;
- training EU magistrates.

Police and customs cooperation

For more than 25 years European countries have worked on different models of cooperation to tackle crime and organized crime groups in the European Community. There was significant development from the establishment of the original Trevi Group in 1976 until the establishment of Europol in 1999.[11] The following examines the development of models of cooperation.

The Trevi Group

In 1976 Trevi was created initially as a forum to exchange information regarding terrorism, and was later expanded to deal with problems of international organized crime and public order. The Trevi working groups were concerned with the implications of the abolition of border controls in 1992, and their recommendations were incorporated into the Schengen Agreement. The new European Drugs Intelligence Unit was established in 1990. With the entry into force of the Maastricht Treaty in 1992, Trevi was incorporated into the Third Pillar under the title of Justice and Home Affairs, a title that would be modified in 2002 as Police and Judicial Cooperation in Criminal Matters.

Europol

In 1992, the Maastricht Treaty established the European Drugs Unit (EDU), an organization devoted to supporting each member state's fight against drugs and associated

86   *J. G. Ibáñez*

money laundering. In July 1999, the EDU evolved into the European Police Office (Europol), and its responsibilities have grown from drugs policing to include such diverse areas of serious crime as illegal immigration, vehicle trafficking, child pornography, forgery, terrorism, and money laundering. The Treaty of Nice increased Europol's functions. Europol was granted authority to work on the collection, storage, processing, analysis, and exchange of relevant information, including information held by law enforcement offices as well as reports on suspicious financial transactions.[12]

Europol supports law enforcement agencies of all member countries in the EU by gathering and analyzing information and intelligence, specifically about people who are members or possible members of criminal organizations that operate internationally. This information is received from a variety of sources including the numerous police forces of the EU and other international crime-fighting organizations such as Interpol. Europol is also charged with the task of developing expertise in certain fields of crime and making these experts available to the countries of the EU when needed. The human resources of Europol are limited and it depends on supplements from other European countries. It is in constant contact with hundreds of different law enforcement organizations.

Since the events of September 11, the role of organizations such as Europol has taken on more importance within the boundaries of international law enforcement. At the European level, Europol leads the fight against terrorism in Europe because of its centralization and its close cooperation with similar organizations in the United States. At the heart of the service is a vast computer database that when fully operational will make it much easier to track down, and to keep track of, known and suspected criminals and stolen objects. It will provide authorized law enforcement officers in all EU member states with instant access to millions of commonly shared data files.

Europol's responsibilities have quickly expanded, and it now deals with a wide range of issues where two or more EU member states are affected. These include illegal trafficking in drugs, stolen vehicles, and human beings, as well as illegal immigration networks, sexual exploitation of women and children, pornography, forgery, smuggling of radioactive and nuclear materials, terrorism, money laundering, and counterfeiting of the euro.

European Police College

The European Police College (CEPOL) was established by the Council of Ministers in 2000.[13] Its principal goal is to provide cross-border training of senior police officers, thereby optimizing and reinforcing cooperation among relevant national institutes and organizations. CEPOL also is to support and develop an integrated EU approach on the cross-border problems faced by its member states in their fight against crime and the maintenance of law and order and public security.

Drugs and the EU

All EU member states agree on the need to tackle the organized criminals who either smuggle narcotics and psychotropic substances into the EU or—as is the

International organized crime operating in Western Europe 87

case of certain synthetic drugs—manufacture them illegally in laboratories within the European Union.[14]

Since 1994 Europol has been able to provide intelligence and analytical support to investigations into drug-smuggling operations. All EU countries supported an initiative to set up a drug observatory, the European Monitoring Centre for Drugs and Drug Addiction. Based in Lisbon, this agency provides regular reports on the level of drug use in all Europe. The EU has also designed measures to reduce drug production and trafficking in many parts of the world.

Schengen Agreement

In 1995, Germany, France, Belgium, the Netherlands, and Luxembourg signed the Schengen Agreement to establish an area with no internal border controls and where police and judicial cooperation would be improved. Currently, the "Schengen area" covers 15 countries: Austria, Belgium, Denmark, Finland, France, Germany, Iceland, Italy, Greece, Luxembourg, Netherlands, Norway, Portugal, Spain, and Sweden. All of these countries except Norway and Iceland are European Union members.[15]

Since 2000, the Schengen Agreement has been incorporated into the EU Treaty. Ireland and the UK, which already had their own common travel area, still remain out of the Schengen Agreement. The Schengen Agreement and Europol are central to the fight against drugs and crime within the European Union.

The "communitarised" benefits of Schengen—a common policy on visas and effective controls at the EU's external borders—contribute to the protection of internal security within the borderless Schengen community. Far from trying to create a fortress, these measures in fact make entry into and travel within the European Union easier for any legitimate person, while attempting to thwart the activities of criminal organizations that exploit human beings.

Although the "open borders" element of the Schengen Agreement is perhaps its best-known aspect, it also contains a number of other important provisions that attempt to compensate for the elimination of internal borders. These "compensatory measures" require that countries at the edge of the Schengen zone ensure that their external borders are properly policed. Once a person is inside the Schengen area, that individual is free to move around wherever he or she wants within this area. Member states have, therefore, argued that it is vital that border checks at the area's external frontiers are rigorous enough to stop illegal immigration, drug smuggling, and other unlawful activities. In other words, each state that carries out checks at external borders has to take into account the common interest and security of all EU members states. At the external frontiers of the Schengen area, all EU citizens need only show an identity card or passport to be allowed to enter. The nationals of many third countries may also enter the Schengen area on presenting their passports.

SIS

All border controls were to have been abolished within the Schengen area by 2004. To facilitate the security of external borders, a new Information System for the

88   J. G. Ibáñez

Exchange of Data on Suspected Criminals (SIS) was introduced and became fully operational in 2005. SIS is a complex database that enables the appropriate law enforcement and legal authorities to exchange data for investigations on persons and objects. For example, information may be shared on people wanted for arrest or extradition and information on stolen vehicles or stolen works of art. Independent supervisory authorities have been put in place in the member states to check that information entered into the SIS does not violate data protection rules.

This system is vital for the proper and effective work of Europol and Schengen. The Schengen provisions also provide for better coordination among police services and judicial authorities to fight effectively against organized crime.

The need for a complementary approach to tackle organized crime gained ground during the 1990s when the idea of an integrated judicial body for European member states was developed as a way to fight transnational crime.[16]

The idea of a "European legal area" has been gaining ground since the 1987 Single European Act, which included the concept of a European Community without frontiers in the Treaty of Rome. The Treaty of Maastricht added cooperation in civil and criminal matters to Title VI as areas of common interest to the European Union member states. Later, the Treaties of Amsterdam and Nice preserved cooperation in criminal matters in the Third Pillar and spelled out its objectives, including the fight against crime.

The EU Treaty underlines the importance of fighting organized crime. It contains provisions for coordinating the national rules on offenses and penalties applicable to organized crime, terrorism, and drug trafficking. The Tampere European Council in 1999 stated its firm intention of stepping up the fight against serious forms of organized and transnational crime. In particular, it stressed the need for further preventive measures and closer cooperation at the EU level.

Efforts to find agreement on common definitions, offenses, and penalties in criminal law would concentrate initially on a limited number of particularly important sectors such as financial crime, drug trafficking, trafficking in human beings, crime using advanced technology, and crime against the environment. The Council also underlined the need for specific action to combat money laundering. There have been exchange and training programs in this area, such as the Grotius program for legal practitioners (1996–2000) and the Falcone program for judges and public prosecutors involved in fighting organized crime (1998–2002). These programs are designed to improve mutual understanding of the member states' legal systems, exchange information, and encourage cooperation among the professionals concerned.

In May 2000 the Council of EU adopted the convention on mutual assistance in criminal matters.

Judicial cooperation

Eurojust

At the special Justice and Home Affairs summit in Tampere in October 1999, EU governments agreed to set up a special team of legal and judicial experts, known as

International organized crime operating in Western Europe 89

Eurojust, to smooth the way and help coordinate the investigation and prosecution of serious cross-border crime.[17] Previously, this judicial body worked alongside the European Judicial Network (EJN), which began work in 1998. The EJN acts as a central coordinating group among EU lawyers and judges working on criminal cases and tries to help them exchange information rapidly and effectively.

Since 2001, Eurojust is made up of a team of senior lawyers, prosecutors, and/or magistrates from member states. Team members are expected to know the legal systems of member countries, have rapid access to information from diverse countries, and are entitled to engage in direct dialogue with national authorities. Eurojust actively intervenes in cross-border cases analyzed by Europol that call for immediate legal advice and assistance from investigators and prosecutors in different member states. European judicial cooperation in criminal matters is also extended to international organizations such as the Council of Europe, the United Nations, and the G8 grouping of the world's seven richest countries plus Russia.

The heteronomous and diverse national criminal procedures must be accommodated as member states gradually harmonize rules on criminal matters and penal sanctions. The aim is not, therefore, to establish a supranational judicial and law enforcement system, but to intensify contacts among legal practitioners and law enforcement officials, encouraging trust rather than rivalry and harmonizing where necessary while coordinating where the latter option is more effective.

The European judicial area must be understood as a framework open to all forms of international cooperation, first and foremost those established within the Council of Europe. The European Judicial Network is a light structure that comprises 190 "points of contact" intended to fight transnational crime, particularly organized crime. The "points of contact" are intermediaries intended to assist in judicial cooperation among member states. They are available to local judicial authorities and the judicial authorities of other member states to allow them to establish direct contacts with each other. The points are determined by the member states and reflect the internal structure of their judicial system, including investigating judges and/or public prosecutors. The number of these varies from two for Greece to 36 for France.

Eurojust works as a vital point of contact. Its members are active intermediaries with the task of facilitating judicial cooperation among the member states, particularly in actions to combat serious crime. European experience has taught that language and legal or technical problems hinder effective cooperation in criminal matters. The European Judicial Network intervenes to resolve these problems by serving as an intermediary among judicial authorities in the various member states. The judicial network also created a "Judicial Atlas." This "atlas" is a computer system allowing magistrates to identify with great speed and ease the authority in a member state competent to receive a request for cooperation. One of the basic activities performed is to improve judicial cooperation in cases where a series of requests from the local judicial authorities in a member state necessitates coordinated action in another. Network members intervene to authorize and coordinate cross-border operations such as controlled deliveries and cross-border surveillance.

Aside from its supportive role in matters of judicial cooperation, the Joint Action Plan provides for periodic meetings of the network. As a rule, these meetings take

90   *J. G. Ibáñez*

place three times a year. Each presidency of the EU organizes one in its country and the third takes place at the beginning of the year in Brussels. Eurojust provides better understanding of foreign law and prompts interesting discussions on comparative law. This better understanding of the operation of the judicial systems of other member states contributes to reducing the number of obstacles to judicial cooperation.

The European Arrest Warrant

The European Arrest Warrant replaced the traditional extradition mechanism in 2004. This judicial "path of action" was developed to ensure judicial cooperation between states in order to prevent a criminal from finding refuge on the territory of another EU state. It has been a major leap in favor of European cooperation, bearing in mind the initial strong opposition presented by the Italian government and former Prime Minister Berlusconi. In fact, it has been a revolutionary cooperation formula among judicial authorities that does not include the involvement of the government during the European judicial extradition proceeding.

The European Arrest Warrant is a judicial decision delivered by a member state for the arrest and surrender by another member state of a requested person. In keeping with the underlying principles of mutual recognition, its objective is to allow throughout the Union the execution of decisions in criminal matters delivered by a judicial authority of a member state. The arrest warrant does not cover all offenses; there is a threshold beyond which it does not apply. Arrest warrants can be issued only if, under the law of the issuing member state, the act is punishable by a custodial sentence of at least 12 months or if there has been an order imposing sanctions of at least four months.[18] The judicial authority of the state of execution will make provisions for surrendering the person. It must verify that the necessary conditions for executing the mandate and for surrendering the person have been properly met.

Communication between member states is direct, for example, from judge to judge. In contrast with the classic rules on extradition, the mechanism of the European arrest warrant abolishes the intervention of the diplomatic authorities, and even that of the ministries of justice. As mentioned above, the abolition of all political intervention constitutes the main difference with extradition, a system where the executive power controls the procedure.

The creation of the European Arrest Warrant represents a true step forward in the field of mutual assistance in criminal matters. Eliminating interference from political powers or establishing a time limit to execute a warrant represents real progress in comparison with the old system of extradition.[19]

Mutual recognition of judicial decision in criminal matters: background

Mutual recognition was already being applied successfully in the Community with the creation of the Single Market in 1986. The process was given a real boost by the Tampere European Council of October 1999. The heads of state or government

International organized crime operating in Western Europe 91

went on record to say that mutual recognition of judicial decisions had to become the cornerstone of judicial cooperation in the Union.

The principle of mutual recognition means full execution of a judgment handed down by the judicial authorities of another member state, although is not an absolute principle. In practice it runs up against different types of restrictions. Mutual recognition is also linked to the process of the approximation of criminal law; the two methods, mutual recognition and approximation of legal legislation, work in tandem to help create the area of freedom, security, and justice.

As states remain fully sovereign on criminal matters, foreign decisions have no weight. Judgments handed down in another member state are based on a different legal order founded on different values. For that reason, a country is not obliged to execute decisions reflecting values that are not its own. This principle was challenged because, with European integration, the values defended by national criminal laws converged. In a context of building an area of freedom, security, and justice, mutual recognition has the goal of guaranteeing a legal effect for decisions taken by any member state throughout the Union. It allows a decision delivered in a member state to be applied unconditionally by another member state.

The implementation of the principle of mutual recognition of decisions in criminal matters implies reciprocal trust by member states in each other's criminal justice systems. Building this system of confidence and trust depends on two elements:

- The different legal systems must be based on a common foundation of democratic principles, respect for human rights, and fundamental freedoms. The inseparability of fundamental rights from mutual recognition is highlighted by the Commission's Green Paper on procedural guarantees for suspects and defendants.[20] We must not forget that all the EU members are also members of the Council of Europe and are state signatories of the European Convention of Human Rights (Rome, 1950), which implicate a common legal concept of fundamental liberties and rights for all European member states.
- There has to be a certain degree of commonality between the different systems. Mutual trust will be fostered as national legal systems converge. Harmonization is meant to reduce differences in laws and contribute to a common definition of criminal policy. Mutual recognition pursues the opposite objective, namely, that of getting the different legal system to coincide while preserving their differences.

Assistance to victims in criminal matters

Victims of crime have a right to protection, and this is a right that should be ensured by the Union to achieve the objective of freedom, security, and justice. The protection of victims of crime can be expressed in two complementary forms: compensation for harm suffered and provision of material, psychological, medical, and social assistance.

Pursuant to Article 29 of the EU treaty, the European Union acts as guarantor for the European citizen's security. This article provides that the goal of the area of

92   J. G. Ibáñez

freedom, security, and justice is to offer citizens a high level of safety. Protection of victims of crime is in keeping with the extension of the right to freedom of movement of persons. The citizen can exercise this right only if the state authorities have introduced measures for protection and compensation according to objective criteria, independent of nationality.

OLAF: fighting crime within the European institutions

The European Anti-Fraud Office (OLAF) was created in 1999 to compensate for the lack of an official body to fight fraud against the Community's financial interests, estimated to amount to 10 percent of its total budget in the early 1990s. In 1997, the emergence of irregularities within the European institutions themselves clearly pointed to the need for an entirely new inter-institutional body with the standing of a legal persona and charged with conducting independent investigations into infringements within the institutions.[21]

From June 2001 to June 2002, the Office opened 552 new cases of internal investigations relating to activities within the Community's institutions, 30 percent more than during the previous two years. Internal investigations account for approximately 10 percent of the cases handled, the majority of which concern the Commission. This trend has been confirmed for the period 2002–5.[22] External investigations are conducted in close collaboration with competent authorities from the member states concerned. These authorities must be kept informed on the investigation and may participate in it if they wish to do so. When carrying out its investigations, OLAF enjoys a right of access to the premises of economic actors and of the institutions, and a right of communication for any information it deems useful. Investigations are opened by a decision of the director-general of OLAF, who may act either on his or her own initiative or at the request of a member state concerned by an external investigation.

Conclusions and challenges

Crime does not respect national borders. Organized criminals are becoming increasingly sophisticated and regularly use EU-wide or international networks to carry out their activities. Faced with this reality, EU governments have realized during the last 30 years that they cannot effectively tackle international organized crime by relying solely on national law enforcement agencies. As the European Commission emphasizes, money is crime's lifeblood. Criminal organizations exist to make money. The EU's police, customs, and judicial agencies are at the forefront of the fight against crime and complement national efforts against organized crime.

Cooperation and flow of information is the answer

As we have seen, the interconnected functioning of Eurojust, Schengen, OLAF, and Europol will make cooperation among European law enforcement bodies more effective.

International organized crime operating in Western Europe 93

The establishment of transparent and direct links among Eurojust, Europol, and OLAF would increase the effectiveness of the fight against crime within the European Union. Nevertheless, the achievement of a Europe without frontiers has also given room to a European crime without frontiers, as Hugo Brady, research fellow at the Centre for European Reform in London, claims.[23] The member states, aware of the increased levels of crime, have promised to reform information sharing among their law-enforcement authorities by adhering to a "principle of availability" by 2008. This means that police forces will no longer plaintively have to request information from each other. Meanwhile, the governments will continue an ongoing effort to align national criminal laws more closely throughout the EU. In a way, the historical premise for European countries prompts member state to work together to avoid the repetition of confrontation. This "forces" Europeans to work on the process of European integration, to always look forward with no possibilities of ever stepping back. Europe is building on its democratic principles. It is overcoming the haunting memory of its history. Now European citizens demand a democratic response to the globalized phenomenon of international crime and terrorism. The response given by the citizens to the terrorist attacks in Madrid on March 11, 2004 and in London on July 7, 2005 showed that the response of European Union member states must be based on the rule of law, respect for human rights, and a strong and intense institutional cooperation among member states.

Notes

1 The European Union is a supranational and integrating organization that has taken on responsibilities of the member states. But the European Union is not a state or a nation, such as the United States, the United Kingdom, or Spain. The aim of the European Union is to create an area for peace and welfare, based on freedom, security, and justice; and on a free market economy, a dynamic and plural economy that promotes the development of an important Union market and free competence among economic operators. The prospect of economic development is influenced by the use of sustainable development policies that include economic, social, and environmental aspects; scientific and technical progress; law and social protection. The principle of solidarity among member states aims at guaranteeing social and economic cohesion among the European societies. Jean Monnet, one of the founding fathers of the European Communities, said on April 4, 1952, "We are not making a coalition of States, but are uniting people." See European Commission, *A Constitution for Europe*, p. 6.

2 The European Union treaty was passed in 1992 in the city of Maastricht, Netherlands, and meant the evolution from the European Economic Communities to a more polit- ical and closer organization to European citizens. The EU Treaty has gone through two amendment processes: the EU Treaty of Amsterdam 2000 and the current EU Treaty, Treaty of Nice 2002.

3 See Chapter VI, EU Treaty, <europa.eu/generalreport/er/2003/pt0753.htm> (accessed February 23, 2007).

4 The Organized Crime Control Act, adopted by the United States in 1970, defines organ- ized crime as "The unlawful activities of a highly organized, disciplined association." Nevertheless, organized crime is characterized by some specific qualities: durability over time, diversified interests, strong hierarchical structure, capital accumulation, reinvest- ment, access to political protection, and the use of violence to protect interests. Klaus Von Lampe refers to "organized crime" as something to be built, not a self-evident

94 *J. G. Ibáñez*

phenomenon," and it is used as a term for diverse phenomena. Von Lampe also claims that the current concept of organized crime is an American invention superimposed on Europe. See K. Von Lampe, *Organized Crime in Europe.*

5 See C. Fijnaut and L. Paoli (eds.), *Organised Crime in Europe.*
6 See Morgan Cloud, "Organized Crime, Rico and the European Union."
7 United Nations, Office on Drugs and Crime. *Drugs and Crime Trends in Europe and Beyond.*
8 See "The Third Horseman: Organized Crime" by John Simpson <http://www.bbc.com> (accessed July 2006).
9 See the survey performed by GfK under the name "Challenges of Europe 2006," GFK-Nürnberg e.V., Nuremberg, 2006, p. 5.
10 See Europol, *Europol Annual Report 2005.*
11 See Police and Judicial Cooperation in the European Union, <http://www.europa.eu.int> (accessed July 2006).
12 See Carrera Hernández and F. Jesús, *La cooperación policial en la Unión Europea: acervo Schengen y Europol.*
13 Decision of the Council of Minister on December 22, 2000, EU, Brussels.
14 See *Report on the Risk Assessment of TMA-2 in the Framework of the Joint Action on New Synthetic Drugs* issued by the European Monitoring Centre for Drugs and Drugs Addiction, Luxembourg.
15 See <http://www.eurovisa.info/SchengenVisa.htm> (accessed July 2006).
16 See M. Bacigalupo Saggese, *La cooperación policial y judicial en materia penal*, (The police and judicial cooperation in criminal matters).
17 See <http://www.ejn-crimjust.eu.int> (accessed July 2006).
18 See 2002/584/JHA: Council Framework Decision of 13 June 2002 on the European arrest warrant and the surrender procedures between member states.
19 In 2003 Spain was one the first European countries to implement the National Law, the European Arrest Warrant. It has been a very efficient procedural tool during the investigation of terrorist attacks in Madrid of March 11, 2004, and for the extradition of alleged members of Al-Qaeda or ETA. See, E. García Coso, "La Aplicación En España De La Euroorden Y Su Aplicación Judicial: Las Limitaciones Impuestas Por Algunos Tribunales Constitucionales Europeos Y La Garantía De Los Derechos Y Libertades Fundamentales."
20 See Commission Green Paper on procedural guarantees for suspects and defendants <http://www.eupsjc.org> (accessed July 2006).
21 See the European Anti-fraud office at <http://ec.europa.eu/anti_fraud/index_en.html> (accessed July 2006).
22 See OLAF Supervisory Committee, Opinion No 1/05 on the Commission staff working document on complementary evaluation of the activities of OLAF, Luxembourg, March 22, 2005.
23 See Hugo Brady, "The EU and the Fight Against Organised Crime," Centre for European Reform, April 2007, <http://www.cer.org.uk/pdf/wp721_org_crime_brady. pdf> (accessed October 14, 2010) and "Europe's Crime Without Frontiers," *Yorkshire Post*, June 21, 2006, <http://www.yorkshirepost.co.uk/> (accessed October 14, 2010).

References

Bacigalupo Saggese, M. (2005) *La cooperación policial y judicial en materia penal* (The Police and Judicial Cooperation in Criminal Matters), Madrid: Colex.

Brady, H. (2007) "The EU and the Fight Against Organised Crime," Centre for European Reform, <http://www.cer.org.uk/pdf/wp721_org_crime_brady.pdf> (accessed October 14, 2010)

International organized crime operating in Western Europe   95

—— (2006) "Europe's Crime Without Frontiers," *Yorkshire Post*, June 21, <http://www.yorkshirepost.co.uk/> (accessed October 14, 2010).

Cloud, M. (2000) "Organized Crime, Rico and the European Union," paper presented at the Emory University School of Law.

European Commission. (2004) *A Constitution for Europe*, Brussels.

European Monitoring Centre for Drugs and Drugs Addiction. (2004) *Report on the Risk Assessment of TMA-2 in the Framework of the Joint Action on New Synthetic Drugs*, Luxembourg: Office for Official Publications of the European Communities.

Europol. (2005) *Europol Annual Report 2005*, Europol, The Hague.

Fijnaut, C. and Paoli L., eds. (2004) *Organised Crime in Europe. Concepts, Patterns and Control Policies in the European Union and Beyond Series: Studies of Organized Crime*, vol. 4, Freiburg, New York: Springer.

García Coso, E. (2006) "La Aplicación En España De La Euroorden Y Su Aplicación Judicial: Las Limitaciones Impuestas Por Algunos Tribunales Constitucionales Europeos Y La Garantía De Los Derechos Y Libertades Fundamentales" in G. Ibáñez, *Derechos Humanos, Globalización y Relaciones Internacionales*, Bogotá: Ediciones Jurídicas Gustavo Ibáñez.

Hernández, C. and Jesús, F. (2003) *La cooperación policial en la Unión Europea: acervo Schengen y Europol*, Madrid: Colex.

United Nations, Office on Drugs and Crime. (2004) *Drugs and Crime Trends in Europe and Beyond*, Vienna, April 29.

Von Lampe, K. (2006) *Organized Crime in Europe*, Berlin: Free University of Berlin.

5 Crime in Japan and its relation to international organized crime

Kan Ueda

Introduction

In the 1980s, Japan was viewed as the only economically developed country in the world that had succeeded in controlling crime. In 1985, for example, the number of penal code offenses known to the police (excluding traffic-related offenses) was 1,607,663, which translates to a rate of 1,328 crimes per 100,000 population. This was dramatically lower than the crime rates of 5,000–7,000 per 100,000 population reported in the United States and Europe during the same period. With a clearance rate of 72.9 percent for penal code offenses as a whole, and 64.2 percent even when traffic-related offenses were excluded, the Japanese police force for the most part enjoyed the full confidence of the general public. Against this background, the annual "White Paper on Crime" published by the Ministry of Justice that year proudly stated:

> Crime in Japan in recent years has generally remained rather low, as a result of the application of criminal justice policies well-suited to the distinctive characteristics of the Japanese environment. This achievement is attracting the attention of countries all over the world.

The phrase "criminal justice policies well-suited to the distinctive characteristics of the Japanese environment" is thought to refer to the following points. First, as a result of the ethnic isolation of the Japanese people due to geographical and historical factors, as well as to social and economic policies such as Japan's extended period of *sakoku* or self-imposed isolation, there was no systematic influx of non-Japanese ethnic groups into Japan for a long period. In the absence of ethnic conflict, Japan evolved a culture that emphasized values such as empathy and harmony rather than conflict and rivalry between "us" and "them," friend and foe. Within family, the Japanese "company," and the local community, human relations were given primary importance. Perhaps most important was the fact that the period of rapid economic expansion that began in Japan in the late 1950s, and the subsequent period of relatively stable economic growth, led to comparatively low rates of unemployment.

Crime rates in general, and property-related offenses in particular, fell steadily or remained stable over a very long period. Under these conditions Japan, while placing severe restrictions on firearms and strict controls on immigration, was able to maintain its traditional policing system.[1] This system consisted of a network of *koban* or neighborhood police stations, and was able to successfully develop a system of criminal administration that featured, at each stage of the process, a variety of measures aimed at avoiding the stigma of criminalization and reducing the need to impose criminal punishments. Most juveniles or others committing minor offenses were not subjected to criminal prosecution and punishment, and even when punishments were applied, actual incarceration was very rare. As a result, on one hand the institutions responsible for controlling crime and administering criminal justice were able to devote their entire energies to battling major crimes. On the other, the barriers to rehabilitation and resocialization of offenders were kept low, helping to prevent many minor delinquents from becoming repeat offenders or professional criminals. This combination of factors helped contribute to the large gap in crime rates, especially violent crime rates, between Japan and other countries.

This sanguine view of the status of crime in Japan disappeared in the early 1990s. In August 1990 the Iraqi army invaded Kuwait, and this was followed by the first Gulf War from January to March of 1991. It was around this time that Japan's so-called "bubble economy" burst, and Japan entered a period of long-term economic stagnation that has come to be known as the "Great Heisei recession." The economy was beset by one problem after another, as non-performing loans exposed weaknesses in Japan's financial system, corporate restructuring and layoffs became widespread, household incomes fell, and unemployment became a serious problem.

The various crime-related indices began to fluctuate alarmingly, stimulating an over-reaction about the danger of crime on the part of the public, and leading to increased demands for implementation of more severe measures to deal with crime. For the first time in decades, crime became a serious social problem, and, as such, an important political issue. This led to a series of revisions to the penal code, imposing more severe punishments for crimes, and at the same time there was a notable increase in the number of surveillance cameras installed along streets in urban areas and in public transport systems, and in the formation of neighborhood crime watch groups. Also during this period the courts began to issue fewer suspended sentences and increased the percentage of sentences involving actual jail time. This in turn has led to a serious state of chronic overcrowding in Japan's correctional facilities, which is reflected in the fact that there are now more than 100 death row inmates awaiting execution in Japanese prisons.

Given the dynamic nature of these crime-related trends, this chapter attempts to clarify which aspects of crime in Japan have changed, which aspects have remained the same, and examines the present status of crime in Japan as it relates to the global problem of international organized crime.

Public safety and crime in Japan

Looking back over crime trends in Japan since the end of World War II, the crime rate (defined as penal code offenses known to the police per 100,000 population, excluding traffic-related violations) reached a peak of 2,000 in 1948, and then

98   K. Ueda

declined steadily for a long period, eventually falling as low as 1,091 in 1973. Thereafter, however, crime began a gradual upward trend, and broke through the 2,000 barrier again in 2001. Considering that these rates still represent a mere fraction of those in Europe or the United States, and that the majority of the increase in crime in recent years consists of minor offenses such as petty larceny or embezzlement, some take the view that this increase in crime rates does not necessarily signify a serious problem. However, we must guard against the dangers of excessive optimism. Japanese society has been changing rapidly in recent years, and the wave of internationalization now sweeping the nation is steadily eroding the effectiveness of those distinctive factors that until now have been credited with keeping crime rates low in Japan. The increased seriousness of the crime problem in this country is a natural consequence of these changes.

Until the end of the 1980s the Japanese government was able to state proudly "Japanese society has achieved a level of security that has made it widely known as one of the safest countries in the world."[2] "Two things are free in Japan: safety and the air we breathe" was an expression used often by ordinary citizens in those days. In such conditions little attention was paid to the dangers of crime in terms of public safety and, in retrospect anyway, relatively few social resources were invested during that period in the wider criminal justice system. As stated above, this situation began to change rapidly during the 1990s as the economic recession and rising unemployment produced a rising sense of frustration throughout the country. Juvenile crime, which had leveled off for a while, began to climb again, and an increase in crimes by foreigners pointed out a growing trend toward "borderless crime."[3]

This all reached a peak in 1995 when the crimes committed by the Aum Shinrikyo religious cult sent shock waves throughout the nation. During this period Japanese society was shaken by a storm of criminal activities that had been virtually unknown in the country, including a spate of robberies of financial institutions, an epidemic of drug-related crimes centered on amphetamines, a series of bizarre murders and sex crimes, corporate terrorism, Internet crimes, and so on. Excessive and rather sensational coverage of these crimes in the mass media heightened anxiety about crime among ordinary citizens.[4] During this same period, the prestige of the police system was damaged by the revelation of several cases in which the failure of police to investigate complaints lodged by citizens led to tragic results, by a seemingly unstoppable decline in clearance rates, and by the inability of the police to solve a number of high-profile crimes. This fueled widespread uneasiness and a sense of powerlessness on the part of ordinary citizens (or perhaps more properly the mass media?) in the face of mounting crime.

Beginning in 2003 many signs began to appear indicating that Japan's economy was on the road to recovery. The most important of these indicators was job creation. As job numbers improved and unemployment fell, a series of statistical indices began to show a downturn in crime levels. However, even as the number of penal code offenses known to the police was dropping, a succession of sensational violent crimes made it difficult to convince the public that the crime situation was improving. Frequent bank robberies, murders involving the dismemberment of the victims, and sensational crimes committed by juveniles followed one another in swift succession. Foreign criminal groups committed a series of robberies, and there were even vague concerns about the possibility of terrorist attacks. Moreover, ordinary citizens did not yet have any direct sense that the long period of economic stagnation was really over. On the contrary, public discontent was mounting at the perceived widening of the gap between rich and poor. Taken together, these factors pushed the public to demand stronger measures to deal with crime and the implementation of harsher penalties for both adult and juvenile offenders.

Recent characteristics of crime in Japan

Crime dynamics

According to recent editions of the Japanese government's "White Paper on Crime" and other sources, over the last ten years the number of penal code offenses known to police (excluding charges of professional negligence related to traffic offenses) has been growing steadily, albeit with some degree of fluctuation, and reached a new postwar peak of 2,853,739 in 2002. This represents an increase of over 150 percent in the last ten years. In addition, the crime rate per 100,000 population (also excluding charges of professional negligence related to traffic offenses) rose by nearly 100 compared with the previous year (2001), setting a new record of 2,240. Although both of these figures fell over the following three years, it is still too early for optimism. However, we should also point out that the total number of persons arrested for crimes in 2002 (excluding crimes involving professional negligence related to traffic offenses) was only 387,234, a figure that has remained largely unchanged over the past ten years.[5] This is partially explained by Japan's low clearance rates, as will be discussed below.

Of course, we cannot comprehend the true state of crime in Japan simply by looking at statistics on the total number of crimes known to the police. What is important is the breakdown of the types of crimes committed. Examining reported penal code offenses in 2005 by type of crime, theft (55.2 percent) was most common, followed by traffic-related crimes involving professional negligence (27.4 percent), destruction of property (6.6 percent), embezzlement (3.1 percent), and fraud (2.7 percent). All other crimes accounted for only 5.0 percent of the total. Further, if we exclude the category of traffic-related crimes involving professional negligence, which are somewhat different in character from other crimes because of their relation to public transport policy, we find that more than 95 percent of all crimes are so-called property crimes, such as theft, destruction of property, embezzlement, and fraud. Figures for violent crime show that 1,392 murders, 5,988 robberies, and 2,076 rapes were committed in 2005, and these levels have all remained relatively stable in recent years. In terms of crime rate, the incidence of these types of serious crimes has held steady at around 1–4 per 100,000 population.[6]

It is easy to see from the above composition ratio that theft and larceny account for a majority of the increase in crime in recent years. It is important, moreover, to look at a breakdown of this category. In 2005, for example, only 14.2 percent of all

100   K. Ueda

thefts involved breaking and entering. The vast majority of such crimes consisted of relatively minor offenses such as stealing bicycles (23.5 percent), motorcycles (6.0 percent), breaking into and stealing items left in automobiles (14.9 percent), or robbing vending machines (5.1 percent).[7] Further, most embezzlement cases fell into the category of "embezzlement of lost articles," which includes things such as borrowing or riding away on someone's bicycle without permission.[8]

Moreover, in 2005 the number of Special Law violations transferred to public prosecutors' offices totaled 864,582. If we exclude Road Traffic Law offenses, which are the major component in this category (735,667, or 85.1 percent of the total), violations of drug-related laws controlling stimulants or poisonous substances were the largest category, accounting for 40.2 percent of the remainder, followed by offenses affecting public security such as violations of the Firearms and Swords control law (13.4 percent), immigration violations involving foreigners (8.7 percent), and violations of public decency laws such as the Anti-prostitution Law (5.4 percent). Both in terms of the overall total, and in terms of the total excluding Road Traffic Law violations, the number of persons arrested for Special Law violations has been declining over the long term. These facts also call into question the assumption that the chronic state of overcrowding in Japan's prisons[9] and correctional facilities in recent years is the result of an explosion in crime.

The clearance rate problem

During the 1990s the major cause of concern to those directly involved in dealing with crime, as well as crime researchers, was the steep decline in clearance rates for penal code offenses. The number of crimes known to the police climbed steadily during this period, while at the same time the clearance rate declined. In 2001 the clearance rate for penal code offenses, excluding violations of the Road Traffic Law, fell to as low as 19.8 percent,[10] which was even lower than that seen during the chaotic period immediately following the end of World War II, and this news sent shock waves through the country. For many years Japan had maintained clearance rates far higher than those in Western countries, and was able to point to this as a proof of the superiority of its policing system. Now yet another indicator of the superiority of Japan's criminal administration policy had disappeared.[11] The extraordinary steepness of this decline is illustrated by the fact that just over ten years earlier, in 1987, Japan had recorded an overall clearance rate of 73.5 percent for all penal code offenses, and 64.1 percent even when Road Traffic Law violations were excluded.

One event that is sometimes considered to have been the turning point that led directly to this sharp fall in clearance rates was the weakening of regional police forces that took place starting in 1989 as a result of the increased deployment of police resources in the Tokyo area to protect against the possibility of terrorist activity during the ceremonies that marked the ascension of the new emperor. However, even after these extraordinary deployments ended, the situation was not easily remedied. Perhaps the reasons for the clearance rate problem were that urbanization was pushing up Japan's so-called floating population as well as the number of

Crime in Japan   101

single-occupant households, the foreign resident population was expanding, and lifestyles based on the idea of individualism were becoming increasingly popular. These factors were making Japanese society more complex and thus making police work more difficult. The limits of the traditional neighborhood police station/substation system, which was based on the idea that the police could keep tabs on everyone living in their jurisdiction, had become clearly apparent, and as such it now appears quite unlikely that Japan will ever again achieve the same level of high clearance rates that it enjoyed in the past.

In 2002 there were some signs of improvement in the clearance rate, and in 2005 the overall rate for all offences rose to 48.2 percent and 28.8 percent when Road Traffic Law violations are excluded. However, there is still a world of difference between these figures and those seen in the past.[12]

The increase in juvenile crime

A look at the age distribution of penal code offenders (excluding cases involving violations of the Road Traffic Law) shows that in 2005 the percentage of crimes committed by juveniles between the ages of 10 and 19 had fallen to 35.4 percent. This may be partly explained by an increase in arrests of adult offenders in recent years, but nevertheless it provides clear confirmation that juvenile arrests for penal code offenses are declining. For 15 years beginning in 1981, except for brief periods, the majority of arrests for penal code violations involved juvenile offenders, so these new statistics indicate that the explosion in juvenile delinquency in Japan has finally run its course.

In retrospect, 1983 marked a sort of watershed in the largest juvenile crime wave that Japan had experienced since the end of World War II. After 1983, juvenile crime began escalating to an entirely different qualitative level as compared to the preceding period. One significant new trend was the increase in crimes by lower-aged children. Formerly, 18 to 19 year olds had committed the majority of juvenile offenses, but now 14 to 15 year olds became the largest group of offenders. Moreover, crimes by younger children, once considered anomalies, now became quite ordinary, as the number of 14 to 15 year olds arrested rose to as high as 1.7 percent of the total population of that age cohort. A third trend was the shift towards theft, with 85 percent of all juvenile crime consisting of larceny and embezzlement, most of which involved the theft of bicycles and motorcycles. Even today it remains unclear what factors were responsible for these characteristic structural changes in juvenile crime, nor have we reached any definitive understanding of how best to cope with this difficult situation.

Juvenile crime today primarily consists of property-related offenses, and the items stolen are not necessities. Today's juvenile offenders do not steal out of need; they commit their crimes rather aimlessly, and often do so in groups. These facts suggest the existence of other fundamental reasons behind the increasing seriousness of the juvenile crime problem. These reasons might include an increased demand for money among children because of the proliferation of products specifically targeting young people, and a decline in the level of education and training both at

102　*K. Ueda*

home and at school. The general trends in society toward unbridled consumerism and the worship of money are clearly affecting the younger generation. At the same time no firm guidelines have been developed regarding the types of wholesome social values and social discipline that should be taught to children to counter these influences, either in terms of content or in terms of who should be responsible for teaching that content. Without addressing these key issues, simply stirring up public anxiety and demanding an increase in juvenile policing and the implementation of harsher punishments is unlikely to achieve many results.[13]

In 2005 the number of juveniles arrested for penal code offenses fell to around 170,000, returning to the level seen in the late 1950s. However, this was likely more of a superficial than a fundamental change, in that it simply reflected the recent decline in the overall juvenile population. The juvenile arrest rate as a percentage of the overall juvenile population has held steady over the past ten years. In addition to theft and other property-related crimes, the number of arrests for violent crimes such as murder and robbery is also falling, but this trend has been obscured by a seemingly endless series of sensational crimes that excite the interest of the general public.[14]

The increase in crimes by foreigners

After the end of World War II both penal code and Special Law offenses by foreigners fluctuated to some degree, but the overall long-term trend was downward. The situation changed quite clearly in 1991, and crimes by foreigners have been rising since that time. The number of cleared cases involving foreigners has risen by 170 percent in the last ten years, and the number of foreigners arrested has grown by 180 percent.

This increase in foreign crime is largely due to an increase in the number of crimes committed by resident foreigners and visa overstayers.[15] In most years about a third of all crimes involving foreigners (31 percent in 2005) have to do with Special Law violations such as visa overstays (Immigration Control and Refugee Recognition Law), but among penal code offenses, the largest number of arrests is for theft, mostly involving residential breaking and entering, car theft, purse snatching, and pick-pocketing.

More than half of the foreigners arrested have overstayed their visas, and most of these are arrested for Special Law offenses such as Immigration Control Law violations. If we exclude these Special Law offenses, it turns out that of penal code crimes committed by foreigners, the percentage committed by visa overstayers is not very large (only 15.3 percent in 2005). On the other hand, a majority of the foreigners arrested for crimes such as residential burglary or robbery through breaking and entering are visa overstayers, so there is indeed a significant involvement of this type of illegal immigrant in those crimes that tend to strike closest to home and create the most fear among the public. In addition, a relatively large percentage of the foreigners arrested for intellectual crimes such as fraud and credit card counterfeiting, as well as violent crimes such as armed robbery, are committed by foreigners who do not possess valid visas.

The "increase in crime by foreigners" is, in one sense, a natural reflection of the process of internationalization that is affecting society as a whole. The term

Crime in Japan 103

"globalization" does not refer simply to an increase in cross-border travel. Rather, insofar as it involves the pursuit of wealth on a global scale by powerful actors such as multinational corporations whose economic pursuits generate turbulent flows of products, capital and information, it is natural that various types of frustrations will arise among groups at each level of the social structure, and that this frustration will find expression in various types of social problems, including crime. From a worldwide perspective, one trend that emerged clearly after the end of the Cold War between East and West was the pursuit by the North of the resources of the South, and the influx of immigrants from the South looking for wealth and employment in the North. In Japan's case this trend is taking the form of an influx of immigrants from Southeast Asia and China. However, Japan's immigration policy is quite severe, and immigration for the purpose of finding employment is basically outlawed. Therefore, many of these new Southeast Asian immigrants end up coming into Japan as so-called "entertainers," "students," or "trainees," but in fact look for jobs as bar hostesses, or work part-time in the food service industry. They do the types of "dirty, difficult or dangerous" jobs that the Japanese tend to avoid, in order to generate as much income as possible in a short period of time. This in itself represents a violation of the Special Law (Immigration Control Law), but many of these people working at unstable jobs and looking to make as much cash as possible end up turning to criminal activity involving prostitution, drugs, or smuggling, and in some cases even go so far as to commit robberies.

Certain districts in major metropolitan centers such as Tokyo and Osaka contain large concentrations of foreigners whose residential and employment status is unstable. For some time their presence has been viewed with concern due to crime-related issues. In more recent years this phenomenon has begun to spread out from the urban centers into surrounding areas, and even to regional cities. This demographic trend forms the backdrop to today's so-called "foreign crime problem." As discussed earlier, although statistics show that the number of foreigners arrested for penal code offenses has been rising in recent years, even more important is the fact that more and more ordinary citizens have themselves actually come into contact, directly or indirectly, with this type of crime in their own neighborhoods. As a result, there is a tendency for the foreign crime problem to be exaggerated. At the same time, however, it is also important to be cognizant of certain alarming trends, such as the recent increase in the number of violent crimes including armed robberies committed by foreigners, crimes committed by foreign criminal groups, and the spread of these types of crimes to regional cities. Against this background one must also face the fact that resident foreigners (legal immigrants) are forming criminal organizations, that international organized crime groups are moving into Japan, and that both of these groups are forming ties with Japanese *boryokudan* gangs.[16]

The boryokudan *(organized crime syndicate) problem*

Every country has criminal groups of one form or other that seek to profit through activities that are detrimental to society, and in Japan the so-called *boryokudan*

104   *K. Ueda*

gangs fall into this category. Post-war membership in these criminal syndicates peaked at more than 180,000 in the early 1960s when *boryokudan* were in their heyday, but then began a long-term decline that ended, ironically, with the passage in May 1991 of a new anti-organized crime law (Law to Prevent Illegal Acts by Members of Organized Crime Syndicates). Thereafter, despite several revisions designed to further strengthen the provisions of the law, and social campaigns aimed at eradication of the problem, *boryokudan* membership has remained largely unchanged for more than ten years, and numbered 86,300 as of the end of 2005.[17]

One significant development during this period has been the dramatic consolidation of power into the hands of a few powerful crime syndicates. Currently, more than 70 percent of all *boryokudan* members belong to one of only three national syndicates, the *Yamaguchi-gumi, Inagawa-gumi*, or the *Sumiyoshi-kai*.

Another recent feature is the diversification of *boryokudan* activity. The *boryokudan* traditionally evolved from gamblers and street peddlers, and their activities were centered on gambling and on sales of goods in open-air stalls at street fairs and festivals. Today, however, their main sources of income are from the sale of illegal drugs, and income from loan or real estate companies posing as legitimate businesses. In addition, however, they are deeply involved in gambling, bookmaking, the sale of narcotic and stimulant drugs, labor racketeering, entertainment, protection rackets, loan sharking, debt collection, negotiation of automobile accident claims, eviction of tenants, *sokaiya* (corporate blackmail), human trafficking, the sale of pornographic materials, and so on. In other words they may be likened to a conglomerate involved in every type of illegal activity designed to take advantage of the human frailty for gambling, for money, or for sexual gratification.[18]

Reflecting this diversification in the activities of the *boryokudan*, the types of crimes committed by these groups have also undergone a change. Formerly most *boryokudan* arrests were typically for violent crimes such as murder, robbery. rape, unlawful assembly with dangerous weapons, battery, assault, blackmail, and so on, but now they are more likely to be arrested for relatively minor offenses. In recent years about 30,000 *boryokudan* members have been arrested annually, and of these about 7,000 are usually charged with violating the Stimulants Control Law, and about 3,000 are charged with larceny.

However, the aspect of *boryokudan* criminal activity that is presently attracting the most attention and causing the greatest concern is its internationalization, and the development of ties with foreign criminal organizations. For some time is has been well known that most drug-related crimes are carried out by *boryokudan* in cooperation with a large number of foreign criminal organizations. A notable development more recently is the relationship between *boryokudan* activities and crimes committed by foreign residents. Illegal immigration (illegal entry, false marriages, illegal visa procurement), illegal employment after entry, prostitution, and other activities are extremely difficult without the help of the *boryokudan*, and these activities enable the *boryokudan* to establish cooperative ties with other criminal organizations both inside and outside Japan.

International organized crime and Japan

The problem of drug-related crime

Smuggling of contraband, criminals escaping to other countries, acts of piracy against multiple countries, and similar types of international crimes have been known in the past. What is different today is that a huge expansion in economic activity and dramatic advances in modes of transportation and means of communication have greatly increased the cross-border flow of people and materials, expanded the scope of people's desires, and intensified conflicts between people. These new factors have pushed international crime to a new stage of development in today's borderless society.

The classic type of international crime, and one that continues to plague countries all over the world, involves the problem of illegal drugs. In Japan, the most widespread and therefore most serious problem involves stimulant drugs, and nearly all the illegal drugs sold in Japan[19] are smuggled into Japan from overseas and are sold to users primarily through *boryokudan* gangs.

In 2005 the number of people arrested for stimulant drug offenses totaled 13,346, and 93 percent of these cases involved either use or possession. The total number of arrests for the smuggling or sale of stimulants was only about 870. In the same year 2,063 persons were arrested for violation of the Cannabis Control Law, 606 for violation of the Narcotics Control Law, and 13 for offenses related to the Opium Law. It is clear from these figures that the drug problem in Japan is far less serious than that in other countries. According to the United Nations' "World Drug Report 2006," approximately 4 percent of all people between 15 and 64 use cannabis (marijuana), and 1 percent use cocaine (28 percent smoke tobacco).

As for the sources of the illegal drugs found in Japan, stimulants generally originate in China and Thailand; marijuana tends to come from South Africa or Belgium, cannabis resin from India and Israel, and MDMA from Holland and France. In the past, large quantities of stimulants were smuggled into the country from North Korea, and MDMA via a Russian route, but restrictions on port calls by North Korean ships as a result of economic sanctions, and a strengthening of cooperative efforts between Japanese and Russian authorities to crack down on drug trafficking, appear to have been effective to some degree. However, given Japan's lengthy coastline, the development of high-speed boats equipped with GPS satellite technology, and the spread of cell phones, it is extremely difficult to prevent this type of crime. Many drugs are also smuggled into the country on commercial airline flights in hand baggage, or strapped to the passenger's body, or by means of international mail or parcel delivery services.

In the past, Japan's efforts to combat drugs have been focused almost exclusively on the *boryokudan*, and very little attention has been paid to the overseas suppliers. However, the illegal drug trade is being conducted on a cross-border basis by criminal drug trafficking groups, and represents a problem that cannot be solved through the efforts of any one country acting alone. In fact, at present nearly all of the stimulants and other illegal drugs that are a problem in Japan are smuggled

106 K. Ueda

into the country from overseas by international drug-trafficking organizations, and strategies that ignore this fact are doomed to failure. Only recently have the Japanese police begun efforts to develop a system of international cooperation with the police forces in surrounding countries, and we are only now starting to see international cooperation through exchanges of investigators, exchanges of information at international conferences, and through the provision of technical assistance to help neighboring countries investigate drug-related crimes.[20]

Countermeasures against terrorist crimes in Japan

More than ten years have passed since the religious cult calling itself *Aum Shinrikyo* perpetrated the first major (by international standards) terrorist attack to take place in Japan. The crimes committed by this group included the release of sarin nerve gas in a neighborhood in Matsumoto City and in subway cars in Tokyo, killing 19 people and causing serious bodily harm to 6,000 others; the planting of devices designed to release poison gas in underground shopping arcades in Tokyo; the murder of a lawyer who had been leading a movement opposed to the cult, together with the rest of his family members; and murders of disgruntled cult members. The background leading up to the wide-ranging crimes committed by this cult was discussed later from every angle in a veritable flood of articles and editorials, mass media broadcasts, and novels, but we still do not have a complete picture of what happened. The leader of the cult, Chizuo Matsumoto, maintained silence throughout the court proceedings against him, and eventually fell into a state of mental illness that rendered him unable to provide any useful information to the court. He was nevertheless sentenced to death by the Tokyo High Court in September 2006, a sentence that has since been confirmed. In all likelihood Matsumoto and the sarin gas attacks will all be pushed into the background and eventually forgotten.

At the end of the year following the *Aum Shinrikyo* incidents, the official residence of the Japanese ambassador to Peru was taken over by a militant group. After four months, the so-called Japanese embassy hostage crisis was brought to a conclusion by means of an extraordinary rescue effort carried out by Peruvian army special forces, which succeeded in freeing all of the hostages and killing all of the criminals. As soon as the crisis was over, the public in Japan soon lost interest in the case.

As these two incidents illustrate, most Japanese still consider terrorist crimes to be something that happens in other countries, and they are not seriously worried about terrorism. The September 2001 terror attacks in the United States were naturally of great concern to many Japanese, but how well they have understood the seriousness of the problem is open to question. It would be unforgivable, however, to believe that Japan is immune from such attacks. In this age of globalization, wherever a large-scale attack takes place, it is only natural to expect that Japanese citizens will be among the victims, and there is no guarantee that the brunt of the attack might not be directed at Japan itself. In nearby Southeast Asia, as recently as October 2005, coordinated terrorist attacks took place at restaurants on the Indonesian island of Bali, killing 23 and injuring 146. It appears that officials of the extremist Islamic group *Jemaah Islamiyah* were involved in this attack. This same group has been responsible for many other terrorist bomb attacks, including the October 2002 attack in Bali that killed 202 and injured more than 300. In Europe, a coordinated attack on the subway and bus systems in central London killed 56 and injured approximately 700 in July 2005, an attack that was apparently timed to coincide with the G-8 summit meeting being held in that country. Two weeks later a second terrorist bomb attack took place that again targeted central London's subway and bus systems. It was sheer luck that no Japanese were injured in these attacks.

In October 2003 a statement released by Osama bin Laden listed Japan among the countries targeted for attack. Further, a statement by bin Laden that appeared on a website in May 2004 promised a reward of 500 grams of gold for the murder of citizens from any nation aligned with the United States, including Japan. Further, the process of globalization has created increased opportunities for Japanese companies and Japanese citizens to conduct activities overseas, and it is easy to see that this has increased the risk that Japanese citizens or interests overseas might become the focus of a terrorist attack. U.S. military facilities have often been the target of terrorist attacks by Islamic radicals, and there are many such facilities in Japan. It is not impossible to conceive that a group of fanatic Islamic fundamentalists might try to attack a U.S. military base in Japan, or facilities of the Japanese government, which is an ally of the United States. There is an even higher risk that a fanatical group based inside Japan might try to blow up a nuclear power plant, disseminate infectious agents or poisonous substances, or damage computer networks.

It was against this background that a French national with connections to Al-Qaeda was discovered to have been traveling repeatedly to and from Japan using a false passport. Many foreigners from Islamic countries presently reside in Japan and have formed communities around the country. There is concern that Islamic extremists may attempt to infiltrate these communities and try to procure funds, equipment, and materials, and may take advantage of various opportunities to promote their radical agenda among the younger generation.

As far as anti-terrorism countermeasures are concerned, Japan's response has been quite limited. In 1995 the "Law on the Prevention of Bodily Harm by Sarin and other Substances" was passed. This was followed in 1999 by the enactment of two other special laws, the "Law to Increase Penalties for Organized Crime, and to Impound the Proceeds of Criminal Activity," and the "Law to Allow Intercepts of Telephone and Other Communications in Criminal Investigations."[21] Later, measures to strengthen witness protection were incorporated into a revision of the Criminal Procedure Code. This has been the extent of Japan's response to the terrorist threat. Japan has no comprehensive set of laws designed to deal specifically with terrorism, and enforcement has been based on the Penal Code, Criminal Procedure Code, and various Special Law regulations such as the penal provisions of the Explosives Control Law, and so forth.

It was under these circumstances that Japan took a first step toward establishment of effective countermeasures against international crime by being among the first to sign the United Nations Convention on Organized Crime that was adopted by the General Assembly in November 2000[22]. This was the first universal convention

108　*K. Ueda*

designed to provide a comprehensive basic framework for fighting international organized crime, and it is intended to form the legal basis for development of future global strategies to combat such crime. This convention specifies penalties for participation in organized criminal groups, laundering funds acquired through illegal activities, corruption, and obstruction of justice; establishes mechanisms to combat money laundering; and provides a legal basis for mutual assistance, extradition of criminals, impounding of proceeds from criminal activity, technical assistance, and others. It is quite clear that the range of punishable offenses under this Convention goes far beyond that specified in Japan's present Penal Code, and therefore a number of fundamental legal problems are certain to arise in future.[23]

However, Japan began taking some steps to remedy this situation after the 9/11 terrorist attacks in the United States. For example, Japan moved to ratify the International Convention for the Suppression of Terrorist Bombings and the International Convention for the Suppression of the Financing of Terrorism, after first quickly establishing the necessary domestic legal framework by expanding the scope of its punishments for violations of the Explosives Control Law, introducing punishments for crimes committed overseas, and enacting a "Law Regarding Punishments for Provision of Funds Used to Commit Criminal Acts Intended to Threaten the Public."The National Police Agency has also implemented a wide range of anti-terrorism countermeasures. Intelligence-gathering activities have been reinforced, special anti-terrorism units have been established, security has been upgraded at key facilities, strategies have been implemented to counter bio-terrorism and prevent hijacking, and a highly flexible "Cyber Force" unit has been created to counter the threat of cyber terrorism.[24]

Where does Japan go from here? Summary and conclusions

Japan's citizens long believed that Japan was a safe country, and they took their personal safety for granted. A steady stream of murders that captured the attention of the mass media, a seemingly unending series of bribery cases involving high-ranking public officials, and an increase in juvenile crime did generate a certain amount of public anxiety. But the overall crime rate remained low, and the overwhelming majority of crimes known to the police were relatively minor property-related offences. For a long time the Japanese could say with confidence that "two things in Japan are free: public safety and drinking water."

However, things began to change in the 1990s. Against the background of a decelerating economy, rapidly aging population, "internationalization," and other factors, crime trends began to show some alarming changes. Violent crimes that had formerly been very rare, such as hold-ups, especially armed robberies involving the use of firearms, robberies of financial institutions, and others began to appear in the news on a daily basis. Drug offenses, centered primarily on the use of illegal stimulants, penetrated various social strata including juveniles, and there seemed to be no end to violent crimes by juveniles, including murder and robbery. Public confidence was shaken by a series of scandals involving the police, and by a shockingly steep fall in clearance rates, and Japan's prisons began to experience chronic overcrowding. The public became increasingly concerned that the crime prevention mechanisms that had formerly worked so effectively in Japan were becoming dysfunctional. It is clear, however, that what is particularly remarkable about these concerns and fears is that they became so widespread throughout the general public, despite the fact that the actual state of crime in Japan was far less serious than was commonly supposed. Now, however, the situation has progressed to the stage where it would no longer be wise to simply dismiss the matter as a case of mass hysteria. Rather, it is important that we focus adequate attention on the various factors that were responsible for this phenomenon.

The problem facing Japan today is that crime has undergone a qualitative change as a result of factors such as a loss in confidence in the state of the economy, the widespread breakdown of conventionally accepted values among young people, the loss in homogeneity of Japanese society as a result of the large-scale influx of foreigners, the sharp increase in interchanges among people as a result of internationalization, and the increasingly borderless nature of many fields of human endeavor. As a consequence, conventional crime prevention measures are becoming ineffective. For many, many years Japanese men spent their early childhood in a society where parents and teachers were held in high esteem, and although they may have faced severe competition during their adolescence to enter the best schools, and may later have had to struggle to earn promotions within their companies, most Japanese men took it for granted that they could enjoy lifetime employment and regular pay raises. This lifestyle is gradually beginning to sound like something out of a fairy tale. These men are finding that the people who live in their neighborhoods and the circumstances that they find themselves in are not at all what they used to be. The various forces that, until now, have served to keep crime under control in Japan are disappearing one by one.

The fundamental factor responsible for these changes is the process of globalization that is affecting every aspect of the Japanese economy and Japanese society. Dramatic increases in the flows of people, money, materials, and information between countries is causing people's lifestyles and even their ways of thinking to become "borderless" in nature, and this also true of the phenomenon of crime. In fact, even when we look at something as basic as the movements of criminals and the logistics of transporting stolen property, it is clear that at every level of criminal activity, from large-scale international terrorism, to drug trafficking and car theft, all the way down to organized pick-pocketing, crime around the world is becoming increasingly interrelated, and Japan is rapidly becoming one more link in this international criminal network. That being the case, it is also clear that Japan's conventional strategies for dealing with crime will no longer be adequate. Japan must face up to its present crime problem, learn from the experience of other countries in this field, and strengthen its international cooperation. Only by developing crime prevention measures based on new standards and new methods will we be able to protect the lives, persons, and property of our citizens and guarantee their safety. It is important that we make the problem of ensuring "human security" our most urgent priority.

110   *K. Ueda*

Globalization has made it imperative to promote cooperative efforts to deal with terrorism and international organized crime, and it is essential that we take steps to prevent Japan from becoming a convenient stopover point for international criminal organizations. However, this must be accomplished in compliance with Japanese law and in harmony with Japan's legal culture. Should new tools be required to deal with these challenges, it is important to follow appropriate procedures to ensure that the need for such measures is fully explained, and to seek the understanding of all concerned parties before their introduction. Moreover, with regard to certain criminal activities that in the past have not received the emphasis they deserved, such as the production and distribution of child pornography, the exportation of stolen cars, the involvement of foreign subsidiaries of Japanese companies in environmental crimes or bribery, and the overseas activities of Japanese *yakuza*, the government and citizens of Japan must be prepared to shoulder their international responsibilities and make every effort to stamp out these offenses.

In this process, what should be emphasized on the domestic level is the need to develop a criminal administration policy that gives due consideration to the views of the public. In its basic outline, such a "citizen-based" approach will likely call, on the one hand, for deployment of a police force adequate to ensure that the public may go about their lives free from fear, and on the other will require that citizens themselves join forces and play an active role in reforming and strengthening the various protective functions that help to prevent crime in this society.

Notes

1 There are a total of 275,000 policemen in Japan, and the overall system of police administration is based on 15,000 neighborhood police stations (*koban*) and substations (*chuzaisho*) that are scattered throughout the country. The koban in urban districts generally have two or three officers on duty at all times, and the *chuzaisho*, which tend to be located in more remote regions, are staffed by a single officer who lives at the station with his family. This distributed policing system enables police to carry out criminal investigations and crime prevention activities based on a thorough understanding of all the residents in their districts, and it is the most distinctive feature of the Japanese police. Cf. D. H. Bayley, *Forces of Order: Policing Modern Japan.*
2 "White Paper on Crime," Ministry of Justice, 1989 edition, p. 258.
3 Based on "White Paper on Crime," Ministry of Justice, 1992 edition.
4 According to the results of a large-scale study by the Research Foundation for Safe Society (2005), when ordinary citizens were asked "Do you think Japan is safer now than one year ago, or less safe?" 75.4 percent of the respondents answered "Less safe," while 16.9 percent answered "No change." However, when asked, "Is the neighborhood you live in safer now than it was one year ago, or less safe?" 66.0 percent answered "No change," while only 18.8 percent responded "Less safe." From these results it appears that although most people's immediate surroundings remain largely unchanged, their impression from media coverage is that public safety is getting worse in the country as a whole.
5 A brief review of crime trends in the post-war period in Japan shows that after reaching a peak of 160,000 in 1948–9 (the crime rate in 1948 for Penal Code offenses was 2,000 per 100,000 population), crimes known to the police (penal code offenses, not including cases involving professional negligence) began a long-term decline until they reached their post-war low in 1973 (1.19 million penal code offenses; resulting in a crime rate

Crime in Japan 111

of 1,091). After this point crime rates began a long-term upward trend. The number of crimes set a new post-war record in 1993, and after falling slightly in 1994 they turned upward again in 1995, and have been setting new records every year since.

6 The totals for each of the different types of crimes known to the police shown in Japan's official crime statistics include crimes of preparation, attempted crimes, soliciting, and abetting.

7 One reason for the low number of theft-related crimes is that, as these figures indicate, residential burglary is uncommon. This is because most households keep very little cash at home. Another factor is that the market in Japan for used goods is small or non-existent, which means that is very difficult in Japan to convert stolen household goods or home electric appliances into cash. However, there are some indications that Japanese attitudes toward used goods are beginning to change as Internet auction businesses steadily penetrate Japanese society.

8 Based on Japan's "White Paper on Crime," Ministry of Justice, 2006 edition.

9 According to the 2006 edition of Japan's "White Paper on Crime," the number of new convicts in 2005 totaled 32,789, an increase of 2.2 percent compared with the previous year. The total number of convicts in Japanese prisons as of the end of 2005 was 68,319, which represents 116 percent of total prison capacity. Even if we include facilities for persons who are in jail awaiting settlement of their cases, the total number of persons under confinement in Japanese penal facilities is still 104 percent of total capacity. This chronic state of overcrowding has been quite notable since 2000, and prisons around the country have had to implement emergency measures, such as housing eight prisoners in cells designed for six, bringing bunk beds into community cells, converting meeting rooms to cells, or cafeteria spaces into inmate facilities. The government has also been forced to move forward quickly with plans to construct new prisons.

10 Clearance rates vary depending on the type of crime committed. As a rule, the clearance rate for violent crimes is generally high (94.1 percent for murder, 48.7 percent for robbery, 63 percent for rape, etc.), while that for larceny, which comprises the majority of crimes, is only 15.7 percent.

11 According to the 2002 edition of Japan's "White Paper on Crime," as of 2000 the arrest rates for general penal code offenses were higher in Germany (53.2 percent), France (26.7 percent), and England (24.4 percent), than in Japan (23.6 percent). The arrest rate in the United States was 20.5 percent.

12 Clearance rates are a function of the number of crimes known to police and the total number of arrests, so care is needed when evaluating the degree to which this figure reflects the actual status of crime. Over the past ten years although the number of persons arrested for penal code offenses has actually been rising, the clearance rate has been falling sharply. The reason for this is that suspects in custody are not being adequately investigated to determine their involvement in other unsolved crimes. Therefore it is important to recognize that the increases or decreases in some of these crime indices do not necessarily represent actual changes in the state of crime in Japan.

13 Japan's Juvenile Law defines three types of delinquent acts, namely penal code offenses committed by juveniles, "crimes" committed by juveniles below the age of 14 (who are therefore not considered criminally responsible), and other behaviors that might lead to the commission of a crime. In practice, however, only the first two are treated as delinquency.

14 Based on Japan's "White Paper on Crime," Ministry of Justice, 2006 edition.

15 According to the Ministry of Justice, there were 194,000 foreign visitors in Japan who were known to have overstayed their visas as of January 2006. This is down by approximately 100,000 from its peak, due largely to the stagnation of the Japanese economy. However, the true number of illegal immigrants is thought to be much higher. Official statistics make a distinction between "foreign visitors to Japan" and "long-term foreign residents." The latter category consists primarily of Koreans who settled in Japan as the result of historical circumstances.

112 *K. Ueda*

16 Based on Japan's "White Paper on Crime," Ministry of Justice, 2006 edition.

17 Despite their socially destructive nature and their clear involvement in many crimes, the fact that *boryokudan* gangs continue to operate with impunity in Japan is due in part to the continuing fascination with the historical and cultural fantasy known as the *yakuza*. It is also undeniable that secret ties between the *boryokudan* and the conservative government during the period immediately before and after World War II is another key factor. Today, however, the main reason that the *boryokudan* continue to exist is that there is a certain level of demand in society for the antisocial services that they provide.

18 The annual revenues generated by the *boryokudan* by supplying these types of socially destructive services are estimated by the National Police Agency to total as much as one trillion yen. The majority of this income is from the sale of stimulants and other illegal drugs, followed in order by gambling and bookmaking, protection rackets (bouncers), violent civil intervention, violent corporate intervention, and others.

19 There have been some incidents in which morphine has been stolen from hospitals and later sold, and some cases in which marijuana growing wild in certain parts of Hokkaido has been harvested, dried, and sold.

20 For example, in February 2005 the 11th Asian Drug Enforcement Conference was convened in Tokyo, attended by representatives of 28 countries, two territories, and one international agency. In September and October 2005 the National Police Agency and the Japan International Cooperation Agency jointly sponsored a drug enforcement seminar to which top officials from 17 countries in Asia and Central and South America were invited for the purpose of exchanging information about drug enforcement, and to facilitate the transfer of Japanese investigative technology to law enforcement agencies in these countries.

21 There was strong opposition to these laws on the grounds that they "infringed on fundamental human rights" and that there was "serious potential for abuse." However, they were narrowly approved by the Diet after the government and ruling party offered compromise amendments, particularly to the Communications Interception Law, "restricting the period of implementation to approximately ten years" and "limiting its application to typical organized crimes". The Communications Interception Law calls for the government to report to the Diet annually on "the number of requests made by public prosecutors or judicial police for warrants to intercept telecommunications, the number of such warrants issued, and the number of such warrants executed." According to these reports no such warrants have been executed since 2000.

22 The Convention includes the draft resolution together with supplementary Protocols to suppress illegal trafficking in firearms, illegal immigration, and trafficking in persons. All the Protocols were adopted by May 2002.

23 With the signing of this Convention it became incumbent upon Japan to establish legal jurisdiction for crimes such as conspiracy to commit serious offenses, money laundering, and obstruction of justice, and to establish a legal framework to allow for international cooperation in the confiscation of the proceeds of crimes, and extradition of criminals. The Japanese government therefore submitted to the 2004 Ordinary Diet Session a bill to partially amend some laws to better cope with "international and organized crime, and the increased sophistication of information processing technology," but deliberations in the Diet became bogged down, and the bill still remained under consideration in the 2006 session. There has been strong criticism that the scope of activities considered punishable as "conspiracy" under the new bill is too wide and too vague. There has been of flood of objections and protests against this legislation from the Japan Bar Association, regional bar associations, social organizations of various types, groups, and individuals involved in crime research, as well as from the general public.

24 In December 2004 the Japanese government's Headquarters for Prevention of International Crime and International Terrorism drew up an Action Plan for the Prevention of Terrorist Acts. This action plan was designed to ensure that Japan did not leave open any "loopholes" for international terrorism. The plan includes 16 "measures

that should be implemented urgently for the prevention of terrorism" that were based on a study of anti-terrorism practices that have been effective in other major countries. The Plan specified which Ministries should institute which measures, as well as the time period for implementation. The National Policy Agency drew up proposed legislation that is scheduled to be submitted to the 2007 Ordinary Diet Session. Based on this Action Plan, in March 2006 the Cabinet approved a partial amendment of the Immigration Control and Refugee Recognition Law to require all foreigners except those holding Special Permanent Resident status to provide fingerprints and other personal information to establish their identity. They also proposed amending the "Law for Prevention of Infectious Disease and Treatment of Infected Persons" to establish a system for the control of infectious agents that might be used for bio-terrorism. Of these, the former amendment became law in May 2006.

References

Bayley, D. H. (1991) *Forces of Order: Policing Modern Japan*, revised edition, Berkeley: University of California Press.

Ministry of Justice (Japan). (1989, 1992, 2002, 2006) "White Paper on Crime," Ministry of Justice.

6 Drug trafficking in Korea

Sung-Kwon Cho

Introduction

Although military security, highlighted by confrontations between powerful countries, was the most important issue of the international community in the twentieth century, the security of human beings, which stems from the confrontation between nations and crime organizations, is rapidly becoming a crucial issue for the international community of the twenty-first century. Such a change has already appeared with the rapid upsurge of illegal drug sales by super-national criminal organizations that have rapidly globalized in the post-Cold War period.

After the terror of 9/11 in 2001, the criminal organization/drug-trafficking nexus, as well as the terror/drug-trafficking nexus, became a new and worldwide phenomenon. In response to this, the United States started to regard the illegal narcotics trade and terrorism as the most threatening factors of the twenty-first century's new world order.[1] This implies that the traditional concept of security, which once mainly assumed a narrow perspective of military security, has expanded since the end of the Cold War to include non-military forms of security such as protecting against threats related to the illegal international narcotics trade.

South Korea is a peninsula in northeastern Asia geopolitically located between China, with is large territory on the Asian continent, and Japan, an island country. Its geopolitical location makes South Korea a transit country for drugs between China, which produces narcotics, and Japan, which consumes them. The "War on Crime" movement in 1990 strengthened the role of South Korea as a transit drug market. Before the end of the "War on Crime" movement in 1992, the South Korean government arrested more than 100 illicit manufacturers and narcotics traffickers within the country. The domestic narcotics trade soon faced stiff competition. As a result of South Korea's globalization policy, there had been an increase in the number of legal and illegal immigrants from Southeast Asia, resulting in a rising quantity of illegally imported drugs. The narcotics users have multiplied and expanded to new sectors of society including the middle-class and high-class users.

In this chapter, I analyze the trends of the illegal narcotics trade in Korea. The trade will be examined with respect to consumption, distribution, and supply. The most widely sold narcotic in Korea is methamphetamine, which represents about 70 percent of all drug crimes. I also analyze consumption tendencies according to the occupation, age, sex, educational background, and reason for consumption of the users. The role of super-national criminal organizations in Korea's neighboring countries demands great attention in understanding the problems of distribution and supply. These international criminal organizations connect to domestic criminal organizations in Korea to sell smaller quantities of illegal drugs. However, these national organizations have a great potential of becoming larger criminal organizations in the future.

Second, I analyze counter-narcotics policies in Korea. In short, the drug control policy in Korea is one of strong criminalization. Narcotic addicts are mainly considered as criminals in Korea, although interest in treatment and rehabilitation of addicts has recently increased. Laws and institutions controlling narcotics will also be discussed.

Tendencies and analysis of drug trafficking

Consumption of drugs in Korea

There has been an evolution of drugs that have been abused in Korea. Initially, the primary illegally used drug in the 1950s was opium. In the 1960s, abuse was centered on methadone, which emerged as a medical substitute for opium. This was followed in the 1970s by marijuana; and in the 1980s by methamphetamine. However, illegal drugs in the domestic market have become more diverse because new illicit drugs are manufactured, such as ecstasy, which is a replacement for methamphetamine, which flows in from foreign countries to target a market of drug users in their twenties and thirties. All of this is a result of globalization. Methamphetamine has been one of the most popular drugs since the 1990s. In particular, ecstasy, which was initially discovered in 1999 in Korea, has a high probability of becoming one of the main illicit drugs of the future because its retail price is cheaper than that of methamphetamine and it is easier to buy. In addition, young drug users think that ecstasy is not addictive. There are several other illegal narcotics, such as LSD, GHB, ketamine, amphetamine, and the yaba tablet from Thailand. These drugs are called designer drugs or club drugs, like ecstasy, and small amounts of them are currently circulating through Korea. Table 6.1 shows the trends in drug seizures for the main narcotics sold in Korea.

In the past, foreigners or international drug-trafficking organizations mainly used Korea as an intermediate stopover between eastern Asia, which produced heroin, and the American market that consumed the heroin. There are almost no heroin users in Korea. Since 1998, heroin smuggled from China, Thailand, and Bangladesh has been continuously confiscated in Korea as have the precursor chemicals used to produce heroin. In 2003, there were only three seizures of nitric acid, which is a raw material used for heroin. Now, the nitric acid exported to Afghanistan passes through Iran. Illegal cocaine sales were initially discovered in Korea in 1990. Mainly South Americans or Korean-South Americans illegally exported cocaine to Japan via Korea.

Table 6.1 Confiscations of main narcotic drugs (unit: ecstasy tablet), others (kg)

Drug Type	Year									
	1996	1997	1998	1999	2000	2001	2002	2003	2004	2005
Opium	0.6	6.8	1.0	3.1	3.4	0.2	0.3	25.3	1.7	0
Heroine	1.8	0.6	2.1	0.3	0.4	0.6	1.1	0	0	0
Cocaine	0.8	11.2	2.1	2.3	1.8	0.1	1.2	0.9	0	0
Methamphetamine (pilophone)	33.3	24.9	28.3	29.2	46.1	169.6	36.8	64.7	12.2	19.3
Ecstasy	0	0	0	0	8,786	1,672	39,011	37,784	20,388	10,744
Marijuana	44.4	59.5	32.8	39.4	106.5	283.9	194.8	37.3	36.2	18.4
Hesisi	0	0.6	0.9	2.0	0.6	4.3	0.8	3.3	11.4	11.5
Total Amount	–	–	–	–	–	–	274	171	82	50

Source: Supreme Prosecutors' Office, *Crime Report of Illegal Narcotic Drug*, 2001, p. 28; Supreme Prosecutors' Office, *Crime Report of Illegal Narcotic Drugs*, 2006, p. 114.

Korea was a major producer of methamphetamine in the 1980s. However, most domestic producers of methamphetamines disappeared in the 1990s because of the "War on Crime" of the Noh Tae-Woo government (1988–92). Since then, the technical experts who make methamphetamine have moved to China where raw materials and labor are cheap. They have been exporting methamphetamine to Japan and Korea from their Chinese production bases.

Before 1995, the quantity of illegally imported marijuana was small; most instances involved 10 or 20 grams intended for individual users. However, the scale of illegally imported marijuana has increased drastically and its import has been transformed into a serious business since 1996. Since 2003 individual users make use of international mail to illegally import marijuana.

Table 6.2 Yearly price for illegal sales of methamphetamine (pilophone) (unit: 10,000 won, region: Seoul)

Year Section	96.12	97.12	98.12	99.12	00.12	01.12	02.12	03.12	04.12	05.12
Retail price per gram	158	110	80	100	30	34	40	30	130	90
Price for one-time use (0.03 g)	10	15	9	11.5	9	9	10	10	9	9

Source: Supreme Prosecutors' Office, *Crime Report of Illegal Narcotic Drugs*, 2006, p. 83.

Table 6.3 Illegal importation of new narcotic drugs (unit: tablet)

Year Section		2001	2002	2003	2004	2005
Yaba	Thailand	2,018	0	380	0	18
MDMA	Russia	0	38,637	0	0	0
	Canada	0	549	745	512	66
	U.S.A.	545	32	289	78	81
	Netherlands	0	54	0	0	0
	Thailand	890	660	0	3	6
	France	0	0	0	19,675	0
	China	0	0	2,000	0	828
LSD	Canada	0	0	900	0	0
Ketamine	China	0	0	0	0	125
2C-B	China	0	0	900	0	293
Total		3,453	39,932	5,214	20,268	1,417

Source: Supreme Prosecutors' Office, *Crime Report of Illegal Narcotic Drugs*, 2006, p. 125.

118   S.-K. Cho

Ecstasy and LSC, newly developed narcotics, are most frequently used by members of the younger generations who have high educational levels. Students who have studied abroad and English lecturers from foreign countries are frequent users. Annual confiscation of these drugs averaged 82 kg per year after 1996. However, the total amount confiscated increased significantly, up to 159 kg in 2000, and two-thirds of the total amount was brought from foreign countries.[2] In particular, methamphetamine changed from being a domestic product (total amount manufactured between 1979 and 1988 was 533 kg) to being an imported product (total amount manufactured between 1989 and 2000: 1,101 kg). The total amount of methamphetamine manufactured practically doubled.[3] Table 6.2 shows the retail price and price per one-time use of methamphetamine, now one of the most widely used narcotics in Korea.

The number of criminals in Korea charged with narcotics offenses increased to 4,000 in 1988 and then temporarily dipped in 1990 due to the "War on Crime" program. Since then, the number has increased again. As Table 6.4 shows, there were approximately 6,000 drug offenders in 1996, 7,000 in 1997, and 8,000 in 1998. The number initially rose above 10,000 in 1999 and remained at that level from 2000 to 2002. However, it has dropped to approximately 7,000 since 2003 because of strong enforcement.

During the last ten years, 20 percent of all drug offenders use marijuana, 10 percent of them use more serious narcotics (opium, heroin, and cocaine) and 70 percent use psychotropic drugs (mainly methamphetamine), which means that the psychotropic drugs now represent a major part of the narcotics problem in South Korea. The number of criminals who use methamphetamine increased continuously after 1995. Although the number decreased temporarily because of crackdowns in 2003, it has increased again gradually since 2004.

In Table 6.5 the crackdown on drug offenders is divided into categories. The first involves the individual level including illicit cultivation (such as farmers who raise opium for individual use), illicit use, and illicit possession by individuals. The other dimension involves organizations that produce drugs as a business (such as illicit manufacture, smuggling, and illicit sale). Overall, the individual level accounts for 50–70 percent of all narcotics used in Korea. Illicit sales by organizations, involving distribution and sales of drugs, comprises approximately 10 to 20 percent of the domestic market. Illicit sales by organizations are gradually increasing, but individual narcotics use has decreased gradually since 2001 when individual use was at its peak.

Table 6.6 shows that the number of foreigners arrested for drug-related crimes began to increase rapidly after 2001 due to Korean government policy to promote tourism for foreigners. The Korean government deregulated customs procedures and extended the possible length of visits by foreign workers. Due to this policy, the number of illegal foreign workers who used narcotic drugs increased. However, the number of foreign drug criminals decreased in 2005 as a result of the Department of Justice's strong controls on illegal foreign workers.[4] Most foreigners arrested for drug crimes were for offenses related to consumption. They mainly used marijuana before 1999 but the use of psychotropic drugs has increased since 2000. This

Table 6.4 Crackdown on narcotic drug criminals (unit: person)

Year Section		1996	1997	1998	1999	2000	2001	2002	2003	2004	2005
Number of Narcotic Drug Criminals		6,189	6,947	8,350	10,589	10,304	10,102	10,673	7,546	7,747	7,154
Type of Narcotic Drug	Marijuana	1,272 (21%)	1,301 (19%)	1,606 (19%)	2,187 (21%)	2,284 (22%)	1,482 (15%)	1,965 (19%)	1,608 (21%)	1,231 (16%)	1,032 (14%)
	Narcotic Drug	1,235 (20%)	1,201 (17%)	892 (11%)	923 (9%)	954 (9%)	661 (6%)	790 (7%)	1,211 (16%)	1,203 (15%)	768 (11%)
	Psychotropic Drug	3,682 (59%)	4,445 (64%)	5,852 (70%)	7,479 (70%)	7,066 (69%)	7,959 (79%)	7,918 (74%)	4,727 (63%)	5,313 (69%)	5,354 (75%)

Note: "Narcotic drug' refers to opium, heroin, and cocaine and "psychotropic drug" refers to methamphetamine.
Sources: Supreme Prosecutors' Office, *Crime Report of Illegal Narcotic Drugs*, 2001, p. 25; Supreme Prosecutors' Office, *Crime Report of Illegal Narcotic Drugs*, 2006, p. 111.

Table 6.5 Arrests of offenders for different drug crimes

Type of Offense		Year								
		1997	*1998*	*1999*	*2000*	*2001*	*2002*	*2003*	*2004*	*2005*
Organized Activity	Production	11	0	5	8	4	4	2	0	0
	Smuggling	161	79	110	190	114	137	201	185	161
	Distribution	**682 (10%)**	**841 (10%)**	**1,127 (10%)**	**1,178 (10%)**	**1,066 (11%)**	**1,329 (13%)**	**978 (13%)**	**1,054 (14%)**	**1,270 (18%)**
Individual Use	Cultivation	1,150	866	909	983	414	498	788	911	608
	Consumption	**4,045 (58%)**	**5,777 (69%)**	**7,321 (69%)**	**6,858 (67%)**	**7,167 (71%)**	**7,251 (68%)**	**4,520 (60%)**	**4,215 (54%)**	**3,872 (54%)**
	Possession	435	569	744	575	552	549	524	796	687
Other		463	218	373	512	785	905	533	586	556
Total Amount		6,947	8,350	10,589	10,304	10,102	10,673	7,546	7747	7,154

Source: Supreme Prosecutors' Office, *Crime Report of Illegal Narcotic Drugs*, 1998–2006.

Table 6.6 Arrests of foreigners for drug offenses

Drug Type	Year									
	1996	1997	1998	1999	2000	2001	2002	2003	2004	2005
Narcotic Drug	9	6	14	3	3	12	21	30	**74**	27
Psychotropic Drug	2	12	0	**29**	**13**	28	**40**	21	58	56
Marijuana	**12**	**24**	**14**	28	7	**30**	27	**35**	71	**79**
Total	23	42	28	60	23	70	88	86	203	162

Sources: Supreme Prosecutors' Office, *Crime Report of Illegal Narcotic Drugs*, 2001, p. 39; Supreme Prosecutors' Office, *Crime Report of Illegal Narcotic Drugs*, 2006, p. 127.

phenomenon reflects the increasing numbers of Chinese criminals selling methamphetamine. Recently, criminals from the Republic of South Africa and Nigeria have trafficked large amounts of marijuana to Korea, using it as a transit country. They also used Korea as a stopover en route to Japan where there are many marijuana users and there is less government enforcement.[5]

Domestic narcotics use has been analyzed including determination of the occupation, age, sex, education, and the reasons for use of the abusers. Thirty-nine percent of drug users were unemployed, and employed drug users work as manual laborers and in agriculture, commerce, and the hospitality industry. Each of these areas of employment contributed approximately 10 percent of users between 1996 and 2000.[6] From 2001 to 2005, there was a significant change in the profiles of drug users. Drug consumers spread from that of manual laborers to various occupational groups, and included salaried (business) men, wholesale and retail business, and service business employees.[7]

Second, considering the age of consumers in 2000, 52 percent of users of narcotics were over 60 whereas 72 percent of psychotropic drug users were 30 to 40 years of age, and 68 percent of marijuana users were between 30 and 40 years old.[8] From 1996 to 2000, the number of drug users who were between 30 and 40 gradually increased, specifically to 53 percent in 1996, 54 percent in 1997, 59 percent in 1998, 64 percent in 1999, and 66 percent in 2000.[9] In 2005, 44 percent of narcotic drug users were over 60, while 74 percent of psychotropic drug users and 62 percent of marijuana users were aged 30–40. So there was not much change in the demographic profile between 2000 and 2005.[10] From 2001 to 2005, on average 66 percent of all narcotic drug users were between the ages of 30 and 40, individuals who should be actively employed.[11]

Third, between 1996 and 2000, an average of 80 percent of narcotic users were men and 20 percent were women. The ratios of male to female users were 40/60 for narcotic drugs, 80/20 for psychotropic drug, and 90/10 for marijuana.[12] From 2001 to 2005, an average of 80 percent of narcotic drug users were male and 20 percent were female. The ratio of male to female users was 50/50 for narcotic drugs, 80/20 for psychotropic drugs, and 90/10 for marijuana.[13]

122   *S.-K. Cho*

Fourth, examining consumption tendencies by educational background showed that, in 2001, 91 percent of drug users, regardless of narcotic drug type, had low educational levels, below the level of high school graduates.[14] In 2005, 85 percent of drug users, regardless of narcotics used, had less education than a high school graduate. Although the educational level slightly improved, the vast majority of drug users had less than a high school education.[15]

Finally, analyzing consumption tendencies according to reasons for use shows that, in 2001, 31 percent of users were motivated by curiosity, 27 percent by temptation, 17 percent by addiction, and 12 percent by profit.[16] However, in 2005, 26 percent were motivated by addiction, 17 percent by temptation, 10 percent by profit, and 9 percent by curiosity. Addiction was the most common factor in causing an individual to use narcotic drugs.[17]

Distribution of narcotic drugs: the role of domestic crime organizations

From the 1960s to the Kim Young-Sam government (1993–7), illicit narcotic sales were carried out by professional organizations. However, after the slot machine business was made illegal in 1996, crime organizations tried to find a new means to earn money. The first involvement of Korean organized crime groups in narcotics sales was discovered in 1996.[18] Most of the criminals were dealers selling to individual consumers, but some of them became involved with illegal production and smuggling. Crime organizations became more involved in the narcotics business during the Kim Dae-Jung government (1998–2002). During these years, there was some fluctuation in the number of arrests and in the number of crime groups subject to police action. For example, in 1999, 29 criminals from 23 different organizations were arrested; 17 from 13 organizations in 2000; 54 from 28 organizations in 2001; and 49 from 32 organizations in 2002. The number of the arrests made during the subsequent Roh-Moo-Hyun government generally showed an increase: although the numbers were small in 2003, six individuals from five organizations, the numbers were much higher in the following years. Fifty were arrested from 35 organizations in 2004, and 37 from 34 organizations in 2005.[19]

In 2001, methamphetamine production, by both drug and criminal organizations, was first disclosed.[20] The criminal organizations involved were the clubs Seven-star, Dangamdong, U-tae, Seo-myun, Twentieth Century, Daeshin-dong, and Dongsung-ro in the Busan and Daegoo area. After 2004, these organizations became more international and were directly and systematically involved with methamphetamine trafficking with such foreign groups as the *yakuza* in Japan, the Sam-hap in Hong Kong and Taiwan, and Los Angeles-based Korean crime organizations in the United States.[21] The drug trade did not represent a significant share of the activities of criminal organizations from 1996 to 2000.[22] Much of drug crime in the past five years has been focused on individual crime such as consumption, representing on average 55 percent of all crime, rather than the organizational dimension such as illicit production, smuggling, and illicit sales.[23] This raises a very urgent issue because violent crime organizations could soon intervene in the domestic trafficking market. If this happens, the domestic narcotic drug market will be completely changed. Because of the possible intervention of violent crime organizations, the Supreme Prosecutors' Office created the Narcotics Department in 2001, and combined the Narcotics and Violent Crime Departments to create a new department—the Narcotics and Violent Crime Department. All these changes are to curtail the involvement of criminal organizations in the drug trade.

There are two basic reasons for the increased involvement of crime organizations in the drug trade and these should be analyzed in depth. First, law enforcement agencies are able to oversee tax evasion emanating from pleasure stores, game rooms, private lenders, and gambling operations, traditional sources of illegal funds for crime organizations. This is possible because the Korean government completed an electronic data system to monitor those businesses. Consequently, it became necessary for the crime organizations to find new sources of illegal funds.

Second, new small-scale organizations have increased their involvement in the drug trade, exceeding that of traditional criminal organizations. The cause of this phenomenon might be that new small-scale organizations, not territorially based, never had access to the traditional sources of illegal funds of criminal organizations. For them the drug trade was an easy way to get a huge amount of money in a short period.[24]

Supplying narcotics: the role of international criminal organizations and of North Korea

As mentioned previously, the typical pattern of methamphetamine trafficking in Northeastern Asia was that drug organizations in Korea imported ephedrine, a raw material, from China, refined it, and produced methamphetamine in Korea. They then illegally exported it to Japan. However, this was before the "War on Crime" in 1990. After the "War on Crime," domestic drug organizations collapsed because methamphetamine producers in Korea escaped to China where there was abundant cheap labor and materials.[25] From there, they refined and produced methamphetamine and illegally exported it to Japan, where the price is relatively expensive, using Korea as a transit country. As Table 6.7 shows, since 1996 most of the methamphetamine that is consumed in Korea has come from China.

Until now, China has been the only country that plays the role of both producer and intermediary in northeastern Asia. In particular, China is part of the Golden Triangle region. The opium and heroin produced in China and Myanmar, which shares a 2000 km border with China, are distributed to the United States, Australia, and third world nations via China, Korea, Japan, and Guam.[26] In addition to opium and heroin, methamphetamine production in China has increased since the mid-1990s. Because of the increase, China's government has revised its criminal laws. The illicit sale of methamphetamine is now treated as a serious crime, as are illicit sales of chemical ingredients needed to process opium and heroin. Nonetheless, the production of amphetamine-type stimulants, such as methamphetamine and ecstasy, is rapidly increasing. Moreover, the first ecstasy production facility was closed down in China in 1998.

Table 6.7 Source countries for Chinese-produced methamphetamine (in kilos)

Countries	Year									
	1996	1997	1998	1999	2000	2001	2002	2003	2004	2005
China	**18.0 (76%)**	**20.9 (81%)**	**14.8 (91%)**	**10.2 (70%)**	**46.2 (99%)**	**151.8 (99%)**	**68.6 (99%)**	**57.3 (97%)**	**6.4 (63%)**	**10.8 (81%)**
Japan	5.0	0.8	0	0.4	0	0	0.5	0.1	0	0
Hong Kong	0.5	3.2	0	2.2	0	0	0	1.5	3.7	0.2
Philippines	0.1	0.7	0.3	1.2	0.3	0	0	1.5	3.7	0.2
Taiwan	0	0	1.2	1.0	0	0	0	0	0	0
Canada	0	0	0	0	0	0	0	0	0	2.0
Total	23.7	25.7	16.3	14.6	46.5	151.9	69.1	58.9	10.1	13.3

Sources: Supreme Prosecutors' Office, *Crime Report of Illegal Narcotic Drugs*, 2001, p. 34; Supreme Prosecutors' Office, *Crime Report of Illegal Narcotic Drugs*, 2006, p. 119.

In a word, Korea is playing a role of an intermediary, instead of that of a consumption country, because Korea does not have a big domestic illegal drug market compared to that of Japan or other neighboring countries. Korea is a middle-man connecting production countries, such as China (methamphetamine), Southeast Asia (heroin), and Middle and South America (cocaine), to consumption countries, such as Japan, Hong Kong, the United States, Russia, and Europe. Also, since 1999 Korea has emerged as an intermediary for the chemicals used to produce methamphetamine, heroin, and cocaine. For example, 10 tons and 12 tons of potassium permanganate, which was being transferred from China to Colombia, were discovered and disposed of in Korea in March and May of 1999, respectively.

The core of the Northeast Asian drug trade is comprised of super-national crime organizations such as the Samhap Club and the Black Society Club from China, *yakuza* from Japan, and the Russian mafia. Fifty percent of the major super-national crime organizations are centralized in Northeast Asia. The Samhap Club is a conventional organization from China, which transfers heroin from Northeast Asian countries to the United States via China and Korea. In 2000, the club was discovered to be transporting 100,000 tablets for distribution to the United States. The *yakuza* controls 95 percent of illicit sales and distribution of methamphetamine in Japan. It is assumed that the proceeds of drug trafficking make up over 50 percent of their total earnings.[27] In Russia, organized crime groups control almost all elements of the drug trade—cultivation, production, distribution, and money laundering. This is called a "mafiocracy."[28]

Drug trafficking in North Asia is not only controlled by drug organizations. North Korea as a country assumes a role in drug trafficking. The North Korean government is engaged in state-directed drug trafficking or it indirectly uses criminal organizations as a surrogate to avoid being directly tied to the drug trade. After methamphetamine from North Korea was initially disclosed in Japan in 1997, an additional 14 of the 26 incidents of drug trafficking related to North Korea were connected to methamphetamine;[29] nine of which were disclosed in Japan. Because of this, the U.S. Department of Defense has regarded North Korea as "a country of concern" since 1998, when the DOD initially made public the direct involvement of the North Korean government in the drug trade.

Another serious problem is that super-national criminal organizations in Northeast Asia would prefer narcotic drugs from North Korea because of the proximity of consumers (e.g. Japan), the low wholesale price (per kilogram), and its high purity (over 90 percent). Because North Koreans sell large amounts of domestically produced narcotics while avoiding the surveillance of the international community, they can sell them at relatively low prices. Super-national criminal organizations can buy large amounts of narcotics from them at low prices. One detected trade revealed that heroin made in North Korea circulated to Fiji through a criminal organization in China. This case reveals the high likelihood that North Koreans are selling to super-national criminal organizations.

Narcotics policy

Since 1945, the main Korean policy relating to narcotics has been one of strong criminalization. The Supreme Prosecutors' Office regards "a policy of a high price for narcotics" as an absolute principle of any drug enforcement. These policies show that drug policies are mainly concerned about enforcement and criminalization rather than treatment and rehabilitation, even though treatment and rehabilitation policies improved during the 1990s.[30] In 1999, the Supreme Prosecutors' Office established a national narcotics drug extermination strategy, which was the first national drug control strategy in 50 years. In 2001, the National Narcotics Drug Policy Committee was established under the Prime Minister's office, under Prime Minister order No. 424. The chief of the Office for Government Policy Coordination became chairman, and the committee makes comprehensive policies and coordinates or modifies national narcotics drug policy in coordination with other organizations.[31]

Briefly examining the changes in domestic laws regulating narcotics drugs reveals that the first narcotics law was the "Narcotic Drug Regulation" law enacted in 1945. During the 1950s, the Narcotic Drug Law was enacted because of the use of opium. In the 1960s, the Toxic Chemical Law was enacted, due to the abuse of methadone. In the 1970s, the Habitual Medicine Control Law and Marijuana Control Law were enacted because of marijuana use. In the 1980s, the Psychotropic Drug Control Law was enacted because of the abuse of methamphetamine. In the 1990s, the Detrimental Chemical Substance Control Law was enacted because the inhalation of Bhutan gas and strong glues became social problems. In 2000, the Narcotic Drug Control Law, which combined the Narcotic Drug Law, the Marijuana Control Law, and the Psychotropic Drug Control Law was enacted and has been in force since that time.[32] There are two additional laws that have been enacted and are presently used: the Narcotic Drug Illegal Transaction Prohibition Law (1995) and the Special Crime Aggregated Punishment and the Criminal Law.[33]

The National Information Service and the Korean Customs Service are the two focal institutions for the crackdown on narcotics by means of law enforcement and prosecution. However, prior to this period, from 1950 to 1989, the primary institution used to address narcotics abuse was the Ministry of Health and Society (currently the Ministry of Health and Welfare). In 1989, the power to conduct drug investigations was transferred from the jurisdiction of the Ministry of Health and Welfare to the Ministry of Justice (the Narcotic Drug Branch, Violent Crime Department, Supreme Prosecutors' Office), which is a law enforcement institution. In 1995, an international crime information center was established in the National Security Planning Office (currently the National Information Office) for dealing with international drug trafficking. This center does not have investigative power; instead it provides information on narcotics to the Prosecutors' Office. Because the number of criminals involved in drug-related crimes grew to 10,000 in 1999, the status of the Narcotic Drug Section of the Supreme Prosecutors' Office was raised, making it the Narcotic Drug Department in 2001. In 2004, the Narcotic Drug Department and Violent Crime Department were combined into one department called the Narcotic Drug and Violent Crime Department. This Department

Drug trafficking in Korea 127

has the responsibility to control the drug trafficking of criminal organizations. Such growth and development of law enforcement institutions related to drug trafficking reflect an effort to establish systematic national policies because of the increase of domestic consumers of illicit drugs.

In 2002, a Joint Drug Intelligence Task Force was established as a result of an agreement between the Supreme Prosecutors' Office and the Korean Customs Office. This agreement is intended to help control the enormous increase in imported illicit narcotics by drug trafficking organizations and to facilitate the solid cooperation of the two institutions. Information obtained by the Joint Drug Intelligence Task Force is provided to the Joint Drug Team of the Prosecutors' Office and the Customs Office, which operates in 18 local prosecutors' offices (102 people) and 25 customs offices (106 people). Because of this, customs offices have jurisdiction in narcotics investigations.

The Prosecutors' Office focuses on reducing drug supply in an effort to eliminate criminal use of narcotics. The police concentrate their efforts on the consumers of narcotics.[34] Table 6.8 shows that prosecutors arrest approximately 40 percent of drug offenders whereas the police arrest approximately 60 percent. However, prosecutors arrest a larger share of the criminals who are members of drug organizations (over 50 percent in most years) than the police who despite the larger number of arrests

Table 6.8 The share of drug arrests of criminals and members of criminal organizations by the Police and Prosecutors' Office and Customs

Year	*Division*			
	Total criminals arrested for drug crimes (number and % who were members of criminal organizations)	*Arrests by Prosecutors' Office (number and % who were members of criminal organizations)*	*Arrests by Police (number and % who were members of criminal organizations)*	*Arrests by Customs officials (number and % who were members of criminal organizations)*
2000	10,304	4,054 (39%)	6,079 (59%)	171 (2%)
	1,376 (13%)	771 (56%)	514 (37%)	91 (7%)
2001	10,102	4,052 (40%)	5,943 (59%)	107 (1%)
	1,186 (12%)	676 (57%)	466 (39%)	44 (4%)
2002	10,673	4,247 (40%)	6,217 (58%)	209 (2%)
	1,470 (14%)	806 (55%)	587 (40%)	77 (5%)
2004	7,747	2,693 (35%)	4,813 (62%)	241 (3%)
	1,239 (16%)	592 (48%)	602 (48%)	45 (4%)
2005	7,154	2,904 (40%)	4,215 (59%)	35 (1%)
	1,431 (20%)	752 (53%)	666 (46%)	13 (1%)

Sources: Cho, En-Suk and Kim, Kwang-Jun *Proliferation of Narcotic Drugs and Direction of Narcotic Drug Control Policy in 21st Century*, Seoul, 2001, pp. 274–5; Supreme Prosecutors' Office, *Crime Report of Illegal Narcotic Drugs*, 2006, p. 108.

128   *S.-K. Cho*

of drug offenders have fewer offenders (approximately 40 percent annually) who are engaged in organized crime activity such as illicit drug production, importation, and sales. The Prosecutors' Office is more concentrated on the supply of narcotics. Prosecutors have less success in arresting members of criminal organizations because of a shortage of human and financial resources in the Prosecutors' Office and the difficulty of obtaining cooperation from different international and domestic organizations fighting the international narcotics trade. Therefore, the Prosecutors' Office also focuses on the drug users, a role that is the key function of the police.

There is significant variation in the type of sentences awarded for different crimes. Prison sentences were much less likely than probation for narcotics cases initiated by the Prosecutors' Office. Between 2001 and 2005 between 15 percent and 40 percent of offenders received prison rather than probation. In the same period with respect to psychotropic drugs, offenders were much more likely to receive prison sentences. Analyzing data available between 2001 and 2005 indicates that the majority of offenders received prison sentences and in some cases the likelihood of confinement was three times the likelihood of a sentence of probation. In general, marijuana criminals are more likely to receive probation because the Korean government treats them more leniently. Severe sentences were sometimes awarded for marijuana. The explanation for this is that some of the arrests were farmers who were engaged in marijuana cultivation and were not just offenders arrested for personal use.[35] In the case of psychotropic drug criminals, the ratio of prison sentences is increasing gradually. This shows that the Prosecutors' Office has a strong willingness to crack down on methamphetamine, which is a major drug in Korea. Examining the totality of drug sentencing data, it is clear that offenders sentenced for drug crimes are more likely to receive probation rather than a prison sentence.

Sentences for drug offenders have increased slightly. The average time narcotic drug criminals spent in prison and on probation was one-and-a-half years in 2001 and this rose to two years by 2005.[36] Between 1996 and 2000, recidivism for drug crimes increased each year. Between 2001 and 2005, the growth of recidivism rates fluctuated between 31 and 43 percent.[38] This is the case because in the later period arrests for psychotropic drugs comprised an average of more than 30 percent of all drug offenses.[37] The high recidivism rates show that the treatment for drug addiction has not worked well.

In Korea, treatment under protection and treatment under custody is executed by the Narcotic Drugs Management Law and Order of Narcotic Drug Addicts' Treatment under Protection according to the President's order. These are mandatory provisions, and drug addicts who are sentenced to probation are required to be treated free for 12 months. A typical treatment institution is the Drug Addicts' Clinic of the National Boo-Gok Hospital. Treatment custody is a mandatory treatment system for drug addicts who have been sentenced to more than 20 days of imprisonment. The drug addicts are required to finish their terms of imprisonment after the mandatory treatment. A representative treatment institution is the Drug Addicts' Rehabilitation Center under National Gong-Ju Treatment Custody. The number of drug addicts under the treatment increased yearly from 1996 to 2005 because of the increased number of users of psychotropic drugs arrested.

Nevertheless, the effectiveness of treatment rendered under protection and custody is very minimal because the percentage of arrested drug offenders is only 1–2 percent of the total even though the total number of criminals treated is rapidly increasing. In 2005, the proportion doubled over the previous year because the Supreme Prosecutors' Office gave the incentive of promotion for prosecutors who enforced treatment under protection and custody. Moreover, because there is no rehabilitation and treatment provided for the addicts in prison, the level of recidivism is continuously increasing.

Conclusion

The purpose of this study is to examine trends in the drug problem in Korea by analyzing consumption, distribution, and supply of narcotic drugs. From this analysis, it was found that ecstasy is becoming a widely used narcotic drug in Korea, just as it is in Western countries, although methamphetamine remains a widely used narcotic. Also, the increasing involvement of criminal organizations in the narcotics trade could have serious consequences in Korea. If criminal organizations intervene more fully into drug trafficking, connections between domestic criminal organizations and super-national criminal organizations will become a requirement rather than a choice. These changes in the trade are already evident in changes in the use of narcotics consumed. For example, ecstasy use has increased since the mid-1990s. There are also changes in drug suppliers including those from China but also those that are farther away and a greater number of international drug organizations.

Drug control policies in Korea have mainly taken the form of a criminalization policy; however, decriminalization of trafficking and consumption of soft narcotic drugs (for example, marijuana) will be a hot issue, as it is in Europe. These changes could gradually transform Korean drug policy from one focused on a criminal response that concentrates on punishing drug offenders to a more treatment-oriented perspective, which would be more concerned with medical care. Korea is seen as a country with limited drug problems compared to other Northeast Asian countries.[39] The Korean government and civil society should try to keep earning this assessment and continue cooperating with other Asian countries for more practical and efficient control of narcotic drugs.

Notes

1 Joseph J. Romm, *Defining National Security The Non-Military Aspects*, p. 6.
2 Supreme Prosecutors' Office, *Crime Report of Illegal Narcotic Drugs*, 2001, pp. 1–18.
3 Ibid., p. 171.
4 Supreme Prosecutors' Office, *Crime Report of Illegal Narcotic Drugs*, 2006, p. 126.
5 Ibid., p. 132.
6 Supreme Prosecutors' Office, *Crime Report of Illegal Narcotic Drugs*, 2001, p. 55.
7 Supreme Prosecutors' Office, *Crime Report of Illegal Narcotic Drugs*, 2006, p. 155.
8 Supreme Prosecutors' Office, *Crime Report of Illegal Narcotic Drugs*, 2001, p. 61.
9 Ibid.

130 S.-K. Cho

10 Supreme Prosecutors' Office, *Crime Report of Illegal Narcotic Drugs*, 2006, p. 159.
11 Ibid., p. 160.
12 Supreme Prosecutors' Office, *Crime Report of Illegal Narcotic Drugs*, 2001, p. 76.
13 Supreme Prosecutors' Office, *Crime Report of Illegal Narcotic Drugs*, 2006, p. 164.
14 Supreme Prosecutors' Office, *Crime Report of Illegal Narcotic Drugs*, 2001, p. 78.
15 Supreme Prosecutors' Office, *Crime Report of Illegal Narcotic Drugs*, 2006, p. 166.
16 Supreme Prosecutors' Office, *Crime Report of Illegal Narcotic Drugs*, 2001, p. 79.
17 Supreme Prosecutors' Office, *Crime Report of Illegal Narcotic Drugs*, 2006, p. 167.
18 *The Seoul Shinmun*, September 21, 1997.
19 Supreme Prosecutors' Office, *Crime Report of Illegal Narcotic Drugs*, 2003, p. 24; Supreme Prosecutors' Office, *Crime Report of Illegal Narcotic Drugs*, 2006, p. 134.
20 *Yonhap News*, May 20, 2001.
21 Supreme Prosecutors' Office, *Crime Report of Illegal Narcotic Drugs*, 2006, pp. 133–48.
22 The ratio of narcotic criminals to crime organizations in the totality of narcotics offenders was 0.5 percent in 1996, 0.6 percent in 1997, 0.3 percent in 1998, 0.3 percent in 1999, and 0.2 percent in 2000. Eun-suk Cho and Kwang-jun Kim, *Proliferation of Narcotic Drugs and Direction of Narcotic Drug Control Policy in 21st Century*, Seoul, p. 134.
23 Supreme Prosecutors' Office, *Crime Report of Narcotic Drugs*, 2006, p. 135.
24 Sung-Kweon Cho, *The History of Korean Crime Organizations: Crime Organization and Political Power*, pp. 161–2.
25 In 2001, the government of China imposed a death sentence on Korean methamphetamine producers. Six of 25 Korean narcotic drug criminals were sentenced to death in 2002. *Yonhap News*, January 13, 2003.
26 U.S. Department of State, *International Narcotics Control Strategic Report*, 2003, pp. viii–18.
27 Ibid., p. viii–29.
28 CSIS Task Force Report, *Russian Organized Crime*, pp. 42–5.
29 Woo-Sang Kim and Sung-Kwon Cho, "Human security in the Korean Peninsula: A Case of the North Korean Drug Trafficking."
30 En-Suk Cho and Kwang-Jun Kim, *Proliferation of Narcotic Drugs*, pp. 313–14.
31 In 2005, the National Narcotic Drug Policy Committee was renamed as the Narcotic Drug Policy Committee and the chairman stepped down from the position of chief officer to deputy manager.
32 According to the Narcotics Drug Control Law, (1) a person who imports, exports, produces, and sells narcotic drugs, (2) a person who imports, exports, produces, and sells raw material for narcotic drugs, (3) a person who sells, compounds, prescribes, and delivers narcotic drugs to those under age, will receive life imprisonment or more than five years imprisonment, and if the person earns money or is a habitual criminal, then he will receive more than 10 years imprisonment with a maximum sentence of execution.
33 The Special Law is enacted to abide by regulations related to punishment for money laundering, confiscation of illicit proceeds, surrender of criminals, controlled deliveries of drugs and of raw materials, prohibition of illegal maritime transactions, regulation of the international post, and so forth.
34 En-Seok Cho and Kwang-Jun Kim, *Proliferation of Narcotic Drugs*, p. 274.
35 Supreme Prosecutors' Office, *Crime Report of Illegal Narcotic Drugs*, 2006, pp. 177–8. The ratio between prison and probation sentences for those arrested for marijuana was 51/46 in 2001, 64/32 in 2002, 32/59 in 2003, 33/60 in 2004, and 34/57 in 2005.
36 Supreme Prosecutors' Office, *Crime Report of Illegal Narcotic Drugs*, 2006, p. 181.
37 Supreme Prosecutors' Office, *Crime Report of Illegal Narcotic Drugs*, 2001, p. 103.
38 Supreme Prosecutors' Office, *Crime Report of Illegal Narcotic Drugs*, 2006, p. 186.
39 Bureau of International Narcotics and Law Enforcement Affairs, "2010 International Narcotics Control Strategy Report (INCSR)," South Korea report, <http://www.state.gov/p/inl/rls/nrcrpt/2010/vol1/137199.htm> (accessed April 8, 2010).

References

Bureau of International Narcotics and Law Enforcement Affairs. (2010) "2010 International Narcotics Control Strategy Report (INCSR)," South Korea report, <http://www.state.gov/p/inl/rls/nrcrpt/2010/vol1/137199.htm> (accessed April 8, 2010).

CSIS (Center for Strategic and International Studies). (1997) *Russian Organized Crime. CSIS Task Force Report*. Washington, D.C., CSIS.

Eun-suk Cho and Kwang-jun Kim. (2001) *Proliferation of Narcotic Drugs and Direction of Narcotic Drug Control Policy in 21st Century*. Seoul, Korea: Korean Institute of Criminology.

Romm, J. J. (1993) *Defining National Security: The Non-Military Aspects*, New York: Council on Foreign Relations Press.

Sung-Kweon Cho. (2006) *The History of Korean Crime Organizations: Crime Organization and Political Power*, Seoul, Korea: Hansung University Press.

Supreme Prosecutors' Office. (2001, 2003, 2006) *Crime Report of Illegal Narcotic Drugs*.

U.S. Department of State. (2003) *International Narcotics Control Strategic Report*, Washington, D.C.: U.S. Department of State.

Woo-Sang Kim and Sung-Kwon Cho (2003) "Human security in the Korean Peninsula: A Case of the North Korean Drug Trafficking," *Global Economic Review* 32, no. 3: 23–39.

Part III
Human smuggling and trafficking

7 International trafficking
An important component of transnational crime

Louise Shelley

Introduction

Human trafficking has been one of the most rapidly growing forms of transnational crime. Its growth has been explained by the demand for cheap labor, the enormous profitability of this trade, and the ready supply of people ready to be trafficked. But this chapter suggests that there are important political, economic, and social reasons that have given rise to human trafficking that are often overlooked in the discussion of the problem.

The neglect of human security by many countries has made many citizens vulnerable to traffickers as they seek a better life away from their current conditions. The internationalization of corruption, the rise of regional conflicts since the end of the Cold War, and the rise of globalization that has enhanced the economic differences between rich and poor have all contributed to the availability of people to be trafficked. Simultaneously, the increased penalties and prosecutions of drug traffickers have made trafficking a desirable alternative for many transnational criminals.

Although the trade in human beings has existed on a global scale for centuries, globalization has brought profound economic and demographic changes.[1] With economic globalization and growing international migration, human trafficking has become an increasingly important component of this larger movement of impoverished people. Marginalization of many rural communities, an ever more competitive globalized economy, the decline of small scale agriculture, the imbalance in demographics between the developed and developing world all help explain the rise of people ready to be trafficked.[2]

Defining the problem

After years of negotiation, in 2000 the member states of the United Nations finally responded to the enormous growth in human trafficking, by adopting the Protocol to Prevent, Suppress and Punish Trafficking in Persons, Especially Women and Children. This protocol defines trafficking as:

> The recruitment, transportation, transfer, harboring or receipt of persons, by means of threat or use of force or other forms of coercion, of abduction, of fraud, deception, of the abuse of power or of a position of vulnerability or of

136 *L. Shelley*

the giving or receiving of payments or benefits to achieve the consent of a person having control over another person, for the purpose of exploitation. Exploitation shall include, at a minimum, the exploitation of the prostitution of others or other forms of sexual exploitation, forced labor or services, slavery or practices similar to slavery, servitude or the removal of organs.

The Protocol accompanies the United Nations Convention on Transnational Crime, which is highly significant as it defines the problem of human trafficking within the context of transnational crime. Its status as one of the protocols within this convention recognizes the central relevance of the problem to international crime.

Very broad approximations of the size of the trafficking problem by the U.S. government estimate that some 600,000 to 800,000 people were trafficked worldwide in 2003, of which 80 percent were female and 70 percent were trafficked for sexual exploitation.[3] These crimes are now globalized. Almost every country in the world is involved in human trafficking either as a source, host, or transit country; indeed, some countries function in all three categories simultaneously. In many parts of the world, trafficking occurs within the context of large-scale migration with some of the migrants, especially women and children, winding up as trafficking victims.[4] This is due in large part to the enormous population migrations into and from the major cities of Africa, Latin America, and Asia. Europe is also facing increasing illegal migration from Africa, Latin America, and Asia, with an estimated 400,000 entering Europe illegally each year.[5] The United States alone is estimated to have ten million illegal migrants and some give even higher estimates.

The rise of the illicit global economy

Trafficking has become an important component of the expanding illicit global economy. Globalization has facilitated the rise of all forms of transnational crime and the internationalization of corruption. The growth of corruption in recent decades, facilitated by the globalization of the international financial system, appears to be very highly correlated with trafficking. Many countries that are rated among the most corrupt in Transparency International's Corruption Perception Index, such as Indonesia, Russia, Ukraine, Nigeria, Pakistan, and the Philippines[6] are major source countries for both male and female trafficking victims. There are several reasons that this correlation exists.

Corrupt leaders have been able to steal large sums from their citizens, moving these monies to offshore locales from where they are difficult to recover. Appropriating such significant resources from the country's treasury undermines the human security of the citizens. Convicted money launderer Pavel Lazarenko, the former Prime Minister of Ukraine, was accused of stealing in excess of one-half billion dollars from his country's treasury.[7] Theft on such a large scale occurred in many other poor countries, leaving its citizens vulnerable to exploitation. Among the most egregious examples of this kind of embezzlement occurred in Pakistan, where President Bhutto's husband was convicted of massive corruption, and in the Philippines, where the Marcos family stole billions that remain unrecovered in offshore locales.[8] In addition, the Suharto family corruption in Indonesia contributed significantly to the economic collapse of that country. It is hardly surprising that significant problems of labor and sexual trafficking have occurred in those countries where the state does not provide for its citizens' human security.

Corruption has numerous other negative consequences. It reduces economic investment and growth, leading to poor and often irrational economic decisions. Programs for economic development in rural areas are often not successful because resources for development are diverted by corrupt national and regional leaders. Corruption contributes to distorted economic policies and decisions that fail to address the problems of rural poverty such as healthcare and access to education.[9] Corruption results, for example, in the construction of schools because of pay-offs provided by the contractors. Yet often there are no teachers available to teach in these new facilities and no money for books or for transport to ensure that the children are able to reach the schools and receive an education. This affects all rural children but particularly affects girls because any available resources are more often provided to male children.

Corruption combined with crony capitalism is particularly pernicious. Illustrative of this is the situation in the Philippines, where only a few families dominate most of the economy, providing citizens little opportunity to obtain capital.[10] Some of these prominent families are also involved in human smuggling operations.[11] Hundreds of thousands of Filipino women labor overseas to obtain money for their families back home, and a portion of these women are trafficked into the sex trade. Yet trafficking in the Philippines is diverse, consisting also of labor trafficking and trafficking for adoption and sexual exploitation of children.[12]

The rise of human trafficking

Trafficking in women and laborers has become part of the larger global illicit economy. Agile criminal groups have entered into the trafficking business because the capital needed to engage in this business is low, the chance of detection is limited, and one can conduct this business in most regions of the world with few obstacles. The crime groups specialize in forging needed documents, contracting with transporters, and bribing government officials in order to move individuals across borders.[13] In the rare case of apprehension of a member of an organization, the overall operation can survive because the flexible network structure allows the organization to survive in the face of arrests of individual members.

With globalization, trafficked men, women, and children are often found far from their countries of origin. In some parts of the world, trafficking occurs within the country or the region of origin. However, trafficked people are increasingly traveling long distances to their ultimate destination. This has been seen particularly in Asian countries where Chinese are moved long distances to Europe or Asia and Pakistanis are moved to various destinations in Europe and the Middle East. Women from the former Soviet Union are trafficked to Europe, the Middle East, Asia, Latin America, and North America.[14] Women from the Dominican Republic are trafficked to Spain; Italy is the primary recipient country of women trafficked from Nigeria.

138 *L. Shelley*

Enhanced communications in a globalized world has facilitated the growth of human trafficking. The rise of the Internet has had a major impact, as organized crime groups in India and Russia are able to buy and sell women with the ease of a mouse-click. In the countries of the former USSR, hundreds of thousands of websites exist, promoting brides and sexual services, and in Europe, websites promote sex tourism, particularly in Latin America and Asia. These activities are facilitated by well-developed organized crime groups in Southeast Asia and Latin America.

Diverse trafficking organizers disperse their victims to different international locales. Chinese groups are significantly involved in the sex industry in Thailand and neighboring countries.[15] Thai women are trafficked by Thai and other Asian crime groups to Japan and the United States. Japanese organized crime, *yakuza*, are major actors in the Asian sex trade,[16] organizing sex tourism to Thailand and importing girls from Thailand, the Philippines, and Russia to Japan. Not as well known in the international crime literature is Indian organized crime, which is involved in the international trade of girls from Nepal and Bangladesh to major urban centers, particularly Mumbai.[17]

Trafficking is a much more important part of the criminal equation of the larger crime groups in Africa, Asia, and the former Soviet Union than those in Latin America or Europe. In Latin America, trafficking is more common among the lesser known crime groups of the Dominican Republic. In Europe, Albanian crime groups and smaller Slavic groups predominate. In Asia, as previously mentioned, pre-eminent crime groups, such as the *yakuza* in Japan and the triads of China, often traffic women. The triads are major human smugglers, often moving Southern Chinese to exploitative work situations where individuals are indentured for years to pay off their debts. Apart from these major groups, smaller but important crime groups in Pakistan, Nepal, Bangladesh, Sri Lanka, and India rely on trafficking to make their profits.[18] In all regions, the crime groups are able to function effectively because they cultivate close links to law enforcement. In some societies, law enforcement officials themselves are part of the crime groups that traffic the women. In other cases, a significant part of the policemen's income is derived through the perpetuation of trafficking.[19]

Transnational criminals have seen tremendous business opportunities in the human trafficking arena. They are rarely prosecuted, not only because of their ability to neutralize law enforcement, but also because the controls that exist are state based, while the crime groups are transnational. In contrast to the illegal drug trade, human smugglers and traffickers earn enormous profits but are rarely prosecuted. Furthermore, their assets are seldom confiscated.

Conditions facilitating trafficking

Human trafficking has grown with globalization, failed development strategies, more porous borders, and increased number of refugees. Trafficking is often caused by deep-seated poverty, the low status of women in many societies, and the failure of governments to address the human security needs of their citizens. Crime

International trafficking 139

groups exploit the vulnerability of girls and women, who are often left out of the legal economy and lack legal protections.

Political conflicts contribute to increased trafficking, which has grown dramatically during armed conflicts in countries such as in Myanmar, Indonesia, and the Balkans. Periods of political transition, as will be discussed more fully later, are also highly conducive to the rise of trafficking. Destabilizing political corruption such as occurred in the Philippines and Nigeria also is conducive to the rise of trafficking. The introduction of peacekeepers in post-conflict situations also leads to the trafficking of local women and the importation of trafficked women for sexual exploitation.

Other causal factors of trafficking include the discrimination that women and girls face in many societies and their lack of economic and educational opportunities. Insufficient attention has been paid to the rise of transnational organized crime, its increasing violence, and powerful links to the political and law enforcement structures in many regions where trafficking has grown.[20]

Gender issues

Gender issues affect every aspect of trafficking analysis—social, political, and economic. Women and female children are vulnerable to trafficking because of their low social status, the lack of investment in children, and the view in some societies that females can be used to advance a family's economic situation. Even in the past, women were sent abroad to earn money. But the phenomenon has grown dramatically with increased population mobility; women have been sent abroad to earn money for their families. While this is the case more in Southeast Asia than in other regions of the world, in Africa, Latin America, and the former Soviet states women have become vulnerable to traffickers because of their need to support their families. Trafficking their wives and daughters is one way that families provide for their financial well-being.[21]

Japan has a long history of socially accepted prostitution.[22] When Japan was a poor country in the nineteenth and early twentieth centuries, women were exported to other countries. In recent years, however, the pattern has reversed, with more than 100,000 women from Thailand and the Philippines trafficked into the Japanese sex industry each year.[23]

As the Asian Development Bank Report explained,

> Gender discrimination and the low status of women across South Asia also results in women and girls having fewer options or means available to them to counter the deceptions of traffickers and are most likely to suffer from stigmatization once they return from such experiences.[24]

There are ongoing problems of lack of access to education, little investment in education for girls, and often a strong preference given to the education of male children over female. Unsafe school environments, prevalent in many areas of Southeast Asia, increase vulnerability to sexual exploitation.[25]

140 *L. Shelley*

Discrimination against women is also a major causal factor of trafficking in Latin America, Africa, and the former USSR. In the regions of the former USSR, many of the trafficked women have education but face tremendous problems in finding viable employment that provides sufficient wages to support their families.

The barriers to education faced by girls, which is particularly acute in rural areas, limit opportunities for girls' employment and decently paid work outside the home. In a report on trafficking in the tri-border area near Thailand, sex workers had the lowest educational level of any cohort studied. Of those surveyed, 22 percent had never attended school at all and 41.5 percent had only some exposure to primary education. These barriers create a class of "disposable people" as Kevin Bales has described them.[26] Their low educational level increases their vulnerability, often leaving them unable to keep track of their supposed earnings, which increases their vulnerability to exploitation by brothel keepers.[27] In Afghanistan, the inability of women to study during the years of Taliban rule has left women particularly vulnerable in the unstable current economic environment. Furthermore, the violence against women without access to protection has made them particularly vulnerable to all forms of sexual exploitation including trafficking.[28]

The trafficking problem from Eastern Europe and the former Soviet Union, where the majority of trafficked women have a high school education or even more, suggests that investment in female education does not safeguard against trafficking. But the absence of female education, such as exists in Asia, Latin America, and Africa, makes girls economically vulnerable, often unreachable by anti-trafficking programs and unable to understand the full risks of being trafficked.

Economic factors

The economic factors contributing to trafficking are not limited to simple poverty. With the increasing globalization of the international agricultural economy, it is becoming increasingly difficult for rural families to survive on small plots of land. Consequently, many of the girls trafficked into prostitution come from poor rural families or ones such as Sri Lanka, Indonesia, and the Balkans whose communities have seen recent ethnic and regional conflict. The sale of girls often becomes a means for family members to generate funds to make capital improvements on their land, as is often the case in Thailand.[29] The sale of a daughter may provide for the healthcare of male family members in India, or sustain a family barely surviving in the Dominican Republic.

Poverty, access to capital, and employment

Traffickers work most effectively in urban slums and rural villages where young girls and their families are living in poverty. Many analyses of trafficking point to the very strong correlation between familial poverty and the likelihood of being trafficked or sold into the sex industry.[30] In much of the world, women have difficulty obtaining access to capital. The well-known Gameen bank in Bangladesh has demonstrated the impact of providing small-scale credit to women, but there are many other countries where women are systematically excluded from access to capital to start or develop businesses. Discrimination in the job market makes it very difficult for many women to obtain jobs or advance beyond the lowest level of employment, and pushes them to work in sectors where they are the most vulnerable to labor and sexual exploitation.[31] Without the ability to function as small scale traders, women then become vulnerable to trafficking.[32]

Illustrative of this dynamic is child and female employment in the Nepali carpet industry, where Nepali girls are subject to sexual exploitation and then are trafficked directly into the sex business.[33] Uneducated children are also forced into the most dangerous economic sectors such as construction, fishing, or indirect sex work.[34] Other very difficult sectors where children are frequently exploited include gold polishing, mining, and quarrying.[35] In the United Arab Emirates, children have been trafficked into the dangerous work of camel jockeys.[36]

Economic development and crises

Although economic development in Asia has been very rapid in some countries, many others, such as Myanmar, Afghanistan, and Bangladesh, remain among the poorest in the world. A similarly unequal economic development process has occurred between Latin America and North America. Enormous disparity exists between the countries of Western Europe and North and sub-Saharan Africa. These disparities in wealth and income have been highly significant in the development of the sex industry. Certain regions have become magnets for girls from less economically developed areas. The enormous income disparities among countries in a relatively small region contribute to the sex trade. The lack of employment and economic development in Myanmar, Cambodia, and Laos has provided a steady stream of young girls and women for the Thai sex industry.[37] The customers of these girls in the sex industry in Thailand are not only local men but also men who come from the more prosperous countries of Asia, the Middle East, Europe, and North America.[38] Increasingly, the same can be said for girls from Nepal and Bangladesh who are trafficked into India. Young women are trafficked from Latin America into North America. Traffickers move both women and men from Africa to Western Europe, the men into labor exploitation and the women into situations of sexual exploitation.

Severe economic crises occurred in Asia, Latin America, and the former socialist world in the late 1990s and beginning of the twenty-first century. Women and girls have suffered disproportionately during these economic crises. The tsunami in Indonesia, the economic crisis in Thailand, and the conflicts in Iraq and Afghanistan have contributed significantly to the rise in trafficking.[39] Families no longer able to support family members, or facing overwhelming debts, often find the solution to their economic problems is the sale of their children, particularly their girls, to traffickers.[40]

Many parts of Asia have sought development capital often without concern as to its source. Japanese *yakuza* have purchased golf courses in Southeast Asia, thereby establishing the underlying foundation for sex tourism.[41] There has been no

142 *L. Shelley*

attempt to discourage the investment of this capital, which has distorted economic development and contributed to a rise in trafficking.

Sex trafficking thrives today because there is a large financial incentive for this activity to continue. As Colligan-Taylor notes, "An alliance is formed between local governments in search of foreign currency, and both local and foreign business-men willing to invest in the sex-travel industry."[42] The sex industry, particularly in Thailand, is viewed as a form of development capital.[43]

Political factors

Political transitions and trafficking

The end of the Cold War has had an enormous influence on trafficking. The most important consequences are the politico-economic transitions under way in the formerly communist states and the concomitant rise of regional conflicts. Among the most noted examples of the correlation between trafficking and regional con-flict are the conflicts in East Timor and Sri Lanka, the insurgency in Myanmar,[44] the ongoing insurgencies in Nepal and Bhutan, and the rebellions in the southern Philippines. These conflicts have resulted in the displacement of women but also in the diversion of government energies away from the social welfare of their citizens in order to maintain power and suppress rebellions. Women and children, of low priority to these governments, are particularly vulnerable in these conflict regions.

The social dislocation caused by the collapse of the communist systems has con-tributed to trafficking in a myriad of ways. Not only has there been a weakening of national border controls, thereby permitting the flow of girls and young women to more affluent countries in the region, but there has also been a significant decline in these economies. The rise of trafficking in the communist countries of Southeast Asia bears some similarity to that which is occurring in Eastern Europe and the successor states to the USSR where large scale trafficking is occurring in countries that had made enormous efforts to stamp out prostitution.[45]

In societies in transition, particularly former socialist societies, there is a femi-nization of poverty as the social protections provided to women and children were eliminated with the end of the socialist system and no social support system was put in their place. Many of the countries in Southeast Asia are moving away from socialism and losing the social protections for women that once were part of these cultures. The feminization of poverty in the states of Cambodia, Laos, and Vietnam and in the Yunnan region of China may explain the increasing number of girls and women trafficked from these countries and regions.[46] The intense corruption of the long-term Communist governments of Laos, Cambodia, Vietnam, and China has meant that there has been a mutuality of cooperation between government leaders, law enforcement agencies, and human traffickers. In some of these Asian com-munist countries, the leadership itself is helping to supply and run the brothels.[47]

Trafficking in women grew rapidly in Russia and Ukraine at the end of the Soviet regime and during the early years of the post-Soviet transition.[48] The poorly conceived post-Soviet transition proved particularly traumatic for women. The

International trafficking 143

elimination of job security, the decline of the economy, and the collapse of the social welfare state combined to place women in an extremely precarious situation, with limited opportunities to function in the legitimate economy and support their families. The speedy privatization process deprived women of jobs as enterprises downsized their work forces and the corrupt bureaucrats and members of organized crime acquired most of the countries' wealth. Women in Russia and Ukraine were left without employment or property, a fact readily exploited by the traffickers.

Political control and border areas

Many border regions around the world are outside the control of central authorities, permitting large-scale smuggling and trafficking of individuals. In many Asian multi-border areas, there is an absence of governmental control, where the crime groups and the smugglers are the dominant powers. Illustrative of this is the Golden Triangle region, in which human trafficking from Cambodia, Laos, Myanmar, and southern China flows into northern Thailand.[49] In some parts of this border area, such as between Cambodia and Thailand, there are no-man's lands with no one taking responsibility for law enforcement. In an area of Cambodia four hours from Bangkok, a casino industry second only in scale to Macao has developed with the brothels to go with it.[50] Other examples of this dynamic are the Indian–Bangladesh and Indian–Nepal border areas, where a whole culture of smuggling and organized crime has developed. The same can be said for parts of Afghanistan, where a whole smuggling culture related to the drug trade has developed in border areas, which also has been adapted for human smuggling and trafficking purposes.

These patterns are not unique to Asia. In Morocco, for example, smuggling networks of men to Europe have also been adapted for human trafficking, as has occurred in France and Spain, where young Moroccans have been smuggled to southern France for the last two decades.[51] The border areas of the former Soviet Union are extremely porous, permitting both large-scale illegal migration within the countries of the former USSR and the creation of transit routes from Asia to Europe. Similarly, the U.S.–Mexico border has large sections that are poorly policed, allowing large numbers of illegal crossings. The Transdniestra area of Moldova between Ukraine and Moldova, which has declared itself independent from the central government, is an important source and transit point for traffickers as well as many other illicit commodities.

War, political instability, and peacekeeping

The problem of trafficking is exacerbated by the presence of peacekeepers and military personnel in conflict regions. With the rise of regional conflicts, particularly since the end of the Cold War, there has been a proliferation of international peace-keeping missions throughout the world. In the absence of sufficient controls over the peacekeepers and of disciplinary action against peacekeepers for frequenting brothels with trafficked women, the presence of peacekeepers contributes signifi-cantly to the rise of trafficking. Peacekeepers in East Timor provide a demand for

144   *L. Shelley*

sex workers, and similar problems exist in Korea, where women are trafficked from Russia and Southeast Asia to service servicemen stationed there, as the Korean chapter points out.[52] The peacekeepers, by frequenting brothels and giving money to organized crime, are institutionalizing the phenomenon of trafficking within these societies. This is undermining the long-term objectives of the peacekeepers.

Absence of political will

There are many other political factors that contribute to the pervasiveness of trafficking throughout the world. First, there is the absence of political will. Some of the governments of source, transit, and destination countries for human trafficking are highly authoritarian and are more interested in maintaining political power than in serving their citizens and providing for their security. In some of these countries, the money from trafficking is an essential element of the political system. As has been shown by the research of Pasuk Phongpaichit in Thailand, the profits from trafficking help fund political parties and campaigns.[53] With the enormous dependence of the political process on this source of money, there is no domestic political incentive to address this problem. Only international political pressure concerning the spread of AIDS, the UN protocol, and United States *Trafficking in Persons Report* may motivate some of these foreign governments to address the issue of human trafficking.

Social-cultural factors

Traditional cultural mores

Diverse social and cultural factors contribute to the rise of trafficking, including problems of discrimination against minority groups and long-standing cultural mores that provide conditions favorable to human trafficking. For example, some Asian cultures have long-standing cultural practices such as child marriage or sending children away from home communities in search of better opportunities.[54] These traditions can be exploited by traffickers, thereby placing children in a vulnerable position.

Because the stigma against prostitution is not as strong in some parts of Asia and Africa as in other parts of the world, some families sell their daughters into prostitution as a solution to economic dislocation or a family financial crisis. In many countries, the social status of women and girls is not high; therefore, employment in nightclubs or the sexual entertainment business does not result in dishonor to the family. This allows the girls to return to their families. An example of this occurs in Northern Thailand, where women return to their families when they are ill and no longer employable as prostitutes.[55] In Africa, before the advent of AIDS many women worked as sex workers to earn money to start businesses.

The absence of affordable health services in most of the developing world places young women and girls in a vulnerable status by making families dependent on their income in order to afford healthcare. In some cases, girls are being placed

International trafficking   145

into bondage where they provide sexual services for a defined period of time to finance the healthcare of more senior family members.[56] This is particularly frequent in India.

Urbanization, migration, and culture change

Urbanization and international migration within countries often leads to the breakdown of traditional values, thereby increasing the risk of trafficking. Long-held social and cultural values can be weakened by exposure to mass media, promotion of materialism, and exposure to new and foreign cultures through tourism. There are also major social and psychological factors contributing to increased vulnerability to trafficking including: family homelessness, parental illness, divorce, death of a parent, and abandonment of the family by the father. All of these factors limit a family's ability to take care of its children, who may run away. At other times, they may be left to take care of themselves.

The difficult adjustment to urban life may result in greater rates of alcoholism, which compounds the likelihood of children's exposure to violence.[57] This violence may occur within the family or within the work place, such as the sweatshops where young workers are often sexually exploited. This exploitation is often a transition to trafficking.

The decline of rural areas and increasing urbanization forces many young men to migrate to cities. Far from their families and unable to afford to marry or have their wives with them, they create a great demand for the services of prostitutes. This phenomenon of trafficked women serving migrant laborers is a phenomenon observed in the United States, Western Europe, and Russia. Under these circumstances, trafficked women migrants are serving illegal labor migrants. One illegal world exists within another.

Racial and ethnic discrimination

Problems related to ethnic discrimination contribute to the rise of trafficking. The Hill Tribes of northern Thailand lack citizenship and, under these circumstances, are not granted access to social services or education, which would allow them to obtain decent employment. Compounding their problems is the fact that the crop substitution programs that have been introduced in these communities have failed to provide as much income as their cultivation of such crops as poppy. Daughters are often sold into prostitution because their families cannot survive through legitimate means.[58]

The relationship between discrimination and trafficking is not confined to Thailand. Elsewhere in South Asia, prostitution is also "a social problem caused by extreme under-development and caste discrimination in a strictly hierarchical society."[59]

The problem of discrimination leading to greater vulnerability to trafficking is also a problem in Europe and the United States. In Moldova, there is a particularly high level of trafficking among gypsy and Gagauz minorities in that country.

146   *L. Shelley*

Within the United States, black juvenile girls are much more likely than their white counterparts to be victims of trafficking. The same can be said for Native American girls in Canada.

HIV/AIDS

The proliferation of HIV/AIDS has contributed to the increase in trafficking, especially of children. Many traffickers and those who exploit younger victims believe that they are less likely to be carriers of the infection. This increases demand for younger children, some of whom are trafficked even under the age of ten. They are then considered "worn out" by the time that they reach 16.[60] The HIV/AIDS reality is quite different from the perception. Young children who are not fully developed are even more vulnerable than adults to infection.

HIV/AIDS has resulted in a rise in the number of single family homes, of orphans, and of parents who are ill and cannot support their families. This has resulted in even greater pressure on young people to become wage earners, which, combined with the social stigma attached to AIDS, leaves children increasingly vulnerable to trafficking.

Trafficked girls are particularly vulnerable to contracting venereal diseases and AIDS.[61] Young trafficked girls cannot control the conditions of their sexual relations with clients and are particularly vulnerable to lesions during sexual relations, which increases their likelihood to contract AIDS. As their symptoms become visible, they are no longer able to serve clients. Therefore, the brothel keepers need to continuously search for new girls to restock their brothels. In Asia, for example, this has resulted in the traffickers recruiting their victims in ever more remote parts of Asia that had not previously been a central part of the trafficking problem.[62]

Conclusion

Human trafficking is a growing and central element of international organized crime. The disparity between the developed and the developing world is a prime driving force for this growth. The tardiness with which the international community has responded to this problem has made many organized criminals switch to this area of criminal activity from drug trafficking and other forms of illicit activity. Some crime groups traffic in human beings at the same time that they engage in other criminal activity. Therefore, human beings may move drugs and arms at the same time that they are trafficked.

As discussed in this chapter, there are many diverse conditions that have led to the proliferation of trafficking and the rise of potential victims. The failure to pay adequate attention to human security in a globalized world has resulted in the enormous rise of all forms of human trafficking.

Many conditions accompanying globalization, such as the increasing disparity between developed and developing countries, have been conducive to the rise in trafficking. The increase in regional conflicts since the end of the Cold War has resulted in many individuals vulnerable to traffickers. The rise of AIDS in recent decades has also resulted in many more victims being sought in more remote areas and younger victims, thought to be unaffected by the disease, being recruited.

The decline of borders and border controls has facilitated the illicit movement of people across enormous distances. Victims are increasingly trafficked enormous distances to their ultimate destinations. The victims of this trafficking are disproportionately the poor, without access to education or capital, and all too often the victims of ethnic or other minorities who are least able to defend themselves. The cross-national nature of the trafficking networks means that when an individual is trafficked, he or she is unlikely to return to their home communities in the future.

Much international policy has sought to focus on human trafficking as a crime problem. The development of an international protocol against human trafficking within the context of an international convention on transnational crime is evidence of the legal approach to the problem. But as this chapter reveals, an anti-trafficking strategy requires a much broader approach than one based on law enforcement. Rather, an anti-trafficking strategy must focus on human security.

Anti-corruption policies in government, on borders, and in the political process are central to preventing and prosecuting trafficking. Military interventions and the introduction of peacekeepers must be accompanied by strategies that seek to address human trafficking before it becomes a serious problem.

The rise of regional conflicts in recent decades and the highly destructive conflicts in Iraq and Afghanistan assure that there will continue to be a large supply of trafficking victims in the coming years. There is an imperative need to understand how rural poverty, civil and regional conflict, and displacement contribute to the growth of organized crime and human trafficking, in particular. Until we enhance our understanding of the complexity of the human trafficking phenomenon and its links to organized crime, we are condemned to witness an enormous growth in the phenomenon and in the human suffering connected with it

The collapse of the Soviet Union and the post-communist transitions in Eastern Europe and in parts of Southeast Asia have resulted in hundreds of thousands of victims of sexual trafficking and many male victims of labor trafficking. The failure to understand how the decline or collapse of social welfare supports, particularly for women and children, contributes to the trafficking of people, in particular women, is the result of short-sighted economic policies that define "economic efficiency" in terms of costs to the enterprises but not in terms of costs to the people. It is this short-sighted perspective that has placed millions in jeopardy and created a large population vulnerable to exploitation by traffickers.

The rise of human trafficking is not a transitional problem of the late twentieth and early twenty-first centuries. It is a consequence of globalization and an emphasis on military as opposed to human security. Increased communications, mobility, and international commerce have facilitated the illicit movement of people. With the decline of international borders, state capacity to address human trafficking is limited. Yet inadequate attention is being paid to the economic and social needs of people, which makes them vulnerable to traffickers. Therefore, the growth and endurance of human trafficking will remain a serious problem in coming decades. Despite concerted efforts to control the organized crime that plays such a pivotal role

148　*L. Shelley*

in the rise of all forms of trafficking, law enforcement alone cannot combat a problem that is the result of deep structural change in the world. A much broader human security approach is needed to forestall the continued rise of human trafficking.

Notes

1　M. Cusimano Love, "Global Problems, Global Solutions."
2　Shafqat Munir, "Report Trafficking South Asia and Pakistan, HIMAL South Asian," <www.himalmag.com/2003/september/report_2.htm> (accessed November 10 2003).
3　U.S. Department of State, *Trafficking in Persons Report June 2004*, p. 2.
4　Human Rights Watch/Asia, "Rape for Profit: Trafficking of Nepali Girls and Women to India's Brothels"; S. P. Singh, "Transnational Organized Crime: The Indian Perspective," *Annual Report for 2000 and Resource Material Series No. 59*, Tokyo: Unafei, 2002, <http://www.unafei.or.jo/pdf/no59/ch.29/pdf> (accessed January 31, 2004).
5　P. Smucker, "Sahara Town Booms with People Smuggling."
6　"Corrupt Political Elites and Unscrupulous Investors Kill Sustainable Growth in its Tracks, Highlights New Index," <http://www.transparency.org/pressreleases_ archive/2002/2002.08.28.cpi.en.html> (accessed January 20, 2004).
7　Ibid.
8　M. Johnston, "Public Officials, Private Interests and Sustainable Democracy: When Politics and Corruption Meet."
9　S. Rose-Ackerman, "The Political Economy of Corruption."
10　J. T. Sidel, *Capital, Coercion and Crime Bossism in the Philippines*.
11　Ibid., pp. 119–20.
12　International Organization of Migration, *Combating Trafficking in South-East Asia: A Review of Policy and Programme Responses*.
13　R. W. Lee III, "Transnational Organized Crime: An Overview."
14　B. Lintner, "The Russian Mafia in Asia," <http://www.asiapacificms.com/articles/ russian_mafia> (accessed January 31, 2004) and interviews with Russian law enforcement personnel.
15　B. Lintner, *Blood Brothers: The Criminal Underworld of Asia*, pp. 222–3.
16　D. Kaplan and A. Dubro, *Yakuza: Japan's Criminal Underworld*.
17　Singh, "Transnational organized crime: The Indian perspective."
18　S. M. Tumbahamphe and B. Bhattarai, "Trafficking of Women in South Asia," <www. ecouncil.ac.cr/about/contrib/women/youth/english/traffic1.htm> (accessed November 10, 2003).
19　P. Phongpaichit, *et al.*, *Guns, Girls, Gambling, Ganja*, p. 211.
20　Ibid.; M. Macan-Markar, "Human Trafficking: Asia's Persistent Tragedy," *Asia Times Online*, October 10, 2002, <www.atimes.com/Asian_Economy/DJ10Dk01.html> (accessed November 10, 2003).
21　International Organization of Migration, *Combating Trafficking in South-East Asia*, p. 50.
22　K. Colligan-Taylor, Introduction to *Sandakan Brothel No. 8*, pp. xx–xxvii.
23　Ibid.
24　Asian Development Bank, *Combating Trafficking of Women and Children in South Asia*, p. 5.
25　Economic and Social Commission for Asia and the Pacific, "Sexually Abused and Sexually Exploited Children and Youth in the Greater Mekong Subregion: A Qualitative Assessment of their Health Needs and Available Services," St/ESCAP/2045, New York: United Nations, 2000, foreword.
26　K. Bales, *Disposable People: New Slavery in the Global Economy*.
27　J. W. Yoon, "Situation Analysis Report of Trafficking and Migration in World Vision Foundation Thailand's Three Border Sites along the Thai-Burmese Border."

International trafficking 149

28 Amnesty International Press Release, "Afghanistan: No Justice and Security for Women," October 6, 2003, <http://web.amnesty.org/library/Index/ENGASA110252003?open&of= ENG-AFG> (accessed January 19, 2004).
29 Oren Ginzburg, "TRACE Trafficking from Community to Exploitation," p. 16.
30 S. Williams and R. Masika, "Editorial," in R. Masika, ed., *Gender, Trafficking and Slavery*; Macan-Markar, "Human Trafficking."
31 International Labour Organization, Gender Promotion Program, *Preventing Discrimination, Exploitation and Abuse of Women Migrant Workers, An Information Guide*.
32 Interview with head of Ghanaian NGO providing capital to women to prevent trafficking, October 2004.
33 Human Rights Watch/Asia, "Rape for Profit."
34 R. Baker, R. Hinton, and S. Crawford, "The Sexual Exploitation of Working Children: Guidelines for Action to Eliminate the Worst Forms of Child Labor."
35 Asian Development Bank, "Combating Trafficking of Women and Children in South Asia," p. 9; C. Wille, "Thailand-Lao People's Democratic Republic and Thailand-Myanmar Border Areas Trafficking in Children into the Worst Form of Child Labour: A Rapid Assessment, Asian Research Center for Migration."
36 U.S. State Department, "Trafficking in Persons Report 2004," p. 204.
37 Asian Development Bank, *Combating Trafficking of Women and Children in South Asia*. World Vision, Situation analysis report of trafficking and migration.
38 B. Lintner, "Asia's Sex Trap," <http://www.asiapacificms.com/articles/fallen_angels> (accessed January 19, 2004).
39 Interview with Dorothy Rosenberg, 1999.
40 Lintner, "Asia's Sex Trap."
41 Kaplan and Dubro, *Yakuza: Japan's Criminal Underworld*.
42 Colligan-Taylor, *Sandakan Brothel No.8*, p. xxvii.
43 Interview with President of Mahidol University, March 1992, when author was part of a USIA sponsored program and a curriculum was being instituted at the university on crime, including combating trafficking. He commented on the difficulties of instituting this program and was subsequently removed from his position for such statements.
44 Burma/Myanmar Trafficking from *The Factbook on Global Sexual Exploitation* <www. catwinternational.org/fb/Burma_Myanmar.html> (accessed November 10, 2003).
45 L. Shelley, "Post-Communist Transitions and the Illegal Movement of People: Chinese Smuggling and Russian Trafficking in Women."
46 International Organization of Migration, *Combating Trafficking in South-East Asia A Review of Policy and Programme Responses*; B Lintner, "Illegal Aliens Smuggling to and through Southeast Asia," 2000, <http://www.asiapacificms.com/papers/pdf/ gt_alien_smuggling.pdf> (accessed January 20, 2004).
47 Lintner, *Blood Brothers*.
48 See S. Stoecker, "The Rise in Human Trafficking and the Role of Organized Crime"; L. Shelley, "The Trade in People in and from the former Soviet Union."
49 Asian Development Bank, *Combating Trafficking*.
50 B. Lintner, "Betting on the Border," <http://www.asiapacificms.com/articles/cambodia_ casinos> (accessed January 20, 2004).
51 Testimony of Mmes Zohra Azirou, Celine Manceau and Georgina Vaz Cabral, April 25, 2001 published in *L'esclavage en France aujourd'hui*, no. 1, Les Documents d"information de L'Assemblee Nationale, No.3459, 2001, pp. 38–9.
52 Congressman Chris Smith has brought attention to this problem.
53 Phongpaichit *et al.*, *Guns, Girls, Gambling, Ganja*, pp. 3–7.
54 Asian Development Bank, *Combating Trafficking*.
55 Ibid.
56 Economic and Social Commission for Asia and the Pacific, "Sexually Abused and Sexually Exploited Children and Youth in the Greater Mekong Subregion: A Qualitative Assessment of their Health Needs and Available Services."

150 *L. Shelley*

57 Ibid.
58 *Trading Women*, a 2003 film of David Feingold, <http://www.voanews.com/Khmer/archive/2003–07/a-2003–07–29–1-1.cfm>. An article on the film (accessed May 20, 2007).
59 B. Lintner, "Asia's Sex Trap."
60 Economic and Social Commission for Asia and the Pacific, "Sexually Abused and Sexually Exploited Children and Youth in the Greater Mekong Subregion."
61 Ibid.
62 International Organization of Migration, Combating Trafficking in South-East Asia. A Review of Policy and Programme Responses No. 2 IOM Migration Research Series, <http://www.old.iom.int/documents/publication/en/mrs_2_2000.pdf> (accessed May 21, 2007).

References

Amnesty International. (2003), "Afghanistan: No Justice and Security for Women," October 6, <http://web.amnesty.org/library/Index/ENGASA110252003?open&of=ENG-AFG> (accessed January 19, 2004).
Asian Development Bank. (2002) *Combating Trafficking of Women and Children in South Asia*, Asia Development Bank, ADB headquarters, May 27–29, report released July 2002.
Baker, R., Hinton, R. and Crawford, S. (2001) "The Sexual Exploitation of Working Children: Guidelines for Action to Eliminate the Worst Forms of Child Labor," University of Edinburgh: Department of Social Anthropology, February.
Bales, K. (1999) *Disposable People: New Slavery in the Global Economy*, Berkeley: University of California Press.
Colligan-Taylor, K. (1999) Introduction, in T. Yamazaki, *Sandakan Brothel No 8: An Episode in the History of Lower Class Japanese Women*, Armonk and London: M.E. Sharpe, pp. xx–xxvii.
Economic and Social Commission for Asia and the Pacific. (2000) "Sexually Abused and Sexually Exploited Children and Youth in the Greater Mekong Subregion: A Qualitative Assessment of their Health Needs and Available Services," St/ESCAP/2045, New York: United Nations.
Ginzburg, O. (2003) "TRACE Trafficking from Community to Exploitation," UNICEF/UNIAP, May 12.
Human Rights Watch/Asia. (1995) "Rape for Profit: Trafficking of Nepali Girls and Women to India's Brothels," *Human Rights Watch*, 12(5A).
International Labour Organization, Gender Promotion Program. (Undated) *Preventing Discrimination, Exploitation and Abuse of Women Migrant Workers, An Information Guide*, Booklet 6, "Trafficking of Women and Girls," Geneva: ILO.
International Organization of Migration. (2000) *Combating Trafficking in South-East Asia: A Review of Policy and Programme Responses*, Geneva.
Johnston, M. (1997) "Public Officials, Private Interests and Sustainable Democracy: When Politics and Corruption Meet," in K. A. Elliott, ed., *Corruption and the Global Economy*, Washington, D.C.: Institute for International Economics, pp. 61–82.
Kaplan, D. and Dubro, A. (2003) *Yakuza: Japan's Criminal Underworld*, Berkeley: University of California Press.
Lee III, R. W. (1999) "Transnational Organized Crime: An Overview," in *Transnational Crime in the Americas*, T. Farer, ed., New York: Routledge, pp. 1–17.
Lintner, B. (2000) "Illegal Aliens Smuggling to and through Southeast Asia," <http://www.asiapacificms.com/papers/pdf/gt_alien_smuggling.pdf> (accessed January 20, 2004).

International trafficking   151

Lintner, B. (2003) *Blood Brothers: The Criminal Underworld of Asia*, New York: Palgrave Macmillan.

Lintner, B. (2004) "Asia's Sex Trap," <http://www.asiapacificms.com/articles/fallen_angels> (accessed January 20, 2004).

Lintner, B. (2004) "Betting on the Border," <http://www.asiapacificms.com/articles/cambodia_casinos> (accessed January 20, 2004).

Love, M. Cusimano. (2003) "Global Problems, Global Solutions," in M. Cusimano Love, ed., *Beyond Sovereignty Issues for a Global Agenda*, 2nd edn., Belmont, WA: Wadsworth/Thomson, pp. 1–42.

Macan-Markar, M. (2002) "Human Trafficking: Asia's Persistent Tragedy," *Asia Times Online*, October 10, <www.atimes.com/Asian_Economy/DJ10Dk01.html> (accessed November 10, 2003).

Phongpaichit, P., *et al.* (1998) *Guns, Girls, Gambling, Ganja*, Chiang Mai: Silkworm Books.

Rose-Ackerman, S. (1997) "The Political Economy of Corruption," in K. A. Elliott, ed., *Corruption and the Global Economy*, Washington, D.C.: Institute for International Economics, pp. 31–4.

Shelley, L. (2002) "Post-Communist Transitions and the Illegal Movement of People: Chinese Smuggling and Russian Trafficking in Women," *Annals of Scholarship* 14, no. 2: 71–84.

Shelley, L. (2003) "The Trade in People in and from the former Soviet Union," *Crime, Law and Social Change* 40: 231–49.

Sidel, J. T. (1999) *Capital, Coercion and Crime Bossism in the Philippines*, Stanford: Stanford University Press.

Singh, S. P. (2002) "Transnational Organized Crime: The Indian Perspective," *Annual Report for 2000 and Resource Material Series No. 59*, Tokyo: Unafei, <http://www.unafei.or.jo/pdf/no59/ch.29/pdf> (accessed January 31, 2004).

Smucker, P. (2004) "Sahara Town Booms with People Smuggling," *International Herald Tribune*, October 25, p. 2.

Stoecker, S. (2000) "The Rise in Human Trafficking and the Role of Organized Crime," *Demokratizatsiya* 8, no. 1: 129–44.

U.S. Department of State. (2004) *Trafficking in Persons Report June 2004*, Washington, D.C.: U.S. Department of State.

Wille, C. (2001) "Thailand-Lao People's Democratic Republic and Thailand-Myanmar Border Areas Trafficking in Children into the Worst Form of Child Labour: A Rapid Assessment, Asian Research Center for Migration," prepared for International Labour Organization, Geneva, November.

Williams, S. and Masika, R. (2002) "Editorial," in R. Masika, ed., *Gender, Trafficking and Slavery*, Oxford: Oxfam, pp. 5–6.

Yoon, J. W. (2002) "Situation Analysis Report of Trafficking and Migration in World Vision Foundation Thailand's Three Border Sites along the Thai-Burmese Border," World Vision Foundation of Thailand and of Myanmar, January.

8 Foreign women's life and work in the entertainment sector of Korea from the human trafficking perspective

Dong-Hoon Seol and Geon-Soo Han

Introduction

According to the *Trafficking in Persons Report 2007* of the U.S. Department of State, the Republic of Korea is a country of origin, transit, and destination for trafficking in human beings. There are foreign women from the Philippines, Russia, and the former Soviet states of central Asia and Eastern Europe in the sex industry of Korea. Many foreign women migrate to economically advanced countries such as Japan and the United States through Korea. Korean women also are trafficked to Japan, the United States, and Australia. These phenomena have not changed since 2001 when the report became an annual publication.

Korea was ranked in Tier 3, together with 23 other countries in the report of 2001. The following excerpt illustrates the situation in Korea:

South Korea (Tier 3)

South Korea is a country of origin and transit for trafficking in human beings. Young female Koreans are trafficked primarily for sexual exploitation, mainly to the United States, but also to other western countries and Japan. Female aliens from many countries, primarily Chinese women, are trafficked through Korea to the United States and many other parts of the world. In addition to trafficking by air, much transit traffic occurs in South Korean territorial waters by ship.

While South Korea is a leader in the region on human rights and democracy generally, the Government has done little to combat this relatively new and worsening problem of trafficking in human beings. Although it does prosecute alien smuggling activities such as visa fraud and possession or sale of fraudulent civil documents, there are no laws that specifically address trafficking. There are statutes against kidnapping and sale or purchase of sexual services with a juvenile, and maximum penalties for these are commensurate with those for rape. Although corruption occurs, there is no evidence that government officials are involved in trafficking in human beings. Aliens are treated as immigration violators and deported. No government assistance is available for trafficking victims or to support NGOs involved in assisting trafficking victims.[1]

Foreign women's life and work in the entertainment sector of Korea 153

The Korean government made various legal efforts to prohibit human trafficking. The Department of State's 2007 Report upgraded the rank of Korea to Tier 1, acknowledging the government's efforts since the 2002 Report. The U.S. government mentioned reasons for this upgrade such as the organization of a Counter-trafficking Committee by government agencies, increase in support for NGOs concerned with trafficking in human beings, intensified public campaigns to prevent trafficking in human beings, and the passing of numerous legal provisions to stop trafficking, even though there is no official law to specifically eradicate trafficking. These changes are illustrated in the Report of 2007.

REPUBLIC OF KOREA (Tier 1)

The Republic of Korea (R.O.K.) is primarily a source country for the trafficking of women and girls internally and to the United States (often through Canada and Mexico), Japan, Hong Kong, Guam, Australia, New Zealand, Canada, and Western Europe for the purpose of commercial sexual exploitation. Women from Russia, Uzbekistan, Kazakhstan, the People's Republic of China (P.R.C.), the Philippines, Thailand, and other Southeast Asian countries are trafficked for sexual exploitation to South Korea. A growing number of these foreign victims were trafficked to the R.O.K. for sexual or labor exploitation through brokered international marriages to South Korean men. South Korean men are a significant source of demand for child sex tourism in Southeast Asia and the Pacific Islands.

The Government of the Republic of Korea fully complies with the minimum standards for the elimination of trafficking. Over the last year, the government continued vigorous law enforcement efforts against sex trafficking and commercial sexual exploitation, and expanded protections offered to victims of sex trafficking. The government demonstrated appreciation for the perceived increase in transnational sex trafficking of South Korean women to the United States by increasing cooperative efforts with U.S. law enforcement investigators. These advances, however, were not adequately matched by an awareness of potential labor trafficking among South Korea's large foreign labor force. The South Korean government should take steps to ensure that the new Employment Placement System of labor recruitment offers greater protections to foreign workers by investigating and prosecuting cases of forced labor among migrant workers victims.[2]

Numerous efforts have been made by the Korean government and civil societies to prevent human trafficking. The National Assembly of the Republic of Korea legislated the Special Laws on Sex Trade including the "Act on the Prevention of Prostitution and Protection of Victims thereof" and the "Act on the Punishment of Procuring Prostitution and Associated" on March 2, 2004. The laws have been in effect since September 23, 2004.

The special laws reflect international standards that consider sex trade as violence perpetrated on women. The laws established tougher penalties on brothel

154 *D.-H. Seol and G.-S. Han*

owners and buyers, while protecting prostituted victims. New laws emphasize the responsibility of the state to protect women's human rights. In addition, the Special Laws on Sex Trade called for the Korean government to establish support centers providing shelters for sex trafficking victims and prostitutes. The shelters also provide medical and legal help and vocational training.

International societies also acknowledged the changes and efforts of Korea. The 2006 report of the UN Office on Drugs and Crime, *Trafficking in Persons: Global Patterns*, ranked Korea as low in origin, very low in transit, and medium in destination among five levels in human trafficking. According to this report, inbound human trafficking is the most serious problem in Korea. This chapter will illustrate the situation of trafficking of foreign women in Korea based on empirical research data.

Data and method

There has been no systematic research on the human trafficking situation in Korea since passage of the Special Laws on Sex Trade. The statistics in this chapter are based on nationwide survey research in 2003 supported by the Ministry of Gender Equality and Family. In this research, we examined immigration processes and employment conditions of migrant women working in the sex and entertainment sector in Korea. The research was conducted in Seoul, Gyeonggi province (including Uijeongbu, Dongducheon, and Anyang), Busan and Changwon in Gyeongnam province, and Gunsan in Jeonbuk province. We tried to obtain objective results by encompassing metropolitan Seoul and Busan, middle and small cities, and rural areas, U.S. military camp towns, and non-military areas. In total, 195 migrant women—89 from the former Soviet Union (CIS), including Russia, Uzbekistan, Kazakhstan, Kyrgyzstan and others, and 106 Filipinas (from the Philippines)—responded to the survey. Also, 32 women (17 CIS women and 15 Filipinas) among the survey respondents agreed to have in-depth interviews with researchers. The survey was carried out during the three-month period between August 25 and November 24, 2003.

This chapter includes additional analysis on the current changes of human trafficking in Korea since the Special Laws on Sex Trade of 2004. Because there are no new research works on this subject, we use articles from the news media and official police reports of criminal investigations.

Immigration process in the Korean sex and entertainment business

Source of information on employment in Korea

For most of the women (86.6 percent), Korea is their first country of labor migration. Only 13.4 percent of the women answered that they had worked abroad before Korea for a period of a month or more. Table 8.1 shows the respondents' knowledge of Korea before their migration.

Foreign women's life and work in the entertainment sector of Korea 155

Table 8.1 Awareness of Korea prior to migration (%)

	Total	*The CIS*	*Philippines*
(N)	*(192)*	*(86)*	*(106)*
Not at all	40.6	21.3	54.3
A little	50.0	57.3	44.8
Very well	9.4	21.3	1.0
Total	100.0	100.0	100.0

The interviews revealed that most of the women had desired Korea or Japan for their migration. In fact, many of the women had expected to be sent to Japan, rather than Korea. Korea entered the women's migration decisions as a possible destination usually in the context of their inability to secure an entertainment visa for Japan. Most commonly, the women are convinced to go to Korea because it is relatively easy. They normally need to wait only two weeks before they can depart, compared with Japan, where it can take at least eight months to obtain the necessary documentation. The relative ease of getting a visa for Korea as compared with Japan often made this an attractive alternative for women intending to migrate as entertainers. In addition, recruiters and managers often tell the women that Korea is similar to, or better than, Japan.

> I read a newspaper article in Antenna. It said a woman had been to Japan and succeeded in earning a lot of money. There were nice pictures and an agency address in Vladivostok. The article said the job was good, not related to sex at all and people were kind. You could earn a lot of money and, plus, the rent and food was free. The agency had connections to Korea and Japan. I went to see the agency in Vladivostok and people there were very kind. They told me about the work on the stage and about being a good hostess to customers. The work they described was to assist customers with drinks, to talk, sing, prepare ashtrays, and so forth. They told me that Korea was a better choice than Japan as it took less time to get a visa. The salary was US$400 but you could make approximately US$1,000 a month including tips.
>
> (Case #105, 33 years old, Russia)

Without exception, however, all the Filipinas who had previously worked in Japan stated that Korea was much worse than Japan and was not like Japan at all. Russian participants who had worked in Europe pointed out the inferior treatment in Korea as well. Many of the Russians complained about the inadequate or unfair treatment from their club managers. The women in Korea are engaged in the entertainment business because they have no other options or because they had no information about the work before starting it, rather than because they prefer or had experience in the entertainment business. Especially in Russia, the rumor is that women who go abroad to work in factories end up falling into prostitution. This leads Russian women to believe that entertainment agencies advertised on TV or in magazines are safer routes than other types of migration.

> They say that it is too expensive to get an industrial trainee visa and that chances are there is no such company or factory when you come to Korea. In some other cases, you come to Korea with an industrial trainee visa only to find that it was originally a tourist visa. Employment contracts are all in English but the people who need jobs outside the country are those who could not afford to learn English. So many people end up with being illegal aliens.
>
> (Case #107, 29 years old, Russia)

Entertainment agencies do extensive promotion through TV commercials or newspaper advertisements. This is one of the major reasons that women are attracted to the entertainment business. The agencies tell them that jobs are easy to get and they are required to pay as little as US$50 visa fee in the beginning. Table 8.2 shows how the women learned about work in Korea.

The following are some of the stories of how the women from the CIS countries first learned about Korea and the entertainment business. They would believe what they heard from people around them. If any of their acquaintances had been to Korea and said it was okay, that was enough.

> Once, after my divorce, my parents-in-law asked me, 'Why don't you go abroad and see the world? Your friends came back and bought apartments, you saw that. It seems better for you to go as well.' Those friends had spent about two years abroad. They said they had drunk whisky or juice and sometimes had gone on bar fines [left to provide sexual services] with the customers but never been forced to do so. They said many of them had boyfriends there and got much support from them emotionally and financially. My niece and her

Table 8.2 Source of information on work in Korea (%)

	Total	The CIS	Philippines
(N)	(192)	(86)	(106)
Friend	43.8	38.4	48.1
Mass media	22.4	27.9	17.9
Broker or recruiting agency	17.7	9.3	24.5
Acquaintance	9.4	19.8	.9
Family/relatives	5.7	3.5	7.5
Others	1.0	1.2	.9
Total	100.0	100.0	100.0

Foreign women's life and work in the entertainment sector of Korea   157

friends had worked in Japan and they also told me it had been really good and easy. As I heard Korea was the same as Japan, I decided to come to Korea.

(Case #107, 29 years old, Russia)

The story reflects the lack of a formal source of information in Russia. They say, "In Vladivostok, two in every five have worked in Korea." Nonetheless, the general public learns only from friends or friends of their friends. They are the source of most information in the women's decision to migrate. Thus, many of the Russian women know almost nothing when they arrive in Korea. In addition, recruiting agencies in the home countries increasingly hire women who had worked in the entertainment sector in Korea to work for them. The validity of the information these women would give to women candidates is questionable. Yulia, who entered Korea in 2001, told this story:

Once I met Lupov, who had been to Korea as a dancer for three months. She stopped working when her manager fell in love with her. Then she started working as a recruiter in an agency in Russia. She told me about the work I would be supposed to do at the tables. Customers are interested in Russian women and your job is to willingly serve them and spend time with them. The life is easy and comfortable and you can make a lot of money with tips. In a short video she showed me, women were dancing and customers were enjoying their time drinking and dancing at clubs. There were pictures of the office of the agency as well. After listening to her, I decided to give it a try for a term of six months and signed the contract. I had never met any other women than her.

(Case #115, 28 years old, Russia)

Victoria was seeking a job when she came across a recruitment advertisement in Russia. She applied for a job, but she never dreamed she would get it so easily.

I saw a TV commercial about working in Korea one day. It was a 'hostess job.' There I saw posters and the address and phone numbers of the agency that recruited people for Korea and Japan. I made an appointment by phone and visited the office. The explanation was simply that the work in Korea was good and well paying. She said that all the expenses in the process were to be paid for me by the agency. There were many people from neighboring areas in the office. They all said there was no problem with going to Korea and the work was OK. Like me, however, nobody in the office considered it seriously as a job offer. I waited for a few months but I never believed I would go to Korea. But then they contacted me and said, 'Now you are going,' and I signed the contract they handed me.

(Case #111, 25 years old, Russia)

Filipina respondents can be categorized into three groups according to their sources of information: those who had never worked in the entertainment sector, those who

158 D.-H. Seol and G.-S. Han

had worked in the Philippines as a singer or a dancer, and those who had made a living with striptease or prostitution.

There are three common processes by which women in the Philippines are recruited for Korea. The first is for recruitment agents to go to provinces, approach women, and tell them that they can help them go abroad. This strategy is normally utilized for women who have had no previous experience working at clubs, as entertainers or prostitutes. Heather describes this in the following way:

> When they recruit a girl they don't tell her what's their job. They just go from province to province and look for good-looking girls—some of them are not good-looking, anyway. And some of them tell other girls. They say, 'Hey, you want to go abroad?' They give the girl the name of a promoter and the girl goes to an audition. They say to the girls, 'Oh, you'll be just like a star.'
> (Case #601, 28 years old, Philippines)[3]

Kelly told of her experience:

> This Korean woman came to my house where I was living one day. I was asleep and she knocked on the door. I answered it and she said to me, 'Do you want to go to another country? It's fast. Just a couple of weeks and you can go.' This woman, she spoke very good Tagalog. I thought it sounded like a good idea and easy to make money. So I went to the agency, which was on the ninth floor of this building in Santa Cruz.
> (Case #211, 18 years old, Philippines)

Kelly said that the woman came to her house because she was sharing with four other women at the time. One of her housemates had told the recruiter that she was living with some girls who might be interested in going to Korea.

The second most common method of recruitment is for a person known to the woman (a friend, relative, or manager of agencies training entertainers) to suggest that she go to Korea. Entertainment agencies train women to be professional entertainers and assist them in passing their Artist Record Book examinations in exchange for a fee. One participant in this research, Emily, said that she heard from a friend about working in Korea. Her friend had said, "It's easy to go to Korea. It only takes two weeks. The work is easy. You just serve drinks and dance with guys." Emily's friend had not been to Korea, but this was what she had heard. Indeed, such narratives of Korea as an easy place to make a lot of money, as a place that is comparatively easy to go to, and as a place where the work to be performed is very clearly expressed as serving drinks, chatting to and dancing with customers, are circulated widely among women who wish to migrate abroad to work. Normally, the women will go to a specific agency in the Philippines that is recommended by the recruiter or a friend or relative.

Finally, women are recruited through print advertisements that circulate either in the media (for example, newspapers) or on signboards and walls on the street. These advertisements are posted by both entertainment agencies and promotion agencies.

Foreign women's life and work in the entertainment sector of Korea 159

Immigration paths and networks

The majority (93.6 percent) of the migrant women in our research had travelled to Korea with a passport under their original name; 98.8 percent among the women from the CIS countries and 89.5 percent among the Filipinas. Those who travelled with a fake passport were usually minors (16 to 17 years old). A few cases were found where fake passports were used even though the women were of legal age at the time of entry. The women could only speculate as to why they were issued false passports when they were of legal age, and two reasons prevailed in their explanations. First, the exceedingly high cost of a false passport would entail a substantial fee that would add to the women's migration debts; and second, if women did not have a passport but were to migrate quickly they were issued a passport belonging to another woman in which the photograph had been changed.

Table 8.3 shows the types of visas obtained by women from CIS countries and the Philippines and the types of visas under which they migrated to Korea.

When women from the CIS countries get Korean visas, they travel to Korea in a group of as small as three or as big as ten, accompanied by a Russian agent or a manager from Korea. In cases where they travel with a Russian agent, a Korean manager would come to the airport to pick them up and escort them to the office or to their accommodations.

All of the Filipina participants either came directly to Korea or via Hong Kong or Bangkok, where they received their E-6 visas. None of the women who came to Korea via Hong Kong or Bangkok personally appeared at the Korean Embassy to apply for their E-6 visa; their manager performed this task. In 2000 it became clear that the promotion agencies were utilizing the Korean Embassies in Hong Kong and Bangkok as a means of facilitating the entry of Filipinas into Korea on E-6 visas, even where they were clearly not professional entertainers. The 11 Filipinas of Cases #301 to #311 shared the same route to Korea in 2002. They first travelled from the Philippines to Thailand as tourists, acquired Korean E-6 visas at the Korean Embassy in Bangkok and then travelled to Korea. The following is Kyla describing the procedure:

Table 8.3 Type of visa (%)

	Total	*The CIS*	*Philippines*
(N)	*(187)*	*(82)*	*(105)*
Entertainment (E-6)	90.9	85.4	95.2
Tourist or other types of short-term visa	8.0	13.4	3.8
Fiancée	0.5	0.0	1.0
Others	0.5	1.2	0.0
Total	100.0	100.0	100.0

160   D.-H. Seol and G.-S. Han

We travelled to Bangkok on tourist visa. The immigration office of the Philippines would not allow our departure because they were suspicious of us having only US$100 with us and saying we were travelling to Thailand. They required us to prove that we had more money with us. So we stayed at a hotel in Manila and called Mr. K, a Korean agent. Then he tried to take us out via Cebu, where he found they had no international flights. So he called people at the club to bring us some money. We were distributed 7,500 pesos each and then we were able to travel to Bangkok. We travelled by ourselves to Bangkok, where we met another Korean, Mr. P, at noon. He took the money back. Our Korean visas were ready in two days in Bangkok. We just gave them our photos and birth certificates and got our passports issued with E-6 visa. The application form, we filled them out and they asked us no questions at the Korean Embassy.

(Case #309, 27 years old, Philippines)

After this procedure was recognized, agents no longer used these routes to bring women into Korea. Of those arriving since late 2001 not one woman interviewed for the research stated that she travelled via Bangkok or Hong Kong, but came directly to Korea. This indicates the ability of promotion agents to respond quickly to changed circumstances for the movement of women to Korea. Similarly, while women tended to come in large groups before late 2001, since that time women generally state that they travel together in smaller groups (two to six persons), especially if they are dancers who usually perform in a group, or alone, as in the cases of women entering as singers.

Most of the costs incurred in the process of migration to Korea were initially paid by the agencies. Only 12.6 percent of the participants paid for all of their costs to come to Korea, 18.0 percent of the women paid part of their costs and the rest was taken care of by their agencies, and 69.4 percent paid none of their costs. Where the costs were paid in part or in full by someone else, this person was normally the promotion agent in Korea and/or the Philippines. The most common case was one in which women would pay for the costs of their photographs (which was given to the promotion agency in the Philippines for their use in placing a woman in Korea), their passport (if they did not have one already), and their visa.

The average cost the women paid for their travel to Korea is US$1,574.30. Regionally compared, Filipinas paid US$1,953.99, which is a lot more than was paid by women from the CIS countries, US$1,096.16. How the costs are paid can be categorized into three different types. The following is an analysis of how much the women are supposed to pay in each case.

The first type is where the woman pays all the costs incurred in the migration process. The average cost in this case was US$760.97. The discrepancy between the cost borne by the Filipinas and the women from the CIS countries was the biggest in this case. The Filipinas paid an average of US$1,959.50 whereas the women from the CIS countries paid US$508.65.

The second type is to share the cost between the woman and her agency. In this case, the average of total costs was US$954.95. Again, Filipinas turned out to have

Foreign women's life and work in the entertainment sector of Korea   161

paid more than the others. They paid an average of US$1,624.17 and the women from the CIS countries paid US$704.00. The average cost borne by a woman was US$300.41 while that of an agency was US$654.55.

In the last type, where an agency covered all costs incurred, the average was US$1,882.52. Again, Filipinas are found to pay back a little more than the women from the CIS countries: US$1,987.10 and US$1,637.60, respectively. The promotion agents normally pay for the women's round-trip airfares to Korea and often loan them money to purchase costumes, other clothes, and makeup for their first few week in Korea before they have income. In addition, women also have to pay an agency fee to their promoter, the exact amount of which is often not disclosed to the women and can be arbitrarily altered by the promoter. All the costs borne by the promotion agents are added to a woman's migration debt, usually at a highly inflated figure.

When women whose costs were totally borne by the agencies were asked whether they must pay the costs out of their salaries once in Korea, 66.7 percent of them answered "yes" and 23.1 percent answered "no." The remaining 10.2 percent answered "I do not know." In cases of those who answered "no," the women did not see anything deducted from their accounts, but the agencies were still collecting the costs. The agencies take back what they invested (the costs incurred in the process of migration). It is interesting that the percentage of those who answer "yes" is much higher among Filipinas than among the women from the CIS countries: 84.1 percent and 11.5 percent, respectively. It is related to the fact that more Filipinas were recruited in the third type where the agencies paid the total costs initially.

Women must normally pay these costs out of their salaries once in Korea. More than half (55.6 percent) of the respondents answered that they were paying back a certain amount every month. The rest (44.4 percent) were also paying back the costs, although they did not know how much they were paying each month. The average amount of money they had to pay back was 1,279,200 won: 660,000 won among the women from the CIS countries and 1,313,600 won among the Filipinas.

According to the research conducted by the National Human Rights Commission of Korea in 2002, it costs US$3,815.4 on average for one migrant worker to come to Korea.[4] The average migration cost for a woman worker in the entertainment business is US$1,574.30. In sum, it costs significantly less for a woman to enter Korea and start working in the entertainment business than for a migrant worker seeking a job in manufacturing, construction, agriculture, forestry, or fishing in Korea. This can be interpreted in two ways. First, the promotion agencies are willing to bear the burden incurred in the migration process as a reasonable investment to run a profitable business. This is plausible in the sense that the cost per woman would be less than US$2,000, as it requires only the visa fee, airfare, and the agency fee. Second, the agencies deliberately make advance payment, which then becomes the women's debts. Most (87.4 percent) of the women in the research are indebted to their agents, and the amount is much bigger than the agents originally paid. As the women cannot break from the agencies before they pay back all the debts, the debts become a very useful system to force the women to become involved

162 *D.-H. Seol and G.-S. Han*

in prostitution. Both scenarios were easily evident during the interviews with the women, although it is hard to show which is more prevalent.

Employment status and working conditions

Employment status

The types of sex-related jobs in which migrant women workers in the entertainment business are engaged are classified as follows: clubs catering to U.S. military personnel (U.S. GIs) in *kijichon* or the U.S. military camp town areas; foreigners-only clubs in tourist zones, such as "Texas Town" in Busan; clubs in mixed areas such as Itaewon in Seoul; and other nightclubs, Karaokes, and Room salons catering to Koreans all over the country.

As shown in Table 8.4, the majority of the respondents answered that they worked at nightclubs, followed by kijichon areas. Most of the women from the CIS countries work at nightclubs, while Filipinas are found at kijichon clubs. It is notable that the women from the CIS countries, rather than the Filipinas, are largely employed at the clubs catering to Korean customers. Filipinas are employed mostly at kijichon clubs catering to U.S. GIs. This is because of the Filipinas' fluency in English and Korean customers' preference for white women. The women from the CIS countries are distributed to both kijichon clubs for U.S. GIs and clubs for Koreans. Therefore, it is convenient to separate Filipinas from the women from the CIS countries in studying foreign women's employment status in Korea.

The women from the CIS countries are located at Korean clubs such as nightclubs, Karaokes and Room salons; American clubs in kijichon; and clubs in Itaewon or in "Texas Town" in Busan. Unlike the Filipinas who are concentrated at American clubs in northern Gyeonggi province where many kijichons are located, the women from the CIS countries are found more at Korean clubs, dispersed throughout the country. Kijichon clubs and Korean clubs are similar in that both of them demand sexual service in the form of entertaining (sitting at the table with the customers) and the bar fine (prostitution, euphemized as "second round" in Korean). The

Table 8.4 Place of work (%)

	Total	The CIS	Philippines
(N)	*(188)*	*(83)*	*(105)*
Nightclub	55.3	83.1	33.3
Kijichon club	39.4	6.0	65.7
Motel	0.5	1.2	0.0
Room salon	0.5	1.2	0.0
Others	4.3	8.4	1.0
Total	100.0	100.0	100.0

Foreign women's life and work in the entertainment sector of Korea   163

difference is that the women's duties at Korean clubs are dancing and entertaining the customers at the same time whereas entertaining is prioritized at kijichon clubs. The relationship between the migrant women workers and the other workers at clubs, including waiters and "mamasans," is another difference between the two types of clubs.

Most Filipina participants in this research were employed at kijichon clubs catering to U.S. GIs. The women have various duties at the clubs, regardless of what kinds of sexual services the clubs offer to the customers. In addition, they also work as waitresses at the clubs and all of them describe one of their central activities as "someone to talk to, dance with or drink with customers." The provision of all other services would occur inside the clubs: either in the main club area, in separate VIP rooms adjacent to it or upstairs from the main club area. Customers would normally come to the clubs to purchase the services of the women, although women could be "bar fined" to customers, meaning a customer would purchase the time of a particular woman and take her out of the club. In these cases, customers could "date" a woman, taking her out bar hopping, to a restaurant or shopping, or to a hotel for a sexual liaison.

Job descriptions

Table 8.5 shows the results of the survey on the duties of women in their work places. The majority of the respondents stated that they worked as "someone to talk to and dance or drink with customers," followed by "waitressing/serving" and "dancer." Due to the characteristics of the clubs at which the women work, the women from the CIS countries are chiefly titled as dancers while Filipinas work as waitresses. This originates in the difference between the services provided at kijichon clubs and those at Korean clubs such as nightclubs.

As to the venue for meeting the customers, 95.8 percent of the respondents answered that they meet their customers "at a fixed place." Regionally disaggregated,

Table 8.5 Job descriptions (multiple responses) (%)

	Total	The CIS	Philippines
(N)	(188)	(83)	(105)
Someone to talk to, dance or drink with customers	71.8	50.6	88.6
Server/waitress	58.0	15.7	91.4
Dancer	43.1	61.4	28.6
Sexual service provider	33.5	6.0	55.2
Singer	15.4	3.6	24.8
Musician	1.6	0.0	2.9

164   *D.-H. Seol and G.-S. Han*

it is found that 94.2 percent of the women from the CIS countries and 96.7 percent of the Filipinas meet their customers "at a fixed place."

When asked whether they were working full-time or part-time, 97.2 percent of the respondents answered that they worked full-time. Regionally disaggregated, 96.2 percent of the women from the CIS countries and 98.0 percent of the Filipinas turn out to be full-time workers, showing little difference between the two groups. Although small in percentage (2.8 percent), some participants answered that they were currently working part-time. They are Filipinas working as factory workers or salespersons and some of the women from the CIS countries who are students at the same time as working at clubs.

To the question if they ever have worked in any line of business other than entertainment in Korea, 90.1 percent of the women answered "no." Among the women from the CIS countries, 1.4 percent of them answered "yes" while 16.1 percent of the Filipinas gave the same answer, showing that more Filipinas have some experience in other kinds of work than their counterparts. Among the respondents who have experience working in other fields, 75.0 percent stated that they had worked in factories. Many Filipinas have worked in various types of work other than in factories (75.0 percent).

The jobs that the women are required to perform differ across clubs. In most cases, the women were told in signing their contracts that their work would be primarily "to dance with the customers, get orders, and perform entertainment." Hanna, one of the interviewees, states as follows:

Table 8.6 Services that migrant women offer (multiple responses) (%)

	Total	CIS women	Filipinas
(N)	(167)	(64)	(103)
Dancing	73.7	73.4	73.8
Selling juice, drinks, beverages	64.7	35.9	82.5
Serving	60.5	32.8	77.7
Customer's touching/fondling	53.9	29.7	68.9
Sexual intercourse	33.5	12.5	46.6
Sexy dancing on stage	32.9	6.3	49.5
Singing	32.3	39.1	28.2
Sitting on customer's lap	26.9	1.6	42.7
Hand-job	12.6	1.6	19.4
Blow-job	9.0	1.6	13.6
Others	3.6	9.4	0.0

Foreign women's life and work in the entertainment sector of Korea 165

The contract said we would be a waitress, entertain and talk like that. But then when I come here we have to sit down on their [customers'] laps, lap dance, VIP, and going out on bar fines. Only sometimes VIP and bar fines. They don't push us—it's our choice. But we need the money.

(Case #209, 26 years old, Philippines)

The women perform various duties such as dance, table service, and sexual services on a daily basis. Providing sexual services is as high as 33.5 percent. Among the women from the CIS countries, dancing takes the highest percentage with 73.4 percent while selling juice, alcoholic drinks or other beverage takes the highest among the Filipinas with 82.5 percent. Each of the women's jobs that is, performing "sexy" dance, entertaining, and sexual services, is examined in detail.

"Sexy" dance

All the women who participated in this research said that they were required to start working as soon as they arrived in Korea. The women from the CIS countries who were sent to clubs catering to Korean customers, in particular said that they had to dance on the stages from the very first day. They found it shocking to dance in bikinis in front of many people, which was also very different from what they had heard before coming to Korea.

The first club I worked at in Korea was Club A in Andong, Gyeongbuk province. It served Korean customers and the manner was shocking. I never imagined standing on such a high stage. The lighting was overwhelming and it was as beautiful as in a real show. The work was very hard in the beginning. I had difficulties in dancing with high heels on such a stage, as I never had any experience like that. We worked from 7:30 p.m. to 4 a.m. and danced for three to four hours every night. DJs took pity on us and sometimes played the music longer so that we could take a break while the customers danced.

(Case #105, 33 years old, Russia)

In some of the clubs the women dance in costumes, and at other clubs they have to strip dance. Strip dancing is not included in any of the job descriptions given in their contracts. Linda, who found dancing the worst of all her duties at Club MZ, states: "I'm shy. I don't want to see all the guys [look] at my body. It's okay to go to VIP room, but I don't want to dance. But I have no choice. If you want the money, you have to do like that." (Case #212, 28 years old, Philippines)

At Club YA, the women were also forced to dance. Kelly explained that the strip shows normally started at 9 p.m. each night. Each woman has a song and when her song is being played she must get up on the stage and dance. The woman must strip completely naked.

We have to run quickly [when our song is playing], otherwise we would be punished. We would get so cold in winter and we would all go to the heater

166 *D.-H. Seol and G.-S. Han*

before the customers arrived. But when the mamasan sees this she would turn the heater off and tell us to get up on stage and practice our dancing. Because, you know, none of us knew how to dance when we came to Korea.

(Case #211, 18 years old, Philippines)

Other clubs, such as Club PB, do not force the women to dance or perform strip shows. Nonetheless, apart from the strip and stage dancing which take place at some of the clubs, all the clubs force the women to lap dance. Lap dancing is tied to the drink system in that the girl must cajole a customer into buying her a drink. In order to do this she should perform a lap dance on him. As Kelly states, at Club YA, the mamasan instructed the women in the following way:

When you sit with a GI you have to sit on his lap facing him [straddled over his legs] and dance—even before he buys you a drink. If after one minute he doesn't buy you a drink, you have to get up and go to another customer and do the same thing until a GI buys you a drink.

(Case #211, 18 years old, Philippines)

The only duty that was agreed to by all the women in the contracts they signed was waitressing. Nonetheless, none of the women who participated in this research realized that this also entailed sitting on the customer's lap and letting him fondle her. Many women experience incredible stress in approaching a customer and asking him to buy her a drink.

Entertaining

Women from the CIS countries at nightclubs catering mainly to Korean customers sit at tables upon customers' requests and get tips from them. The women had expected that their job at the tables would be talking with the customers. However, what the Korean customers want to do is fondle them or touch them beneath their clothes. At most nightclubs and Room salons, the women are supposed to sing or dance with customers, who then in many cases try to fondle the women.

Clubs in kijichon areas offer more kinds of sexual services. The U.S. GIs either buy juice for the women and talk with them or enjoy various sexual services provided. The women play card games and talk with the customers or go further to perform hand-jobs or blow-jobs. They cater to different customer groups including Koreans, U.S. GIs, and migrant workers and provide various sexual services as each group has different needs, tastes, and attitudes toward women. Clubs have different distribution of customers in terms of nationality, with Koreans at the clubs at which women from the CIS countries work and Americans at the clubs where Filipinas work (see Table 8.7). The makeup of the customers' age group is 39.7 percent in their thirties, 38.6 percent in their twenties, and 18.6 percent in their forties.

In general, the Filipinas interviewed for this research preferred American GI customers to other customers because many GIs were sympathetic to their situation and often gave them money or bought them food and personal items—even if the

Foreign women's life and work in the entertainment sector of Korea   167

Table 8.7 Distribution of customers by nationality (%)

	Total	The CIS	Philippines
(N)	(161)	(61)	(100)
Americans	54.6	9.0	82.9
Koreans	36.2	81.4	8.2
Migrant workers	6.3	3.0	8.3
Others	2.9	6.5	0.6
Total	100.0	100.0	100.0

GI was not the boyfriend of one of the girls. However, not all GIs are understanding or supportive and many openly abuse the women at the clubs. Kelly (Case #211, 18 years old, Philippines), for example, stated that "Often the GI would beat me before having sex with me." Gina from Club PB also recounted the types of expectations (and perceptions) her GI customers have about her job at the club. When asked what she had to do when a customer bought her a drink, she stated:

> If a customer is drunk he tries to touch you. I say, 'Don't touch me.' He says something like, 'Why? You're working at a club, right? I can do whatever I like with you.' I don't want it like this because I have no respect. I want respect.
>
> (Case #207, 26 years old, Philippines)

The women at the clubs state that they do not like South Asian customers because they do not have much money. Hanna (Case #602, 26 years old, Philippines) stated, "They smell bad." The customers from other nationalities are normally not allowed at the clubs until the GIs have returned to base to meet their nightly curfew. At Club UC, Hanna stated if there was a lockdown or if there were no GI customers, the mamasan would let customers from other nationalities enter:

> If there is a lockdown [meaning the GIs are restricted to base], the mamasan would let the migrant factory workers come into the club early. One time she forced us to go on a bar fine with two Bangladeshi guys. They smelled bad, so we told them to take a shower. While they were taking a shower we ran away back to the club.
>
> (Case #602, 26 years old, Philippines)

The women from the CIS countries and the Philippines working at kijichon clubs have a strong idea that they cater only to Americans and show aversion to entertaining Asian men or migrant workers whose social status in Korea is considered inferior to American men. In spite of the women's prejudice against migrant workers, some of the women have them as patrons or boyfriends and they sometimes end up living together.

168 D.-H. Seol and G.-S. Han

The women from the CIS countries described how shocked they were when they realized that they were supposed to perform exotic dances on stage, and how they suffered from the conflicts in relationships with their club owners, waiters, mamasans, Korean customers, or their Korean boyfriends. They often interpret these conflicts and misunderstandings as "cultural differences." They particularly understand Korean male customers' unique behaviors as part of "Korean" drinking culture.

> I cried a lot when I was working at clubs. I could not speak the language and the way they drank was too strange to me. I did not drink while sitting at the tables. Korean people were normal when they did not drink. But when they had drunk, they turned crazy. They put their hands or mike in my underwear; climbed up on the tables; and peed in front of others.
>
> (Case #103, 23 years old, Russia)

Alla, who worked at a kijichon club, heard from her mamasan that the harassment from the customers was the way Koreans were. She was told to accustom herself to the way it was because she had come to Korea to work.

> I saw Americans two days and after that only Koreans, Bangladeshis, and Pakistanis came to the club. They forced us to drink. Especially the Koreans made us drink and groped our bodies. They bit us, pinched us, and hit us on the heads. Mamasan said it was OK and it was 'the Korean way of love.' She told us that we would get accustomed to it. Her husband was always drinking at night as well.
>
> (Case #101, 25 years old, Russia)

Although migrant women think the Korean male culture of drinking "very strange," they accustom themselves to it and develop their own strategies of survival.

> Korean men drink a lot and get drunk very quickly. Sometimes they lose themselves at clubs. When we get customers who are very rude or violent, we make him drink a lot till he sleeps. At most of the clubs we are supposed to serve them at the table until they leave but we are allowed to leave after two hours when they get very irritating or violent. We can still get our money for the table. Usually customers want to touch the girls and hug them. When it gets uncontrollable, we ask questions to them about their families and wives so that they talk more. Or we start singing or go to the restroom. In extreme cases, we bring the club managers and solve the problem.
>
> (Case #115, 28 years old, Russia)

Prostitution ("bar fine")

Betty (Case #305, 23 years old, Philippines), who was rescued from Club XY in a kijichon area, wrote in her diary of April 3, 2002, "My goodness! The work we

Foreign women's life and work in the entertainment sector of Korea 169

have to do here is prostitution. We are all frightened realizing this." It is not easy for the women who identify themselves as entertainers to accept sexual services as part of their regular job. Most of the participants in the interview had not been informed beforehand of the sexual service of the so called "bar fine" or "go out" that they were to provide, and have very negative perceptions of it because they are forced by the club owner or manager to perform the sexual service against their will. However, they cannot avoid such services as the club owners would abuse them, shouting, "When you came here [Korea], making money is most important, isn't it?" and force them to "go out." Veronika from Uzbekistan recalls her first experience when she was asked to go out with a customer while working at a kijichon club:

> Mr. Kang told us when we were in Tashkent, 'All you have to do is just dance, no drink, no sex.' But mamasan had a different story when we started working at the club. One day she told me to go out on a bar fine and I said no. Then she told me, 'Do you know how much I pay to keep you? I pay 1,200,000 won to your manager every month.' My salary was 470,000 won. That was the first time I ever knew that the manager was making such a lot of money from me.
>
> (Case #110, 23 years old, Uzbekistan)

In the case mentioned above, the club owner takes it for granted that he has the right to use the bodies of the women because he pays money to the women's managers in addition to the regular salary to the women. Agency managers tend to persuade the club owners not to force the women to "go out" when they do not want to, but at the same time they persuade or threaten the women to comply with whatever the club owners demand. If the women refuse to comply with what they are told to do, the managers usually transfer them to another club.

The bar fine can generally be arranged on demand of customers for a certain amount of payment and on "special" occasions the club owners arrange it without any payment. Milena (Case #114, 25 years old, Russia) stated, "When they are short of money, some girls would deal with customers by themselves and go out with them." These cases are where the women have prior experiences of working at Korean clubs and are working at a club in Seoul where they can move around on their own without being supervised. Ksenia, who was forced to provide sexual services to the club owner's friend or a person in power in that area, states:

> It was forced only when they were important customers. You would have trouble if you don't go out. But I was never paid for it. One of the girls was kicked out of the club for good for refusing to go out. They had promised to pay us for that but we never got anything.
>
> (Case #108, 25 years old, Russia)

Irina was positioned at a kijichon club. She explains how she was "tricked" into signing a voluntary pledge for bar fines:

I was not able to communicate with the customer but I was still sitting at the table drinking with him. Then mamasan asked me to approach her. She said the Bangladeshi man I was drinking with wanted to 'buy' me for one day. She also said that everybody did it and there was nothing to be afraid of. Her daughter-in-law was a Russian and she made her translate for me. 'That customer loves you so much that he wants to go around with you. It is not sleeping with him. Follow him with Lena as he is accompanied with his friend as well.' So I was about to go out and she handed me a piece of paper and asked me to sign it. They made me write in Russian: 'I voluntarily go out on a bar fine.' Then mamasan's son wrote the same sentence in Korean at the bottom. As I asked them why I was supposed to write it, they asked me back, 'What if somebody blames us for forcing you later? That's why.' I never knew it was illegal and I was responsible for it if caught by the police. Nobody told me that prostitution was banned in Korea. I just did what they told me to. The first month was terrible. I rarely slept at my place, as I was always on a bar fine. During the weekends, I went on two to three bar fines a day. I had no time even to take a shower in between and mamasan was making me hurry as there was always another man waiting when I came back from one. Now she was forcing me to go on bar fines, saying, 'Do well when you have sex with them so that we can keep them coming back.' Customers said that they paid a lot of money but I never got anything for selling juice and going out on a bar fine. Mamasan would tell me that she deducted the money for what she spent for me, such as on costumes.

(Case #107, 29 years old, Russia)

Daria is from Vladivostok. She says that women are sometimes "lent" to other agencies and forced to prostitute when there is a great demand of women. "My agency sometimes lends girls to other agencies. And they make it clear not to talk about it to others because it was prostitution work." (Case #103, 23 years old, Russia)

Generally, the women hate Korean customers the most. Ann (Case #201, 27 years old, Philippines) fled from Club YW in Songtan, Gyeonggi province, with four other Filipinas in 2002. She had a lot to say about bar fines. She says Korean customers are extremely violent and always want sex. Once she had escaped from a man on a bar fine as he was too drunk. Another time, she had a quarrel with her mamasan when she made Ann go out for very little money. When she was forced to go out she pretended she was having her period in order to avoid sex: "I was wearing panty liner that day and I spread tomato sauce on it to make it look like blood. It was very unpleasant and sticky but was much better than having sex with him." (Case #201, 27 years old, Philippines)

Ann used to have conversations with her colleagues about bar fines, whether it would be OK to go out if you like the customers. Her colleagues would say to her, "We are not prostitutes." Whenever they said that, her mamasan would yell at them not to say such a thing. Joan, who worked at Club VD in Songtan, shares the same opinion of Korean customers: "They are rude. They are extremely drunk when

Foreign women's life and work in the entertainment sector of Korea 171

they come to our club and they try to touch our bodies. They want bar fines but we don't do that. We never do as they want." (Case #210, 23 years old, Philippines)

The clubs the women refer to as "good clubs" are those where they do not force bar fines. "Most cases we sold juice. We played billiards or cards with the customers. They did not force us to drink. They have gin-Coke and we pour them. They did not force bar fines. It was the best." (Case #101, 25 years old, Russia)

The women "break from prostitution" when they get a boyfriend, a partner to live with, or get married. When they get a boyfriend, whether it is a Korean or a Bangladeshi, they are required to quit the club. Then they look for factory work or stay at home and do housework. Veronika (Case #110, 25 years old, Uzbekistan) met her Ghanaian partner when she was working in Paju, Gyeonggi province, for the first time. She is now working at a factory and living with him. She is a typical case of breaking away from clubs.

> I was new in Korea and did not know anything. One day I went to a shop to charge money for my cell phone and Mark, who happened to be there, helped me. We met several times afterward. Once he visited me at the club and I was drunk that time. He told me to stop working there. The other day when I was feeling ill because of the drinks, he again told me to stop working there. So I asked him to help me escape. At dawn he came to the place where I was staying and I fled with my bags. So we started living together at his place and now I am working at a factory.
>
> (Case #110, 25 years old, Uzbekistan)

However, those who changed their job from the entertainment business to others feel insecure as they work illegally and the workload at factories is quite heavy. One tells of her hardships:

> I have worked at this factory for three months but I still find the work very hard. They shift the working hours every week. If you work during the day this week, you work during the night next week. I had always wanted to lose weight but I guess I should not be all happy for losing 6 kg after this short time.
>
> (Case #113, 27 years old, Uzbekistan)

Breaking away from clubs is a possible option when the women make use of their private network such as boyfriends. However, it is only a temporary solution, as they have no alternatives other than leading an unstable life as illegal migrant workers, repeatedly shifting between temporary employment and unemployment.

Working conditions

The women usually work from 6 p.m. to 3 a.m. without any break. The work always starts at the same time, but as long as the customers stay, they have to work until 4 or 5 in the morning. The average working hours of the women are 8.37 hours on weekdays and 9.76 hours on weekends. By regional groups, Filipinas' working

172   D.-H. Seol and G.-S. Han

hours are 7.89 on weekdays and 10.34 hours on weekends, and those of the women from the CIS countries are 8.90 hours on weekdays and 8.92 hours on weekends. It suggests that Filipinas' work hours can vary significantly, depending on the days of the week.

The hours women work at kijichon clubs vary from a minimum of six hours per night during the week and seven to eight hours per night during weekends to an extremely high 14 hours per night during the week to 18 hours during weekends. On weekday nights women would normally start to work between 5 and 6 p.m. and finish at midnight or 1 a.m. During weekends, however, the women normally start to work at 1 or 2 p.m. and could finish anywhere between 2 and 7 a.m. the next day. No Filipina participant in this research ever received any overtime pay for working these longer hours, even though a standard employment contract for the women normally states that overtime would be paid at the prevailing rate in Korea. As with exercising the right to end their contracts early or receive the salary agreed to in their contracts, the overtime clause in their contracts was, without exception, not upheld.

At Club YA where a Filipina participant was working, working hours were particularly long. From Friday through Sunday the women worked approximately 15 hours a night (from 2 p.m. to 5 a.m.), and on weeknights from 4 p.m. to 2 a.m. Kelly (Case #211, 18 years old, Philippines), who had worked at this club, said that the girls slept on average less than five hours a night on weekends and always felt tired. None of the clubs paid the women overtime for the exceptionally long hours of work.

Among the women engaged in the interviews, no one could keep their working hours or have day offs as their contracts state. Inna, who came to Korea in June 2003 from Kyrgyzstan and was working at a kijichon club, said the hardest thing while working in Korea was "working overtime" and described her daily life as follows:

> The contract says we work from 6 p.m. to midnight. But they make us work from 1 p.m. to 3 a.m. in the morning. If you are working at a club in Korea, your life is always the same every day. You finish your work at 3 a.m. and get a shower, and then it's already 4 or 5 a.m. because we don't have enough showers and it takes long until it's your turn after other girls. So we go to bed around 5 a.m. Clubs open around 1 p.m. Then he [the club manager] comes to open the club and wakes us up. "Hey, wake up," says he along with some violent words. "Get up! Get dressed and come down quickly!" We don't have enough time to get dressed and put on makeup. "You are all dead!" He says we are all fat and there is no need to eat. The bar is downstairs, and we work there until 5 to 6 p.m. Then we go upstairs again and change into miniskirts and boots in a minute. The work continues until 3 a.m. Any club, it is the same.
> (Case #106, 24 years old, Kyrgyzstan)

At clubs catering to Korean customers, the women are required to go outside for one or two more hours when their club work finishes at 2 or 3 a.m. to distribute leaflets advertising the club.

Foreign women's life and work in the entertainment sector of Korea   173

We work from 8 p.m. to 3 a.m. But if you are new to this club or the club is just starting business, you have to work extra to distribute leaflets on the streets for about a week with the waiters. They take you to a dinner when the promotion finishes.

(Case #113, 27 years old, Uzbekistan)

The women working at Korean clubs have only one day off during New Year's holidays and another on Memorial Day, and the women at kijichon clubs have one day off a month. Thus, only a few have more than one day off a month. To the question on the average days off a month they get, 36.8 percent of the participants answered as having "no day off." Those taking "one day off" a month was the same, 36.8 percent.

Among the women from the CIS countries, 52.9 percent take "no day off," while 44.4 percent of Filipinas take "one day off". Interestingly, those taking "three days off" or "four days off" were not found among Filipinas but comprised up to 11.8 percent of the women from CIS countries.

Even though one can have a day off, it cannot be scheduled beforehand. The women would not be told they are having a day off until the morning of that day, thus they would have no time to arrange any outing or activity, such as meeting their boyfriends. Several women also complained that a day off meant only until 10 p.m. in the evening, at which time they would have to be back at the club and ready to start work, which means that in effect they did not really have a full day off.

Generally, the women have some free time during any normal working day, usually between noon and three in the afternoon, when they could go out of the clubs as they please. Some of the participants stated that they were not free to go out unaccompanied by someone from the club, who the women referred to as a "bodyguard." Even the women who could go out unaccompanied during their free time would be monitored while out since the club owner or manager would call them on their cell phones to check where they were, and often they were subject to a penalty if they returned to the club or their apartment later than the time allowed by the club owner. Table 8.8 shows the responses to the question whether they were free to leave their club during their free time.

As a result of extremely long working hours, few, if any, day offs, and limited free time, women complained of constant fatigue. Long working hours and limited

Table 8.8 Freedom to go out during free time (%)

	Total	*The CIS*	*Philippines*
(N)	*(163)*	*(70)*	*(93)*
Yes	61.3	71.4	53.8
No	38.7	28.6	46.2
Total	100.0	100.0	100.0

174   D.-H. Seol and G.-S. Han

Table 8.9 Desired job in Korea (%)

	Total	The CIS	Philippines
(N)	(47)	(9)	(38)
Factory worker	87.2	66.7	92.1
Housewife	4.3	11.1	2.6
Restaurant worker	2.1	11.1	.0
Others	6.4	11.1	5.3
Total	100.0	100.0	100.0

free time also meant that meal times were disrupted and irregular, with women often eating their evening meal after finishing work (around 1 a.m.) or during work time when the club was quiet (usually early in the evening). Many women stated that they only had one meal a day because they got up too late for breakfast and were not permitted to eat at night while working.

The hardships the women experience while working at clubs affect their future plans. As shown above, they want to return home or find other jobs. For future jobs in Korea, "factory workers" is the most popular among both of the groups (see Table 8.9). This result indicates the unfavorable circumstances in which the women workers find themselves in Korea.

Income

The average basic salary is 466,400 won among the women from the CIS countries and 416,100 won among Filipinas (see Table 8.10). Most of the women or 84.5 percent get their income on a monthly basis. Weekly (9.2 percent), daily (9.9 percent), and irregular payments (7.0 percent) are usually accompanied with a monthly payment.

Table 8.10 Composition of monthly income (10,000 won (%))

	Total		The CIS		Philippines	
(N)	(148)		(66)		(82)	
Base salary	43.85	(55.9)	46.64	(58.6)	41.61	(53.7)
Juice or drink commission	15.71	(20.0)	.71	(0.9)	27.78	(35.8)
Table fee	9.18	(11.7)	20.18	(25.6)	.33	(0.4)
Commission on bar fine	5.30	(6.8)	2.82	(3.5)	7.30	(9.4)
Tip	4.42	(5.6)	9.26	(11.6)	.52	(0.7)
Monthly total	78.47	(100.0)	79.61	(100.0)	77.55	(100.0)

Foreign women's life and work in the entertainment sector of Korea 175

Two of the Filipinas working at a club in Gunsan, Jeonbuk province, with whom the research team met were not working that evening. They explained, "Mamasan is sick today. That's why the club is closed now. But she took 60,000 won from each of us for having one day off, even though it was because of her that we don't work today!" According to them, this commonly happens at clubs in Gunsan. At all the clubs in a kijichon area, the women can take a day off only if she pays the bar fine for herself, resulting in a deduction from her income or increasing her debt. Ann from Songtan, Gyeonggi province, tells the researchers a similar story:

> I had to pay US$200 for my own night off. I never have a night off. I had to pay on my own to have one night off. In May I went on a lunch date and ate at McDonald's with a guy. It was 12 o'clock in the afternoon and we only ate in a restaurant! I got a US$200 penalty for that! Oh, if I get drunk at work, it's a US$200 penalty. That happened in May. The penalties equaled all the money that was owed to me in May [for drinks and bar fines]. I never got paid because of the penalty. I took a day off and that was when I had that date.
>
> (Case #201, 27 years old, Philippines)

Tipping is a general practice at Korean clubs, and the women from the CIS countries live on their tips. However, it is very rare to get a tip at kijichon clubs. One of the participants in the in-depth-interview stated that she got a 40,000 won tip from a Korean customer for her sexual service. As explained above, the women working at kijichon clubs earn money by selling juice to customers or their boyfriends or rely on the money they give the women, rather than on tips for providing special services.

While some clubs force the women to go out on bar fines or to VIP rooms, others leave the women to decide by themselves. If, however, the women do not provide sexual services, they suffer financially. Gemma, one of the respondents, states:

> My boss doesn't push me to go on a bar fine. She says, 'It's up to you. If you want to make extra money then go—it's not my decision.' I don't go on bar fines, but I don't have any money because of that.
>
> (Case #203, 26 years old, Philippines)

Besides the amount of money the women actually get every month, forced savings is another problem. The club owners open a savings account under the women's names but only the club owner or the manager can withdraw the money. For instance, the women cannot withdraw her money because the bank books bear the club owner's signature. If the women raised objection to this forced savings, the response was that it was just for the women's sake and that they would get it back when they returned to their home countries. Not all the clubs force the women to save their salary. It seems as though it is for the women's sake, but actually this practice forces the women to provide sexual services by leaving them always short of money.

Of the respondents, 15.3 percent answered that their salary was kept in compulsory savings. The fact that more Filipinas (18.9 percent) are forced to save their salary than the women from the CIS countries (9.7 percent) suggests that the

176   *D.-H. Seol and G.-S. Han*

practice is more common among the clubs in kijichon areas. The amount of forced savings is on average 397,700 won a month. Again, Filipinas are forced to save more than the women from the CIS countries: 473,100 won and 196,700 won, respectively.

Conclusion: aftermath of the 2004 Special Laws on Sex Trade

Korea has been a destination country for human trafficking since the late 1990s. From that time the Association of Special Tourism Business (ASTB) provided Filipina women to the clubs in U.S. military camp towns. This association imported foreign women disguised as entertainers. They abused the Entertainer's visa, originally introduced for artists, sports stars, and professional entertainers such as musicians, dancers, and actors. ASTB recruited 1,093 women from Russia and the Philippines between 1996 and 1999. One club owner in Songtan, Gyeonggi province, a U.S. military camp town, said that he paid 700,000 won (approximately US$730) for the "introduction fee" of five women.[5]

The president of ASTB fabricated official documents and accepted 160 million won (US$165,000) for his brokerage commission. He was prosecuted for fabricating documents, not for human trafficking. ASTB changed its name to the Association of Tourism Facilities Business for Foreigners in 2003.

The Ministry of Justice stopped issuing E-6 visas to dancers working in clubs in June 2003. The club owners and brokers responded to the new visa policy by using the singer category to get E-6 visas. Migrant brokers imported foreign women as singers, avoiding the government's prohibition of issuing visas to dancers. A Korean newspaper reported that most foreign singers working in the clubs did not sing by themselves. They lip-synched to taped music. Russian women who got E-6 visas as singers actually sang only twice in three days, but normally danced every day in clubs.[6] The Korea Media Rating Board, which rates foreign artists' performances in Korea so that they can get E-6 visas, said that if performers had proper documents they could not refuse their application. The Korean government should pay more careful attention to the management of E-6 visas.

Recently, transnational marriage has become a route for human trafficking. The Seoul Metropolitan Police Agency announced the criminal investigation of a human trafficking case on November 27, 2005. A Korean man who is the owner of a barbershop recruited Mongolian women seeking job opportunities abroad. He used international marriage visas for importing the women. He forced them to prostitute themselves at his barbershop and robbed them of money. He told the women that if they worked at his barbershop they could make several thousand dollars per month and forced them to prostitute themselves more than 8,000 times.[7] Human trafficking brokers paid money for false marriages and foreign women had to pay for this by working as prostitutes. In this case, four Mongolian women were trafficked and confined without their passports by traffickers. There are other cases of false marriage. Some foreign women disappeared from their family and began to work in the sex trade shops by their own decision. They used an international marriage to get an entrance visa and work in Korea.[8]

Foreign women's life and work in the entertainment sector of Korea 177

The Trafficking in Persons Report 2007 of the U.S. Department of State also criticized current business activities of Korean transnational marriage agencies. Marriage brokers' advertisements, such as "they never run away." are cited as important evidence of human trafficking. It means foreign marriage migrants do not have the right to make decisions in their marriage relationship, such as getting divorced.

Two main changes have occurred in the patterns of the sex trade in Korea since the introduction of the Special Laws on Sex Trade in 2004. First, the number of foreign women prostitutes has decreased, but they continue to operate in the hidden sector. Because entertainer's visas were blocked by the Korean government, the brokers seem to abuse tourist and marriage visas. There are continuing police investigations into the prostitution of foreign women. Brothel owners use Internet chat sites or distribute leaflets to locate customers. Russian women who have been arrested and deported re-enter with different names.

Second, the prostitution of foreign women in U.S. military camp towns has not changed. According to the Korean National Assembly's parliamentary inspection of the administration in 2004, there were 899 prostitutes in five U.S. military camp towns—Uijeongbu, Dongducheon, Paju, Pyeongtaek and Songtan in Gyeonggi province. Among them, 88 (9.8 percent) were Koreans, and 811 (90.2 percent) were foreigners—81 Russians and 730 Filipina. Most of foreigners are victims of human trafficking. They came to Korea to make money without the knowledge that they might be forced to work as prostitutes. Even though they can ask the help of the Korean government, foreign women tend not to report their cases. They have to support family members at home, so instead they choose to stay and work in Korea.

As the reports of the U.S. Department of State indicate, Korea has tried to establish a system to prevent human trafficking. Even though human trafficking has not disappeared in Korea, the Korean government and civil societies have contributed to a change in the situation. These efforts are recognized by Korea being rated as a Tier 1 country in the Trafficking in Persons Report. As the efforts to exterminate human trafficking increase, so do the number of criminal investigations. Therefore, the actual number of criminal cases does not represent the current human rights conditions. Human trafficking proceeds based on hidden connections. In this regard, the efforts of the Korean government to root out human trafficking are noteworthy.

Notes

1 *Trafficking in Persons Report 2001*, U.S. Department of State, 2001, p. 97.
2 *Trafficking in Person Report 2007*, U.S. Department of State, 2007, p. 129.
3 Case #601 and #602 were interviewed by the Korea Church Women United (KCWU) research team in 2002.
4 D.-H. Seol, H.-Y. Choi, and G.-S. Han, *Foreign Workers' Human Rights in Korea*, p. 55.
5 Y.-H. Oh, "Philippine Hostesses Imported to the U.S. Military Camp Towns in Korea."
6 "Russian Hostesses Admitted as Singers," *The Hankyoreh*, July 15, 2005.
7 Seoul Metropolitan Police Agency, "Mongolian Women Having Fake Marriage with Korean Men Were Enforced to Do Prostitution at a Corrupt Barbershop," Press Release No.1054, November 27, 2005.
8 Korean Broadcast System, *News 9*, October 17, 2006.

References

Association for Foreign Workers' Human Rights (FWR). (2000) *Report on Russian Migrant Women in Entertainment Sites in Busan*, Busan: FWR.

Back, Jae Hee. (2000) "A Study on the Migrant Women into Korean Sex Industry: With a Focus on Filipinas in Military Camp Towns." Unpublished MA thesis, Department of Women's Studies, Ewha Woman's University, Seoul, Korea. (In Korean)

Back, Jae Hee. (2002) "I'm an Entertainer, I'm not a Sex Worker." in *Courageous Women Riding on Wolves*, ed. Magdalena House for Women of the Street. Seoul: Samin Books, pp. 191–228. (In Korean)

Cheng, Sealing. (2000) "Assuming Manhood: Prostitution and Patriotic Passions in Korea," *East Asia: An International Quarterly* 18, no. 4: 40–78.

Cheng, Sealing. (2002) "Trafficked Women, GIs and Love in US Military Camp Towns in Korea," in *Courageous Women Riding on Wolves*, ed. Magdalena House for Women of the Street, Seoul: Samin Books, pp. 229–55. (In Korean)

Han, Geon-Soo, and Dong-Hoon Seol. (2006) *Matchmaking Agencies in Korea and Their Regulation Policies*. Gwacheon: Ministry of Health and Welfare. (In Korean)

Kang, Ok-Kyung, Hyun Sun Kim, and Su-Kyung Jeon. (2001) *Survey of Prostitution in Gyeonggi Province and the Anti-prostitution Policy Research*. Dongducheon: Saewoomtuh, the Center for Prostituted Women. (In Korean)

Kim, Eun-Shil. (2002) "Globalization, Nation-State and Women's Sexualities," *Women's Studies Review* 19: 29–46. (In Korean)

Kim, Hyun Mee. (2001) "Is Global Society a New Form of Caste Society? The Spread of Global Capitalism and the Emergence of Gendered Class," *Radical Review* 7 (Spring): 76–96. (In Korean)

Korea Church Women United (KCWU). (1999) *The Fieldwork Report on Trafficked Women in Korea*, Seoul: KCWU. (In Korean)

Korea Church Women United (KCWU). (2002) *The 2nd Fieldwork Report on Trafficked Women in Korea: With a Focus on Filipinas in Military Camp Towns*, Seoul: KCWU. (In Korean)

Lee, June J. H. (2002) *A Review of Data on Trafficking in the Republic of Korea*. Geneva: International Organization for Migration.

Lee, June J. H. (2005) "Human Trafficking in East Asia: Current Trends, Data Collection, and Knowledge Gaps." *International Migration* 43, no. 1/2: 165–201.

Lee, Kum-Yeon Cecilia. (2002) "The Realities and Solutions of International Trafficking in Foreign Women in Korea," in *Proceedings from a Round-table Conference for Reporting the Realities of Prostitution in US Military Camp Towns in Korea, and Stopping Trafficking in Women*. Seoul: KWAU, Saewoomtuh, the Center for Prostituted Women, and HRSWM, pp. 25–32. (In Korean)

MacIntyre, Donald. (2002) "Base Instincts: Filipina and Russian Women Are Being Sold into Sexual Slavery in the Seedy Bars and Nightclubs that Serve US Military Bases in South Korea." *Time*, Asia Edition, August 12.

Oh, Yeon-Ho. (1998) "Filipina Hostesses Imported to the U.S. Military Camp Towns in Korea." *Monthly Mal [The Voice of People]* 143 (May): 162–73.

Salt, John, and Stein, Jeremy. (1997) "Migration as a Business: The Case of Trafficking," *International Migration* 35(4): 467–94.

Seol, Dong-Hoon, Hong-Yop Choi, and Geon-Soo Han. (2002) *Foreign Workers' Human Rights in Korea*, Seoul: National Human Rights Commission of Korea. (In Korean)

Seol, Dong-Hoon, Hyun Mee Kim, Geon-Soo Han, Hyun Ung Goh, and Sallie Wilton Yea.

(2003a) *Research on Migrant Women in Entertainment Sector in Korea*, Seoul: Ministry of Gender Equality. (In Korean)

Seol, Dong-Hoon, Hyun Mee Kim, Geon-Soo Han, Hyun Ung Goh, and Sallie Wilton Yea. (2003b) *Foreign Women Entertainers' Work and Life in Korea*, Seoul: Korean Sociological Association. (In Korean)

Seol, Dong-Hoon. (2004) "International Sex Trafficking in Women in Korea: Its Causes, Consequences, and Countermeasures," *Asian Journal of Women's Studies* 10, no. 2: 7–47.

U.S. Department of State. (2001) *Trafficking in Persons Report 2001*, Washington, DC: U.S. Department of State.

U.S. Department of State. (2007) *Trafficking in Persons Report 2007*, Washington, DC: U.S. Department of State.

UN Office on Drugs and Crime (UNODC). (2006) *Trafficking in Persons: Global Patterns, 2006*, New York: UNODC.

9 Trafficking in persons in the Americas

An overview

John T. Picarelli

In examining trafficking in persons in the Americas, we find the one form of transnational crime that is both historically and empirically significant. The trade in human beings is closely related to the historical evolution of every country in the Americas, given that trade in human beings plagued the Americas for more than 600 years. The overlap between the trade in slaves and colonial policies continues to leave its mark today. Markets for slavery operate today as they did in the 1700s. Trafficking routes follow the same patterns as the routes slavers used in the 1800s. Debt bondage schemes continue to ensnare migrants as they did in the 1900s.

The combination of socio-economic conditions, geopolitical situations, historical legacies, and organizational capabilities provides the way to explore contemporary trafficking in the Americas. The opening section explores how the transatlantic slave trade and other forms of the trade in human beings left an indelible legacy on the operation and organization of the contemporary trade in human beings. The next section outlines the socio-economic and geopolitical factors that also contribute to the contemporary trade in three regional settings—Latin America and the Caribbean, South America, and North America. The third section focuses on exploring how the trade is organized, providing examples of the two most prominent types of trafficking networks in the Americas. South and North American trade in human beings is active, widespread, and comprises numerous forms of exploitation throughout the region.

A short history of trafficking in the Americas

Trafficking in persons has a long history in the Americas. The trade in human beings in the Americas began legally in 1502 when Portuguese traders brought the first African slaves to the Caribbean. Well into the 1600s, Portuguese traders dominated the trade in human beings, transporting slaves from Portuguese-controlled slave ports in present-day Angola not only to their own colonies in Brazil but also to Spanish colonies throughout the Americas. By the seventeenth century, more European powers had joined the trade and expanded its reach to the Caribbean and North America. By the end of the 1600s and throughout the 1700s, mercantilist competition between the great European powers translated into vast increases in the number of African slaves brought to and sold in the Americas. Reflecting its

Trafficking in persons in the Americas 181

rise to prominence as the leading power of the time, Britain became the dominant slave trading nation in the 1700s. All told, the European powers trafficked close to 10 million African slaves into the Americas between 1502 and 1807.[1]

The trade in human beings underwent radical change in the 1800s. The global abolitionist movement that arose in the late 1700s managed to bring about a relatively swift change in the trade in human beings, followed closely by abolition of chattel slavery. By the early 1800s, the major European powers agreed to end their participation in the slave trade. Great Britain set the tone by banning the slave trade in 1807, closely followed by the United States in 1808 and the Netherlands in 1814. By the 1830s, a global prohibition regime against the trade in African slaves and slavery in general had begun to take hold,[2] although slaves already in the United States remained in bondage.

The end of chattel slavery did not bring an immediate end to the trade in African slaves nor did it end the trade in human beings for other forms of servitude. Rather, the trade in human beings began an evolution in the 1800s that is still felt today in the Americas and indeed worldwide. European states organized a trade in indentured servants from India and debt bondsmen from China as partial substitutes for African slaves in the American colonies. Although European states tried to remove the abuses in this system through regulation, colonial masters and human traders by and large returned to the egregious abuses of the African slave trade.[3] But the trade in chattel slaves also contributed to the formation of sex trafficking routes. The slave trade was dominated by men in colonial ports along the Atlantic who themselves created a significant demand for the importation and enslavement of women for prostitution.[4]

State involvement in the trade in human beings to the Americas had by and large ended by World War I. Yet its four century legacy continues to influence contemporary trafficking. The belief structures that legitimized and justified the trade in human beings are an important though often overlooked factor in slavery's longevity. A market is a social institution that provides information to facilitate purchasing and selling, and thus even slave markets are embedded in social structures.[5] In the Americas, traders in human beings believed that Africans were natural slaves and thus predestined for slavery. It was Aristotle who first opined that a natural slave was "a barbarian whose inclination was to defer and who was distinguished by brawn, not brain," and thus required "the direction of those who were gifted with . . . intelligence and civilization."[6] Reproduced throughout history, this belief allowed traders in the Americas to determine "who is to be considered an outsider and therefore enslavable and who is an insider and thus unenslavable."[7] In 1700 a Massachusetts slaveholder, Judge John Saffin, wrote a pamphlet defending the right to hold slaves by noting that since Africans enslave one another for sale to the British, it proves them to be natural slaves worthy of trade and sale. Traffickers would later use such arguments to justify the enslavement of Indian indentured servants, Italian debt bondsmen, and even women from Eastern Europe for sexual exploitation.

A network of clandestine traders existed during the transatlantic trade and serves as the precedent for contemporary traffickers. Throughout the transatlantic slave

182 *J. T. Picarelli*

trade, small groups of entrepreneurs participated in an illicit trade in slaves in order to avoid paying taxes or abiding by regulations. In the 1640s, the Dutch began smuggling slaves into Spanish colonies at a time when the Portuguese held a vast majority of the trade. In the 1670s, Bermuda served as a black market transshipment station where slaves were offloaded from ships transiting to other markets and later shipped to the colonies commanding the highest prices for slaves. But the illicit trade in human beings expanded to become the majority of the trade in the 1800s as states began to crack down on the trade in human beings. For example, between 1821 and 1833, more than 300 clandestine French slave traders brought some 105,000 African slaves into the French West Indies.[8]

History is not only relevant when exploring the trade in human beings in the Americas; it is required. The sheer volume of literature written on the historical trade in human beings is a testament to its importance historically and currently. The markets, the routes, the organizations, and even the beliefs of traffickers have historical resilience and shape contemporary trafficking. The historical perspective combined with analysis of socio-economic and geopolitical factors provides an important perspective to understand contemporary trafficking in persons.

Scope of human trafficking

The depth and breadth of the historical trade in human beings in the Americas gave way to significant forms of trafficking in modern times. Poverty and unemployment, the most frequently cited root causes of trafficking, are especially important in explaining trafficking. As women increasingly become heads of households in the Americas, they and their offspring are placed in enhanced risk of encountering traffickers.[9] Other factors that are often cited as root causes of trafficking in the region include low rates of education, high rates of illiteracy, and corruption. Geopolitics also has a role to play in trafficking in the Americas. The high rates of migrant smuggling from south to north in the Americas serve as a chronic source of individuals at risk of befalling to traffickers. A number of trafficking cases in the United States have involved victims who were sold into bondage by smugglers.[10]

Exploring the regional mixture of historical precedents and modern realities has helped shape the way trafficking manifests itself throughout the different regions of the Americas. In South America, one finds not only supply and transit states but also demand for trafficking, a reflection of its history as a major destination for both labor and sexual slaves throughout the centuries. In the Caribbean, the rise of the tourism industry as a primary source of national income has resulted in expanded demand for prostitutes satisfied by sex trafficking. Finally, North America's high demand for both sex and labor trafficking reflects its historical legacy as a major market for human traders as much as its socio-economic primacy in the Americas.

South America

Trafficking is pervasive in South America. The International Labour Organization estimates that 25,000 Brazilians are victims of labor trafficking and 75,000

Trafficking in persons in the Americas 183

more Brazilian women and girls in Europe are victims of sex trafficking. South America represents a region with a mix of source, transit, and destination countries. Trafficking routes crisscross South America, with numerous routes heading into and out of the region as well. Some syndicates traffic human beings into South America from the Caribbean and Latin America, while other victims are sent from South America to North America, Europe, and Asia.

Table 9.1 presents the countries that serve as source, transit, or destination for trafficked persons. The prevalence of certain forms of trafficking is presented. The table reveals that sexual exploitation is the predominant form of trafficking in South America. In 2002, for example, the foreign minister of the Dominican Republic asked the Argentine government to investigate traffickers promising Dominican women paying jobs as domestic servants but enslaving them in brothels upon arrival in Buenos Aires.[11] Likewise, Colombian police arrested Claudia Milena-Serna in 2003 on charges that she was recruiting women in southwestern Colombia for traffickers who were sending the women to Japan for sexual exploitation.[12]

Although sex trafficking is most often mentioned in Table 9.1, a fair amount of labor exploitation also occurs in South America. Kevin Bales documented widespread slavery in the Brazilian mining and charcoal production industries, the latter feeding the increasing demand for domestic steel production.[13] A 2001 intelligence report from the Canadian Consulate in Miami alerted its staff that children from Haiti were being trafficked into Suriname via the Caribbean island of Curacao and forced to work on farms for no pay.

Table 9.1 Forms and routes of trafficking in South America

	Routes			*Victims*		*Types of Trafficking*	
	Source	*Transit*	*Destination*	*Men*	*Women*	*Sexual*	*Labor*
Argentina			X	X	X	X	
Bolivia	X	X		X	X	X	X
Brazil	X		X	X	X	X	X
Chile	X		X	X	X	X	
Colombia	X	X			X	X	
Ecuador	X	X	X	X	X	X	X
Guyana	X	X	X		X	X	
Paraguay	X				X	X	
Peru	X				X	X	
Suriname		X	X		X	X	
Venezuela	X	X	X		X	X	

Source: U.S. Trafficking in Persons Report, 2004.

184   *J. T. Picarelli*

Table 9.1 also illustrates the geographic distribution of trafficking. The countries of South America serve primarily as source states, but roughly half of the countries are either transit or destination states as well. As evidenced in some of the examples already presented, there is indeed a market for sexual and labor exploitation within certain regions of South America. Likewise, what is not well represented in the table is that trafficking is a phenomenon that can occur within a country's borders. For example, a significant number of Brazilian victims of labor trafficking are from other regions of Brazil, and numerous Chilean children are trafficked internally for the purposes of sexual exploitation. In short, trafficking in persons in South America is largely a regional phenomenon with only limited ties to global trafficking syndicates.

Latin America and the Caribbean

Trafficking is also widespread in Central America and the Caribbean. Like South America, almost every country in the region is affected in some way or another by human trafficking. Unlike South America, however, Caribbean traffickers focus on inter-regional and international routes. Trafficking routes are tied to regional patterns of migration that pervade Latin America and the Caribbean and to the bustling tourism industry that fuels sexual exploitation and sex tourism. The strong correlation between migration flows and trafficking in this region is clearly demonstrated by the high number of countries that are used as staging areas for victims being sent to South America, the United States, or Canada. The statistics for trafficking in Central America and the Caribbean demonstrate that it is a significant problem for the region. For example, some 50,000 Dominican women overseas are suspected to be working as prostitutes, with a significant percentage being trafficking victims, while some 30,000 minors work in the Dominican Republic as prostitutes with even stronger suspicions of trafficking.[14]

Table 9.2 provides a breakdown of the predominant forms of and routes for trafficking in the region. Once again, sexual exploitation appears as the pre-eminent form of trafficking. Numerous reports point to women who are trying to migrate illegally into the United States being enslaved in Mexican brothels. In a 2002 case, U.S. authorities raided some half-dozen bars and other locations in and around Fort Worth, Texas, to liberate "scores" of Honduran women and girls who had been enslaved for sexual exploitation.[15]

Labor trafficking is another problem that plagues the region. In the Dominican Republic, large numbers of men and children are trafficked to work in agriculture, particularly in sugar cane fields—in much the same way that African men and children were enslaved in the 1700s and 1800s to work the sugar cane plantations.[16] However, to illustrate that not all labor trafficking is internal, consider the case of Juan Carlos Soto. An illegal migrant from Mexico, Soto was sentenced to 23 years in prison in January 2004 for holding women from El Salvador and Nicaragua as slaves, working them as domestic servants during the day and raping them at night.[17]

Other forms of trafficking exist in the region that are not easily represented in Table 9.2. One of the more insidious forms of trafficking that has come to

Trafficking in persons in the Americas   185

Table 9.2 Forms and routes of trafficking in Latin America and the Caribbean

	Routes			Victims		Types of Trafficking	
	Source	Transit	Destination	Men	Women	Sexual	Labor
Belize		X	X	X	X	X	X
Costa Rica		X	X		X	X	
Cuba	Internal				X	X	X
Dominican Republic	X	X	X	X	X	X	X
El Salvador	X	X	X	X	X	X	X
Guatemala	X	X	X		X	X	
Honduras	X	X			X	X	
Jamaica	Internal				X	X	
Nicaragua	X	X			X	X	
Panama		X	X		X	X	

Source: *U.S. Trafficking in Persons Report*, 2004.

light in recent years is the trafficking of infants. In 2003, authorities in Costa Rica arrested numerous members of a trafficking syndicate that was trafficking Guatemalan babies into the United States. Under the guise of an adoption agency named International Adoption Resource, the syndicate was linked to some 85 cases of infant trafficking, selling the babies for up to $80,000 in the United States and $40,000 in Japan. The trafficking syndicate had paid some $630 to $2,200 each for the babies.[18] The Caribbean is also home to extensive child sex tourism industries.[19]

Finally, Table 9.2 demonstrates that trafficking is far more differentiated in Central America and the Caribbean than in South America. The countries of Central America and the Caribbean are nearly equally source, transit, and destination countries. Their strategic location, astride migration routes into South America, the United States, and Canada, is a strong causal factor. However, the historical impact of the pervasive trade in human beings is clearly at work here as well. The trafficking of women to Spain from the Dominican Republic and other Caribbean states follows trade patterns that are hundreds of years old. In short, the trafficking in persons in Central America and the Caribbean has strong historical ties and follows historical precedents.

North America and the United States

The different historical, socio-economic, and geopolitical conditions found in the countries of North America drive significant differences in the way trafficking manifests itself. But this is not always the case. Mexico is a strong source and

186   *J. T. Picarelli*

transit state for men, women, and children for all forms of trafficking. Tied to strong migrant smuggling networks operating on the southwest border of the United States, smuggling gangs known as *coyotes* and *polleros* have been known to frequently aid or engage directly in trafficking rings.[20] In one infamous case, *US v Cadena*, a group of Mexican migrant smugglers trafficked numerous women from Mexico into the United States for sexual exploitation. The women were forced to work in brothels housed in portable trailers that followed migrant workers from Mexico working the fields in southern Florida.[21]

Canada, on the other hand, is a strong transit and destination country primarily for sexual exploitation. Liberal migration and prostitution laws have recently combined to fuel an increasing problem with trafficking into and through Canada. The Protection Project noted in its 2002 *Human Rights Report on Trafficking of Persons* that Chinese and Vietnamese trafficking syndicates paid $8,000 per head to recruiters for women to sell to brothels in Canada for $15,000 each. The liberal border security prior to September 11 also allowed sex trafficking syndicates to "circuit" trafficking victims between major U.S. and Canadian cities, thus increasing profits for the crime groups.

Trafficking in persons in North America, however, is dominated by the demand for sexual and labor trafficking in the United States. The strength of the U.S. economy, the American history with the trade, and the embedded interests of crime groups are all significant reasons that drive the trafficking of persons into the United States. Trafficking routes into the United States originate from across the globe, with the largest groups of victims arriving from Southeast Asia, the former Soviet Union, and Latin America. Few cases exist of the United States serving as a source or transit country for trafficking syndicates outside of cases of internal trafficking.

Whether for sexual or labor exploitation, trafficking syndicates are estimated to bring 50,000 men, women, and children into the United States every year for various forms of slavery. A range of recent prosecutions illustrates the widespread forms of trafficking into the United States:

- In *U.S. v. Alamin and Akhter*, a Bangladeshi couple trafficked a victim from Saudi Arabia to the United States to work for them as a live-in housekeeper and nanny, forcing the victim to perform domestic work for little or no pay. The couple repeatedly beat the victim and threatened to harm her family in Bangladesh if she ran away.[22]
- In *U.S. v. Satia and Nanji*, two defendants were convicted of holding a teenage Cameroonian girl in involuntary servitude and illegally harboring her in their home for use as a domestic servant. The defendants recruited the 14-year-old female Cameroonian national to the United States with false promises of attending a U.S. school. When the young girl arrived, she was isolated in the defendants' home and forced through threats, sexual assaults, and physical abuse to work for them for several years as their personal servant.[23]
- In *U.S. v. Sardar and Nadira Gasanov*, an Uzbek couple who worked as professors in Texas were convicted of recruiting two women from Uzbekistan into the United States under false pretenses, then pressuring them to work in strip

clubs and bars in El Paso, Texas, in order to pay back an alleged $300,000 smuggling fee. The victims were stripped of their passports and required to work seven days a week.[24]

- In *U.S. v. Quinton Williams*, a case of internal trafficking, the operator of a prostitution business transported a 16-year-old juvenile and adult victims cross-country by car to Indiana, Texas, Arizona, and Nevada, where he supervised their prostitution activities and collected and kept all of their earnings.[25]

Such cases are indicative of the breadth of trafficking found in the United States. By coincidence, each of the cases also illustrates that not all trafficking cases in the United States are perpetrated by major transnational criminal organizations.

Trafficking organizations

Trafficking in persons is a network-oriented activity comprised of numerous roles—some essential that must occur for the network to function, some that are less important, and some that are peripheral. A network is comprised of various components that can be linked in a variety of ways. The network components can be people, organizations, computers, and other physical entities, or they can be non-physical, such as roles that people assume within the network. The networks are linked usually through their communications or by transfers of money, persons, or goods. Analysts often focus on network structures to identify and understand organizations, but the idea of networks can also be applied to international transactions.

A network model of trafficking syndicates

A trafficking network can be broken down by examining the roles that various members assume within the network. The various roles can be useful as they provide flexibility in trying to model trafficking networks. For example, either persons or organizations can fulfill the roles that make up a network. These same entities can fulfill more than one role in the network. Figure 9.1 is a presentation of what a basic trafficking network could look like. The diagram demonstrates that there are two categories of network components. The core network components (inside the shaded oval on the diagram) contain the essential activities necessary for the network to function.

Other activities are sometimes also undertaken in conjunction with a trafficking network, and the network components located outside the core represent the other activities. One of the more interesting of the peripheral network components is the role of leader. A leader of a trafficking network may provide the resources, such as money, vehicles, or false documents that establish or help a trafficking network to function effectively. The leader may also oversee the operations of the trafficking network or order the kinds of victims wanted. The reason this network component is outside the core of the diagram is that leadership may not always be a unique role.

There can be different forms of trafficking in persons networks. There may be demand-driven networks. These can consist of a brothel owner requesting an

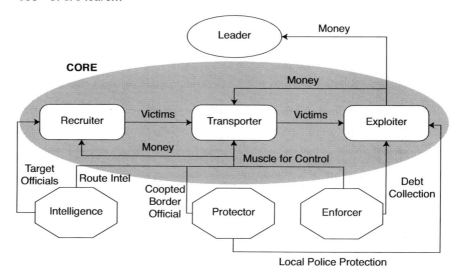

Figure 9.1 Generic human trafficking network.

infusion of new girls for his brothels or a plantation owner needing new agricultural workers from overseas. Another kind of trafficking network is a distribution network where recruiters supply domestic agents with victims. These agents then supply exploiters with laborers. When a leadership role does exist outside of the core network, it is often insulated and other members of the network may not know the identity of the person or group fulfilling that role.

Other peripheral roles may be found in larger, more sophisticated trafficking networks. A protector shields the network from law enforcement or other forms of state interference. As trafficking networks grow larger, in terms of both geographic scope and economic size, they often require protection. Protection is most often provided through corruption, but can also take the form of physical security (for example, hiring gunmen to protect assets). Enforcers often provide two important services. First, for recruiters, transporters, and exploiters, enforcers manage and control trafficked persons, often playing an especially important role in the latter stages of trafficking.[26] Violence and threats of violence are used to control the victims. Second, exploiters often call upon enforcers to serve in the capacity of debt collectors. More exploiters are needed as the size and scope of trafficking networks increase.

Finally, it is not uncommon to find an intelligence function within trafficking networks. The nature of the intelligence function may vary. For example, transporters hire border specialists who survey border security and determine the best time and place for making an illegal crossing. Exploiters also hire persons to collect background information on government or law enforcement officials to determine if they will accept bribes. The intelligence services of traffickers may also consist of a small number of persons with numerous informants and access to highly sophisticated equipment and information systems, such as radios or cell phones.

Trafficking in persons in the Americas 189

As the diagram demonstrates, the roles are connected by transactions that take place among network members. Representative transactions are illustrated in the diagram, including monetary exchanges, flows of information, and the movement and exchange of persons. The connections between network components can be tangible or intangible; therefore, the investigator of a trafficking network (as well as other forms of organized crime) should pay close attention to other related network activities, such as business dealings and phone conversations, that suspects conduct, and the investigator should include those activities in the design of the network model.

Entrepreneurial trafficking syndicates: the Mishulovich Group

Trafficking syndicates largely fall into one of two categories. Entrepreneurial trafficking organizations are small in size, with only a handful of perpetrators fulfilling one or more roles. Thus, it is not uncommon to find two or three perpetrators acting simultaneously as recruiters, transporters, and exploiters—essentially traveling abroad to recruit persons for trafficking schemes they are operating and escorting the victims to their final destination. The small size of these trafficking organizations limits the number of persons they can traffic or exploit at any one given time. Trafficking organizations are likely to conduct other illicit activities such as money laundering or document fraud. Even though entrepreneurial groups are generally tight-knit and reluctant to trust outsiders, they will engage outside specialists to perform these tasks.

Entrepreneurial groups often use simple and unsophisticated measures to traffic people. First, they are much more likely to recruit victims solely in a single country to which they are linked by prior citizenship or ethnic heritage. The victim is then trafficked to an area where they reside or maintain some form of business. Entrepreneurial networks use commercial forms of transport such as airlines, trains, or buses to move their victims. Employing seemingly legitimate methods helps to circumvent immigration controls. Entrepreneurial traffickers use many subterfuges to obtain visas for their victims. Frequently, the trafficked person is compelled to overstay their visa after they arrive in the destination state. Entrepreneurial traffickers may also exploit open and poorly patrolled borders to move people from one place to another. Although entrepreneurial trafficking groups are small in size and may only sporadically engage in trafficking, they can cause significant harm to victims and can earn substantial profits in a short period of time.

Alex Mishulovich, arrested in 1997 as the leader of a trafficking syndicate, brought women from Latvia into the United States for sexual exploitation. Mishulovich was a naturalized U.S. citizen from Russia living in the Chicago suburb of Lincolnwood. His group consisted of his wife, Rudite Pede; a cabdriver, Serguie Tcharouchine; a U.S. lawyer living in Riga, Douglas Slain; and an entrepreneur, Vadim Gorr. The victims were five women from Latvia that prosecutors referred to as Agnese, Agita, Vika, Linda, and Tatiana.[27]

Mishulovich and Tcharouchine struck upon the idea of recruiting women in Latvia to bring to the United States to work for them in strip clubs and elsewhere.

190   *J. T. Picarelli*

Both had been to Latvia before and felt that Riga was full of beautiful women susceptible to recruitment into trafficking. The prosecutors for this case believed that Tcharouchine had trafficked women before and taught Mishulovich how to do it. In October 1996, Mishulovich arrived in Latvia and hired Pede to act as his girlfriend and help him recruit the women in Riga. Mishulovich recruited women by stating that he owned a nightclub and was in need of dancers. He promised the victims an elegant lifestyle and a salary of up to $60,000 a week in the United States. Having recruited the victims, he helped them obtain U.S. tourist visas on false pretenses and then had them fly to Chicago, where they were met by Tcharouchine.

The subsequent phase of the trafficking enterprise was exploitation. Mishulovich and Tcharouchine provided false documents to local clubs to secure employment for the victims. The men forced the victims to watch the movies *Striptease* and *Showgirls* to learn how to dance erotically. The victims were disgusted with what they saw and Mishulovich threatened that his Chechen mafia friends would kill their family members if they did not comply. One woman suffered a concussion from a beating by Mishulovich. Subsequently, Mishulovich and his partners drove the women to various nightclubs on a nightly basis, picking them up after work and taking a significant portion of their earnings every night. The victims earned between $500 and $800 per night and were allowed to keep only $20 per night. By July 1997, Mishulovich began to worry that the victims would inform local authorities about him. He returned the women's passports and bought them tickets back to Latvia. A subsequent attempt to traffic women from Belarus by Mishulovich and an associate failed because the women were denied American visas. In September 1998, Mishulovich and his co-conspirators were arrested.

This case demonstrates that a small group of individuals with some local knowledge could traffic women to make significant profits. This case recalls the practices of earlier traffickers as traders in humans often historically operated as small groups of entrepreneurs.

Snakeheads, etc: a corporate trafficking model

The other major form of trafficking is that of a corporate syndicate that is often linked to a larger transnational crime group that may also engage in drugs and arms smuggling. Corporate trafficking networks contain significant numbers of perpetrators and have significant geographical breadth. Unlike entrepreneurial groups, corporate trafficking syndicates are comprised of crime groups that each perform a specific role or roles in the network. Moreover, these networks require other illicit services in order to operate. Such services include protection, enforcement, document fraud, money laundering, and intelligence collection.

The major transnational networks traffic their victims differently from the smaller entrepreneurial groups. Transnational networks move larger numbers of trafficked persons and operate on a continuous basis. Corporate groups are more innovative as they are constantly searching for new routes and additional ports of entry to exploit. To support their activities, they need to collect and analyze intelligence. The transnational groups use numerous trafficking routes to service multiple destinations and

Trafficking in persons in the Americas 191

transport significant numbers of victims. This heterogeneity of trafficking routes increases the potential that the traffickers will exploit the same routes as traffickers of illicit commodities. To increase profitability, the groups may simultaneously engage in other criminal acts along with the trafficking.

An excellent illustration of the corporate model was brought to light in April 2000 when U.S. authorities discovered a sophisticated global trafficking syndicate bringing Chinese men and women into the United States for labor and sexual exploitation.[28] The syndicate was organized and led by a Triad crime group located in China's Fujian Province. The trafficking process for this particular group began with recruiting migrants wishing to enter the United States illegally. A Snakehead gang located in the city of Fuzhou in China's Fujian Province recruited the migrants, who were willing to pay a fee of $37,000 to the Snakeheads for transport and smuggling into the United States. Figure 9.2 is a graphical representation of what transpired next, based on the transactional model described above.

The recruiters sent the migrants from China to Guatemala. During the long journey, former members of the Cambodian Khmer Rouge guerillas guarded the migrants, a necessary precaution given the risk of rebellion against the abhorrent conditions aboard the unseaworthy vessel during the long trip across the Pacific. Upon arrival in Guatemala, a Taiwanese gang took control of the group and (for a fee) brought them to Guatemala City. After a brief stay, the migrants were driven into Mexico and handed off to a Mexican migrant smuggling group. For a fee of $5,000 per head, the coyotes led the group across the U.S. border with Mexico and reunited them with U.S.-based representatives of the Fuzhou Snakehead gang. From there, the Snakeheads split the group, taking some to Los Angeles and others to Houston.[29]

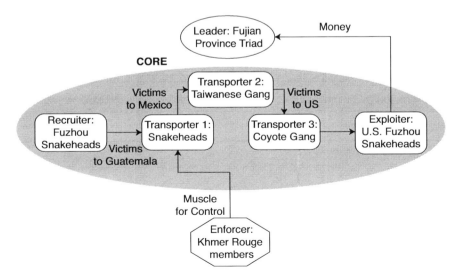

Figure 9.2 Corporate trafficking syndicate example.

192　*J. T. Picarelli*

When the victims had been placed in safehouses, the Snakeheads took control of them. The Snakeheads informed the migrants that the fees owed to them had increased from $37,000 to $50,000. In this way, the snakeheads were able to leverage the vulnerability of the migrants and place them into debt bondage. Those who were able to pay the increased sum or who obtained loans from their families back in China were released. Those who could not afford the increase, however, were threatened with forms of exploitation such as being forced onto the streets to deal narcotics.[30] Many of the migrants never did make it to New York City—their original destination.

Conclusion

The long history of the trade in human beings, starting with the transatlantic trade in the 1500s, sets trafficking in the Americas apart from trafficking in other regions. Poverty, unemployment, and issues related to gender discrimination fuel trafficking in the Americas in much the same way it fuels trafficking elsewhere in the world. But the long history of the trade in human beings in the Americas provides a unique influence on the way that trafficking occurs in the Americas today. Labor trafficking practices and routes mirror those that began in the transatlantic slave trade and the later trade in indentured servants from Asia. Reports of sex trafficking in the Americas bear uncanny parallels with reports from the late 1800s, with women brought from overseas to brothels in the major urban areas of the Americas. The trafficking that occurs within the Americas also has historical precursors.

Further analysis of the trade in human beings in the Americas could unlock important lessons applicable elsewhere in the globe. The influence of history on the trade in human beings in the Americas adds a layer of complexity to our understanding of trafficking. One cannot develop a simple and distilled model of trafficking in the Americas. Trafficking in the Americas is not solely the result of poverty, of gender discrimination, or of geopolitical forces. Rather, it is the result of all these factors *and* historical precedents. Regions such as Europe, Southeast Asia, and Africa all contain similar historical periods of slavery that, when put to similar rigor, should yield insights into how trafficking manifests itself today. But nowhere is that history as intense, as widespread, and as long as one finds in the Americas. For this reason, further study of the interplay between historical and contemporary factors driving the trade in human beings in the Americas could yield benefits far beyond the Western Hemisphere.

Notes

1　P. Lovejoy, *Transformations in Slavery*.
2　P. Andreas and E. Nadelmann, *Policing the Globe: Criminalization and Crime Control in International Relations*; E. Nadelmann, "Global Prohibition Regimes: The Evolution of Norms in International Society."
3　D. Galenson, "The Rise and Fall of Indentured Servitude in the Americas"; D. Northrup, *Indentured Labor in the Age of Imperialism, 1834–1922*.

Trafficking in persons in the Americas 193

4 E. Bristow, *Prostitution and Prejudice: The Jewish Fight Against White Slavery 1870–1939*; I. Vincent, *Bodies and Souls: The Tragic Plight of Three Jewish Women Forced into Prostitution in the Americas*.
5 K. Polanyi, *The Great Transformation: The Political and Economic Origins of Our Time*.
6 R. Blackburn, *The Making of New World Slavery: From the Baroque to the Modern, 1492–1800*.
7 D. Eltis, *The Rise of African Slavery in the Americas*.
8 Ibid.
9 "In Modern Bondage: Sex Trafficking in the Americas," International Human Rights Law Institute, 2002.
10 Ibid.
11 "Smuggling of Dominican Women to Argentina investigated," *EFE*, 26 April 2002.
12 M. Nakamoto, "Tokyo Under Fire for Turning Blind Eye to Trafficking in Women."
13 K. Bales, *Disposable People: New Slavery in the Global Economy*.
14 A. Salicrup, "Uncharted Migration: OAS Rapid Assessment Report of Trafficking in Persons from the Dominican Republic into Puerto Rico."
15 T. Bensman, "Sex Slave Ring Broken Up."
16 Development and Peace and Anti-Slavery International, *Debt Bondage: Slavery Around the World*.
17 T. Eastland, "Traffick."
18 M. O'Matz and S. Hernandez, "State Reviews Files of Overseas Adoptions at Coral Springs Firm"; A. Fantz, "Interpol Hunts Baby-Smuggling Suspect."
19 P. Pattullo, *Last Resorts: The Cost of Tourism in the Caribbean*.
20 "Coyote" is one of the nicknames that migrants and law enforcement have given to Mexican gangs and organized crime groups that specialize in smuggling migrants across the Southwest border of the United States. Another frequently employed term is *pollero*.
21 M. Navarro, "Group Forced Illegal Aliens into Prostitution, US Says"; S. Smith, "Women Smuggled into US, Forced into Prostitution try to Recoup $1M."
22 T. Mrozek, "Los Angeles Couple Charged in Slavery Case."
23 L. Sun, "Modern Day Slavery Prompts Rescue Efforts."
24 C. Gray, "Two Arrested in US for Trade in 'Exotic Dancers.'"
25 U.S. Department of Justice, U.S. Attorney, District of Nevada, "Man Convicted of Transporting Females to Las Vegas for Prostitution."
26 Trafficking is a three-phase operation, starting with recruitment, then transport of the victim, and concluding with exploitation.
27 T. Kinney, "*U.S. vs. Alex Mishulovich*: A Case Study Under the Involuntary Servitude Statute, 18 U.S.C. 1584."
28 T. McCarthy, "Coming to America: The Long Harsh Odyssey of a Chinese Man Smuggled from Fujian Province to New Jersey."
29 Ibid.
30 Ibid.

References

Andreas, P. and Nadelmann, E. (2006) *Policing the Globe: Criminalization and Crime Control in International Relations*, New York: Oxford University Press.
Bales, K. (1999) *Disposable People: New Slavery in the Global Economy*, Berkeley: University of California Press.
Bensman, T. (2002) "Sex Slave Ring Broken Up," *Dallas Morning News*, May 18, p. 34A.
Blackburn, R. (1997) *The Making of New World Slavery: From the Baroque to the Modern, 1492–1800*, London: Verso.

194 *J. T. Picarelli*

Bristow, E. (1982) *Prostitution and Prejudice: The Jewish Fight Against White Slavery 1870–1939*, New York: Schocken Books.

Development and Peace and Anti-Slavery International. (1999) *Debt Bondage: Slavery Around the World*, Montreal: Development and Peace.

Eastland, T. (2004) "Traffick," *Daily Standard*, February 12.

Eltis, D. (2000) *The Rise of African Slavery in the Americas*, Cambridge: Cambridge University Press.

Fantz, A. (2003) "Interpol Hunts Baby-Smuggling Suspect," *Miami Herald*, December 9.

Galenson, D. (1984) "The Rise and Fall of Indentured Servitude in the Americas," *Journal of Economic History* 44, no. 1: 1–26.

Gray, C. (2001) "Two Arrested in US for Trade in 'Exotic Dancers,'" *The Independent*, August 18.

Kinney, T. (2002) "*U.S. vs. Alex Mishulovich*: A Case Study Under the Involuntary Servitude Statute, 18 U.S.C. 1584", February 22, Johns Hopkins School of International Service.

Lovejoy, P. (2000) *Transformations in Slavery*, Cambridge: Cambridge University Press.

McCarthy, T. (2000) "Coming to America: The Long Harsh Odyssey of a Chinese Man Smuggled from Fujian Province to New Jersey," *Time*, May 1.

Mrozek, T. (2000) "Los Angeles Couple Charged in Slavery Case," Office of the U.S. Attorney of the Central District of California.

Nadelmann, E. (1990) "Global Prohibition Regimes: The Evolution of Norms in International Society," *International Organization* 44, no. 4: 479–526.

Nakamoto, M. (2003) "Tokyo Under Fire for Turning Blind Eye to Trafficking in Women," *Financial Times*, February 6.

Navarro, M. (1998) "Group Forced Illegal Aliens into Prostitution, US Says," *New York Times*, April 24.

Northrup, D. (1995) "Indentured Labor in the Age of Imperialism, 1834–1922", in M. Adas, E. Burke III, and P. D. Curtin eds., *Studies in Comparative World History*, New York: Cambridge University Press.

O'Matz, M. and Hernandez, S. (2003) "State Reviews Files of Overseas Adoptions at Coral Springs Firm," *South Florida Sun Sentinel*, December 9.

Pattullo, P. (1996) *Last Resorts: The Cost of Tourism in the Caribbean*. London: Cassell.

Polanyi, K. (1944) *The Great Transformation: The Political and Economic Origins of Our Time*, Boston: Beacon Press.

Salicrup, A. (2006) "Uncharted Migration: OAS Rapid Assessment Report of Trafficking in Persons from the Dominican Republic into Puerto Rico," Organization of American States.

Smith, S. (1999) "Women Smuggled into US, Forced into Prostitution try to Recoup $1M," *Broward Daily Business Review*, April 9, p. B9.

Sun, L. (2004) "Modern Day Slavery Prompts Rescue Efforts," *Washington Post*, May 3.

U.S. Department of Justice, U.S. Attorney, District of Nevada. (2003) "Man Convicted of Transporting Females to Las Vegas for Prostitution," <http://www.usdoj.gov/usao/nv/home/pressrelease/april2003/williams403.htm> (accessed May 15, 2007).

Vincent, I. (2005) *Bodies and Souls: The Tragic Plight of Three Jewish Women Forced into Prostitution in the Americas*, New York: William Morrow.

Part IV

Responding to human smuggling and trafficking

10 The EU combat against illegal immigration, smuggling, and trafficking in human beings

Its impact on Spanish law

Emiliano García Coso

Introduction

Cooperation between the member states of the European Union in the fight against organized crime began in the decade of the 1970s with the creation of the Trevi Group in 1976. This inter-governmental group was joined in 1985 by the Schengen Agreement with a view to eliminating the internal borders among the signatory states, free movement of persons, and cooperation in matters concerning police and security. However, the collaboration mechanisms against organized crime came about from the individual sovereignty of the states and were outside the scope of the European Community.

The creation of a single area with no borders, made up of the member states of the EU, was agreed to in the Single European Act of 1986 for the free movement of persons, goods, services, and capital, as well as the progressive elimination of border controls. This act soon gave rise to the need to establish common legal bases to combat organized crime at the European level. European and foreign criminal organizations profited from the suppression of physical frontiers and police controls. The member states saw how organized crime took advantage of the globalization of economic relationships and, thus, from an increase in the movement of persons, capital, and goods. In addition, they were aware that the diversity of legislations and judicial and police authorities and the sovereign limitations on their actions within the European area could be used to increase their profit and their fields of action.

The progressive consolidation of the European area with no internal borders highlights the need to renounce the individualized regulations and actions of the member states in order to combat organized crime and its activities. The European Union Organised Crime Situation Report describes organized crime as follows:

> In order to speak about organised crime at least six of the following characteristics need to be present, four of which must be those numbered 1, 3, 5, and 11: 1. Collaboration of more than 2 people; 2. Each with own appointed tasks; 3. For a prolonged or indefinite period of time (refers to the stability and (potential) durability); 4. Using some form of discipline and control; 5. Suspected of the commission of serious criminal offences; 6. Operating at an international level; 7. Using violence or other measures suitable for

198 *E. G. Coso*

intimidations; 8. Using commercial or businesslike structures; 9. Engaged in money laundering; 10. Exerting influence on politics, the media, public administration, judicial authorities or the economy; 11. Determined by the pursuit of profit and/or power.[1]

The substantial achievements reached at the EU level show that cooperation within the scope of the EU[2] is the best way to effectively combat European and foreign organized crime. The Council Joint Action of December 21, 1998, in relation to the penalization of participation in a criminal organization in the member states of the EU, states that a criminal organization:

> shall mean a structured association, established over a period of time, of more than two persons, acting in concert with a view to committing offences which are punishable by deprivation of liberty of a maximum of at least four year or a more serious penalty; whether such offences are an end in themselves or a means of obtaining material benefits and, where appropriate, of improperly influencing the operation of public authorities: the offences referred to in the first subparagraph include those mentioned in article 2 of the Europol Convention and in the Annex thereto and carrying a sentence at least equivalent of that provided for in the first subparagraph.

In this chapter, I will show how the necessary European legislation has been drafted and built up in order to fight against this type of crime within the European area through successive reforms to the European Community Treaty and its limitations. Emphasis will be given to the regulation and combat of illegal immigration as an activity of organized crime, which is increasing due to the financial returns and the short prison sentences imposed. Thus, our starting point is illegal immigration[3] in its twofold aspect of smuggling immigrants and the traffic of human beings[4] that, despite the fact that they are different legal concepts, can be complementary activities.

Treaties constituting the EU and their use to fight against organized illegal immigration

As mentioned above, the impact of globalization,[5] the reduction of internal border controls in the European area, and the pressure of the migratory flows toward Europe led to illegal immigration becoming an attractive activity for organized crime. This criminal activity is combined with others as it uses networks, means of transport, companies, and routes similar to those used for drug trafficking to traffic human beings (especially women and children). It is often combined with money laundering. Faced with this situation, the member states of the EU became aware of the need to act at the European level to address this transnational threat using the same type of legal and police instruments.

The first step was taken with the reform introduced into the foundational treaties of the EU by the Treaty of Maastricht of 1992. The objective of this reform was to

The EU combat against illegal immigration   199

develop closer cooperation among the member states regarding matters of justice and ministries of interior. For this reason, a Third Pillar was created within the institutional structure of the EU, through the Council of Ministers, to coordinate their actions and positions on matters involving intergovernmental collaboration.

Chapter VI of the European Union Treaty was part of this Third Pillar. It states that immigration, drugs, international fraud, judicial cooperation as regards civil and criminal issues, and police cooperation for the prevention of and the fight against terrorism, drug trafficking, and other types of international delinquency (the former Article K1, the present Article 29 of the European Union Treaty) should be regarded as matters of common interest.

Combined action on these matters was made through recommendations that are not binding on the states, Common Actions, Common Positions (Article 34 of UE Treaty, establishes new norms, such as the Framework Decision). Their execution and efficacy depended on each state. As can be seen, civil and criminal questions were mixed together with immigration[6] rather than with other spheres of criminal activity.

The framework of intergovernmental cooperation and the arrangements used to pursue common interests were incompatible with the solidity, resources, and networks used by transnational organized crime. Nevertheless, the maintenance of contacts among the member states reaffirmed the need to increase cooperation and agree to common legal bases to combat organized crime.[7] Significant gaps existed between the legal situations raised by the European Union Treaty and the Treaty of the European Community. In addition, the Third Pillar of the EU Treaty provided the institutions of the European Community with limited functions, while the states predominated. Thus the Luxembourg Court of Justice could intervene only with express authorization (Article 35 of EU Treaty), the European Parliament was only notified and the European Commission had only a limited right of regulatory initiative shared with the member states, which could reach agreements concerning Chapter VI only with unanimous decisions.

To alleviate the operative deficiencies of this legislative situation, the member states agreed that the EU should become an area of freedom, security, and justice. Therefore, they decided to reform the European Community Treaty and the European Union Treaty through the Treaty of Amsterdam of 1997, which came into force in 1999. Thus, some competences or matters in Chapter VI of the European Union Treaty (Articles 61–69) were transferred to the European Community Treaty.[8] Specifically included were asylum, immigration, its dimension of the fight against illegal immigration, and judicial cooperation in civil matters. However, the European Union Treaty (Articles 29–31)[9] kept the fight against drug addiction, international criminality, international fraud, and police and judicial cooperation as regards criminal questions. This duality of legal bases split between the European Community Treaty and the European Union Treaty gave rise to difficulties and obstacles in achieving an authentic European area of freedom, security, and justice.

It is obvious that the member states are solely responsible for this legal situation, which is favorable to the criminal organization and permits them to diversify into complementary criminal activities such as illegal immigration and drug trafficking.

200   E. G. Coso

That the transfer of immigration questions to the First Pillar was not accompanied by the simultaneous transfer of questions of security, police, organized crime, and judicial cooperation, which remained under the Third Pillar, is to be criticized. The maintenance of complementary functions under two separate pillars creates gaps and flaws in the systems of police control of the member states. This increases the possibilities for organized crime to act across frontiers by taking advantage of existing infrastructures and networks without legal impediments.

Within the framework of the meetings of the European Council, the heads of state and the government of the EU became aware of these problems and attempted to reduce their negative impact on the European area of liberty, security, and justice by taking action, making plans, and giving directives to the Council of Ministers of the EU and the European Commission. Especially relevant was the Plan of Action agreed to in Vienna in 1999 where it was established that the action of the EU

> means first of all that criminal behaviour should be approached in an equally efficient way throughout the Union: terrorism, corruption, traffic in human beings, organised crime, should be the subject of minimum common rules relating to the constituent elements of criminal acts.[10]

The European Council of Tampere led to a qualitative leap in the awareness of the heads of state and government as they committed themselves to creating an area of freedom, security, and justice in the EU. A statement was issued that

> The European Council has decided to address illegal immigration at its origin, by combating especially those who are involved in the traffic of human beings and the economic exploitation of migrants. It urges the adoption of legislation which lays down strict sanctions for this serious offence. Based on a proposal of the Commission, the Council is invited to adopt legislation to this effect before the end of 2000. The member states, together with Europol, should direct their efforts at detecting and dismantling the criminal networks implicated. The rights of the victims of these activities must be safeguarded, and special attention must be given to the problems of women and children.[11]

After the Tampere Council of Europe (1999), discussion on the European legislative proposals against organized crime and its criminal activities began from a perspective that might guarantee security and the values of freedom and justice. These are fundamental values as they are linked to human rights. However, the discussion and drafting of Community legislation in this area has entered a phase where only security predominates. The reason for this modification in the balance of values arose as a consequence of the terrorist attacks of September 11, 2001, which shocked the whole world.

From that time on, a radical change in immigration and its legislation has become perceptible. Before September 11, it was understood that legislation had no criminal implications for immigrants, only for the traffickers. However, the flaws detected in residence permits and the migratory pressure from third countries, including Muslim countries—the terrorists were Islamic radicals—led to a security reaction. There was concern that a clear relationship existed between illegal immigration, terrorism, a lack of security, and delinquency. This resulted in the drafting of European legislation to combat direct and indirect criminal activities related to illegal migration, and helped lead to a policy on returning all illegal immigrants and strengthening Europe's external border controls. From this point, the fight against illegal immigration in the context of combating smuggling and trafficking became a political priority for the member states. This policy was consolidated in subsequent European Councils, especially the Councils of Seville in June 2002 and Thessaloniki in June 2003. More recently the Hague Programme in 2005[12] established ten priorities for the coming years to consolidate the area of liberty, security, and freedom.

After 2001, and especially in 2002, the member states of the EU agreed to adopt common legal measures to combat all the manifestations of organized crime in a more coordinated and efficient way.[13] The main problem of this agreement was that it was adopted as the Framework Decisions of the Third Pillar of the EU Treaty, which means they are not directly effective as there was not binding adoption by all member states. Despite the common objective of the member states to combat criminality, they maintain two different legal bases (the Treaty of the European Community and the Treaty of the European Union). They adopt specific Community measures against illegal immigration[14] regarding its smuggling dimension and indirectly regarding trafficking. They also adopt measures to address security, police, and judicial cooperation against smuggling and trafficking.

The next part focuses on the particular measures adopted to combat illegal immigration as an important focus of criminal activity at the European Union level and its implications to Spain. Spain is an important case study in this area because of its high rates of smuggling and trafficking activities.

Legal measures of the EU to combat illegal immigration, smuggling, and trafficking

Migration in itself is not illegal. However, migration becomes illegal when the persons themselves or with the help of organized criminal groups enter the states of the European Union secretly, move about, remain, and work illegally. It is very difficult to determine the number of immigrants who enter or attempt to enter member states of the EU illegally because of the clandestine nature of the activity and the increasing participation of professional crime groups that facilitate illegal immigrants. Chinese organized crime groups mainly aid the illegal immigration of their compatriots, as do the organized Moroccan groups involved in drug trafficking that traffic persons across the Straits of Gibraltar, and more recently the Senegalese groups involved in traffic of persons from African countries toward the Spanish coast. *EU Organised Crime Report 2002* established that organized crime involvement in illegal immigration and trafficking in human beings is also growing because of the increased difficulties illegal immigrants face trying to enter the EU, the high profits involved, and the relatively mild sentences imposed on the perpetrators if they are caught and sentenced.[15]

202 *E. G. Coso*

This criminal activity does not affect only one member state. All the states are implicated, as when the external border controls of the EU have been passed[16] the existence of the Schengen area enables illegal immigrants and the criminal organizations that assist them to move about without any police border controls. The death of immigrants in *pateras* or *cayucos* (boats) trying to arrive at the Spanish coast or Schengen Territory is evidence of the extreme measures used to try to smuggle individuals into Europe.[17]

In recent years there has been a substantial increase in illegal entries organized by facilitators. These facilitators provide transport, temporary refuge, false travel documents, information, protection, and other services from the country of origin, and passage through the transit country until the immigrants reach the European destination country. The price of these smuggling services is very high and a large number of the illegal immigrants have to burden themselves with debt or sell all their belongings before setting out for Europe. If they cannot pay, the immigrants become victims of the traffickers. The smugglers exploit them in illicit activities such as prostitution, piracy, and drug trafficking. They use them in "three D-jobs"—dirty, difficult, and dangerous—until the illegal immigrants finish paying back their debt. Illegal immigrants are often the victims of kidnapping, forcing family members to pay more money. On other occasions the families are threatened in the countries of origin to force those who have immigrated to pay money.

This situation makes it difficult to know exactly when illegal immigration involves a crime of smuggling or one of trafficking. It also leads to other criminal conduct in the country of origin involving either victims or accomplices. The EU has attempted to respond to this with legislative measures. The objective of these measures is to try to approximate the legislation of the member states and establish the required cooperation mechanisms among police and judges in the member states through Europol and Eurojust as coordinating bodies at the European and international level. Eurojust was established

> to improve the effectiveness of the competent authorities in the Member States and cooperation among them in an increasing number of areas: preventing and combating terrorism, unlawful drug-trafficking, trafficking in human beings, crimes involving clandestine immigration networks, illicit trafficking in radioactive and nuclear substances, illicit vehicle trafficking, combating the counterfeiting of the euro, and money-laundering associated with international criminal activities. Europol has the following principal tasks: to facilitate the exchange of information among Member States; to obtain, collate and analyse information and intelligence; to notify the competent authorities of the Member States without delay of information concerning them and of any connections identified between criminal offences; to aid investigations in the Member States; to maintain a computerised system of collected information. Each member state establishes or designates a national unit to carry out the tasks listed above.[18]

Eurojust was established as

a body of the Union with a legal personality. Each Member State must appoint a national member of Eurojust: a prosecutor, judge or police officer (the latter must have competencies equivalent to the judge's or the prosecutor's). The national members mentioned above are subject to the national law of the Member State which appointed them. Furthermore, each Member State determines the length of the term of office as well as the nature of the judicial powers conferred on its national representative. Regarding investigations and prosecutions (concerning at least two Member States) in relation to serious crime, Eurojust has competence for: promoting coordination between the competent authorities of the various Member States; facilitating the implementation of international mutual legal assistance and of extradition requests. Eurojust's competence covers, *inter alia*, the types of crime and offences for which Europol has competence (e.g.: terrorism, drug trafficking, trafficking in human beings, counterfeiting and money laundering, computer crime, fraud and corruption, the laundering of the proceeds of crime, participation in a criminal organisation). Eurojust may fulfill its tasks through one or more of the national members or as a College. Eurojust may ask the authorities of the Member States concerned, *inter alia*, to: undertake an investigation or prosecution; set up a joint investigation team.[19]

The four main routes used for the traffic of illegal immigrants have been identified; these are the Baltic route, the Central European route, the North African route, and the Eastern Mediterranean route from Turkey. Each of these routes implies the use of various means of transport and the transit of several states. This makes it necessary to have European coordination at the international level.

The EU signed the UN Convention against Trans-national Organised Crime (Palermo, December 12–15, 2000) and its two Protocols against Trafficking and Smuggling.[20] In addition, it has made agreements with third party states for the readmission of illegal immigrants or has added readmission clauses to the agreements for economic association and cooperation with the EU.[21] Further, as pointed out by Albrecht,[22] a combination of administrative and criminal law measures has been instituted in the member states of the EU with a view to providing more flexible responses to the crimes committed by immigrants. These sanctions entail prison sentences and expulsion from the territory.

An important example of administrative and criminal legislative measures adopted by the EU was Directive 2001/40 on the mutual recognition of decisions on the expulsion of third country nationals.[23] The general objective was the harmonization of the expulsion measure contemplated in the regulations of member states. The common aim of this EU legal measure was to prevent immigrants from avoiding expulsion by moving to another state.

This directive stipulated that all the member states of the EU, except Denmark, but including Norway and Iceland, undertake to recognize an expulsion decision pronounced by another member state against a foreigner in their own national legislations before December 2, 2002. The reason for the expulsion decision must be one of the following:

204   *E. G. Coso*

- A third country national is the subject of an expulsion decision based on a serious and present threat to public order or to national security and safety. This action is taken in cases of conviction of a third country national by the issuing member state for an offense punishable by a penalty involving deprivation of liberty of at least one year, the existence of serious grounds for believing that a third country national has committed serious criminal offenses, or the existence of solid evidence of his intention to commit such offenses within the territory of a member state.
- A third country national is the subject of an expulsion decision based on failure to comply with national rules on the entry or residence of aliens. In the two cases referred to previously, the expulsion decision must not have been rescinded or suspended by the issuing member state.

This mechanism for the mutual recognition of expulsion decisions was implemented in Spanish legislation under Article 64(3) of Organic Law 4/2000 on the rights and liberties of aliens, although it had failed to comply with the implementation period laid down. In Article 59 of Organic Law 4/2000, the Spanish legislature also provided for assisting victims and providing a certain level of protection for those who collaborate against organized networks.[24]

Directive 2001/51[25] of the EU endeavors to control the phenomenon that could be called legal smuggling. It transfers functions of the border police to transport companies whose destination is the EU. The objective of this directive was that transport companies not carry any aliens into Schengen territory without the required documents. Thus, the transport company will have to comply with controls in the country of origin or transit of the alien, thereby preventing undocumented aliens from traveling. If the transport company does not comply, a sanction will be imposed requiring it to maintain and return the alien at their cost. The transport company may also incur fines that may range from €5,000–€500,000. Member states were obligated to implement this measure before February 11, 2003. Spanish legislation has only partially adopted this directive, but the reform of Organic Law 4/2000 stipulates its complete adoption in Articles 66 and 55.[26]

Specific legal measures of the EU against smuggling

The fight against illegal immigration through smuggling made substantial progress within the context of the EU. This progress was reached with an agreement involving the partial approximation of the criminal and administrative law measures of member states concerning these problems. The main objective of the agreement was the implementation of common sanctions against human smuggling in provisions of both the administrative and criminal codes of the member states. Therefore, action is determined by two different legal bases. One base is made up of Articles 61(a) and 63(3)(b) of the European Community Treaty concerning the aspects of harmonization related to the common definition of facilitating unauthorized entry, transit, and residence in a member state. The other is composed of Articles 29, 31(e) and 34(2)(b) of the European Union Treaty concerning the harmonization of criminal sanctions, the responsibility of the legal person involved, and problems of jurisdiction.

The legal result is evident in two Community legal instruments that are different but complementary and that were to be adopted before December 5, 2004 by the member states, except Denmark, plus Norway and Iceland. One is Council Directive 2002/90 of November 28, 2002 defining the facilitation of unauthorized entry, transit, and residence (hereinafter Directive 2002/90).[27] Under Directive 2002/90, member states are obliged to adopt sanctions that are effective, proportional, and dissuasive for any person who assists a non-Community citizen to enter, cross, or reside in a member's state intentionally or for financial benefit, infringing the laws of the states affected by the illegal entry, transit, or residence. In the event that this involves humanitarian aid, each state can decide whether or not this conduct will be punished. The person who instigates, participates, or attempts to behave in this way will also be punished.[28]

The other is the Council Framework Decision of November 28, 2002 on the strengthening of the penal framework to prevent the facilitation of unauthorized entry, transit, and residence.[29] The Framework Decision stipulates the punishments and sanctions related to this conduct must be effective, proportional, and dissuasive and may even include extradition. The aim was to obtain a common penal definition of this offense in the different criminal codes in each member state. The combination of both instruments permits smuggling to be defined in its administrative and criminal perspectives. Unfortunately, at the end of 2006 many member states had not adopted any national measures implementing the EU legal instruments.

In fact, the measures establish that the persons who participate in the previously described conduct for financial benefit must be punished by the member states with sentences involving a maximum punishment of not less than eight years' imprisonment if the persons implicated belonged to a criminal organization or had put the lives of the persons who are the subject of the activity in danger. These punishments may also entail the confiscation of the means of transport used, disqualification from working in the professional activity involved in the offense, and deportation.[30]

In cases of smuggling in which a legal person participates and benefits financially from this activity, it is stipulated that the member states must adopt the measures needed to ensure responsibility of the legal person in the commission of the offense. Thus, persons who legally have the power to represent the company—those who have authority to make decisions for the company or authority to exercise control over the company—will be held responsible. Also included is the responsibility to control persons who work in the company and carry out the smuggling to the benefit of the company. Obviously, this legal responsibility of legal persons does not exclude the responsibility of the persons who are the perpetrators, instigators, or accomplices with regard to this conduct. Furthermore, the legal person can be sanctioned with measures that exclude him/her from public subsidies, withdraw licenses for exercising commercial activity, and order auditing of his/her activity by judicial authority.[31]

The transnational nature of this criminal activity gives rise to the possibility that conflicts of jurisdiction and problems concerning extradition might arise among

206   E. G. Coso

the member states. In an attempt to solve these problems, it has been established that the states will adopt internal legal measures that recognize its jurisdictional competence to judge the smuggling activities committed totally or partially on its territory by one of its citizens or to the benefit of a legal person established on its territory.[32]

However, the use of these three criteria hinders the delimitation of the competent jurisdiction. Thus, a clause was added that permits each member state to use its discretion to exclude the criteria that a citizen of that state or a company established on its territory carried out the activity in order to claim its jurisdiction. The approval of the Convention on Mutual Assistance in criminal matters[33] made by the member states should reduce these possible problems to a minimum with the temporary handovers laid down in Article 9 of the Convention.

In any case, in order to avoid problems concerning the resolution of the investigation and the trial, it has been established that if a member state is opposed to the extradition of one of its citizens who is implicated, it will have to try this citizen in its courts for the smuggling committed in another member state. In addition, if its citizen is only implicated and his member state is opposed to his extradition, it will have to take the proper national measures for his/her prosecution[34] and notify the state affected of the prosecution in accordance with the proceedings laid down in Article 6 of the European Convention on Extradition of 1957.

To guarantee adequate cooperation, it has been established that each member state that knows of the infringement of the laws on the entry and residence of foreigners from another state must notify this state. If the latter state requests a member state to initiate proceedings for the infringement of its laws on entry and residence, it will have to officially notify the member state of the national provisions that have been infringed.

Combating smuggling from a harmonized European perspective seems to have been consolidated by the legal measures adopted. However, the evaluation of the efficacy of the legislation against the criminal phenomenon will not be known until the member states have adapted their legislation to this Community rule. The deadline was December 5, 2004 (unfortunately, this instrument has not yet been implemented by all member states in their national laws). However, the urgent need to reduce this criminal activity and the consequences for the victims, which is often death as occurs on the Spanish coast, requires the agreed adoption by all the member states.[35]

Specific legal measures of the EU against trafficking

Since 1993, the EU has been committed to combating the criminal trafficking of human beings. Initially, this was applied to women and children, but it has subsequently evolved toward a wider conception of human trafficking.[36] Trafficking represents a serious infringement of human rights and human dignity because it uses violence and threats of violence, and traffickers coerce and enslave vulnerable persons. At the request of the European Commission and in compliance with its international commitments, the member states determined that it was essential to

The EU combat against illegal immigration 207

adopt a common definition of what constitutes the offense of trafficking, including adopting adequate penal sanctions harmonized at the European level.

The legal instrument chosen was a Framework Decision of the Council legally based on Articles 29, 31(e) and 34(2)(b) of the European Union Treaty. The Framework Decision itself established August 1, 2004 as the deadline for the harmonization of this offense. The new feature is that the Framework Decision defines the traffic of human beings for exploitation in any sector of employment. Sexual exploitation now includes pornography—unlike the previous European legal instruments, which referred principally to trafficking with a view to sexual exploitation.

Member states had to include in their trafficking legislation conduct involving the recruitment, transportation, transfer, harboring, and subsequent reception of a person, including exchange or transfer of control over that person where: (1) use is made of coercion, force or threat, including abduction; (2) use is made of deceit or fraud; (3) there is an abuse of authority or of a position of vulnerability, which is such that the person has no real and acceptable alternative but to submit to the abuse involved; or (4) payments or benefits are given or received to achieve the consent of a person having control over another person.[37]

To avoid legal problems related to the will of the victims, it is laid down that when any of these recourses are used the consent of the victim must be considered to be irrelevant, and when minors are the victims, no recourse to the coercive measures described above will be required. Obviously, conduct involving instigation, assistance and cooperation, and the planning of such conduct must be included.

The Framework Decision also stipulated that the penalty for trafficking in any member state must not be less than eight years of imprisonment if the offense is committed in circumstances endangering the life of the victim, against a victim who was particularly vulnerable (under the age of sexual majority, purpose of prostitution or sexual exploitation, including pornography), used serious violence, has caused particularly serious harm, or was committed within the context of a criminal organization.[38] Trafficking and smuggling are subject to equal criminal sanctions despite the fact that in the former there is a predominance of coercion of the victim in order to achieve his exploitation, whereas smuggling involves only a financial objective.

Because the nature of victimization is difficult to detect without the cooperation of the victim, the legislation treats these two activities of organized crime in the same way. The Community legislation is based on different behaviors but it also establishes the same conduct at the European level in order to determine the cases of responsibility as regards legal persons and the sanctions that affect them if they are implicated in trafficking or smuggling.

The most noteworthy difference is that "legal person" is defined with regard to the cases of trafficking. Incomprehensibly, an unexpected sanction is established for cases of smuggling. This sanction consists of the temporary or permanent closing of the commercial establishment used for the trafficking.[39] An identical solution is adopted for the problems of jurisdiction and prosecution of cases of trafficking committed in another member state by citizens who cannot be extradited but must be investigated and tried in the states in which they are citizens.[40]

208   *E. G. Coso*

Another notable difference with regard to the Framework Decision is that it urges the member states to create protection for the victims of trafficking to permit them to cooperate in the investigation of the criminal networks by which they have been exploited. Special treatment is given to victims who are minors and to their families. But the important thing is that this protection of the victims was already included in another Framework Decision[41] and gave rise to Directive 2004/81 to grant short-term permits to the victims of trafficking or smuggling who cooperate with the authorities in order to eliminate these networks.[42] Nevertheless, these permits must not be confused with the possible creation of a European statute for the protection of victims. If the EU wants this cooperation, it will have to extend the period of time granted in its residence permit from six months and make them renewable. The existing short-term protection is insufficient to motivate victims to cooperate actively as this short period only delays their expulsion until the investigation ends.

Spanish penal regulation of illegal immigration regarding smuggling and trafficking

Spain is an active destination for smugglers and traffickers because the networks use Spain as a pointy of entry into Europe. As was stressed above, organized crime is using the traditional routes for drug trafficking to smuggle and traffic illegal immigrants into Europe. The lack of Spanish experience in controlling and regulating migration flows has led to a substantial increase in these criminal offenses. There has been an inadequate response in applying both administrative and penal legislation.[43] Exchange of experiences with its European partners and the harmonization of the regulation of these criminal activities led Spain to adopt Organic Law 11/2003, 29 September. This law provides specific measures concerning the security of citizens, domestic violence, and the social integration of aliens.[44] It replaced existing provisions of the Spanish Criminal Law Code of 1995.

Although Spanish legislation already included penal measures to combat these criminal acts, this Organic Law of the Spanish government complies with Spain's commitments to the European Community and introduces a substantial increase in penalties by establishing a prison sentence of between four and eight years for persons involved in the illegal trafficking of persons, as requested by the previously cited Framework Decision.

Specifically, Spanish legislation for combating smuggling and trafficking is contained in Article 318 *bis*, which was reformed in accordance with European harmonization. Thus, it was established that the person who directly or indirectly promotes, helps, or facilitates illegal trafficking or the clandestine immigration of persons from, in transit, or with Spain as their destination will be punished by a sentence of four to eight years' imprisonment. Therefore, it includes the complete provisions of the Framework Decision for combating smuggling. In addition, persons implicated in illegal trafficking or clandestine immigration with a view to sexually exploiting those trafficked will be punished with sentences of six to ten years' imprisonment. This punishment complies with the requirements imposed by the Framework Decision as regards trafficking.

The Spanish legislature introduced the punishments described at the higher level—from six to eight years in the case of smuggling and from seven to ten years for trafficking—when the persons responsible:

- act with the intention of making a profit;
- use violence, intimidation, deception, etc.;
- abuse a situation of superiority;
- involve the special vulnerability of the victim;
- involve a victim who is a minor or is incapacitated;
- put life, health, or the physical integrity of the persons in danger.

Furthermore, to combat organized crime when the perpetrators belong to organizations or associations, which might even be transitory, and the organizations are involved in criminal activities, the convicted offenders will be sentenced to between eight and ten years' imprisonment, and may possibly be disqualified from working in their professions, trade, industry, or commercial business during the period of the conviction. If the guilty parties are managers or directors or are in charge of the organizations or associations, more serious sentences will be imposed on them as they may be condemned to serve from 10 to 15 years', or even 15 to 20 years' imprisonment.

As can be seen, in regard to punishments, the Spanish legislations complies with the Community legislation and is also committed to the persecution, repression, and condemnation of the persons implicated in smuggling or trafficking activities. When it is a question of legal persons involved in criminal activity, Article 318 of the Organic Law 11/2003 established the same punishments for the directors or the legal persons and those who were aware of the crime but did not prevent the activities within the framework of their business activity.

Finally, the Spanish legislature has also introduced modifications with a view to providing a penal response to aliens living illegally in Spain who commit offenses. Thus, the changes introduced by Organic Law 11/2003 in sections 1, 2, and 3 of Article 89 of Criminal Law Code mean that illegal aliens who commit an offense punishable by imprisonment for less than six years are expelled instead of being imprisoned. If the prison sentence is equal to or greater than six years, when three-quarters of the sentence has been completed or good conduct comes into force, an agreement will be reached to expel the alien with a prohibition that he/she will not enter Spanish territory for a period of ten years.

In conclusion, the Spanish legislature adopted legislation in accordance with the EU model and in advance of the deadline. It also attempted to actively combat organized crime in Spain and in the EU. By substantially increasing the punishments and the financial consequences, it has reduced smuggling and trafficking. The increased risks and punishment have served as a deterrent to their commission.

Conclusion

The fight against organized crime and its activities is one of the priority objectives of the EU and its member states. Despite the difficulties involved in the application

210 E. G. Coso

of two different legal bases (the European Community Treaty and the European Union Treaty), significant progress has been made in Community coordination against organized crime in the last few years through the enactment of various Community legislation instruments. These, combined with the international commitments involving the EU, will soon bear fruit.

This criminal activity must not be addressed merely by regulation, but also by prevention. The latter requires close cooperation with the countries involved in smuggling and trafficking in order to create economic, social, and judicial incentives to deter smuggling at its country of origin. Spain has fulfilled its obligations by adopting penal legislation and has provided for strong penal instruments against organized crime. Its policies have contributed to combating organized crime at the European level. The dream of a united Europe with penal systems coordinated against organized crime is a little closer and the Europe of freedom, security and justice will serve as a reference at the international level.

Notes

1 6204/1/97 (ENFOPOL 35 REV 2) DH H II: The international legal reference for a global recognition of the problem and a comparable approach to tackling it is the UN Convention against Trans-national Organised Crime signed in Palermo on December 12–15, 2000 and its two accompanying Protocols on trafficking in persons and smuggling of migrants, <http/ww.unodc.org> (accessed November 1, 2003). For problems linked to national sovereignty see P. Tak, "Bottlenecks in International Police and Judicial Cooperation in the EU"; H. Aden, "Convergence of Policing Policies and Transnational Policing in Europe."

2 *Official Journal (OJ) of 29.12.1998, L351/1*. An indication of organized crime areas is also given in Article 2 (2) and the Annex to the Europol Convention in which serious forms of international crime are listed, in addition to those already mentioned in Article 2(2) of the same Convention. "Illegal immigrant smuggling and trafficking in human beings" are included among the serious crimes listed.

3 The Europol definition of organized illegal migration, according to its Convention implementing the Schengen Agreement of June 19, 1990, is "activities intended deliberately to facilitate, for financial gain, the entry into, residence or employment in the territory of the Member States of the European Union, contrary to the rules and conditions applicable in the Member States."

4 The UN established the differences between trafficking and smuggling in its two Protocols of UN Convention against Trans-national Organized Crime. In some aspects, trafficking in persons resembles the smuggling of migrants. However, the smuggling, while often undertaken in dangerous or degrading conditions, involves migrants who have consented to the smuggling. On the other hand, trafficking victims have never consented or, if they initially consented, that consent has been rendered meaningless by the coercive, deceptive, or abusive actions of the traffickers. Another major difference is that smuggling ends with the arrival of the migrants at their destination, whereas trafficking involves the ongoing exploitation of the victims in some manner to generate illicit profits for the traffickers. Finally, smuggling is always transnational, whereas trafficking may not be. <http://www.unodc.org> (accessed November 1, 2003).

5 M. Alain, "Transnational Police Cooperation in Europe and in North America: Revisiting the Traditional Border between Internal and External Security Matters, or how Policing is being Globalised."

6 Council Recommendation of December 22, 1995 on harmonizing means of combating illegal immigration and illegal employment and improving the relevant means of

The EU combat against illegal immigration   211

control, *OJ C5*, January 10, 1996; Council Recommendation of September 27, 1996 on combating the illegal employment of third country nationals, *OJ C304*, October 14, 1996.

7 Council Joint Action 96/277/JHA of April 22, 1996 concerning the framework for the exchange of liaison magistrates to improve judicial cooperation between the Member States of the EU, *OJ L105*, April 27, 1996, p. 1. Council Joint Action 96/700 JHA of November 29, 1996 establishing an incentive and exchange programme for persons responsible for combating trade in human beings and sexual exploitation of children (STOP), *OJ L 322*, December 12, 1996, p. 7. Council Joint Action 96/748/JHA of December 16, 1996 extending the mandate given to the Europol Drugs Unit, *OJ L 342*, December 31, 1996, p. 4. Council Joint Action 97/154/JHA of February 24, 1997 concerning action to combat trafficking in human beings and sexual exploitation of children, *OJ L 63*, March 4, 1997, p. 2. Council Joint Action 98/428/JHA of June 29, 1998 on the creation of a European Judicial Network, *OJ L 105*, July 7, 1998, p. 4. Council Joint Action 98/699/JHA of December 3, 1998 on money laundering, the identification, tracing, freezing, seizing and confiscation of the instrumentalities and the proceeds from crime, *OJ L333*, December 9, 1998. Council Joint Action 98/733/JHA of December 21, 1998 on making it a criminal offence to participate in a criminal organization in the Member State of the EU, *OJ L351*, December 29, 1998, p. 1. Council Joint Action 98/427 of June 29, 1998 on good practice in mutual legal assistance in criminal matters, *OJ L 191*, June 7, 1998, p. 1.

8 Article 62(1) Treaty of European Community (TEC) Free internal movement; Article 62(2) TEC External borders; Article 62(3) TEC Freedom to travel of third country nationals; Article 63 (1) TEC Asylum; Article 63(2) TEC Refugees & displaced persons; Article 63(3) TEC immigration policy.

9 Article 29 Treaty of European Union (TEU), Preventing & combating crime; Article 30 (1) TEU Police cooperation; Article 30 (2) TEU Europol; Article. 31 TEU Judicial cooperation in criminal matters; Article 31 (2) Eurojust (legal basis introduced with the Nice Treaty 2003, latest reform of TEC and TEU). M. Kaiafa-Ghandi, "The Development Towards Harmonization within Criminal Law in the European Union: A Citizen's Perspective."

10 Council Recommendation of September 28, 1998 on the prevention of organized crime with reference to the establishment of the comprehensive strategy for combating it, *OJ C408*, December 29, 1998, p. 1. The Amsterdam Treaty provides an institutional framework to develop common action among the member states in the connected fields of police cooperation and judicial cooperation in criminal matters; the Vienna Action Plan on the implementing the Amsterdam Treaty provisions on freedom, security, and justice adopted by the Justice & Home Affairs Council of December 3, 1999, *OJ C19*, January 23, 2000, p. 1, point 18.

11 European Council at Tampere, October 15–16, 1999, point 23. Further in point 5, the European Council declared: "The enjoyment of freedom requires a genuine area of justice, where people can approach courts and authorities in any Member States as easily as in their own. Criminals must find no ways of exploiting differences in the judicial systems of Member States. Judgment and decisions should be respected and enforced throughout the Union. . . . Better compatibility and more convergence between the legal systems of Members States must be achieved."

12 Communication from the Commission to the Council and the European Parliament. The Hague Programme—Ten priorities for the next five years. The Partnership for European renewal in the field of Freedom, Security and Justice [CCM(2005) 184 final—Not published in the Official Journal].

13 Council Decision establishing a European Police College, 20 December 2000, *OJL 336, 30 December 2000*. Council Framework Decision of March 15, 2001 on the standing of victims in criminal proceedings, *OJ L 82*, March 22, 2001. Council Framework Decision of May 28, 2001 on combating fraud and counterfeiting of non-cash means of payment,

212   *E. G. Coso*

OJ L149, June 2, 2002. Council Decision 187/2002 of February 28, 2002 setting up Eurojust with a view to reinforcing the fight against serious crime, *OJ L63*, March 6, 2002. Council Framework Decision of June 13, 2002 on combating terrorism, *OJ L164*, June 22, 2002. Council Framework Decision of June 13, 2002 on joint investigative teams, *OJ L162*, June 20, 2002. Council Framework Decision of June 13, 2002 on the European Arrest Warrant, *OJ L 190*, July 18, 2002. The adoption of the European arrest warrant constitutes the first achievement, and without doubt one of the most important achievements, in the implementation of the program of mutual recognition in criminal matters. On November 21, 2003, at Toledo, Spain, a Home Ministers meeting, in which Spain, France, Portugal, United Kingdom, and Italy participated, agreed to apply the arrest warrant. M. Plachta, "European Arrest Warrant: Revolution in Extradition?"

14 With the reform introduced by the Treaty of Nice 2003, visa, asylum, and immigration policy are to be decided mainly by the co-decision procedure. The shift to qualified majority voting is provided for under Article 63 of the EC Treaty for matters concerning asylum and temporary protection, but subject to prior unanimous adoption of common framework legislation on asylum. The shift to qualified majority voting and co-decision will automatically take place on May 1, 2004 for Article 62 of the EC Treaty—setting out the conditions for free circulation of non-member state nationals legally resident on EU territory—and Article 63 of the EC Treaty—illegal immigration and the repatriation of illegally resident persons.

15 <http/europa.eu.int/comm./justice_home/fsj/police/europo/fsj_police_europol_en.htm> (accessed November 1, 2003).

16 A recent major investigation after the death of many smuggled Chinese (the Dover catastrophe) confirmed that there was a clear division of tasks and a well-defined network that was divided between the country of origin, transit countries, and the country of destination. Each part of the chain functioned with a large degree of independence. The network had a multi-ethnic composition and made use of existing economic and administrative logistic structures. European Commission Staff Working Paper, "Towards a European Strategy to Prevent Organised Crime"; for challenges for investigation and prosecution of criminal networks, see T. Schalken and M. Pronk, "On Joint Investigation Teams, Europol, and Supervision of their Joint Actions."

17 Report of the President of Group X "Freedom, Security and Justice" European Convention, Brussels, December 2, 2002, CONV 426/02, p. 1.

18 Council Act of July 26, 1995 drawing up the Convention on the establishment of a European Police Office (Europol Convention) *JO UE 316*, November 27, 1995.

19 Council Decision of February 28, 2002 setting up Eurojust with a view to reinforcing the fight against serious crime *OJ L 63*, March 6, 2002.

20 The Convention was signed by 147and 131 ratified it, including EC and 23 member states (except Czech Republic, Greece, Ireland, and Luxembourg); 115 states and the EC had signed the Protocol on Trafficking in persons and 111 had ratified it; 111 states and the EC had signed the Protocol on smuggling of migrants and 105 had ratified it. For the current status see: <http//: www.odccp.org/crime_cicp_convention> (accessed February 10, 2007). It is essential to ensure that member states that have not yet ratified the Convention and the two Protocols (Czech Republic, Greece, Ireland, and Luxembourg) do so.

21 Based on the EU's powers under Article 63(3)(b) TEC, the Council authorized the Commission to negotiate Community readmission agreements with 11 third countries: Morocco, Sri Lanka, Russia, Pakistan, Hong Kong, Macao, Ukraine, Albania, Algeria, China, and Turkey. Negotiations have been successfully completed with Hong Kong (November 2001), Macao (October 2002), Sri Lanka (May 2002), Albania (November 2003) and Russia (October 2005). The agreement with Hong Kong was formally signed in November 2002 and concluded in December 2003; it entered into force on March 1, 2004 as the first ever Community readmission agreement. The next agreement to follow was the one with Macao, which entered into force on June 1, 2004. The agreement with Sri Lanka was signed in Colombo in June 2004 and its formal conclusion by the

The EU combat against illegal immigration   213

Council took place in March 2005; it entered into force on May 1, 2005. The agreement with Albania was signed in the margins of the JHA Council of April 14, 2005; its entry into force is expected for 2006. The agreement with Russia was initialled on October 12, 2005 but still needs to be ratified before entering into force. Negotiations are ongoing with Morocco, Turkey, Pakistan, and Ukraine and have not yet started with China and Algeria. Biannual update of the scoreboard to review progress on the creation of an area of freedom, security, and justice in the EU, *COM(2002) 738 final*, p. 22. It is important to note the recent agreement between Europol and U.S. agencies to cooperate. EU–U.S. counter-terrorism cooperation in the area of justice, freedom, and security after September 11, 2001 has been very successful. Concrete results were achieved with the signature of several agreements (see <http://ec.europa.eu/justice_home/fsj/external/usa/fsj_external_usa_en.htm> (accessed January 26, 2007), two Europol–US agreements in December 2001, see <http://www.europol.eu.int/legal/agreements/Agreements/16268-2.pdf> (accessed January 26, 2007), and December 2002 <http://www.europol.eu.int/legal/agreements/Agreements/16268-1.pdf> (accessed January 26, 2007), the latter allowing for sharing of personal data. Following these two agreements, Europol has posted two liaison officers at the European Commission's Delegation in Washington, D.C. In June 2003 the EU–U.S. Summit signed two criminal judicial cooperation agreements on Extradition Agreement and on Mutual Legal Assistance and Extradition <http://ec.europa.eu/comm/external_relations/us/sum06_03/extra.pdf> (accessed January 26, 2007). In addition, contacts have been established between the EU body for judicial cooperation in criminal matters Eurojust and U.S. law enforcement authorities, and a cooperation agreement is under negotiation. The EU and the U.S. further signed an agreement on the transfer of passenger data in May 2004.

22 H-J. Albrecht, "Fortress Europe? Controlling illegal immigration," p. 20.

23 Council Directive 2001/40 of May 28, 2001, on the mutual recognition of decision on the expulsion of third country nationals, *OJ L149*, June 2, 2001. E. García Coso; "Spanish Report of the Directive on the Mutual Recognition of Decisions on the Expulsion of Third Country Nationals."

24 Organic Law on Aliens 8/2000, of December 22, 2000, *Official State Gazette* (BOE) January 23, 2000, Article 64, section 3. For a study of the progress of Directives implementation in Spanish law and in other member states see Carlier and De Bruycker, *Immigration and Asylum Law*.

25 Council Directive 2001/51 of June 28, 2001, whereby the provisions of Article 26 of the convention applying the Schengen Agreement of June 14, 1985 is complemented, *OJ L187*, July 10, 2001. E. García Coso, "Spanish Report on the Transposition of the Directive Supplementing Article 26 of the Schengen Convention."

26 Article 66(3).

27 *OJ L328/17*, December 5, 2002.

28 Articles 1, 2, and 3 of Directive.

29 *OJ L328/1*, December 5, 2002.

30 Article 1 of Framework Decision. There is an exception established in section 4.

31 Articles 2 and 3 of Framework Decision.

32 Article 4 of Framework Decision.

33 Convention of May 29, 2000 on Mutual Assistance in Criminal Matters between the Member States of The European Union, *OJ C197*, July 12, 2000, p. 1. Explanatory Report on the Convention, *OJ C379/7*, December 29, 2000. Final Report on the first evaluation exercise–mutual legal assistance in criminal matters, *OJ C216/14*, August 1, 2001.

34 Article 5 of Framework Decision.

35 For a comprehensive study of the transposition in all member states, see Carlier and De Bruycker, *Immigration and Asylum Law*.

36 Discussion paper on prevention of trafficking in human beings, Brussels, May 17/18, 2001, p. 2. U. Smart, "Human Trafficking: Simply a European Problem?"

214   E. G. Coso

37 Articles 1 and 2 of Council Framework Decision of July 19, 2002 on combating trafficking in human beings, *OJ L203/1*, August 1, 2002.
38 Article 3.
39 Articles 4 and 5 of Council Framework Decision of July 19, 2002 are the model followed to elaborate the Articles of Council Framework Decision of November 28, 2002.
40 Article 6.
41 Council Framework Decision 2001/220/JHA of March 15, 2001 on the standing of victims in criminal proceedings, *OJ L82*, March 22, 2001, p. 1.
42 Council Directive 2004/81/EC of April 29, 2004 on the residence permit issued to third country nationals who are victims of trafficking in human beings or who have been the subject of an action to facilitate illegal immigration, who cooperate with the competent authorities. *OJ L 261*, August 6, 2004, pp. 19–23.
43 C. Gortazar Rotaeche, E. García Coso, and A. Obregon García, "Trafficking in and Smuggling of Human Beings: the Spanish Approach."
44 *Official State Gazette* 234, September 30, 2003.

References

Aden, H. (2001) "Convergence of Policing Policies and Transnational Policing in Europe," *European Journal of Crime, Criminal Law and Criminal Justice* 9, no. 2: 99–112.
Alain, M. (2001) "Transnational Police Cooperation in Europe and in North America: Revisiting the Traditional Border between Internal and External Security Matters, or how Policing is being Globalised," *European Journal of Crime, Criminal Law and Criminal Justice* 9, no. 2: 113–29.
Albrecht, H-J. (2002) "Fortress Europe? Controlling illegal immigration," *European Journal of Crime, Criminal Law and Criminal Justice* 10, no. 1: 1–22.
European Commission Staff Working Paper: Joint Report from Commission Services and EUROPOL. (2001) "Towards a European Strategy to Prevent Organised Crime," SEC: Brussels. *433*, March 13.
García Coso, E. (2005) "Spanish Report of the Directive on the Mutual Recognition of Decisions on the Expulsion of Third Country Nationals," in J. Y. Carlier and P. De Bruycker, *Immigration and Asylum Law of the EU: Current Debates*, Brussels: Bruylant, pp. 252–6.
García Coso, E. (2005) "Spanish Report on the Transposition of the Directive Supplementing Article 26 of the Schengen Convention," in J. Y. Carlier and P. De Bruycker, *Immigration and Asylum Law of the EU: Current Debates*, Brussels: Bruylant, pp. 481–6.
Gortazar Rotaeche, C., García Coso, E. and Obregon García, A. (2006) "Trafficking in and Smuggling of Human Beings: the Spanish Approach", in E. Guild and P. Minderhoud, eds., *Immigration and Criminal Law in the European Union. The Legal Measures and Social Consequences of Criminal Law in Member States on Trafficking and Smuggling in Human Beings*, Leiden: Martinus Nihjoff, pp. 271–324.
Kaiafa-Ghandi, M. (2001) "The Development Towards Harmonization within Criminal Law in the European Union: A Citizen's Perspective," *European Journal of Crime, Criminal Law and Criminal Justice* 9, no. 4: 239–63.
Plachta, M. (2003) "European Arrest Warrant: Revolution in Extradition?" *European Journal of Crime, Criminal Law and Criminal Justice* 11, no. 2: 178–94.
Schalken, T. and Pronk, M. (2002) "On Joint Investigation Teams, Europol, and Supervision of their Joint Actions," *European Journal of Crime, Criminal Law and Criminal Justice* 10, no. 1: 70–82.

Smart, U. (2003) "Human Trafficking: Simply a European Problem?" *European Journal of Crime, Criminal Law and Criminal Justice* 11, no. 2: 164–77.

Tak, P. (2000) "Bottlenecks in International Police and Judicial Cooperation in the EU," *European Journal of Crime, Criminal Law and Criminal Justice* 8, no. 4: 343–60.

11 Japanese experience and response in combating trafficking

Atsushi Kondo

Trafficking in persons and sale of human beings

Both human trafficking and anti-trafficking law have existed since ancient times in Japan. In the seventh century, the buying and selling of *Nuhi*,[1] the lowest class of people, was permitted, a practice influenced by Chinese law. On the other hand, making persons *Nuhi* through abduction and selling was severely punished.[2] Later, the *Nuhi* class dissolved; however, poor peasants would sell their children during a famine. Even in modern Japan, there was a problem of *shôgi*, prostitutes who were often sold by their poor parents. In 1872, the Japanese government proclaimed the "Emancipation Decree for Prostitutes (*Shôgi-Kaihô-Rei*), which prohibited "the sale of human beings."[3] This decree was a by-product of the *Maria Luz* incident. When the Peruvian ship *Maria Luz* called at the port of Yokohama, the Japanese government emancipated Chinese "coolie" laborers who were treated like slaves on the ship while being trafficked from China to Peru. The Peruvian party asserted that the sale of slaves was not prohibited under Japanese law because trafficking of prostitutes was a long-standing Japanese custom.[4] Therefore, the emancipation decree was issued in response to the embarrassing comments by the Peruvian party but there was no true liberation of prostitutes. Thus, it was officially explained that licensed prostitutes were engaged in business by their own will rather than by compulsion; however, they were actually forced to engage in prostitution to repay advance payments.

The licensed prostitution system was completely abolished when the Law on the Prevention of Prostitution was enacted in 1958. This law was implementing legislation to comply with the UN Convention for the Suppression of the Traffic in Persons and the Exploitation of the Prostitutions of Others. This Convention was called "Anti-Sale of Human Beings Convention" (*Jinshin-Baibai-Kinshi-Jôyaku*) in Japan. The term *jinshin-baibai* ("sale of humans") was often used in Japan. Article 226 of the 1907 Penal Code punished the "sale of human beings" for the purpose of transporting people from Japan to foreign countries.

Since the middle of the nineteenth century, many Japanese peasant girls had been trafficked from Japan to China and Southeast Asian countries for the main purpose of prostitution. These girls were called *Karayuki-san*,[5] "Ms. Gone to China." In the middle of the twentieth century, Japan changed from a prostitute "sending country" to a "receiving country." Especially since the 1980s, many women have

Japanese experience and response in combating trafficking 217

been trafficked for the main purpose of prostitution from Southeast Asian countries to Japan and they have been called *Japayuki-san*, "Ms. Gone to Japan." Today, countries of origin of the victims of trafficking in persons are expanding from Asia to Latin America and Eastern Europe.

In November 2000, the United Nations General Assembly adopted the Protocol to Prevent, Suppress and Punish Trafficking in Persons, Especially Women and Children, Supplementing the United Nations Convention against Transnational Organized Crime (hereafter referred to as the UN Protocol). Article 3 of the UN Protocol stipulated the comprehensive definition of trafficking in persons. The Japanese government examined the Japanese translation of the term trafficking in persons and chose the term *jinshin-torihiki*, which is the broad concept including cases without giving or receiving of payments or benefits such as money, instead of the term *jinshin-baibai*, which is the narrow concept excluding such cases. The 2005 revised Penal Code established the crime of "sale of human beings" in the narrow concept and stipulated many regulations regarding trafficking in persons in the broad concept. In addition, the 2005 revised Immigration Control and Refugee Recognition Act (hereafter referred to as the Immigration Control Act) stipulated the definition of the term "trafficking in persons or the like,"[6] and added the criteria of special residence permission for victims of trafficking in persons and deportation for the traffickers.

Human trafficking is often referred to in the traditional term *jinshin-baibai*, "sale of human beings." However, in present legal terms, it is referred to as *jinshin-torihiki*, "dealing of human beings" in the broad sense, including cases without giving or receiving of payments or benefits such as money.

In this chapter I discuss the impact of the UN 2000 Protocol and the U.S. 2004 Report in combating trafficking in Japan, examine the relationship between Japanese legal reform and the UN Protocol, and consider the challenges to overcome remaining problems.

Impact of the 2000 UN Protocol and the 2004 U.S. Report

The number of foreign workers in Japan increased rapidly due to the country's economic growth from the time of the Plaza Agreement in mid-1980.[7] At that time mass media often reported that foreign women working in the Japanese sex industry were put into debt for their airplane ticket and other expenses, their passports were confiscated by their managers, and they were forced into prostitution. "*Japayuki-san*" and the human rights violations of victims of human trafficking were social problems. The 1989 revised Immigration Control Act established the crime of encouragement of illegal employment and this restricted the activities of trafficking brokers. This crime could be punished by imprisonment with or without labor for more than three years and/or a fine not exceeding two million yen (presently three million yen). It was often said that many foreign women with "entertainer" visas were forced to be hostesses and prostitutes. In response to criticism from NGOs, the Ministry of Justice investigated the actual working situation of foreigners with "entertainer" visas in 1995 and revised the Ministry

218   *A. Kondo*

of Justice Ordinance to Provide the Criteria for Landing Permission (hereinafter referred to as the Ministry of Justice Ordinance). This ordinance gave strict criteria for accepting the "entertainer" in the sex-related and amusement (entertainment) industries and made a clear distinction between reception and entertainment in 1996. Although the number of new entrants with "entertainer" visas decreased, the number who overstayed these visas increased.[8] In addition, the number of new entrants with "entertainer" visas has increased again since 1997. At that time there was no well-organized investigation of human trafficking in Japan and it is not clear whether or not the number of victims of human trafficking decreased;[9] however, it was no longer a general concern.

In the 2000s, concern was again raised over human trafficking. After the UN General Assembly adopted the UN Protocol in 2000, a Japanese NGO published the book, *Trafficking in Persons and Japan as a Big Receiving Country*[10] in 2001. Although the National Police Agency had been compiling statistics on trafficking since 2000, the UN Committee on the Elimination of Discrimination against Women requested Japan "to provide in its next report comprehensive information and data on the trafficking of women and girls as well as on measures taken in this regard."[11] As for trafficking in children, in 2000 the UN General Assembly adopted the Optional Protocol to the Convention on the Rights of the Child on the Sale of Children, Child Prostitution and Child Pornography. Prior to the signature of this Protocol, the Japanese Parliament established the Law Punishing Acts Related to Child Prostitution and Child Pornography, and for Protecting Children and its Supplementary Provision in 1999. Article 8 of this law stipulates that a person who buys or sells a child shall be punished by imprisonment with labor for not less than one year and not more than ten years in cases of child prostitution and by imprisonment with labor for a limited term of not less than two years (maximum 20 years) in cases of trafficking in children from the residing country to another country. Regarding trafficking in persons, the Japanese government signed the UN Protocol in 2002 and Parliament approved the UN Protocol and amended the trafficking-related laws for the purpose of ratification of the UN Protocol in 2005.[12]

In addition, the U.S. Department of State published the fourth annual Trafficking in Persons Report in June 2004 (hereafter referred to as the U.S. Report),[13] which placed Japan on the "Watch List"—the second worst rank for combating human trafficking—and encouraged the Japanese government to amend the Penal Code. The U.S. Report pointed out the following problems in Japan:

> Japan must speed its review of anti-trafficking legislation and ensure trafficking-related punishments are commensurate with the severity of the crimes. . . . The government currently employs the Penal Code and a variety of labor, immigration, and child welfare/protection statutes to carry out limited trafficking-related prosecutions. These laws provide for up to 10-year prison terms and steep fines, but actual penalties have been far less severe. . . . Over the past year, the Japanese government offered victims of sexual slavery little in the way of legal advice, psychological or financial support. Generally, victims were deported as illegal aliens.

Japanese experience and response in combating trafficking 219

In April 2004, the government established the Inter-Ministerial Liaison Committee (Task Force) regarding measures to combat trafficking in persons. The Task Force—consisting of the Cabinet Secretariat, Cabinet Office, National Police Agency, Ministry of Justice, Ministry of Foreign Affairs, and Ministry of Health, Labor and Welfare—adopted the National Action Plan of Measures to Combat Trafficking in Persons in December 2004.[14] The Japanese Parliament revised the Penal Code in June 2005.

Why were the punishments not commensurate with the severity of human trafficking before the 2005 revision of the Penal Code in Japan? Let us examine the typical case of "Sony." A Japanese broker who was called by the alias of "Sony" recruited and supplied two Colombian women aged 16 and 23 to the "stripping theatre" where they had to dance wearing almost nothing and act as prostitutes in rooms behind the stage. The broker was arrested on the suspicion of the crimes of "recruiting harmful work" and "promoting illegal employment." Pursuant to Article 63 of the Employment Security Law, a person who engages in labor recruitment by means of violence or with an intention of having workers do work harmful to public health or morals shall be punished by imprisonment with labor for a limited term of not less than one year and not more than ten years or a fine of not less than 200,000 yen and not more than three million yen. Under Article 73–2 of the Immigration Control Act, a person who has recruited foreigners in illegal work shall be punished by imprisonment with labor for not more than three years and/or a fine of not less than 200,000 yen and not more than two million (at present three million) yen. In the Sony case in 2003, the Tokyo District Court decided on punishment of only imprisonment with labor for one year and ten months. Indeed, it confirmed that he had a criminal record of promoting illegal employment, he had recruited and supplied between 70 and 80 Colombian women, and their work included prostitution; however, it concluded that they worked by their own volition and there was no evidence of violence, threat, and so forth.[15] However, Sony had previous convictions and so was given a prison sentence. Most offenders were given suspended sentences with no jail but a fine instead;[16] victims of trafficking were often given suspended sentences for illegal employment and were deported.[17] Thus, in Japan before the trafficking-related laws revision of 2005, offenders' punishment was light and there were few protections for the victims.

Relation between trafficking-related laws revision of 2005 and the UN Protocol

The UN Protocol has three main parts: (1) criminal sanctions; (2) protection of victims; (3) prevention. Article 3 of the Protocol defines "trafficking in persons" in the viewpoints of purpose, means, and acts. The purpose is exploitation, which includes, at a minimum, the exploitation of the prostitution of others or other forms of sexual exploitation, forced labor or services, slavery or practices similar to slavery, servitude, or the removal of organs. Its means are the threat or use of force or other forms of coercion, abduction, fraud, or deception, the abuse of power or of a position of vulnerability, or the giving or receiving of payments or benefits to

220   *A. Kondo*

achieve the consent of a person having control over another person. Its acts are the recruitment, transportation, transfer, harboring, or receipt of persons. The consent of a trafficked victim to exploitation is irrelevant where any of the means listed above are used. Trafficking in children under 18 years of age is considered a crime even if there is no means listed above.

Let us examine the Japanese legal reform, comparing it to the UN Protocol. The Penal Code, the Code of Criminal Procedure, the Immigration Control Act, and the Law for Punishment of Organized Crimes, Control of Crime Proceeds and Other Matters (hereinafter referred to as the Organized Crime Punishment Law) were amended in June 2005, the Ministry of Justice Ordinance for the status of residence for "entertainer" was amended in February 2005, and the Law on Control and Improvement of Amusement Business was amended in October 2005.

The purpose of "threat to the life or body" is added to kidnapping crime

Even in the previous Penal Code, kidnapping of minors (Article 224) and kidnapping for profit, indecency, or marriage (Article 225) had some similarity to the concept of human trafficking. A person who kidnaps a minor by force or enticement shall be punished by imprisonment with labor for not less than three months but not more than seven years. A person who kidnaps another by force or enticement for the purpose of profit, indecency, marriage, or threat to life or body shall be punished by imprisonment with labor for not less than one year but not more than ten years.

However, kidnapping for the purpose of "the removal of organs" (in Article 3 of the Protocol) does not necessarily correspond to the purpose of profit if the organs are transplanted into a member of the trafficking gang.[19] Therefore, the revised Article 225 added the purpose of "threat to the life or body" in which "the removal of organs" shall be included.[20] Kidnapping refers to the act of "recruitment" in Article 3 of the Protocol. Although the "threat or use of force or other forms of coercion, of abduction, fraud, deception, abuse of power, or of a position of vulnerability" includes kidnapping, "giving or receiving of payments or benefits to achieve the consent of a person having control over another person" does not include kidnapping.

Establishment of the crime of sale of human beings

It also was necessary to include new regulations on the crime of buying or selling of human beings (Articles 226–2) for the act of recruitment by means of "giving or receiving of payments or benefits to achieve the consent of a person having control over another person" as set forth in the UN Protocol. A person who buys or sells another shall be punished by imprisonment with labor for not less than three months but not more than five years. A person who buys or sells a minor shall be punished by imprisonment with labor for not less than three months but not more than seven years, for the sake of strengthening the protection of minors. A person who buys or sells another, for the purpose of profit or the like, shall be punished by imprisonment with labor for not less than one year but not more than ten years, in order to align it with kidnapping for profit.

Expansion of the scope of conduct punishable for transportation of kidnapped persons

In the previous Penal Code, transportation of kidnapped persons (Article 226) dealt with transporting victims out of Japan, *Karayuki-san*. However, in the present situation it is necessary to cope with transportation of victims into Japan, *Japayuki-san*. Therefore, the revised Penal Code changed the term from "from Japan" to "from the Country where they were." A person who sells or buys others for the purpose of transporting them from the country where they were to another country shall be punished by imprisonment with labor for not less than two years (maximum 20 years) in the new Article 226–3. The term "from the country where they were" includes the transportation of kidnapped persons who are traveling abroad.

Article 4 of the Protocol applies to the prosecution of international organized crimes; therefore, the Penal Code is required to extend the punishment target to the transportation of kidnapped persons from one country to another. However, the punishment target is not necessary to cover all the crimes committed outside the territory of Japan because the Protocol does not demand punishment for the transportation of kidnapped persons by foreigners from one foreign country to another foreign country. Regarding the crime of transportation of kidnapped persons committed outside the territory of Japan, the Penal Code shall apply to any Japanese citizens who committed the crime in Article 3 and to any non-Japanese citizens who committed the crime against a Japanese citizen outside the territory of Japan.

Establishing the crime of transfer of kidnapped persons

In the previous Penal Code, the punishment targets were the acts of "receipt," "harboring," and "enabling to escape" of kidnapped persons (Article 227). In the revised Penal Code, the punishment targets were extended to the acts of "transfer" and "transportation" (Article 227). The term "harboring" refers to the act of offering a place to hide kidnapped persons. Other acts of impeding the discovery of a kidnapped person, including giving false information, are covered by the term "enabling to escape." Article 227–3 of the Penal Code does not punish enabling to escape for the purpose of profit. This does not violate personal liberty, and Article 3—related to Article 5 of the Protocol—does not demand the criminalizing of the act of enabling to escape.[21]

Concealment or receipt of crime proceeds

The Annexed Table of the Organized Crime Punishment Law was amended to designate as an offense trafficking in persons for concealment or receipt of crime proceeds. A person who conceals crime proceeds or the like shall be imprisoned with labor for not more than five years or fined not more than three million yen,

222   A. Kondo

or both (Article 10–1). Any person who knowingly receives crime proceeds or the like shall be imprisoned with labor for not more than three years or fined not more than one million yen, or both (Article 11).

This amendment is required to cover the offense for money laundering, as stipulated in the Article 1–3, 5, and 6 of the UN Protocol.

Examination of witness through the video link system

In the previous Code of Criminal Procedure (Article 157–4), examination of a witness could occur by having the witness in a place other than the courtroom and using devices that allowed communication by images and sounds in cases of sex crimes such as rape and kidnapping for the purpose of indecency or marriage. This was called the video link system, and was introduced to ease the psychological burden on a witness testifying in open court. The revised Code of Criminal Procedure (Article 157–4) extended the use of the video link system to the victims of the sale of human beings for the purpose of indecency and marriage because they are supposed to have suffered sexual harm.

Special residence permission for victims

Special residence permission is important for the protection of victims. Pursuant to the 2005 amendment of the Immigration Control Act, the Minister of Justice may grant special residence permission (Article 50–1-3) or special landing permission (Article 12–1-2) to an irregular resident if he or she resides in Japan or has entered Japan "under the control of another due to trafficking in persons." On the other hand, those who have committed trafficking in persons may be deported (Article 24–4-c) or denied permission for landing in Japan (Article 5–1-7–2).[22]

This amendment corresponds to Article 7 of the UN Protocol, which stipulated that "each State Party shall consider adopting legislative or other appropriate measures that permit victims of trafficking in persons to remain in its territory, temporarily or permanently, in appropriate cases." The UN Protocol applied the voluntary rule method "in appropriate cases," and kept the State Party's discretion of deportation. The special residence permission in the Immigration Control Act grants wide discretion to the Minister of Justice.

Strict control of sex-related and amusement businesses

Because many victims of trafficking in persons have been employed in sex-related and amusement businesses, the Law on the Control and Improvement of Amusement Business was amended to crack down on illegal employment in such businesses. To prevent trafficking brokers from managing the sex-related and amusement business, the crime of human trafficking justifies disqualification of sex-related and amusement business permits and business suspension (Article 4–1-2). To inhibit illicit work, owners of sex-related and amusement businesses shall verify the immigration status of foreign employees whom they recruit (Article 36–2).

Japanese experience and response in combating trafficking 223

This amendment is considered to correspond with Article 9 of the UN Protocol, which requires countries to "adopt or strengthen legislative or other measures . . . to discourage the demand that fosters all forms of exploitation of persons, especially women and children, that leads to trafficking."

Strict review for visas for "entertainers"

It has been recognized that many people who entered Japan with "entertainer" visas were not engaged as entertainers but rather as hostesses in sex-related and amusement businesses and some of them were forced into prostitution.[23] To prevent entertainer visas from being abused by traffickers of persons, the Ministry of Justice Ordinance to Provide for Criteria for Visa was amended in February 2005 to delete the provision that applicants who intend to engage in performances for "entertainer" visas shall "meet the standards set by a foreign national or local government agency or an equivalent public or private organization."[24] Those who qualify as entertainers are generally required to have spent a minimum of two years studying or have experience relevant to the specified type of performance. A further amendment that tightened the disqualification standard for the operators, managers or other regular employees of the inviting organizations and established a more strict obligation of payment of salaries (at least 200,000 yen) on contracts with entertainers was issued in March 2006.

These amendments are also considered to correspond with Article 9 of the UN Protocol. The number of new entrants with "entertainer" visas declined from 2004 to 2006, especially in the case of Filipinas, where it dropped sharply, as shown in Table 11.1.

Challenges for the future

It is recognized that Japan made progress in 2005 to advance the criminalization of trafficking in persons, protection of the trafficked victims, and prevention of human trafficking. Previously, suspended sentences were often given to traffickers, and even in the case of a second offense case, such as that of "Sony" mentioned above, the court handed down only imprisonment with labor for one year and ten months. Since enforcement of the revised Penal Code in July 2005, assessment of cases has changed. The Nagano District Court applied the crime of sale of human beings (Article 226–2) for the first time in Japan, and handed down a sentence of imprisonment with labor for five years to the owner of snack bar who bought two Indonesian women for the

Table 11.1 The number of new entrants on "entertainer" visas (2004–6)

Year	2004	2005	2006
Total number	134,879	99,342	48,250
Of which Filipinas	82,741	47,765	8,607

Source: Ministry of Justice.

224　*A. Kondo*

purpose of profit and imprisonment with labor for three years and six months to the brokers who sold them.[25] Previously, regardless of their regular or irregular residence status, the victims of human trafficking were deported for violation of the Immigration Control Act. Presently, the Ministry of Justice is inclined to grant special residence permission to the victims who are irregular residents, as shown in Table 11.2, under the revised Immigration Control Act. Furthermore, the Japanese government has produced one million pamphlets in seven languages informing potential victims where to seek help, and has funded programs in countries of origin of victims or by international organizations such as UNICEF and ILO.

Many problems remain to be resolved. For instance, the U.S. Report in 2006 kept Japan in Tier 2, which does not fully comply with the minimum standards for the elimination of trafficking, even if it is not the Watch List in which Japan was included in the 2004 Report. The reasons for the negative assessment were that in 2005

> three of the 64 offenders convicted for trafficking-related offenses served prison sentences, ranging from four to five years' imprisonment and significant fines. In line with Japanese judicial practice, most other offenders were given suspended sentences, which generally entailed a fine and no jail sentence as long as the offender refrains from committing another crime during a set period of time.

As for the protection of victims, "the number identified is still relatively low . . . more coordinated referral mechanisms and a dedicated trafficking shelter would improve the services available to victims."

In order to strengthen the protection of victims of trafficking in persons, the opposition party had submitted a bill to Parliament,[26] which was not passed. However, on

Table 11.2 The number of special residence permission and regular residence granted to trafficking victims (2005–6)

Year	Special Residence Permission			Regular Residence		
	2005	2006	Total	2005	2006	Total
Philippines	22	10	32	25	19	44
Thailand	17	2	19		1	1
Indonesia	4	14	18	37		37
Colombia	4		4			
Korea		1	1			
Romania				4		4
China				2		2
Total	47	27	74	68	20	88

Source: The Immigration Bureau in the Ministry of Justice.

Japanese experience and response in combating trafficking 225

the occasion of the passage of a government bill both the House of Representatives and the House of Councilors referred to the supplementary resolutions for the main purpose of comprehensive legislation to improve the protection of victims. The staff of the International Organization for Migration (IOM) noted four problems to be solved: (1) the establishment of a local liaison council of related organizations; (2) temporary protection for potential victims; (3) temporary or long-term support for victims who will not want to return; and (4) securing shelter for male victims.[27]

Regarding long-term support, there is a problem that the operation of special residence permission in Japan always presupposed that victims will return to their countries of origin. Indeed, in the parliamentary discussion on introducing special residence permission for trafficking victims when amending the Immigration Control Act, it was explained that the victims may possibly be in danger if they return to their countries of origin.[28] However, the victims of trafficking in persons were always granted temporary residence status as "designated activity" without presupposing long-term residence. Therefore, they cannot be covered under the National Health Insurance Act, which is applied to foreign residents who are presupposed to live in Japan for more than one year, and they cannot be covered under the Livelihood Protection Act, which is applied to foreign residents with the status of permanent residents, spouses or children of Japanese citizens, spouses or children of permanent residents, and quasi-permanent residents.[29]

Women's Consulting Offices have been established in each prefecture pursuant to Article 34 of the Prostitution Prevention Law. Since 2004 they have been formally used to provide appropriate protection for trafficked victims as temporary shelters, although a few informal cases existed previously, as shown in Table 11.3. However, generally, men cannot enter the public and private shelters. Currently, it is reported that all protected victims of human trafficking in Japan are sexually exploited women. However, for example, 93,837 persons entered Japan with a residence status of "trainee" in 2006. The idea of the trainee system is the transfer of technology to developing countries, but in reality there are many cases of small businesses that are troubled with a labor shortage inviting cheap unskilled foreign workers.[30] Some trainees, who are charged guarantee money and are in debt to brokers in their countries of origin, are forced to work a long time under the control of the receiving company that prevents them from escaping by keeping their passports and forced saving. This is called "Disguised Human Trafficking."[31]

Table 11.3 The number of victims protected at Women's Consulting Office

FY2001	1 (1 Thai)
FY2002	2 (2 Thai)
FY2003	6 (3 Thai and 3 Filipinas)
FY2004	24 (15 Thai, 4 Taiwanese, 3 Indonesians, 1 Colombian, 1 Korean)
FY2005	112 (59 Filipinas, 40 Indonesians, 6 Taiwanese, 4 Thai, etc.)

Source: Ministry of Foreign Affairs, "The Recent Actions Japan has taken to combat TIP." Available at: <http://www.mofa.go.jp/policy/i_crime/people/action0508.html>

226   *A. Kondo*

It should be noted that men are also potential victims of trafficking, and efforts should be made to improve the working environment in Japan.

In the Women's Consulting Offices, protected persons can stay for only two weeks in general (four weeks in prolonged cases). When they enter the private shelters via the Women's Consulting Offices, they can receive a temporary protection consignment per diem (about 6,500 yen a day). The Ministry of Health, Labor and Welfare subsidized 52 victims out of 112 in FY 2005. However, the private shelters' budgets are constantly short. Therefore, NGOs such as the Japan Federation of Bar Associations, the Japan Network against Trafficking in Persons and the Solidarity Network with Migrants Japan recommended that the Japanese government establish a special facility, a "Support Center for Victims of Trafficking in Persons" (tentative name), to provide effective protection with professional staff, public funds, and damage recovery programs.[32] However, the number of protected victims declined from 117 in 2005 to 58 in 2006 as shown in Table 11.4; therefore, the government explained that it was difficult to establish the specified support center.

Table 11.4 Number of identified trafficking cases and victims

Year	2000	2001	2002	2003	2004	2005	2006
Number of cases	80	64	4	51	79	81	72
Number of arrested persons	55	40	28	41	58	83	78
Number of brokers	16	9	7	8	23	26	24
Number of victims	104	65	55	83	77	117	58
Philippines	4	12	2		13	40	30
Indonesia	3	4		3		44	14
Taiwan	3	7	3	12	5	4	10
Thailand	73	39	40	21	48	21	3
South Korea	1				3	1	1
Romania						4	
Australia						1	
Estonia						1	
Colombia	1	3	6	43	5	1	
Russia	12				2		
Laos					1		
China	7		4	2			
Cambodia				2			

Source: National Police Agency.

Japanese experience and response in combating trafficking 227

In addition, the NGOs recommended that the government establish a trafficking victims' recognition system, which will grant victims temporary residence permission for recovery and reflection to decide whether to return to their home country or remain in Japan, and quasi-permanent residence permission if they wish to remain in Japan. This should open the way to reside permanently in Japan, depending on the circumstances of the victims.

For instance, in the United States, victims of a severe form of trafficking in persons and suffering extreme hardship involving unusual and severe harm upon removal may be granted a temporary residence permit with social assistance, and after three years they may be granted a permanent residence permit under the Immigration and Nationality Act and the Trafficking Victims Protection (Reauthorization) Act. In Belgium, if a victim files a complaint after a 45-day "reflection delay" (suspended expulsion order), a three-month and then a six-month residence permit with social assistance will be renewed until the end of criminal proceedings, and permanent residence status may be granted on the condition of the case closing, staying in Belgium for at least two years, and social integration under the 1994 Circular.[33] In Italy, pursuant to Article 18 of the Immigration Act, a victim may be granted a renewable six-month residence permit with social assistance, and if after 18 months the victim can show promise of employment and can demonstrate a degree of integration into Italian society, permanent residence status may be granted.[34] In the Netherlands, the reflection period is granted for three months, and the temporary residence permit with social assistance is granted for the duration of the criminal investigation and the trial. In contrast to the United States, Belgium, and Italy, in general victims are asked to leave the territory after the completion of the judicial process; however, permanent residence status may be granted on humanitarian grounds of the risk of reprisal.[35]

Presently, Article 5 of the Charter of Fundamental Rights of the European Union prohibits trafficking in human beings, as well as slavery, servitude, and forced or compulsory labor. In 1865, the U.S. Constitution prohibited slavery and involuntary servitude. Influenced by the United States, Article 18 of the Japanese Constitution prohibits bondage of any kind and involuntary servitude. Combating human trafficking is not only required by international laws such as the Protocol but also is covered by constitutional laws. Section 101 of the U.S. Trafficking Victims Protection Act stipulates that "the purposes of this division are to combat trafficking in persons, a contemporary manifestation of slavery whose victims are predominantly women and children, to ensure just and effective punishment of traffickers, and to protect their victims." Under the Japanese Constitution the government is required to enact the Trafficking Victims Protection Act because trafficking victims shall not be held in bondage of any kind (Article 18), their right to life, liberty, and the pursuit of happiness shall be the supreme consideration in legislation (Article 13), and they shall have freedom of residence to the extent that it does not interfere with the public welfare (Article 22).[36]

228   *A. Kondo*

Notes

1 Masajirô Takigawa, *Ritsu-Ryô Senmin Sei no Kenkyû* (A Study of the "Lowborn" People under the *Ritsu-Ryô* Codes), p. 416, referred to *"Nuhi"* as "slavery" because a *Nu* (a male slave) and a *Hi* (a female slave) were owned by other persons and were forced to work for other persons. Generally speaking, *Nuhi* were referred to as "half-person and half-thing" and distinct from the Roman slaves because *Nuhi* had the right to own lands and goods, the right to marriage and the freedom of life without being killed by their owners, even if they were objects for sale and inheritance. See Ryosuke Ishii, *Nihon Hôseishi Gaisetsu* (The Outline of Japanese Legal History), p. 80.

2 *Yôrô-Ritsu: Ryakujin-Jô* (Penal Code of the *Yôrô* era: article on abduction of persons) in Kokushi Taikei Henshûkai (ed.), *Kokushi Taikei. (National History Collection) Newly revised and enlarged version. Vol. 22*, p. 74; See Hidemasa Maki, *Nihon Hôseishi ni okeru Jinshin-Baibai no Kenkyû* (A Study of Sale of Persons in the History of Japanese Law), pp. 30–8. The second oldest official Japanese history book, *Nihonshoki*, noted that even if peasants asked to sell their children during a famine, the Imperial Government refused permission. See W. G. Aston, *Nihongi: Chronicles of Japan from the Earliest Times to A.D. 697*, p. 332.

3 *Dajôkan Fukoku* No. 295. See Hidemasa Maki, *Jinshin-Baibai* (Sale of Persons), p. 5.

4 Gaimushô Chôsa Bu (The Research Bureau in the Ministry of Foreign Affairs), *Dai-Nihon-Gaikô-Bunsho* (Diplomatic Documents of Great Japan), p. 448. See Yasuzo Kitamura, "Evolution of Anti-trafficking in Persons and Practice in Japan: A Historical Perspective."

5 Katsumi Mori, *Jinshin-Baibai* (Sale of Persons), p. 50 ff.; Kazue Moriwaki, *Karayuki-san* (Japanese Prostitutes Gone to China and Southeast Asian Countries), p. 18 ff.

6 Pursuant to Article 2(7) of the Immigration Control Act, the term "trafficking in persons or the like" means any of the following acts:
(a) The kidnapping or the buying or selling of persons for the purpose of making a profit, committing an indecent act or causing injury to their life or physical being, or delivering, receiving, transporting or harboring such persons who have been kidnapped or bought or sold;
(b) Except for the acts set forth in Sub-item (a), placing persons under the age of 18 under one's own control for the purpose of making a profit, committing an indecent act or causing injury to their life or physical being;
(c) Except for the acts set forth in Sub-item (a), delivering persons under the age of 18, knowing that they will be or might be placed under the control of a person who has the purpose of making a profit, committing an indecent act or causing injury to their life or physical being.
This definition used the Japanese legal terms such as the Penal Code and the Child Welfare Law. The term "trafficking in persons or the like" instead of the term "trafficking in persons" was used because the former in the Immigration Control Act had the broader scope than the latter in the UN Protocol.

7 Atsushi Kondo, "The Development of Immigration Policy in Japan."

8 Hômushô Nyûkoku Kanrikyoku (The Immigration Bureau in the Ministry of Justice) *Heisei 10 Nenban Shuutsunyûkoku Kanri* (Immigration Control), pp. 91–5.

9 As for the NGO's research on the trafficking in Thai women, see Human Rights Watch, *OWED JUSTICE: Thai Women Trafficked into Debt Bondage in Japan.*

10 Kyoto YMCA and APT (Asian People Together) (eds.), *Jinshin-Baibai to Ukeire-Taikoku Nippon* (Trafficking in Persons and Japan as a Big Receiving Country).

11 CEDAW/C/2003/II/CRP.3/Add.1/Rev.1, para. 27 f. Committee on the Elimination of Discrimination against Women. Consideration of the fourth and fifth periodic reports of Japan, July 18, 2003.

12 After the relevant laws are amended, the Japanese government will conclude reform proposed by the UN Protocol and the UN Convention Against Transnational Organized

Japanese experience and response in combating trafficking 229

Crime as soon as possible. According to the government, the reform to include the rule of conspiracy in the Law for Punishment of Organized Crimes, Control of Crime Proceeds and Other Matters is indispensable to ratifying the Protocol and the Convention; however, there are many objections to the government's opinion.

13 U.S. Department of State, Trafficking in Persons Report (2004 Report), <http://www.state.gov/g/tip/rls/tiprpt/2004/> (accessed May 7, 2007).

14 Japan's Action Plan of Measures to Combat Trafficking in Persons. <http://www.mofa.go.jp/policy/i_crime/people/action.html> (accessed May 7, 2007).

15 Tokyo District Court, March 28, 2007.

16 According to National Police Agency, penalties for four years (from 2000 to 2003) ranged from one to two years' prison sentence on average (although suspended sentences were often awarded for first arrests), to a maximum of four years without suspension, with fines of usually less than 500,000 yen (approx. US$4,700) up to a maximum of two million yen (approx. US$19,000). See *Human Trafficking for Sexual Exploitation in Japan*, p. 39.

17 In the case of "Sony," 68 Colombian women were arrested and sent to the police or the Immigration Bureau; however, no one was protected in the Women's Consulting Offices. See Keiko Ôtsu, *Josei no Ie HELP kara mieru Josei eno Bôryoku Jinshin-Baibai* (From the Viewpoint of the House for Women, HELP, Violence against Women and Trafficking in Persons), p. 13.

18 There are other important reforms: raising the upper limit of imprisonment with labor for the crime of an unlawful capture and confinement (Article 220 of the Penal Code) from five years to seven years; raising the upper limit of imprisonment with labor for the organized crime of an unlawful capture and confinement (Article 3–1-4 of the Organized Crime Punishment Law) from seven years to ten years; raising the upper limit of the fine for the crime of aiding another to commit illegal entry (Article 74–6 of the Immigration Control Act) from two million yen to three million yen. A non-penal fine not exceeding 500,000 yen in cases of the violation of the obligation for carriers to check passports and other travel documents (Article 76–6 of the Immigration Control Act); provision of information to immigration authorities of other countries (Article 61–9 of the Immigration Control Act).

19 Shin Kukimoto, *"Keihô tô no Ichibu wo Kaisei suru Hôritsu" ni tsuite* (About the "Law on Partial Reform of the Penal Code etc."), p. 87 ff.

20 Same as Articles 226–2-3 and 227–3. According to the UN Protocol, the way to enumerate "purposes such as sexual exploitation, forced labor, and the removal of organs" were considered; however, the concepts of "sexual exploitation" and the "removal of organs" were vague; therefore, the Penal Code stipulated the purpose of "threat to the life or body." See Osamu Sakuma, *"Jinshin no Jiyû ni taisuru Hôseibi ni tsuite"* (On the Law Reform of Personal Laverty), p. 11.

21 Kukimoto, *"Keihô tô no Ichibu wo Kaisei suru Hôritsu"*, p. 100.

22 According to the Immigration Control Office, as the offenders of human trafficking laws, a Filipino was deported in 2005, three Filipinos and a Thai were deported in 2006, and all were women.

23 According to the National Police Agency, the total number of trafficking victims was 117 in 2005. Of that number, 67 women (57.3 percent) entered Japan on "entertainer" visas and 12 women (10.2 percent) entered Japan as "short-term stay." Almost all victims (96.6 percent) were forced to work as hostesses, owed large amounts of money to their "owners," who kept their passports, and were exploited for prostitution. In 2006, the total number of trafficking victims was 58. Among them, the number of "entertainer" visas declined to 18 (31.0 percent), "illegal entry" was 20 (34.5 percent), "short-term stay" was 12 (20.7 percent), "over-stay" was 7 (12.1 percent) and "spouse or child of Japanese citizen" was 1 (1.7 percent).

24 The background of this crackdown was the fact that "in particular those who have entered Japan having fulfilled the criteria for landing permission by holding a certificate issued

230   *A. Kondo*

by the Government of the Philippines, which testifies that the holder is an artist, but in fact does not have ability as an artist. See Japan's Action Plan of Measures to Combat Trafficking in Persons, *supra* note 14, p. 4.

25 According to the report of the Ministry of Foreign Affairs, "the number of prosecutions for buying and selling persons after the Penal Code was amended in June 2005 is 19, and nine offenders were sentenced to imprisonment. The most severe sentence was five years and six months' imprisonment, the mildest one is two years and six months'." *Asahi Newspaper*, March 29, 2006; May 18, 2006. The Recent Actions Japan has taken to combat TIP, <http://www.mofa.go.jp/policy/i_crime/people/action0508.html> (accessed May 7, 2007).

26 Minshutô (the Democratic Party of Japan), *Jinshin-Torihiki tô no Bôshi oyobi Jinshin-Torihiki no Higaisha no Hogo ni kansuru Hôritshu-An* (The Bill on Prevention of Trafficking in Persons or the Like and Protection of Victims of Trafficking in Persons), <http://www.dpj.or.jp/news/files/BOX_0073_hon.pdf> (accessed May 7, 2007).

27 Mayumi Ueno, *Jinshin-Torihiki Mondai to Nihon no Torikumi* (Problem of Trafficking in Persons and Its Approach of Japan), p. 22 ff.

28 See Naoki Hosaka, *Shutsunyûkoku-Kanri oyobi Nanmin-Nintei Hô no Ichibu Kaisei ni tsuite* (On the Partial Reform of the Immigration Control and Refugee Recognition Act), p. 34.

29 See Atsushi Kondo, "Citizenship Rights for Aliens in Japan."

30 As trainees (one year) and as technical interns (two years), foreigners can stay for a maximum of three years. Trainees cannot receive wages (only training allowance), but technical interns may earn wages. Labor laws such as the Labor Standards Law apply to technical interns, but do not apply to trainees. Foreigners whose status is "trainee" and/or "technical intern" must return to their countries of origin after a certain period of residence (maximum three years), even if they want to work longer in Japan. Japanese NGOs referred to this as the "Japanese style rotation system." The Republic of Korea had a similar trainee system and Korean NGOs often referred to it as "modern slavery."

31 Gaikokujin Kenshûsei Mondai Network (Network for the Problem Foreigner Trainees), *Gaikokujin Kenshûsei: Jikyû 300 Yen no Rôdôsha* (Foreigner Trainees: Workers whose hourly wage is 300 yen), p. 168.

32 Nihon Bengoshi Rengôkai (the Japan Federation of Bar Associations), *Jinshin-Torishiki Higaisha no Hogo Shien ni kansuru Hôseibi ni taisuru Teigen* (Proposal for the Law Reform on the Protection and Assistance on Victims of Trafficking in Persons), <http://www.nichibenren.or.jp/ja/opinion/report/data/2004_62.pdf> (accessed May 7, 2007); Japan Network Against Trafficking in Persons, *Jinshin-Baibai wo nakusu tameni: Ukeire-Taikoku Nippon no Kadai* (Combating Trafficking in Persons: Challenges in Japan as a Big Receiving Country), p. 145; *Ijûren "Jose eno Bôryoku" Project* ("End Violence Against Women" Project, SMJ) (ed.), *Domestic Violence to Jinshin-Baibai* (Domestic Violence and Trafficking in Persons), p. 85; Yoko Yoshida, *Nihon ni okeru Jinshin-Torihiki no Kadai* (Challenges of Human Trafficking in Japan).

33 Joanna Apap and Medved Felicita, *Protection Schemes for Victims of Trafficking in Selected EU Member Countries*, p. 41.

34 Ibid., p. 65 ff.

35 Helga Konrad, "Trafficking in Human Beings: A Comparative Account of Legal Provisions in Belgium, Italy, the Netherlands, Sweden and the United States."

36 For the relation between freedom of residence in the Constitution and the special residence permission in the Immigration Control Act, see Atsushi Kondo, *Gaikokujin no Jinken to Shiminken* (Human Rights for Foreigners and Citizenship).

References

Apap, Joanna and Medved, Felicita. (2003) *Protection Schemes for Victims of Trafficking in Selected EU Member Countries*, Candidate and Third Countries, Geneva: IOM.

Japanese experience and response in combating trafficking 231

Aston, W. G. (1972) *Nihongi: Chronicles of Japan from the Earliest Times to A.D. 697*, Rutland: Tuttle.

Gaikokujin Kenshûsei Mondai Network (Network for the Problem Foreigner Trainees). (2006) *Gaikokujin Kenshûsei: Jikyû 300 Yen no Rôdôsha* (Foreigner Trainees: Workers Whose Hourly Wage is 300 yen), Tokyo: Akashi Shoten.

Gaimushô Chôsa Bu (The Research Bureau in the Ministry of Foreign Affairs). (1939) *Dai-Nihon-Gaikô-Bunsho* (Diplomatic Documents of Great Japan), Tokyo: Nihon Kokusai Kyôkai, 1939.

Hômushô Nyûkoku Kanrikyoku (The Immigration Bureau in the Ministry of Justice). (1998) *Heisei 10 Nenban Shuutsunyûkoku Kanri* (Immigration Control), Tokyo: Ôkurashô Insatsukyoku.

Hosaka, Naoki. (2005) *Shutsunyûkoku-Kanri oyobi Nanmin-Nintei Hô no Ichibu Kaisei ni tsuite* (On the Partial Reform of the Immigration Control and Refugee Recognition Act), *Keisatsu Koron* 60, no. 9: 34.

Human Rights Watch. (2000) *OWED JUSTICE: Thai Women Trafficked into Debt Bondage in Japan*, New York: Human Rights Watch.

Human Trafficking for Sexual Exploitation in Japan. (2004) Tokyo: ILO Office in Japan.

Ijûren "Jose eno Bôryoku" Project ("End Violence Against Women" Project, SMJ) ed. (2004) *Domestic Violence to Jinshin-Baibai* (Domestic Violence and Trafficking in Persons), Tokyo: Gendai-Jinbunsha.

Ishii, Ryosuke. (1971) *Nihon Hôseishi Gaisetsu* (The Outline of Japanese Legal History), Tokyo: Sôbunsha.

Japan Network Against Trafficking in Persons. (2001) *Jinshin-Baibai wo nakusu tameni: Ukeire-Taikoku Nippon no Kadai* (Combating Trafficking in Persons: Challenges in Japan as a Big Receiving Country), Tokyo: Akashi Shoten.

Kitamura, Yasuzo. (2006) "Evolution of Anti-trafficking in Persons and Practice in Japan: A Historical Perspective," *Tulane Journal of International and Comparative Law* 14, no. 2: 336–40.

Kokushi Taikei Henshûkai (ed.) (1966) *Kokushi Taikei. (National History Collection) Newly revised and enlarged version. Vol. 22*, Tokyo: Yoshikawa Kôbundô.

Kondo, Atsushi. (2001) "Citizenship Rights for Aliens in Japan," in Atsushi Kondo, ed., *Citizenship in a Global World: Comparing Citizenship Rights for Aliens*, New York: Palgrave, p. 17 ff.

Kondo, Atsushi. (2001) *Gaikokujin no Jinken to Shiminken* (Human Rights for Foreigners and Citizenship), Tokyo: Akashi Shoten.

Kondo, Atsushi. (2002) "The Development of Immigration Policy in Japan," *Asian and Pacific Migration Journal* 11, no. 4: 415–36.

Konrad, Helga. (2006) "Trafficking in Human Beings: A Comparative Account of Legal Provisions in Belgium, Italy, the Netherlands, Sweden and the United States," in Christien L. van den Anker and Jeroen Doomernik, eds., *Trafficking and Women's Rights*, New York: Palgrave, pp. 127–31.

Kukimoto, Shin. (2005) *"Keihô tô no Ichibu wo Kaisei suru Hôritsu" ni tsuite* (About the "Law on Partial Reform of the Penal Code etc."), *Keisatsu-Gaku Ronshû* 58, no. 9.

Kyoto YMCA and APT (Asian People Together), eds. (2001) *Jinshin-Baibai to Ukeire-Taikoku Nippon* (Trafficking in Persons and Japan as a Big Receiving Country), Tokyo: Akashi Shoten.

Maki, Hidemasa. (1961) *Nihon Hôseishi ni okeru Jinshin-Baibai no Kenkyû* (A Study of Sale of Persons in the History of Japanese Law), Tokyo: Yûhikaku.

Maki, Hidemasa. (1971) *Jinshin-Baibai* (Sale of Persons), Tokyo: Yûhikaku.

232   A. Kondo

Mori, Katsumi. (1966) *Jinshin-Baibai* (Sale of Persons), Tokyo: Shivundô.

Moriwaki, Kazue. (1976) *Karayuki-san* (Japanese Prostitutes Gone to China and Southeast Asian Countries), Tokyo: Asahi Shinbun Sha.

Nihon Bengoshi Rengôkai (Japan Federation of Bar Associations). (2004) *Jinshin-Torishiki Higaisha no Hogo Shien ni kansuru Hôseibi ni taisuru Teigen* (Proposal for the Law Reform on the Protection and Assistance on Victims of Trafficking in Persons), <http://www.nichibenren.or.jp/ja/opinion/report/data/2004_62.pdf> (accessed May 7, 2007).

Ôtsu, Keiko. (2005) *Josei no Ie HELP kara mieru Josei eno Bôryoku Jinshin-Baibai* (From the Viewpoint of the House for Women, HELP, Violence against Women and Trafficking in Persons), *Gender and Law* no. 2: 13.

Sakuma, Osamu. (2005) *"Jinshin no Jiyû ni taisuru Hôseibi ni tsuite"* (On the Law Reform of Personal Laverty) *Jurist* no. 1286: 11.

Takigawa, Masajirô. (1967) *Ritsu-Ryô Senmin Sei no Kenkyû* (A Study of the "Lowborn" People under the *Ritsu-Ryô* Codes), Tokyo: Kadokawa Shoten.

Ueno, Mayumi. (2006) *Jinshin-Torihiki Mondai to Nihon no Torikumi* (Problem of Trafficking in Persons and Its Approach of Japan). *Kokusai Jinrhû* (The Immigration Newsmagazine) 229: 22 ff.

Yoshida, Yoko. (2006) *Nihon ni okeru Jinshin-Torihiki no Kadai* (Challenges of Human Trafficking in Japan), in Asia-Pacific Human Rights Information Center, ed., *Jinshin-Baibai no Teppai to Higaisha-Shien ni muketa Torikumi* (Approach for Combating Human Trafficking and Assistance for Trafficking Victims), Tokyo: Gendai Jinbun Sha, pp. 42–7.

12 The trafficking of Thai women to Japan and countermeasures of the Thai government

*Yuriko Saito**

Introduction

It was not until the late 1980s and early 1990s that the phenomenon of human trafficking in Japan became visible. Incidents of human rights being trampled were frequent during this period, with foreign women—such as Filipinos and Thais—being forced into prostitution and serving customers against their will. They were beaten if they refused, exploited, and constantly kept under control. This was also a period when a formerly unknown number of women, after risking their lives to escape the control and violence of the criminals, sought help from embassies. According to the embassies, assistance was sought mainly from two private shelters in the Tokyo area that provided protection and shelter for the women until they could be sent home.[1] The largest group taken in by the shelters in the early 1990s were Thai.

The problem of trafficking in women emerged in the 1990s at the end of the Cold War, an era of accelerating capitalist globalization. Human trafficking emerged along with globalization with greater movement of capital, information, and people and the opening of borders. This problem is a serious one that has coincided with the widening social and economic gap, the deterioration of the environment, and the growth of migration of people through irregular means.

In this chapter, I outline the situation of human trafficking in Japan and explain the problem using case studies of Thai women victims. I will also look at sexual exploitation—the location of many of the victims and the growth of the sex industry in Thailand, which is relevant in the trafficking of Thai women to countries such as Japan—and will discuss anti-trafficking measures implemented by the Thai government. Finally, I will mention cooperative links between Japan and Thailand taking place at various levels, including through international bodies, both governmental and non-governmental. I conclude by discussing one key issue that is needed to overcome the problem of trafficking—the participation of survivors and groups of survivors in policy-making abroad and in their home communities.

---

* Translated by Malaya Ileto.

234   *Y. Saito*

Human trafficking in Japan

Contemporary human trafficking

The reality of foreign women becoming victims of human trafficking in Japan became visible from the late 1980s to the early 1990s, when the media began to raise the issue in the context of criminal cases involving the women.

In 1991, for example, there was an incident in Shimodate, Ibaraki prefecture, when three Thai women suffered abuse and violence and were starved and verbally abused.[1] They had been trafficked and forced into prostitution, and ended up killing their Thai "mama" (the woman running the *snack* business[2]). A snack bar in Japan serves alcohol and some light food. It is typically dark inside and arranged like a lounge, often with a karaoke set. The snack bar is usually managed by a "mama," who deals with the customers and oversees the service given to the customers. Hostesses in the snack bar must work according to the mama's orders. There are many types of snack bars in Japan and they can be found almost everywhere in the country. In most, the hostesses serve the patrons drinks and food while socializing with them on the premises. However, there are also snack bars where the hostesses can be taken out to a hotel for a short time (two hours) or longer (all night) to provide sexual services for clients. Thai women are sent to work in snack bars of this latter type.

A year later, five Thai women in Mobara, Chiba prefecture, killed their Singaporean *mama*, and five others in Shinkoiwa, Tokyo, killed their Taiwanese one. During the Shimodate, Mobara,[3] and Shinkoiwa[4] incidents, as well as those of 1994 in Kuwana,[5] Mie prefecture, and Ichikawa,[6] Chiba prefecture, groups supporting the trafficking victims took a stand, exchanging letters with and visiting the women in jail as well as attending their court hearings. This was done to alert the public to the injustice of the women being treated as perpetrators when they themselves were victims. In each of the cases, the women had been given an opportunity and invitation to work in Japan and had been taken there. Upon arrival they were informed that they had incurred a "debt" and were then forced into sexual exploitation and forced labor under strict control. They were clearly victims.

The book *Shelter/Joseitachi no Kik: Jinshinbaibai kara Domestic Violence made Misura no Juunenkan* (The Crisis of Women in Shelter: Ten Years of Ms'la, from Human Trafficking to Domestic Violence) was published on the tenth anniversary of the shelter by Ms'la, an NGO that runs the Saalaa shelter and consultation service for women of all nationalities. The book records how Ms'la first encountered the Thai trafficking victim Sai in 1991. This encounter became the impetus to establish Saalaa, a shelter for the many foreign women who have fallen victim to human trafficking in Japan. I introduce the story of Sai as a typical case of human trafficking in the early 1990s.

Case study: Sai

In her early twenties, Bangkok-born Sai became a single mother and also took on the burden of supporting her parents. She worked day and night at a jewelry and

The trafficking of Thai women to Japan 235

ornaments store in the city, sometimes forced to take stimulants to cope with the long hours. In 1991, an acquaintance invited her to work in Japan. She was given a Singaporean passport and taken to Japan with several Burmese men and Thai women.

Upon their arrival, however, they were met by a Japanese man who took their passports away. The women were taken to a nearby hotel where their faces and bodies were evaluated, and they were "sold" to Japanese and Thai men who had come to "buy" them. Although Sai had not borrowed a cent, the snack bar owner who "bought" her ordered her to bear a "debt" of 3.5 million yen and forced her into prostitution to repay it. Sai was resold to three different snack bars over the two months after she arrived, and every time incurred a new "debt." In debt, she lost hope, and even contemplated suicide. Sai used her last ounce of strength to write a letter in Thai pleading for help, like a last will and testament that she secretly wrote and gave to one of her customers. The letter was passed on until it reached the Thai NGO Friends of Thai Women Working in Asia (FOWIA).[7] Volunteering there at the time, I translated the letter into Japanese and faxed it to Kalabaw no Kai, an NGO that supports foreign workers in Japan.

Fortunately, members of Kalabaw no Kai were able to find the snack bar where Sai was working. They first posed as customers to confirm her intentions, then they were able to rescue her. Sai stayed at the Ms'la shelter while receiving repatriation assistance. Her problem was not unique. According to a survey report by the Japan Network Against Trafficking in Persons (JNATIP) on trafficking victims in Japan, 197 out of a total of 434 identified victims went to the House of Emergency in Love and Peace (HELP), an Asian Women's Shelter,[8] from 1996 to March 2005. From this data, shelter staff members could see that the number of Thai women who escaped from sexual exploitation and forced labor imposed by human traffickers was increasing. They sought protection and help from the Thai Embassy.

Starting with the time that Sai fell victim to trafficking, the number of foreign women approaching the previously mentioned privately run shelters in Tokyo (HELP and Saalaa) increased significantly. Between 1992 and 2001, the largest national group represented at these shelters was Thai, with 65.4 percent of those at HELP and 53.7 percent at Saalaa being of this nationality.

Rapid increase in Colombian victims in late 1990s

Since 1995, the number of trafficking victims approaching privately run shelters for help has fallen. This is not because the number of victims has decreased, but, rather, that since the mid-1990s there has been a clampdown on undocumented migrants, as well as an economic recession. From the late 1990s, Saalaa and HELP saw a rise in the number of Colombian women seeking help. In an interview around that time in "HELP's Perspective on Twenty Years of Human Trafficking,"[9] HELP director Shoji pointed out that there were many Colombian women who entered Japan via regional airports such as Okinawa or Hiroshima and then were sold from one hot springs resort area to another throughout the country.[10] The trafficking of Colombian women was barely covered by the mass media.

Table 12.1 Trafficking victims at House for Women Saalaa (1992–2001)

	1992	1993	1994	1995	1996	1997	1998	1999	2000	2001	Total
Thailand	40	72	52	17	7	6	5	18	6	10	233
Philippines	2	5	6	13	12	10	9	25	18	14	112
East Asia		1	7		2	2			1	1	14
Other Asian Country		1	1	1	1		1		2	2	9
Latin America			1	1	6	5	4	5	7	14	43
America and Africa						1		1			1
Japan							2	2	8	9	21
Unknown								1			1
											434

Sources: *Josei no Ie Saalaa: Juunen no Ayumi* (A Ten Year History of House for Women Saalaa), House for Women Saalaa, 2002, p. 122.
Survey Report on Human Trafficking in Japan, Japan Network Against Trafficking in Persons (JNATIP), Ochanomizu University 21st Century COE Program "Frontiers of Gender Studies (F-GENS)", 2005, p. 72.

Trafficking of Thai women

Media coverage dwindled particularly from the mid-1990s when it seemed like the problem had gone away. A murder involving a Thai trafficking victim in central Japan surfaced in 2000 to show that human trafficking was still very much alive.[11]

The incident is summarized as follows: After being persistently invited by someone from her hometown, the defendant, 'S', left northeastern Thailand for Japan in March 2000, expecting to work in a Thai restaurant. She was told on arrival that she had incurred a 5.5 million yen "advance payment"[12] and had to work without rest or pay as a prostitute to repay it. When the amount "owed" was almost paid off, the broker who managed S, a Thai resident in Japan, resold her.[13] Again, she incurred an "advance payment." Desperate, in July 2000, S planned her escape with a friend from her hometown who had come to Japan after her and had been deceived by the same broker. They asked where to go for help from a male friend who was a migrant worker from Thailand and already familiar with Japan. For some reason, however, her friend escaped first. Upon learning this, the broker went into a frenzy and called a gang for help to find her and bring her back. S and her migrant worker friend planned to run away after knocking the broker unconscious, but the broker recognized them just before she was hit in the head by a vase, so she called some gang members to tell them. Afraid of being caught by the gang, the migrant worker friend kept beating the broker until he finally killed her. Because of her involvement, S was charged with a robbery resulting in death and sentenced to imprisonment.[14]

S's public trial coincided with the adoption by the United Nations of the UN Protocol to Prevent, Suppress and Punish Trafficking in Persons ("Palermo Protocol"). International, cooperative anti-trafficking efforts were beginning. Despite this, her claim of self-defense as a result of being a victim of kidnapping for profit by international traffickers, of being subject to imprisonment, and being forced into prostitution was rejected. S was sentenced to seven years imprisonment at the first (May 2003) and second (July 2004) trials. Her appeal to the Supreme Court in September 2004 was quickly dismissed in only two months. A month later, the Japanese government introduced the Action Plan of Measures to Combat Trafficking in Persons, which focused on the prosecution of traffickers and the protection of victims.

In S's case, the Bureau of Investigation missed the opportunity to investigate the organized crime aspects of trafficking that were central to the case. It became clear that when victims of human trafficking commit criminal acts as a result of their trafficking, their victimhood is generally not acknowledged and investigations related to trafficking are not carried out.

While on trial in Japan, S worked through a lawyer and the Thai Consulate to bring criminal charges against the broker from her village who had invited her to Japan to work. The trial took place in Thailand, and in December 2004, when Japan's Action Plan was released, three brokers were sentenced to 13 years imprisonment at their first trial. They were sentenced for having committed the following crimes: conspiracy to commit fraud in providing working abroad, fraud

238   Y. Saito

in being intermediaries in prostitution, and conspiracy to commit kidnapping and transportation of persons out of a country for the purpose of prostitution.

While serving her sentence, S suffered severe stomach pains and was diagnosed as suffering from terminal cancer with only a few months to live. There was a strong chance that despite falling victim to trafficking in Japan, she would end up dying in a Japanese prison. S's lawyer and support group made efforts to allow her to go home, and in September 2005, she was deported and returned to Thailand.

Because S had won her criminal case against the brokers, the Thai Ministry of Social Development and Human Security and the Ministry of Justice recognized her as a trafficking victim on her return home. She thus became eligible under the Fund to Support Survivors of Human Trafficking, established in 2003, to receive part of her medical costs for cancer treatments, a sanatorium, and a scholarship for her children. Dissatisfied with this paternalistic treatment, S brought a civil action against the broker who had trafficked her, in an effort to exercise her right to recover from the damage that had been inflicted on her. This was the first time a civil action was brought against a broker in Thailand.

Anti-trafficking measures of the Japanese government

Because of the succession of criminal cases involving human trafficking victims in the early 1990s, Japan became a target of criticism and warnings regarding its lack of awareness of human trafficking of women and its effects on the human rights of women.

For example, the concluding observations of the UN Committee on the Elimination of Discrimination against Women (1994)[15] expressed disappointment that the Japanese report contained no serious reflection on issues concerning the sexual exploitation of women in Japan from other countries in Asia. The Committee requested that the Japanese government take specific and effective measures to combat commercial sexual exploitation and prostitution of immigrant women in Japan. The concluding observations of the UN Committee on Economic, Social and Cultural Rights (1998) also raised concern that the protection of foreign victims was inadequate. There was a need to secure the rights of foreign women in Japan as victims of human trafficking.

In the late 1990s, despite the UN Committee recommendations, the Japanese government took no clear anti-trafficking measures apart from the adoption of the 1999 Law Punishing Acts Related to Child Prostitution and Child Pornography. It was only after Japan signed the Palermo Protocol (attached to the Convention against Transnational Crime) in 2000 that the government began to take action.

I discuss four changes that have been taken place in anti-trafficking policies and in the structure of trafficking since 2000.

First, the nationalities of trafficking victims have diversified. In the 1980s, before the growth in the number of Thai victims, organizations assisting foreigners in Japan had raised the issue that Filipino women entering the country on entertainer visas were being exploited. In the early 1990s, the number of Thai women being trafficked

The trafficking of Thai women to Japan 239

rose rapidly, and from the late 1990s to early 2000s, the number of Colombian women being sexually exploited also rose. Since 2000, there has also been a rise in the number of Indonesian women being trafficked. We can see from this that as the supply side of women that are sexually exploited changes, human trafficking continues to respond to the huge demand for victims for the large sex industry in Japan. Data on trafficking victims released by the National Police Agency since 2001 show their diversification, with victims coming from such diverse countries as Indonesia, China, Taiwan, Romania, Estonia, and Cambodia. A JNATIP report on a survey it carried out in 2005 on the protection and support of trafficking victims pointed out that there is an urgent need for interpreters to help victims communicate in a language they understand during hearings and investigations, in shelters, by those offering protection and aid, and for medical visits and mental counseling.[16]

A second feature of recent changes is that UN bodies and governments began to take anti-trafficking measures. The 2000 Palermo Protocol clarified the definition of the term "human trafficking." In December 2004, the Japanese government released its Action Plan of Measures to Combat Trafficking in Persons, which provides guidelines for its anti-trafficking policies. Also, since then it has implemented various policies toward the eradication of human trafficking, including the revision in 2005 of criminal and immigration laws and ordinances regarding entertainment visas and the issuing of notices requiring the police and public shelters to protect trafficking victims. There is, however, a tendency for the measures to focus on the regulation of migrants rather than the protection of their rights.

The third feature is that as anti-trafficking policies and measures develop, new ways to exploit people are also being created so that the forms of human trafficking are diversifying and again become invisible. I mentioned earlier the clampdown on entertainment visas as a means to prevent the exploitation of foreign women entering Japan. As a result of this effort to combat trafficking, another means was then used by traffickers to get women into Japan. As a result, there is cause to believe that international marriage in now an alternate route being exploited by traffickers to facilitate the entry of foreign victims to Japan. A survey report released by JNATIP in 2007 includes case studies whereby an international marriage agent introduced a woman working in a brothel abroad to a Japanese man seeking a wife. The man paid the finder's fee of millions of yen to an agent to find his son a bride and then raped his foreign daughter-in-law, claiming that he had the right to because he had paid for her. JNATIP is raising the issue that such acts constitute exploitation and human rights violations that fall under human trafficking as defined by the Palermo Protocol.[17]

The fourth point is that the awareness and role of civil society in combating human trafficking in contemporary Japanese society has begun to change as trafficking diversifies. For example, JNATIP, which was founded in 2003, is an NGO that carries out UN lobbying and international advocacy activities, engages in rights protection, and addresses violence against women. It works as a network of concerned individuals, researchers, and organizations to raise social awareness of trafficking through workshops. JNATIP carries out survey reports on the situation of trafficking in Japan as well as providing protection and support to victims. It

240   *Y. Saito*

raises public awareness of trafficking issues by hosting seminars and symposia, and undertakes advocacy work through lobbying Diet members and engages in dialogue with relevant government officials, trying to ensure that victims' concerns are reflected in policy.

Since 2004, the Japanese government's anti-trafficking policies have been carried out by a task force comprised of delegates from various ministries, but in the 2009 U.S. Trafficking in Persons Report, Japan remained in Tier 2, despite the fact that most developed countries are ranked in Tier 1.

The context for human trafficking in Thailand

I have already mentioned that there are many Thai trafficking victims in Japan. I next survey Thailand's background as a sending country for human trafficking. I first discuss the increase in the context of migration and the growth of the sex industry because many of the women trafficked to Japan in the early 1990s had experience working in the Thai sex industry in their late teens, in the 1960s and 1970s.

There is an urgent need for anti-trafficking policies because not only is Thailand a sending country to Asian countries such as Malaysia, Singapore, and Japan, but also to countries in Europe and Africa. It is also a receiving and transit country for those from countries of the Mekong river basin, such as Laos and Myanmar. I thus review the development of Thailand's anti-trafficking measures in light of these circumstances. In particular, I will highlight the 1997 Law Prohibiting Trafficking in Women and Children and revisions under the comprehensive Anti-Trafficking Law passed on January 30, 2008, which no longer limits victimization to women and children.

The context for human trafficking in Thailand: migration and the growth of the sex industry

There are two primary factors contributing to the human trafficking of Thai women. First is the domestic and international migration of workers motivated by the economic gap. They move from poor areas to more affluent places.

1960s to 1970s

From the 1960s to 1970s, domestic migration away from the poverty and impoverishment of marginalized rural farming villages to urban areas to find work became common. This was accompanied by young migrant girls entering the sex industry. Thai political economist Pasuk Phongpaichit has noted that the poverty in northern and northeastern Thailand in the 1960s and 1970s was an important contributing factor spurring the internal migration of women. Many women from the north migrated within the country to undertake sex work.[20]

Northern farming villages in particular, where the terrain is mountainous and productivity is low, had been left behind by the Thai central government efforts since the 1960s to promote national economic and social development. This created

The trafficking of Thai women to Japan   241

an economic gap, with a rise in the population living in absolute poverty.[21] The social norm that women assume responsibility for their families and engage in self-sacrifice to save families from a life of poverty led to some women being encouraged to undertake work in the sex industry in their late teens. This occurred particularly in areas where the community base had weakened because of increasing materialism and demand for consumer goods.

The growing sex industry in Thai cities that drew rural women was influenced by the prevailing international situation. Bangkok bars and massage parlors flourished as places for foreign-affiliated firms (including Japanese ones) to wine and dine guests.[22] With the escalation of the Vietnam War in the late 1960s, the service industry in the eastern coastal city of Pattaya and in the capital, Bangkok, grew. This included the sex industry that provided entertainment, amusement, and comfort to American soldiers.[23] Even after the war, the phenomenon continued. The 1970s saw the amusement areas of Bangkok and Pattaya frequented by tourists from the Middle East enjoying their petrol dollars, as well as by sex tourists coming on tours from Japan. There was also growth in the sex industry in southern border cities such as Hat Yai and Betong because of the economic gap between Thailand and its richer southern neighbors of Malaysia and Singapore.

1980s

From the 1980s, the possibility of earning money motivated women to enter the sex industry. They did not do this only to escape poverty. Women were invited into the sex industry in Bangkok and southern cities by women from their own towns who had returned from stints as prostitutes. The network grew between the regions where many women engaged in the sex industry and the source regions. With this, the prostitution system was established, including the condition of repayment of "advance payments." With the growth of this network, the number of women being trafficked abroad from Thailand, particularly Northern Thailand, to Malaysia and Singapore rose.

From the mid-1980s, spurred by the strong yen and the Japanese bubble economy, many Japanese businesses advanced into Thailand, causing many Thai women to dream of visiting or working in Japan. Those enticing women to Japan wanted their Thai counterparts to focus on women who already had experience working in the sex industry, so that they could be sexually exploited in Japan.

It was also in the 1980s that the "mail order bride" industry flourished, when men in Europe (Germany, Switzerland, the Netherlands, etc.) could pick a bride from a mail order catalog.

In the late 1980s, the gap between urban and rural areas remained, but the Thai economy achieved double digit growth and social policies to promote education and medical care reached even the poor. Therefore, there were fewer Thai women to enter the Thai sex industry. Meanwhile, after the 1988 military *coup d'état* in neighboring Burma, and the continuing political chaos, there was an increase in migrant labor and human trafficking from Myanmar into the Thai sex industry. Migrant work was low paid, hard, dirty, and dangerous. With the bars set up to meet the domestic Thai demand for prostitution, trafficking into the sex industry increased.

242 *Y. Saito*

There were also many young girls from Thailand's mountain areas, who had no sexual experience but became victims of human trafficking as a result of the spread of HIV/AIDS. Therefore, in this period, trafficking into Thai's sex industry was enhanced by girls and women from nearby countries such as Burma, Laos, Cambodia, Vietnam, and Southern China that were less affluent than Thailand. They complement the women drawn from the poor Thai mountain areas.

1990s

The early 1990s saw a continuation of the trends of the late 1980s as Thai women continued to be trafficked to Japan. Phongpaichit has analyzed the social and economic factors regarding Thailand's irregular industries and estimates the incomes of agents sending Thai women to Japan, Taiwan and Germany from 1993 to 1995 as shown in Table 12.2.

In the mid-1990s, the Japanese bubble burst and the economy went into a slump. Japanese authorities clamped down on undocumented migrants by deploying immigration and police authorities. There was a sharp decrease in the number of women trafficked to Japan. Instead women were trafficked to Taiwan and South Korea, whose economies were in better shape.

In the period after the 1997 monetary crisis, women no longer were the poor or those whose families faced difficult economic circumstances. Instead, they were joined by a new class of single women who had good academic qualifications and work skills and came to Japan to pay off debts. They were drawn by the promise of Japan. The number of trafficking victims rose.

Table 12.2 Estimated annual income accruing to agents in migrant fees in major markets for illegal Thai workers, 1993–1995

Country	Type of worker	person/year	Fee/ person(baht)	Total fees (m.baht)
Japan	Male	4–6,000	150–200,000	6–800
	Female sex-worker	6–9,000	800,000	4,800–7,200
Taiwan	Male and Female	100,000	70–100,000	7–10,000
Germany	Female sex-worker	500	140,000	70
Total		110,500– 115,500	12,400–17,070	4,168–5,988

Source: P. Phongpaichit , S. Piriyarangsan and N. Treerat "Trafficking in People" in *Guns, Girls, Gambling, Ganja: Thailand's illegal economy and public policy*, Chiang Mai, 1998, p. 181.

The trafficking of Thai women to Japan   243

2000s: Growth and diversification of the trafficking network abroad

A 2005 survey conducted by JNATIP indicates that there was no monolithic organization carrying out human trafficking. Instead, traffickers were drawn from a network of Thai people in Japan who already had residential status.[24] For example, Thai women who were trafficked in the 1980s and 1990s and had acquired residential status as spouses of Japanese men were now running snack bars and small stores. They were involved in organized prostitution, assisting in trafficking acquaintances and relatives from Thailand to Japan.

At present, traffickers have also become more skillful at evading the watchful eye of Japanese immigration officials. For example, the women enter on short-term visas under the cover of group tours or expensive family holidays. They also travel to the United States and Brazil, then to Europe, entering Japan when they are in transit. The JNATIP report also mentions the case of a woman who had acquired a spouse visa but on her entry to Japan was forced to bear a "debt" and was sold into prostitution.[25]

Thailand's anti-trafficking measures

Contemporary human trafficking

It was first acknowledged that human trafficking was a problem in Thailand in 1984, when a young girl who had been locked in a barred room died in a fire in Phuket, a tourist city in the south.[26] NGOs working for the rights of Thai women investigated the circumstances of the incident, contacted the girl's parents, exposed the facts, and sought imprisonment of the perpetrators. However, the extent of the large-scale cross-border trafficking into Thailand was not brought to light until 1991. At that time 150 Burmese women who had been trafficked into prostitution and labor exploitation were rescued in Ranong Province, a Southern Thailand region.[27] These two incidents made it clear that human trafficking was happening both domestically and across borders, with Thailand serving as a receiving country.

In 1994, the National Commission of Women's Affairs (NCWA) of the Office of the Permanent Secretary of the Prime Minister's Office set up the Subcommittee on Combating Trafficking in Children and Women, comprised of scholars and NGOs, to deal with the trafficking issue as it came to light.

The First State Plan to Eliminate Human Trafficking in Women and Children was promptly created and in 1997 the Law Prohibiting Trafficking in Women and Children came into existence.[28]

In the 1990s, human trafficking and prostitution were considered basically the same thing and there was no clear definition of either. There was no end to the debate on whether sex work performed by adult women was exploitation or a matter of choice. Thai government efforts in the 1990s to make clear anti-trafficking policies were motivated by the worsening situation of child prostitution. Domestic Thai institutions were in place from the 1980s to deal mainly with the issues of child prostitution and human trafficking. In preparation for ratification of the Convention

244   *Y. Saito*

on the Rights of the Child, NCWA's powerful leadership pushed for recognition of the importance of issues concerning women and children in policy-making.

Another facilitating factor was that Thai NGOs had already worked for more than 20 years on the serious problem of child labor and child prostitution. They had a lot of experience in the protection and support of victims, and had cooperated with the government on these issues. It is this cooperative relationship that made possible revisions to the 1996 Law on the Prevention and Prohibition of Prostitution and the enactment of a criminal law that punishes traffickers severely.

MOUs, domestic legal mechanisms and international efforts

Despite the adoption of the previously mentioned laws, issues such as the division of responsibilities and powers, cooperation between government bodies and domestic NGOs remained unclear and hindered the effectiveness of the law.

Thailand's anti-trafficking measures were controlled and promoted by NWAC from the 1990s. They focus mostly on women and children. But, in 2003, jurisdiction was transferred to the Ministry of Social Development and Memorandums of Understanding (MOU) began to be passed one after another both domestically and internationally.[29] Legal mechanisms were also put into place, with the revision of existing laws and the creation of new measures. For example, the Criminal Code was revised in 1999 to prescribe heavier penalties for injuries resulting from forced prostitution and the Child Welfare Law in 2003 required that the child's social reintegration after being trafficked be taken into consideration. Laws to control money laundering (1999) and protect witnesses in criminal trials were also passed.

International efforts included the signing of the Palermo Protocol (2000), as well as the Coordinated Mekong Ministerial Initiative against Trafficking (COMMIT),

Table 12.3 Nationality and number of women and children visitors to Social Development and Welfare Bureau-run facilities (January 1999–July 2004)

Nationality	1998	1999	2000	2001	2002	2003	Total
Cambodia		283	134	134	128	29	708
Burma		55	81	113	220	28	497
Laos	5	43	62	66	74	26	276
China			1	11	11	1	25
Vietnam		2		2		1	5
Other				1	2	3	6
Stateless		2	1	1			4
Total	5	385	279	328	435	89	1521

Source: "Summary Thailand Country Report on Combating Trafficking in Persons" (Thai, English), August 2004, Ministry of Social Development and Human Security and the Office of the Permanent Secretary of the Prime Minister's Office (Thai version), p. 29.

Table 12.4 Number of Thai women returning from abroad using Social Development and Welfare Bureau-run Facilities, according to country repatriated (2000–4)

	2000	2002	2003	2004
China		1		
Taiwan		1		
Singapore		2	7	
Hong Kong	2	4	9	
Japan	4	13	57	31
Malaysia	4	25	49	32
United Kingdom		27	2	2
Lebanon	7			
South Africa		5	25	6
Australia	13	10		
Denmark	2			
Israel	1			
Switzerland	1			
Germany	2			
East Timor	15			
New Zealand	1			
Bahrain	8			
Ireland	1			
South Korea		2		
Philippines	1			
Saudi Arabia	4			
Brunei	2			
France	4			
Italy	1			
Total	21	73	199	94

* Total 387

Source: "Summary Thailand Country Report on Combating Trafficking in Persons" (Thai, English), August 2004, Ministry of Social Development and Human Security and the Office of the Permanent Secretary of the Prime Minister's Office (Thai version), p. 30.

246   Y. Saito

an MOU on human trafficking (2004) at the regional level. This was adopted in 2005 as the Sub-regional Plan of Action.[30]

Tables 12.3 and 12.4 show the number of clients of facilities such as shelters, according to nationality, and the number of Thais using the facilities who had returned from overseas and the country from which they returned.

Introduction of new law on human trafficking in 2008

Despite anti-trafficking efforts of the government, including revisions to the law, the problem worsened.

In 2003, declaring that the extermination of drugs was a state matter, Prime Minister Thaksin stepped up the campaign to stamp out drug traffickers using methods that were seen as high-handed. In much the same way, in 2005, he declared that human trafficking was a state priority. He declared a war to stamp out human traffickers. An anti-trafficking fund,[31] which could be used to help trafficking survivors to become self-supporting, was also established by Prime Minister Thaksin at that time. However, it became clear through the payment process for S, who had already fallen victim to trafficking in Japan, that the application process and authorization procedures for these funds were not clear. People who could access the application and receive money were restricted. Until the process was incorporated into the 2008 Anti-Trafficking Law, it was applied only rarely.[32]

There was a need to tackle the following issues to prevent and control the trafficking problem:

- Address the changes in the affected populations—such as a rise in the number of victims who are from Hill tribes, foreign nationals, stateless, male and transgender.
- Provide support for people affected by trafficking, such as survivors and their families.
- Strengthen legal aid to eliminate complications in using civil law following criminal cases. At present, civil measures are high risk and with limited potential benefits for the victim.
- Raise social awareness in the community.
- Address government corruption and involvement in the trafficking process by government officials.
- Address political instability that contributes to trafficking.

A comprehensive, new anti-trafficking law was developed that did not limit its application to women and children and went beyond simply revising the 1997 law, but Prime Minister Thaksin fell from power following the September 2006 *coup d'état*, leaving the country under an interim government. Despite this, the Law to Prevent and Prohibit Human Trafficking (2008 Anti-Trafficking Law) was passed in November 2007, before the election of the new government, and came into effect on January 30, 2008.

The trafficking of Thai women to Japan 247

Outline and significance of the 2008 Anti-Trafficking Law

The 2008 Anti-Trafficking Law is comprised of "General Remarks" (Part 1),[33] "The Committee for the Prevention and Prohibition of Human Trafficking" (Part 2),[34] "Powers" (Part 3), "Relief and Welfare of the Victims" (Part 4), "The Fund for the Prevention and Prohibition of Human Trafficking" (Part 5) and "Penalties" (Part 6).[35]

Compared to the 1997 law prohibiting trafficking, it should be noted that "Human trafficking" has been redefined and clarifies that exploitation is not necessarily sexual but can also be in the form of forced labor. It also states that gender and nationality are irrelevant when considering whether a person is defined as a victim under the Act.[36] The assistance available to survivors in their repatriation and reintegration, including the application process and rules of the Fund to Support Survivors of Human Trafficking, are made clear in Part 5 (Fund for the Prevention and Prohibition of Human Trafficking).[37]

The amount of protection and support for victims assisting in the prosecution of traffickers has been expanded (such as granting status to non-nationals to remain and work in the country).[38] The powers of public servants dealing with the trafficking issue have been defined. Such public servants are penalized more than others if they are complicit in human trafficking.

The new law provides a stronger framework than before for supporting trafficking survivors and prosecuting traffickers.

Outstanding issues in Thailand's anti-trafficking policies

With the enactment of the Law Prohibiting Trafficking in Women and Children, the revisions to the Law to Prevent and Prohibit Prostitution and the Criminal Code, and the signing of various agreements with related bodies, Thailand's anti-trafficking measures can be said to be among the most systematic and progressive in Southeast Asia. We, however, should not wait to commence monitoring until there are interim reports to determine whether this series of measures has actually succeeded in deterring trafficking and helping to protect and support victims.

Further, regardless of how progressive these measures are, there is nothing limiting the demand side of the problem or addressing the "buyers" in the prostitution businesses or the industries that exploit cheap labor, which are the largest users of trafficked humans. As long as demand in the market exists, the product will change to meet it and new forms of human trafficking and their victims will emerge.

Recent anti-trafficking measures have been inadequate in providing support for those who have been trafficked and need to rebuild their lives and achieve independence. Long-term policies are needed in the future to include the survivors; to learn from their experiences and help them fully recover from their ordeal.

Conclusion

Compared to the time when government responses to trafficking were under fire as lagging behind, current government efforts seem to belong to a different age. Yet

248   *Y. Saito*

there are still many aspects of trafficking that need to be addressed. In particular, the focus is on the criminal justice system and its prosecution of traffickers with much less attention being paid to the protection of the victims' human rights and providing assistance for their recovery. If the economic gap continues to grow between the affluent and those in relative poverty and the causes of human trafficking are not thoroughly addressed, human trafficking cannot be ended.

Human rights violations associated with the crime of trafficking are somewhat similar to the victimization associated with conflict and war. It is difficult for ordinary citizens to take direct action in response to the problem where the crimes are committed by those with power. But with both trafficking and conflict, the ordinary citizen can do things to prevent such terrible things from happening. Further, after conflict or the experience of being trafficked, short-term, mid-term, and long-term support is needed to help victims recover, rebuild their lives, and achieve independence. They must also be empowered. In this way doesn't the issue of human trafficking ultimately connect with peace building?

The empowerment of survivors refers to the inner as well as external empowerment of the victim. Members of society need to create a social environment to make empowerment easier for survivors. Trafficking survivors have already begun to create self-help groups in Thailand,[39] Nepal, India and other places. They have also begun to raise their voices to challenge the societies that create the phenomenon of human trafficking.

If we look at human trafficking as a crime, the victims are seen as powerless, pitiful, and needing help. It is easy to stereotype in this way. But it is specifically because they have experienced trafficking that survivors can recognize peace and security. Should we not regard the support we offer to trafficking survivors in their recovery as important not only in the short-term, but in the medium- to long-term scheme as well? For they hold the potential to act as agents in the protection of human security and in peace building. This is what we need in order to end human trafficking, which threatens human security and peace.

Notes

1 The Shimodate Incident: In September 1991, three Thai women killed their *snack mama* (also Thai) in Shimodate, Ibaraki prefecture. The women had been forced to work as hostesses for no compensation and coerced into prostitution to pay off a "debt" of 3.5 million yen.
2 T. Caouette and Y. Saito, *To Japan and Back: Thai Women Recount their Experiences*, p. 4.
3 Mobara Incident: In September 1992, a Taiwanese snack mama in Mobara City, Ibaraki prefecture, was killed by five Thai women under her control. They had been forced into prostitution as well as performing hostessing, cleaning, and gardening duties to repay a "debt" of 3.8 million yen. They were given little food, existed under a penalty system whereby they were given fines, and intimidated on a daily basis.
4 Shinkoiwa Incident: In May 1992, a Singaporean snack mama in Shinkoiwa, Tokyo, was killed by five Thai women. She had exploited the women, arbitrarily raising their "debt" from 3.5 million yen to 4 million yen to create a new pretext for controlling them when they had nearly completed their payments.

The trafficking of Thai women to Japan 249

5 Kuwana Incident: In January 1994 in Kuwana City, Mie prefecture, a male customer was killed by a Thai woman who had been forced into prostitution, beaten, intimidated, and imprisoned.

6 Ichikawa Incident: In February 1994 in Ichikawa City, Chiba prefecture, a Thai man was killed by a Thai woman. The woman was trying to escape from forced prostitution where she was required to repay 3.8 million yen of "debt." She was captured by friends of the Thai woman running the business, beaten, confined, and raped, then demanded to pay an additional "debt" of 5 million yen.

7 FOIWA was active from 1990 to 1998 but has since ceased operation in Thailand.

8 HELP was established in 1986 to commemorate the 100th anniversary of the establishment of the Kyofukai Japan Christian Women's Organization. It is an emergency shelter for women and children, regardless of nationality or residential status; Japan Network Against Trafficking in Persons, <http://jnatip.blogspot.com/2008/01/about-jnatip.html> (accessed April 1, 2010).

9 Asian Women's Resource Center, "HELP's Perspective on Twenty Years of Human Trafficking," p. 31.

10 The rise in the number of Colombian trafficking victims has been calculated based on records undertaken by social workers of the Colombian embassy from 1997 to 2004 regarding the experiences of and support offered to 148 victims. Statistics and analyses of these records have been published in the chapter on Colombia in the *Survey Report on Human Trafficking in Japan*. According to the report, there were two obvious trends in the rise in number, with the first peak from 1996 to 1997 and again in 2004. The women came from the poorest regions of the country and many of those targeted were in their late teens to early twenties. Before they were brought to Japan, they traveled via other cities in Latin America, Europe (Paris, Madrid, Amsterdam, London) and Asia (Bangkok, Manila, Singapore, Seoul), but not to the United States, because the U.S. does not issue transit visas to Colombians. It is also thought that passports were forged or altered in transit countries to enable easier entry to Japan. The women were told that they would work as dancers, singers, or domestic workers. But as soon as they arrived, they incurred "debts" of 2 to 8 million yen and were sexually exploited at strip clubs and as prostitutes, *Survey Report on Human Trafficking in Japan*, Japan Network Against Trafficking in Persons (JNATIP), Ochanomizu University 21st Century COE Program, Frontiers of Gender Studies (F-GENS), 2005.

11 A detailed account of this incident is available in Mitsuaki Sasaki, "Jinshinbaibai Higaisha no Keiji Saiban, Nani ga Towareteiru no ka: Taijin Josei Jinshinbaibai Jiken o Keiki ni" (What are Criminal Cases of Victims of Human Trafficking About? Using the Case of Trafficking of Thai Women to Explore This Question).

12 A fee imposed by the traffickers on the women. This money is not actually borrowed by the women, but represents business expenses incurred by the traffickers as well as profit.

13 Selling the women to other people running businesses. In some cases, the amount of "debt" they were being forced to repay reverts to the original amount "owed" with each new "owner."

14 A. Sugiura, "Naze Higaisha ga Sabakareru no ka? Yokkaichi Tai Josei Jinshinbaibai Jiken kara Miete Kuru Mono" (Why are the Victims being Tried? What We Can Understand from the Yokkaichi Trafficking Incident of a Thai Woman), pp. 23–4.

15 Concluding Comments of the Committee on the Elimination of Discrimination against Women regarding the Japanese government's second and third periodic report, 633, adopted in 1995. From "*Josei kanren Ho Detabukku*" (Databook on Laws relating to Women), p. 21.

16 JNATIP, "Jinshin baibai higaisha shien no renkei no kouchiku-Chiiki, Kokkyo wo koeta shien ni mukete Chosa oyobi katsudou houkokusho" (Research and Activities Report on the Collaboration Building for supporting Human Trafficking Victims beyond Area and Border), pp. 53–4.

250   Y. Saito

17 Adopted by the UN in Palermo, Italy in 2000. Protocol to Prevent, Suppress and Punish Trafficking in Persons Especially Women and Children, Supplementing the United Nations Convention against Transnational Organized Crime.
18 Pasuk Phongpaichit, Sangsit Phiriyarangsan, and Nualnoi Treerat, *Guns, Girls, Gambling, Ganja: Thailand's Illegal Economy and Public Policy.*
19 Mulaniti Phuying (Foundation for Women), "Kaan kha Ying" (Trafficking in Women).
20 P. Phongpaichit, *Massage Girl.*
21 S.Noriyuki, *Daisansekai ni okeru mou hitotsuno hatten riron: Thai nouson no kiki to saisei no kanousei* (The Alternative Theory in the Third World: A Crisis and Recovery of a Rural Area in Thailand).
22 S. Wongsuphap, *Naanggaam Too Krajok* (Women in Glass Room).
23 Thanh-Dam Truong, *Baishun-Sei roudou no shakai kouzou to kokusai keizai* (Sex, Money and Morality: Prostitution and Tourism in Southeast Asia).
24 JNATIP F-GENS (Frontier of Gender studies COE program, Ochanomizu University, 2005) "Nihon ni okeru Jinsinbaibai higai ni kansuru chousa kenkyu houkokusho" (Research and Study on the Damage of Human Trafficking in Japan).
25 Ibid.
26 S. Chutikul and P. Marshall, "Summary of Thailand Country Report on Combating Trafficking in Persons."
27 Ibid.
28 Y. Saito, "Jinshinbaiba higaisha towa dareka: nihon seihu no 'jinsin torihiki' taisaku ni okeru higaisha ninnchi no kadai" (Who are the Victims of Human Trafficking: the Problem of Victim Recognition in the Human Trafficking measure of Japanese Government).
29 Domestically, the Thai government has concluded MOUs between ministries, between government bodies and civil and international organizations, as well as with nine northern provinces (2003), eight eastern provinces (2006), and 19 northeastern provinces. Internationally, it has concluded two bilateral MOUs with Cambodia (2003) and Laos (2006) as well as the COMMIT MOU (Saito, "Jinshinbaiba higaisha towa dareka," p. 61; Y. Tanaka, Mekongawa ryuuiki-chiiki (GMS) niokeru Jinshintorihiki (Human Trafficking in the Mekong River Basin), p. 15.
30 *Sheruta/Joseitachi no Kiki: Jinshinbaibai kara Domesutikku Baiorensu made Misura no Juunenkan* (The Crisis of Shelters and Women: Ten Years of Mizula from Human Trafficking to Domestic Violence).
31 The rules of operation for the Ministry of Social Development and Human Security's Fund to Support Survivors of Human Trafficking (2005) states that the fund was established mainly to prevent human trafficking and to protect victims and help them gain independence for their reintegration into society.
32 S's case is detailed earlier in this chapter. She died in the middle of the proceedings (May 2006), but as of April 2008, her family continued to fight in her place. It is clear from this that it is not only a matter of applying the process offered by the Fund to Support Survivors of Human Trafficking, but that it is necessary to consider how to support trafficking survivors and the burdens that they have in undertaking complicated and lengthy civil actions.
33 Definition of "human trafficking" and other key terms (Article 4).
34 Members of the Committee for the Prevention and Prohibition of Human Trafficking are the Prime Minister (Chairperson), Deputy Prime Minister (Vice Chairperson), representatives from seven ministries (Defense, Foreign Affairs, Tourism, Sports, Social Development and Human Security, the Cabinet, Justice, and Labor) and four experts, including at least one NGO representative. The Secretary General is the Undersecretary of the Ministry of Social Development and Human Security (Article 15).
35 "Traffickers will be sentenced to 4 to 10 years and fined 80,000 to 200,000 baht. If the victim is 15 to 18 years of age, the sentence will be 6 to 12 years and the fine 100,000 to 240,000 baht. If the victim is under the age of 15, the sentence will be 8 to 16 years

The trafficking of Thai women to Japan 251

and the fine 160,000 to 300,000 baht" (Article 52). If a corporate body is involved in the transaction, the fine will be 200,000 to 1 million baht" (Article 53).

36 Rules regarding general protection and support: "Regardless of differences in sex, age, nationality, ethnicity or customs, the victims' human dignity will be respected and they will be assisted with meals, accommodation, medical treatment, physical and mental rehabilitation, education, training, legal assistance, repatriation or assistance for repatriation and civil action according to law" (Article 33).

37 Guidelines for the Fund for the Prevention and Prohibition of Human Trafficking, which targets trafficking survivors and their families and those vulnerable in the future, are stated in the 2008 Anti-Trafficking Law. This fund was inaugurated during Prime Minister Thaksin's administration as the Fund to Support Survivors of Human Trafficking, in its effort to stamp out human trafficking. But it was difficult to use the funds effectively because the terms of its operations were unclear. In the 2008 Anti-Trafficking Law, the purpose and operating mechanisms of the fund are clarified, and various forms of support are offered, including the protection of trafficking victims and help in their safe repatriation. So far, the fund has covered part of the medical expenses of victims recognized under it, and provided scholarships to cover part of their education expenses. It has also provided scholarships for children considered at high risk for human trafficking.

38 "Victims assisting in the prosecution of traffickers who are non-nationals will be granted special status to remain and work in the country, to allow them to access medical care, rehabilitation and legal assistance" (Article 37).

39 Self-Empowerment Program of Migrant women (SEPOM) was founded in 2001 as a self-help group for women from Chiang Rai in northern Thailand who have been victims of trafficking to Japan.

References

Asian Women's Resource Center. (2005) "HELP's Perspective on Twenty Years of Human Trafficking," *Women's Asia* 21, no. 41, February, p. 31.

Asian Women's Resource Center. (2005) "Jinshinbaibai: Dare ni Totte, Nanika ka Mondai na no ka?" (Human Trafficking: So What's the Problem, and for Whom?), *Women's Asia* 21, no. 4.

Bunprasart, Janjira. (2006) "Bua: Ying thai thii looklwang pai khaa prawenee thii prathet Jipun (yua kaan khaa manut)," *Mum mong Sithi* (in Thai, "Bua: Women Tricked into Forced Prostitution in Japan (Human Trafficking Survivors)" *Human Rights Perspectives*, Thai National Human Rights Commission, January–March.

Caouette, T. and Saito, Y. (1998) *To Japan and Back: Thai Women Recount their Experiences*, International Organization of Migration.

Chutikul, S. and Marshall, P. (2004) "Summary of Thailand Country Report on Combating Trafficking in Persons," Office of the Permanent Secretary Office of the Prime Minister, Ministry of Social Development and Human Security.

Japan Association of International Women's Rights. (1998) "*Josei kanren Ho Detabukku*" (Databook on Laws relating to Women), Japan Association of International Women's Rights, Yuhikaku Publishing.

Japan Network Against Trafficking in Persons. (2007) "Jinshinbaibai Higaisha Shien to Rentai no Kochiku—Chiiki, Kokkyo o Koeta Shien ni Mukete: Chosa oyobi Katsudo Hokoku" (Supporting Trafficking Survivors and Building Cooperation—Working Towards Support Going Beyond Community and State: Survey and Report), Japan Network Against Trafficking in Persons, May.

Japan Network Against Trafficking in Persons and Ochanomizu University. (2005) "Nihon ni okeru Jinshibaibai no Higai ni kan suru Chosa Kenkyu Houkokusho" (Survey Report

252 *Y. Saito*

on Human Trafficking in Japan), Japan Network Against Trafficking in Persons and Ochanomizu University 21st Century COE Program Frontiers of Gender Studies (F-GENS), March.

"Josei no Ie Saalaa: Juunen no Ayumi" (A Ten-Year History of House for Women Saalaa). (2002) House for Women Saalaa.

Kanagawa Women's Space "Ms'La" ed. (2002) *Sheruta/Joseitachi no Kiki: Jinshinbaibai kara Domesutikku Baiorensu made Misura no Juunenkan* (The Crisis of Shelters and Women: Ten Years of Ms'la, from Human Trafficking to Domestic Violence), Tokyo: Akashi Shoten.

Mulaniti Phuying (Foundation for Women). (1997) "Kaan kha Ying" (Trafficking in Women), Bangkok: Media Point Co., Ltd.

Noriyuki, S. (1993) *Daisansekai ni okeru mou hitotsuno hatten riron: Thai nouson no kiki to saisei no kanousei* (The Alternative Theory in the Third World: A Crisis and Recovery of a Rural Area in Thailand), Kokusai Shoin.

Phongpaichit, P. (1982) *Massage Girl*, International Labor Organization, Geneva.

Phongpaichit, P., Phiriyarangsan, S. and Treerat, N. (1998) *Guns, Girls, Gambling, Ganja: Thailand's Illegal Economy and Public Policy*, Chiang Mai: Silkworm.

Saito, Y. (2006) "Jinshinbaiba higaisha towa dareka: nihon seihu no 'jinsin torihiki' taisaku ni okeru higaisha ninnchi no kadai" (Who are the Victims of Human Trafficking: the Problem of Victim Recognization in the Human Trafficking measure of Japanese Government), *Asia Pacific Review 3*.

Sasaki, Mitsuaki. (2007) "Jinshinbaibai Higaisha no Keiji Saiban, Nani ga Towareteiru no ka: Taijin Josei Jinshinbaibai Jiken o Keiki ni" (What are Criminal Cases of Victims of Human Trafficking About? Using the Case of Trafficking of Thai Women to Explore This Question), in Shiro Okubo, ed., *Ningen no Anzen Hosho to Hyuman Torafikingu* (Human Security and Human Trafficking), Tokyo: Nippon-Hyoronsha.

Sheruta/Joseitachi no Kiki: Jinshinbaibai kara Domesutikku Baiorensu made Misura no Juunenkan (The Crisis of Shelters and Women: Ten Years of Mizula from Human Trafficking to Domestic Violence). (2002) Kanagawa Women's Space "Mizula", Tokyo: Akashi Shoten.

Sugiura, Akimichi. (2005) "Naze Higaisha ga Sabakareru no ka? Yokkaichi Tai Josei Jinshinbaibai Jiken kara Miete Kuru Mono" (Why are the Victims being Tried? What We Can Understand from the Yokkaichi Trafficking Incident of a Thai Woman), *Buraku Kaiho*, Buraku Liberation Publishing House, April.

Tanaka, Y. (2008) Mekongawa ryuuiki-chiiki (GMS) niokeru Jinshintorihiki (Human Trafficking in the Mekong River Basin), Network Against Human Trafficking Edition.

Truong, Thanh-Dam. (1993) *Baishun-Sei roudou no shakai kouzou to kokusai keizai* (Sex, Money and Morality: Prostitution and Tourism in Southeast Asia), Tokyo: Akashi shoten.

Wongsuphap, S. (1995) *Naanggaam Too Krajok* (Women in Glass Room), Bangkok: Kled Thai Co., Ltd.

Index

abduction *see* kidnapping
addiction 2, 87, 115, 122, 128–9, 199
Afghanistan 10, 115, 140–1, 143, 147
Al-Qaeda 107
Annan, Kofi 17–18
Arar, Maher 44, 48
Argentina 183
arms: dealing in 36, 82, 146, 190; nuclear 10
assets: confiscation of 65, 138; protection of by criminals 188
asylum 63, 81, 83–4, 199, 212n14
Australia 71, 123, 152–3, 226, 245
Axworthy, Lloyd 21

Bales, Kevin 140, 183
Bangladesh 115, 138, 140–1, 143, 186
Beare, M. E. 36
Beck, U. 73
Belgium 71, 87, 105, 227
Belize 185
Berlusconi, Silvio 90
Bhutan 142
bilateralism 2 *see also* multilateralism
bin Laden, Osama 107
black market 60, 63–4, 67, 82–3, 182
Bolivia 183
border control 5, 43, 47, 64, 83, 85, 87, 142–3, 147, 186, 188–9, 197–8, 201–2, 204, 233, 243
boryokudan gangs 103–5
Boutros-Gali, Boutros 15
Brady, Hugo 93
Brazil 180, 182–4, 243
brothel 142–4, 146, 183–4, 186, 188, 192, 239; keepers 140, 146, 153, 177, 187

Cambodia 27, 141–3, 191, 226, 239, 242, 244
Cameroon 186
Canada 1, 21, 36–40, 42–4, 47, 49, 52, 71, 117, 124, 146, 153, 184–6

Canadian Islamic Congress 49
capital 9, 103; access to 137, 140–1, 147; accumulation of 60; for development 141–2; and human trafficking 137; movement of 81, 197, 233
capitalism 10, 14, 137, 233
Caribbean: and sex tourism 185; and trafficking in persons 180, 182–5
charitable organizations 49–50 *see also* shelters
child: labor 183–4, 243; pornography 2, 82, 86, 110
children: adoption of 60; crimes committed by 101–2; female 139; male 137, 139; rural 137; sale of 141, 216, 218; sexual exploitation of 86, 137, 141, 146, 153, 184–5, 218, 243; as victims 136, 141, 186, 198, 200, 206, 227, 240, 244, 246; vulnerability of 5, 49, 139, 142, 144–7, 183, 220, 223, 243–4
Chile 183–4
China 3, 12, 103, 105, 114–15, 117, 123–5, 129, 138, 142–3, 153, 181, 191–2, 216, 224, 226, 239, 242, 244–5
CIS (Commonwealth of Independent States) 154–6, 159–68, 172–6
civil: law 84, 88, 199, 238, 246; society 13, 16, 20, 70, 129, 239 *see also* NGOs; war 9, 10, 18, 62
clubs: kijichon 162–3, 166–9, 172–3, 175–6; Korean 162–3, 169, 173, 175
cocaine 105, 115–16, 118–19, 125 *see also* drugs
coercion 36, 40, 45, 82, 135, 206–7, 219–20 *see also* force
Cold War 10, 13–14, 25; aftermath of 3, 10, 14–15, 26, 103, 135, 142–3, 146, 233
collective security 17, 25, 27
Colligan-Taylor, K. 142
Colombia 125, 183, 219, 224–6, 235, 239, 242, 249n10

254 *Index*

Commission on Human Security 16, 17, 20
conflict 21, 39, 62, 83, 248; ethnic 96;
  prevention 15; and regions 4, 140, 142–3,
  147
constitutional reform in Japan 24–8
Convention Against Illicit Traffic in Narcotic
  Drugs and Psychotropic Substances
  (Vienna Convention) (UN) 70, 72
Convention Against Transnational
  Organized Crime (UN) 61, 70, 72, 107,
  136, 203, 217, 238
Convention for the Suppression of Terrorist
  Bombings 108
Convention for the Suppression of the
  Financing of Terrorism 108
Convention for the Suppression of the
  Traffic in Persons (UN) 216
Convention on Money Laundering (EU) 61
Convention on the Elimination of All Forms
  of Discrimination Against Women 2, 13
Convention on the Rights of the Child (UN)
  243–4
cooperation: international 2–4, 6, 20, 47, 51,
  72–3, 82, 88–9, 106, 109, 128, 142, 197,
  199, 210; judicial 4, 6, 72, 81–5, 87–91,
  199–201; police 4, 61, 65, 72, 82, 84–5,
  106, 199; of victims 41, 46, 61, 207
coordination: in European Union 82, 85,
  88–9, 199, 201–3, 210; international 20;
  of national agencies 126, 224; of terrorist
  attacks 106–7
'corporate' trafficking 190–2
corruption 3, 46, 51–2, 62, 72, 108, 135–7,
  139, 142–3, 147, 152, 182, 188, 200, 203,
  246
Costa Rica 185
Council of Tampere 81–2, 84–5, 88, 90, 200
criminal justice 2, 5, 37, 41, 44–5, 61, 66,
  91, 96–8, 248
criminal law: Canadian 37, 186; European
  3, 5, 61, 66, 81–2, 84–5, 91, 93, 197–8,
  200–3, 206–7, 209–10; German 65, 68–9;
  and immigration 200–1; Japanese 5, 100,
  102–5, 107–8, 216, 218–22, 225, 238;
  Korean 115, 126, 128, 153–4, 176–7;
  limitations of 2–3; and money laundering
  61, 66, 72, 244; Spanish 204, 208–10; and
  terrorism 37, 43, 70; Thai 240, 243–4,
  246–7; of United States 49; and victims
  3–4, 244
criminalization: of complicit acts 50; of drug
  use 2, 115, 126, 129; of human trafficking
  2, 223, 246; of illegal migration 2, 63,
  70; of intimidation 47; of motive 44; of
  youth 97
Cuba 185

Curacao 183
customs: agencies 92, 126–7; cooperation
  85; officials 82
cyber crime 59, 108

data mining 67
debt bondage 5, 180, 192
delinquency 4–5, 101, 201
democracy 9–14, 17, 73, 152
deportation 41, 152, 205, 217–19, 222, 224, 238
destination: and criminal groups 83; and
  drugs 82; and migrants 62, 155, 192,
  202; of smuggled goods 204, 208; and
  terrorists 39; and trafficked people 137,
  144, 147, 152, 154, 176, 182–6, 189–90,
  208
developed countries 12, 96, 146, 240
developing countries 3, 12, 18, 21, 64, 135,
  144, 146, 225
discrimination 144–5; caste 145; ethnic 40,
  49, 144; gender 13, 139–41, 192, 238;
  religious 40
disease 9–10, 16–18, 20, 146–7
Dominican Republic 137–8, 140, 183–5
drugs: distribution of 86, 114–15, 118,
  120, 122–3, 125, 129, 192; production
  of 4, 87, 114, 125, 128; trafficking of 4,
  46, 51, 61, 67, 72–3, 82, 88, 105, 109,
  114–15, 122–3, 125–9, 135, 138, 143,
  146, 198–9, 201–3, 208, 246; use of 1–2,
  4, 64, 82, 87, 115, 118, 120–2, 128–9 *see
  also* cocaine; ecstasy; heroin; marijuana;
  methamphetamine; opium; psychotropic
  drugs; stimulants

East Timor 142–3, 245
ecstasy 115–16, 118, 123, 129
Ecuador 183
education: access to 137, 139, 145, 147,
  241; and crime 101; and drug use
  115, 118, 121–2; and gender 139–40;
  and immigrants 62, 64; and sexual
  exploitation 140; and trafficking humans
  139–40, 182
El Salvador 184–5
entertainment agencies 156–9
'entrepreneurial' trafficking 189–90
environment, crimes against 51, 67, 82, 88,
  110
environmental change 9–12, 18, 20
Estonia 226, 239
ethnic: cleansing 17–19, 21; communities
  42, 44–5, 59; disputes 15; minorities 39,
  64; profiling 44, 48
Eurojust (European Judicial system) 4, 82,
  85, 88–90, 92–3, 202–3

Index 255

European Anti-Fraud Office (OLAF) 4, 92–3
European Arrest Warrant 90
European Convention on Human Rights 13, 91
European Drugs Unit (EDU) 85–6
European Judicial Network (EJN) 89
European Police College (CEPOL) 86
European Police Office (Europol) 4, 82, 84–9, 92, 198, 200, 202–3
exploitation 36, 136, 180, 192, 223; of communities 40; of immigrants 42, 200; labor 141, 153, 183–4, 186, 191, 243, 247; sexual 86, 136–7, 139–41, 145, 152–3, 181, 183–4, 186, 189–91, 207, 216, 219–20, 233–5, 238–9; of vulnerable groups 45–6
expulsion of illegal migrants 203–4, 208–9, 227
extradition 51, 85, 88, 90, 108, 203, 205–7

famine 9, 12, 216
Fiji 125
financial: benefit 72, 142, 198, 205; institutions 10, 49, 66, 98, 108; markets 11; penalties 65–6; system 11, 49, 61, 97, 136; transactions 43, 48, 86
Finn, P. 45
firearms, restrictions on 97, 99–100; use of 108, 188
force: illegal 135, 161, 166, 169, 175, 202, 207, 219–20; legal 18; military 21, 23–8 *see also* coercion
foreign nationals, rights of 5, 38, 153, 177, 225, 238
foreigners: and crime 2, 98–100, 102–4, 118–22, 197–8, 219; as terrorists 43, 107; as trafficking victims 5–6, 153, 163–76, 234–5, 238–9
Framework Decision 199, 201, 205, 207–8
France 71, 87, 89, 105, 117, 143, 245
fraud 4, 36, 52, 82, 92, 99, 102, 135, 152, 189–90, 199, 203, 207, 219–20, 237
free market, globalization of 9, 11–12, 16
Fyfe, N. 42, 46

G8 countries 10, 89, 107
genocide 17–19, 21
geopolitical factors 114, 180, 182, 185, 192
Germany 60, 63, 68–9, 71, 87, 241–2, 245
globalization 6, 9, 11–13, 15–17, 59–60, 62, 64, 73, 83, 93, 103, 106–7, 109–10, 114–15, 135–8, 140, 146–7, 197–8, 233
Guam 123, 153
Guatemala 185, 191
Guyana 183

Haiti 183
harmonization: of investigative technique 72; of legislation 72, 82, 84, 89, 91, 203–8
Healey, K. M. 45
health 16, 83, 137, 140, 144, 209, 219
heroin 115–16, 118–19, 123, 125
HIV/AIDS 5, 19, 146, 242
Honduras 185
Hong Kong 122, 125, 153, 159–60, 245
human rights 1–2, 5, 9, 13–14, 16–17, 19–23, 27, 29n13, 36, 38, 43, 64, 91, 93, 152, 154, 177, 233, 238; violations 206, 217, 239, 248
humanitarian intervention 18, 27, 205, 227

IMF (International Monetary Fund) 12, 14
immigration 59–60, 53; causes of 62; and crime 5, 62; illegal 60, 70, 81, 86–7, 100, 102–4, 152, 198–208, 242; of labor 62; and lack of control 38, 189; law 43, 84, 154, 200, 218–27, 239; networks 86, 159–62, 202; patterns of 63–4; policy 84–5, 97, 103, 199; and reunion with family members 48; *see also* migration
India 12, 40, 105, 138, 140–1, 143, 145, 181, 248
Indonesia 106, 136–7, 139–41, 224–6, 239
Information System for the Exchange of Data on Suspected Criminals (SIS) 87–8
integration: European 81–2, 91, 93; social 59–60, 63, 208, 227, 244, 247
intelligence, criminal 36–7, 44, 46, 65, 70, 86–7, 108, 183, 202
internal trafficking 153, 184–7, 240
International Covenant on Civil and Political Rights 2, 13
International Covenant on Economic, Social and Cultural Rights 2, 13
International Criminal Court 10, 21
International Labour Organization 182
International Organization for Migration (IOM) 225
Internet 138; chat sites 177; crimes 2, 98; pornography 82
intimidation 36, 39–42, 45–7, 197–8, 209
Iraq 10, 17, 27, 141, 147
Ireland 87, 245
Italy 71, 87, 137, 227, 245

Jamaica 42, 185
Japan 2–6, 9, 19–21, 23–8, 96–110, 114–15, 117, 121–5, 138–9, 141, 151–2, 155, 157, 183, 185, 216–27, 233–43, 245–6
Japan Network Against Trafficking in Persons (JNATIP) 235–6, 239, 243

256 Index

Japayuki-san 217, 221
jinshin-baibai 216–17
jinshin-torihiki 217
judicial: authorities 82, 88–91, 197–8;
   decision 69, 90–1; systems 82, 89–90 *see*
   also cooperation: judicial
justice *see* criminal justice

Kazakhstan 153–4
kidnapping 135, 152, 202, 207, 216,
   219–22, 237–8
Korea, Republic of (South Korea) 2, 4–6,
   12, 114–29, 144, 152–77, 224–6, 242, 245
Kosovo 17
Kotler, I. 44
Kyoto Protocol 10
Kyrgyzstan 154, 172

labor: forced 136, 153, 219, 234–5, 247;
   imprisonment and 219–24; markets
   59–60, 62–3; and migration 62–3, 145,
   153–4; trafficking 137, 147, 153, 182,
   184, 186, 192 *see also* exploitation: labor
Laos 141–3, 226, 240, 242, 244
Latin America 82, 136–41, 180, 183–6, 217, 236
Latvia 189–90
law enforcement 3, 4, 6, 36–9, 41–2, 46,
   51–2, 61, 63–4, 67–70, 72–3, 81–2, 86,
   88–9, 92, 123, 126–7, 138–9, 142, 147–8,
   153, 188 *see also* prosecution
Lazarenko, Pavel 136
liability: corporate 67, 72; individual 66–7

MacArthur, Douglas 24
McLelland, Anne 43
mafia: Chechen 190; Russian 125
marijuana 105, 115–19, 121, 126, 128–9
marriage: brokers 176; child 144; enforced
   220; false 104, 176; international 153,
   176–7, 239; visas 177
Matsumoto, Chizuo 106
methamphetamine 114–19, 121–6, 128–9
Mexico 143, 153, 184–6, 191, 242
migration 59–60, 63; and awareness of
   destination country 154–5; debts 159–61;
   illegal 1–2, 5, 136, 143, 201; internal
   240; international 135, 145, 240; large-
   scale 136; laws 186; networks 63–4;
   recruitment 156; regional patterns of
   184–5; regulation of 208, 233; urban 4 *see*
   also immigration; labor: migration
Milena-Serna, Claudia 183
Millennium Report 17
minority groups 38–43, 45–6, 51, 60, 63–4,
   144–5, 147
Mishulovich, Alex 189–90

Moldova 143, 145
money laundering 61, 66–7, 70, 72, 82, 86,
   88, 108, 125, 136, 189–90, 198, 202–3,
   222, 244
Morocco 143, 212n21
multilateralism 2–3, 16 *see also* bilateralism
multinational corporations 11–12, 14, 103
Myanmar 123, 139, 141–3, 240–1

narcotics *see* drugs
nation-state 6, 12, 14, 16, 59, 64, 184, 189
natural disaster 9–10
Naylor, R. T. 50
neoliberalism 10–12
Nepal 138, 141–3, 248
Netherlands 71, 87, 117, 181, 227, 241
networks 59; computer 107; criminal 59,
   64–5, 67, 92, 109, 137, 204, 208; demand-
   driven 187–8; distribution 188; judicial
   85, 89; of migration 63–4, 86, 159, 202;
   personal 62, 171, 239; police 97; roles
   within 187–8; security 21; trafficking 143,
   147, 180–1, 186–90, 198–200, 208, 241,
   243
New Zealand 71, 153, 245
NGOs (non governmental organizations) 13,
   16, 20, 152, 217–18, 226–7, 234–5, 239,
   243–4 *see also* civil: society
Nicaragua 184–5
Nigeria 121, 136–7, 139
North Korea 105, 123, 125

O'Connor, Dennis 44
Obuchi, Keizo 19
opium 115–16, 118–19, 123, 126
organized crime 4, 9, 36–43, 45–7, 51–2,
   60–2, 65–7, 70, 72, 81–3, 85, 88–9, 92–3,
   103–4, 122, 125, 128, 138, 143–4, 147,
   189, 197–201, 207–10, 237; transnational
   10, 12, 18, 20, 37–9, 51–2, 59–61, 64–5,
   70–2, 82, 85, 92, 97, 103, 105, 108, 110,
   139, 146, 198–9, 221
organs, human 82, 136, 219–20

Pakistan 136–8, 168
Panama 185
Paraguay 183
Passas, Nikos 43
peace doctrine 23–6
peace, right to 9, 14, 23–8
peacekeepers 139, 143–4, 147
peacekeeping 15, 143
Peru 106, 183, 216, 242
Philippines 12, 124, 136–9, 142, 152–6,
   158–60, 162–3, 165–8, 170–6, 224, 226,
   236, 245

Index 257

Phongpaichit, Pasuuk 144, 240, 242
political will 72, 82, 144
pornography 82, 86, 207; child 2, 86, 110
Porteous, S. D. 51
poverty 4, 6, 9–12, 17–20, 137–8, 140, 142, 147, 182, 192, 240–1, 248
prevention: of conflict 15, 23; of crime 45, 48, 61, 63, 88, 90, 105, 109–10, 203–5, 209–10; of hijacking 6, 108; of risk 73; of terrorism 27, 48–9, 199, 202; of trafficking 147, 153, 177, 219, 222–3, 239, 246, 248; of victimization 4, 37, 45
preventive: arrest 47; detention 43, 47; outcomes 66; strategies 70, 82
proceeds of crime 37, 50, 61, 65, 107–8, 125, 177, 203, 221–2 *see also* profit
profiling 39, 43–4, 48, 67, 121
profit 61, 66, 82–3, 103, 122, 135, 138, 144, 161, 186, 189–91, 197–8, 201, 209, 220–1, 224, 237 *see also* proceeds of crime
prosecution 21, 36, 41, 45–6, 50, 52, 61, 65, 67, 89, 97, 126–7, 135, 138, 147, 152–3, 176, 186, 203, 206–7, 218, 221, 237, 247–8 *see also* law enforcement
prostitution 103–4, 145, 177, 181, 186–7, 202, 216–17, 219, 223, 233–5, 237–8, 241, 243, 247; and children 243–4; demand for 62, 144, 168–71, 241; legislation against 153, 207, 216, 218–19, 225, 238, 244, 247; management of 104; and poverty 140, 142, 144–5; social acceptance of 139, 144 *see also* recruitment; sex industry
Protocol Against the Smuggling of Migrants by Land, Sea and Air (UN) 2
Protocol to Prevent, Suppress and Punish Trafficking in Persons (UN) 2, 135, 217
psychotropic drugs 2, 86, 118–19, 121, 126, 128
punishment: cultural difference in 2; and European Arrest Warrant 90; mitigation of 69, 97; range of 108, 220; and rehabilitation 129; severity of 97, 102, 216, 219, 227, 244; terms of 198, 204–5, 208–9, 216–21; of victims 165

rape 99, 104, 152, 222, 239
readmission to home country 203, 212n21
recidivism 128–9
recruitment of exploited persons: for prostitution 146–7, 155–8, 161, 176, 183, 186, 188–90, 219–20; from vulnerable groups 45, 186–7
refugees 10, 17, 19–20, 38, 46, 48, 63, 138
rehabilitation 97, 115, 126, 128

religious factors 10, 22, 39–40, 44, 49, 70, 98, 106
risk: combat 20; control 66, 73; and crime 59, 62, 64, 73; and humanitarian intervention 18; to individuals 9, 42, 48, 63, 140, 227, 233; minimization 42; to national interest 42; of oppression 51; policy 16; of profiling 44; of punishment 209; of terrorism 107; types of 9
Rothschild, Emma 15
routes for trafficking 5, 143, 156, 180–6, 190, 192, 198, 203, 208
Russia 83, 89, 105, 117, 125, 136, 138, 142–5, 152–7, 159, 165, 168–71, 176, 226
Rutherford, Justice (Douglas) 43–4
Rwanda 17

Saffin, John 181
Salford Witness Support Service 46
sanctions: corporate 67, 204; criminal 65–6, 73, 89–90, 200, 203–5, 207, 219; economic 105
Saudi Arabia 136, 245
Schengen Agreement 84–5, 87–8, 92, 197, 202, 204
secret services 65, 69
security: human 1–3, 9, 11, 15–22, 24–5, 28, 36–8, 51–2, 109, 135–8, 146–8, 248; international 3, 38; national 14–15, 18–21, 26, 36, 38, 204
self-defense 23, 26–7, 237; collective 27
Senegal 201
sex industry 5, 138–42, 152; Japanese 217, 239; Thai 233, 240–2 *see also* prostitution
sex tourism 138, 141, 184–5, 241; and children 153
sexually transmitted disease 146 *see also* AIDS/HIV
shadow economies 60, 62–4
shelters 2, 6, 154, 224, 233–4, 239, 242; for male victims 225; private 225–6, 233, 235; public 239
Sheptycki, J. 39, 42
Simpson, John 83
Singapore 12, 19, 240–1, 245
Single Convention on Narcotic Drugs (UN) 2
slavery 136, 180, 183, 186, 219, 227; history of 180–2, 192; sexual 218
smuggling 86, 105, 152; arms 190; drug 81, 86–7, 105, 115, 118, 120, 122, 143, 190; human 2–5, 48, 82, 137–8, 143, 182, 186–7, 191, 201–10,
socialism 10, 142
Soto, Juan Carlos 184
source countries 124, 136, 143–4, 153, 182–6, 241

258 Index

South Africa 13, 105, 121
South Korea *see* Korea, Republic of
sovereignty 12, 18, 21, 83, 197
Soviet Union, collapse of 3, 10, 13, 147
Spain 87, 93–4, 137, 143, 185, 201,
208–10
Sri Lanka 138, 140, 142
Stettinius, Edward 22
stimulants 100, 105, 108, 123, 235
Suriname 183
surveillance: of borders 89; covert 68;
electronic 65, 67; techniques of 43, 69,
97; telecommunications 68
survivors *see* victims
sustainable development 14, 93
Switzerland 71, 241, 245
syndicates: criminal 103–4; trafficking
183–5, 187, 189–91

Taiwan 12, 122, 124, 191, 225–6, 234, 239,
242, 245, 248
Takemi, Keizo 19
terrorism: and corresponding factors 5,
18–19; countering 3, 21, 27, 36–8, 40,
43–4, 46–7, 49–51, 70, 81–3, 85–6, 88,
93, 107–10, 199–203; and globalization
17; reactions to 38–9, 43, 98, 106, 114;
and victims 37; and violence 28
Thailand 6, 105, 115, 117, 138–45, 153,
159–60, 224, 226, 233, 236–8, 240–5,
247–8
Trafficking in Persons Report (TIP) 5, 144,
152, 154, 177, 218–19, 225, 240
transit countries 4, 114, 121, 123, 136,
143–4, 152, 182–6, 202–5, 208, 240,
243
transportation 48, 105, 135, 207, 220–1,
238
Treaty of Amsterdam (Amsterdam Treaty)
81, 84–5, 88, 199
Treaty of Maastricht (Maastricht Treaty)
84–5, 88, 198
Treaty of Nice (Nice Treaty) 81, 84–6, 88
Treaty of Rome 88
Trevi Group 85, 197
triads 60, 138
Turkey 63, 203, 212n21

Ukraine 136, 142–3
undercover policing 65, 67–9, 72
UNDP (United Nations Development
Program) 15–20
unemployment 9, 62–4, 83, 96–8, 171, 182,
192
UNICEF 224
United Arab Emirates 141
United Kingdom (UK) 11, 42, 87, 245
United States (US): crime rate in 96, 98;
and drug trafficking 114, 122–3, 125;
and human trafficking 136, 138, 145–6,
152–3, 182, 184–7, 189–91, 227, 243;
and Japan 20, 24–26, 106–8; and national
security 10–11, 17–18, 42, 44, 49, 86; and
slave trade 181–2
Universal Declaration of Human Rights 2,
13, 23
urbanization 100, 145
Uzbekistan 153–4, 169, 171, 173, 186

Van Duyne, P. C. 38
Venezuela 183
victims: assistance for 3, 5–6, 91–2, 152–3,
204, 224, 227, 238–40, 247–8; protection
of 5, 37, 46–7, 91–2, 153–4, 204, 219,
224–5, 247–8; and special residence 217,
222, 224–5; suffering of 2, 4, 49, 218–19,
224, 234, 237–8
Vietnam 142, 186, 242, 244
visas: common EU policy on 85, 87;
entertainer 155–6, 160, 176–7, 217–18,
223, 238–9; illegal 104; marriage 176–7,
243; and overstayers 102, 189; restrictions
on 48; tourist 156, 160, 176, 190, 243;
trainee 156; visitor 48

weapons 17, 61, 104; biological 14, 18
witnesses: intimidation of 39, 42; protection
of 41, 46–7, 72, 107, 244
World Bank 12, 14

xenophobia 39

yakuza 4, 110, 122, 125, 138, 141

Zaccardelli, Giuliano 37